The Illustrated Encyclopedia of

WORLD TENNIS

John Haylett *and Richard Evans*

Foreword

Whenever I see the word 'Encyclopedia' on a book I always wonder who has had the time and energy, not to mention the discipline, to research such a tome! Faced with this excellent volume on what is virtually the story of tennis through its beginnings as a social sport to the complexities of modern-day professionalism by players and administrators alike, my admiration knows no bounds.

The game of tennis has always been in my blood so perhaps I could be accused of being biased. But the truth is that tennis is a great sport. No matter to what standard one plays, there is good health to be gained through exercise, camaraderie through participation, fun (and frustration) through competition.

Club players may think that the highly paid, fiercely motivated stars of today are a million light years away from their own environment. Not so! Everyone starts the same way — by learning the basics.

Many do not have the talent, the opportunity or the advantages to climb upwards and tennis for them remains a pastime with dreams of what might have been, if only . . .

For the special few the dreams come true. We benefit from the pleasure they give us with their awesome and appealing capabilities. Their dedication and commitment is rewarded with prize-money that is probably outside even their wildest expectations. Now they can also pursue Olympic Gold with the return of tennis to the Olympic Games in 1988, which opens up a new dimension for our sport.

This book will transport you from the garden party atmosphere of Sphairistike, *as the game was originally called, through the growth of competitive tennis, including international team events, to an understanding of the modern game as a highly efficient business.*

It has obviously been designed for reading pleasure, packed as it is with interesting facts, photographs and records.

Tennis is a sport with an appeal for everyone from the young aspirants to the experienced veterans — needless to say, this book caters for them all.

Enjoy it!

Philippe Chatrier
President, International Tennis Federation

House Editor: Donna Wood
Editor: Alison Wormleighton
Art Editor: Gordon Robertson
Production: Craig Chubb
Picture Research: Moira McIlroy

Typeset in 10/11 pt Times by Quadraset Limited
Printed and bound by Dai Nippon in Hong Kong

The contents of this publication are believed correct
at the time of printing. Nevertheless, the Publishers
cannot accept responsibility for errors or omissions,
nor for changes in details given.

Published by The Automobile Association, Fanum House,
Basingstoke, Hampshire RG21 2EA.

© Marshall Cavendish Limited 1989

Distributed in the United Kingdom by the
Publishing Division of The Automobile Association,
Fanum House, Basingstoke, Hampshire RG21 2EA.

ISBN 086 145 8265
AA Ref 12548

Below: A portrait group of the most famous competitors in the Lawn Tennis Championships of 1923, with a numbered key to the names.

(1) R. Lacoste; (2) J.P.D. Wheatley; (3) Mrs Edgington; (4) Mrs Clayton; (5) Dr A.H. Fyzee; (6) M.J.D. Ritchie; (7) T.M. Mavrogordato; (8) The Hon Cecil Campbell; (9) Vincent Richards; (10) A.A. Fyzee; (11) W.M. Johnston; (12) J. Brugnon; (13) H.K. Lester; (14) Mrs Mallory; (15) W.C. Crawley; (16) J. Washer; (17) Mlle Lenglen; (18) P.M. Davson; (19) Miss E.F. Rose; (20) J.B. Gilbert; (21) Miss K. McKane; (22) Max Woosnam; (23) F.T. Hunter; (24) J. Borotra; (25) Miss Ryan; (26) D.M. Greig; (27) Mrs Peacock; (28) R. Lycett; (29) Mrs Satterthwaite; (30) B.I.C. Norton; (31) Gordon Lowe; (32) A.R.F. Kingscote; (33) Mrs Beamish; (34) N. Mishu; and (35) Mrs Craddock.

Contents

The History of Tennis

This chapter traces the development of tennis, from its inception nearly five centuries ago through its many phases, including a long period as a genteel garden party game.
Each of the most important events in the game's history is chronicled here, with vivid descriptions of the personalities and the players who were instrumental in changing the face of tennis and bringing to it a new professionalism.
The game generally referred to today as 'tennis' is in fact more properly termed 'lawn tennis', since 'tennis' is really an indoor game of much older origins, still played on a low-key basis in certain parts of the world. In the US this ancient game, sometimes referred to as the 'sport of kings' because it was played by the crowned heads of France and England in the Middle Ages, is known as court tennis. In Britain it is styled real tennis, and in Australia, royal tennis. The outdoor version that evolved in the 19th century and was patented by Major Wingfield as 'Sphairistike' or 'Lawn Tennis', only became officially known as 'tennis' when the International Lawn Tennis Federation dropped the word 'Lawn' from their title in the late 1970s.

Left: A gentle Victorian game of ladies' doubles. When the new pastime of lawn tennis was introduced in the early 1870s, it was originally restricted to fairly wealthy people who had large enough lawns in their garden on which to lay out a court.

At the West Hants Club in the British seaside town of Bournemouth on 24 April 1968, Mark Cox, an amateur from England, defeated Pancho Gonzales, a professional player from the United States, in the first round of the British Hardcourt Championships.

The match would have passed virtually unnoticed save for the fact that Cox, a young left-hander, had taken advantage of Gonzales's advancing years to score a victory over one of the great players of the previous generation. The result wrote itself into the history books and made headline news around the world because it was the first time an amateur had ever beaten a professional. The British Hardcourts, as the first official tournament of the new open era, offered the first opportunity for an amateur and a professional to walk on to the same tennis court and play an official match.

Thoughts of prize money, if not actual professionalism, have been inherent in the game since the first tennis boom struck nearly five centuries ago, during the reign of François I, in France. Reportedly, during a match between a monk and the king himself, one particularly fine shot by the monk prompted the king to exclaim, 'Ah, well done. That was truly the stroke of a monk!' Quick as a flash, the robed figure shot back, 'If it pleases Your Majesty, it could be the stroke of an abbot!' In lieu of prize money, what better than a rapid rise in holy order?

Ancient ball games

Rewards for excellence at sports involving some form of ball play go back as far as antiquity. Ariston of Carystius was considered so brilliant at the game as it was played in his day that the Athenians offered him the right of citizenship and erected a statue in his honour.

Homer was aware of the game and relates in the *Odyssey* how Nausicaä, with her marble white arms, hit a ball into the river while playing a game with her handmaidens. The description suggests that she was playing with some kind of racket so some relationship to tennis can at least be assumed. Nonetheless, not many searches for the inevitable lost ball have resulted in the discovery of a naked Ulysses emerging from the bulrushes.

In Roman times we are told that Horace and Virgil took a siesta while travelling the road from Rome to Brundusium but that Maecenas, an energetic and fashionable young man of the day, left his companions to go off and play at tennis.

With the lions and gladiators pulling the crowds at the Coliseum, no one thought to build a Roman Wimbledon. The sacking of the city and the decline of the Empire saw the end of any chance of refinement of the sport. It had been little more than an idle pastime for a civilization that, for all the brilliance of its architects and engineers, still thought the only manly way to score a point was to stick spears into people. 'Pila', as it was called by

the Romans, faded into the Dark Ages along with saunas, underground heating and all those other modern comforts that man discarded for such a long time.

The French game 'paume'

It reappeared many centuries later in the form of the French game *paume*. The word means 'palm of the hand', and the game was, in fact, a version of fives, played indoors under rules not very different from the game of Eton or Rugby fives played today. It seems to have appeared in France some time in the 13th century, but the first concrete evidence of its growing hold on the upper strata of society came 200 years later when courts for playing it were erected near the centre of Paris.

Le Petit Temple in the Rue Grenier St Lazare was one of the most famous. It was there that a woman referred to merely as Margot made a big name for herself around 1427 by competing at *paume* and, according to writings of the time, 'holding her own with

Left: Tennis in the Champs Elysées, Paris, around 1800. An arena for the game was built there in 1820 and it became the headquarters for the game in France.

all but the very best of the opposite sex'. For a woman to have challenged men at organized sport in those days was, presumably, unusual to say the least.

Birth of real tennis

By the beginning of the 16th century some form of curved racket was being used instead of the palm to strike the ball. Although *jeu de paume* remained the official name for this increasingly popular sport, the word 'tennis' began to appear.

The derivation of the word is open to speculation. Some favour the theory that it came from the word *tenez* (take) — the receiver 'taking' his opponent's serve — while others suggest that the place name Tennois in the Champagne district of France could have been the source.

At any rate, the game grew in stature and complexity, evolving into the game of real tennis — also called royal tennis or, in the US, court tennis — that is still sometimes played today. (Anyone who tries to understand the complexities of the game of real tennis may feel it was highly appropriate that Henry VIII chose as the site for his real tennis court at Hampton Court Palace the spot right next to the maze. It is not a simple game.)

The sport of kings

Apparently unconcerned that the game had suffered its first recorded fatality when King Louis X expired immediately after a hard rubber in 1316, the French nobility took to the game with a passion. Charles V had an enormous court built at the Louvre occupying two entire floors of the Palace. François I, no doubt with the approval of his monks, built another. In fact, he found the game so compulsive that he even installed one on his battleship. But none of the kings was a match for François's successor, Henry II, who ruled France in the mid 16th century and appears to have been in a class of his own as a ball player. By this time there were well over

Above: A view of the All England Club during the first Wimbledon Championship in 1877. At that time, the net across the court was higher than it is now, and dipped slightly in the middle.

1000 courts in Paris alone, and every French chateau had one.

In England, where a court had been built at Windsor Castle in the 15th century, the game was also catching on and, of course, Henry VIII found time between wives to become a proficient player before his girth got in the way of his backhand. The court he built at Hampton Court Palace is no longer in existence, but one built there by James I a century later, in 1625, is still in use today and is the venue for the British Open real tennis championships.

Even the ill-fated Charles I continued the royal patronage of the game. It is recorded that, as Duke of York in 1619, Charles had an appointment to play tennis at 6 am at St James's Palace.

The real tennis boom of the 15th and 16th centuries appears to have started to peter out in France by the reign of Louis XIII. Nevertheless real tennis even survived the elimination of most of its adherents during the French Revolution.

19th-century revival

The gradual but irreversible interest in organized sports of all types that took place throughout the 19th century encouraged a renewed focus on real tennis in Napoleon's France. An arena for the game was built on the Champs Elysées in 1820 and was used as

the headquarters for a sport still called *paume* until it was moved a few years later to the Luxembourg Gardens, and other courts were also constructed.

By the early 1870s interest in the game in France had started to fade. But few of its former participants could have envisaged, as they hung up their rackets, the extraordinary development of an entirely new form of the sport that would sweep the world before the end of the century.

Major Wingfield's boxes

Already, in December 1873, near his home in Nantclwyd in Wales, Major Walter Clopton Wingfield was giving a party to launch a new game he had invented. Major Wingfield had chosen to call his new game Sphairistike and, before anyone else thought it worthwhile, he patented the name, the game and the paraphernalia to go with it. Sphairistike came in a box — net, posts, rackets and balls, all available from the 'inventor's' sole agents, Messrs French & Co, 46, Churton Street, in Pimlico, London for the affordable but none too cheap price of five guineas.

Even out of its box and set up ready for play, Sphairistike would not be instantly recognizable as the game played by the likes of McEnroe and Becker. According to the Major, the space required for the perfect court was 18 metres (20 yards) each way. Its

shape was that of an hourglass, being wider at both baselines than at the net, and the net itself was much higher — 1.5 m (5 feet) at the posts and only 10 cm (4 inches) lower in the middle, as opposed to just over 1 metre (3 feet 6 inches) today. Scoring was borrowed from the game of rackets, and an uncovered indiarubber ball was used.

For his party Wingfield had produced a little programme containing what he called 'useful hints', such as: 'Hit the ball gently and look well before striking so as to place it in the corner most remote from your adversary. A great deal of side can be imparted to the ball by the proper touch, which, together with a nice appreciation of strength, adds much to the delicacy and science of the game.'

Early tributes

Many of the Major's rules were to change within a year, by which time the All England Croquet Club had adopted the game and the Marylebone Cricket Club had set about re-writing the rules. But initially the new game was welcomed in the press, despite the in-evitable reservations about its name. The *Sporting Gazette* announced: 'While admit-ting Sphairistike to be a barbarous name, the writer wishes to pay passing tribute to the inventor of a new game which adds another to that too limited list of pastimes in which ladies and gentlemen can join.'

The Court Journal was unstinting in its praise. 'Sphairistike or Lawn Tennis, the new rival to croquet, has been most favourably reviewed by all the public journals. They declare that it is a clever adaptation of Tennis; that it will become a national pastime; that no English home, no public grounds, no barracks square, should be without it! We certainly wish it well . . .'

On 31 October 1874 a correspondent in the *Sporting Gazette* wrote, 'I hear from Paris that people are all raving there about Sphairistike. There was a great run on the game as soon as it was discovered that it might be played and understood without the necessity of pronouncing it!'

The extent to which Major Wingfield's promotion paid off can be realized from reading the following press cutting of the time. *The Globe* went right to the heart of the matter when it wrote: 'The owners of country houses have been at their wits' end for some attraction wherewith to fill their lawns in summertime.' *The Globe* also went on to point out that whereas the new game was shorn of much of its beauty and finesse (in comparison to real tennis), it was 'free also of the difficulties that have been so fatal'. In other words this was an easier game in which the whole family could participate. And, indeed, in Major Wingfield's eye this was meant to be a relatively gentle pastime.

Above: A large crowd watches a match on the Centre Court at Wimbledon in 1880. Notice the prominent advertising for an equipment manufacturer on the grandstand: direct advertising later became anathema at Wimbledon.

Precursors to the game

But was Wingfield really the inventor of this wonderful new game? Almost exactly a year after the famous launching party at Nantclwyd, heated correspondence broke out in *The Field* disputing the fact. Many years later, in 1890, a leading authority, C. G. Heathcote, put the whole argument in perspective when he acknowledged that 'Major Wingfield undoubtedly deserves the title of the earliest law-giver as well as much of the credit for civilizing the game by introducing it to the notice of the public.' Heathcote went on to point out, however, that some form of tennis had been practised since time immemorial and that even forms of lawn tennis were played long before Wingfield came up with Sphairistike.

It had evidently become sufficiently popular at the end of the previous century for *Sports Magazine* in 1799 to refer to it as a dangerous rival even to cricket. There are records of a similar game called long tennis being played in 1834, and one club claimed to have been acquainted with it 15 years before it was 'revived' by Wingfield. It is also said to have been played at Sir Walter Scott's country seat, Ancrum, in Roxburghshire in 1864, as well as near Leyton in Essex in 1868. Even the clergy got in on the act, thus sustaining the happy tradition set by those French monks. Sir Arthur Hervey, later Bishop of Bath & Wells, had played a substitute form of tennis on the lawns of his rectory in Suffolk.

One of the earliest reports of real tennis being taken out into the open air to be played in a manner that was later to evolve into the game we know today comes from Nicoll in his book *Progress of Queen Elizabeth I*. 'When Queen Elizabeth was entertained at Elvetham in Hampshire by the Earl of Hertford, after dinner, at about three o'clock, ten of his servants, Somersetshire men, in a square green court before her Majesty's windows, did hang up lines, squaring out the form of a tennis court, and, making a cross in the middle, in the square they played, five to five, with handball, with bord and cord as they tearme it, to the great liking of Her Highness.'

Obviously this bore closer resemblance to handball, considering the number of players on either side, but the mention of 'bord and cord' does suggest that some other implements were used. It is probably reasonable to include the great Queen in the game's list of royal patrons.

So as regards the question of Major Wingfield's 'invention' of the game, it is probably fair to say that he was the first to recognize its possibilities, the first to market it and the first to set it off on the road that led to Wimbledon.

Debt to croquet

Wingfield realized that one of the first tasks in his attempt to popularize the sport was to wean away the advocates of croquet. He did not beat about the bush. 'Croquet, which of

late years has monopolized the attention of the public, lacks the healthy and manly excitement of Sphairistike,' wrote the Major.

It was a point well made but it hardly needed repeating. People were frankly becoming bored with croquet, and they turned to the new game in droves. Yet the debt that lawn tennis — or 'Sticky', as it was nicknamed by those who were tongued-tied by Sphairistike — owes to croquet should not be underestimated. In a very real sense croquet had smoothed the path of its successor on the country house lawns of England.

During the previous decades, as the middle classes started to reap the benefits of the Industrial Revolution, more and more

people had moved into spacious country homes. Always conscious of the need to keep up with society, croquet enthusiasts had been quite ruthless in uprooting trees and grassing flowerbeds in order to create the best croquet lawn in the parish. Having created the space, inadvertently, for the sport that was to take over, the croquet crowd had then gone to work on the texture of their lawns. Gardeners were told to replace soft and mossy turf with a firmer and more lively surface so that the wooden ball could travel more easily to the hoop. Easier for a croquet ball? Certainly — but better still for Wingfield's indiarubber ball, which would have died in the moss and rendered his game useless.

So lawn tennis, assisted by its own inherent merits, made its way into popular favour with remarkable rapidity — courtesy of the game it was replacing. No group of people was quicker to appreciate the switch in popularity than members of the All England Croquet Club and it was the contentious Henry 'Cavendish' Jones who introduced the game to the club at Worple Road in 1875. As an example of just how tight-knit sporting society was in those days before mass communication, the secretary of the All England Croquet Club at the time, J. H. Walsh, was also editor of *The Field*, the magazine in which Cavendish's by-line appeared so often.

After the Sett

Just to show there is no Ill Feeling

Play

The Effect of a " Demon " Service

In the late 1860s, when Jones was attending the weekend parties given by Walsh, croquet was still the fashionable game. After Jones pointed out that his host's lawns and flower beds were becoming ruined as a result, it was agreed that a suitable London site should be found for a proper croquet club. The immediate results were not promising. The Crystal Palace rejected the idea and Walsh considered the asking price of £500 rent for six acres of fields situated between Holland House in Kensington and Addison Road exorbitant. Finally, an alternative was found. The location left something to be desired as it was so far out of town, but at £50 a year rising to £100 in rent for four acres of excellent meadowland along Worple Road in Wimbledon, the deal was too good to refuse.

By June 1870, Jones had the place in a sufficient state of readiness for the All England Croquet Club, as it was called, to stage its first tournament. The following year Jones proposed that Walsh should be elected honorary secretary. No one seemed to object, and indeed Walsh's daughter was soon allowed to join as an honorary member. Given the alacrity with which ladies were admitted as members, thus suggesting a very enlightened attitude for the Victorian age, it seems a pity that it took over a hundred years for a woman, in the person of Virginia Wade, to be elected to the All England Club committee.

Reacting to the sudden interest shown in Sphairistike, Jones suggested to the All England Croquet Club committee that one croquet lawn should be set aside for a lawn tennis court. At a cost of £25 this task was completed on 25 February 1875, and it could be said that the game has never looked back. Certainly Jones's sharp opportunism sounded the death knell for Major Wingfield's influence on the game. In that same year the Marylebone Cricket Club, already on the eve of celebrating its first hundred years, decided to take a hand in a sport that was obviously going to need serious attention. Wingfield was asked to present himself at Lords (the club's ground), where a net had been erected especially for the occasion. There, in his persuasive style, the Major outlined the rules of his game which were accepted in all essential elements, including the hourglass court and racket scoring.

Below: A Centre Court match at Wimbledon in 1888. The main arena at the old Worple Road ground had covered stands on three sides, while the fourth — the nearest to a railway line adjoining the ground — was open.

Left: The men's singles all-comers' final on the Centre Court at Worple Road, Wimbledon, in 1892. Wilfred Baddeley is winning against E.W. Lewis in order to qualify to challenge the holder, Joshua Pim.

New rules

Obviously, however, Wingfield had been forced to make some concessions. In a letter Wingfield wrote to the MCC, he began by saying how much he was indebted to the gentlemen of the tennis committee at Lords and went on, 'I shall cancel my present rules and marking of the court and accept [those of the MCC] en masse.'

Over at Worple Road, George Nicol was appointed the committee member in charge of lawn tennis when four more courts were built in 1876. But it was the dynamic Jones along with Julian Marshall (who would take over from Walsh as club secretary in 1880), and C. G. Heathcote (the brother of J. M. Heathcote, who was a leading player of the day and who invented the original flannel covering for the ball) who emerged as the true founding fathers of the sport as we know it today.

It was this trio which decided to adopt the deuce and advantage real tennis scoring system rather than the rackets scoring of 15 points up which had been recommended and adopted by the MCC on 24 June 1875. Under the MCC system only the server could advance his score.

Just as importantly, Jones, Marshall and Heathcote also decreed that the server should have two chances on each point, thus sowing the seed for the development of the ace, which has been used to such devastating effect ever since by the likes of Tilden, Gonzales, Hoad and Becker. These were, as John Barrett so rightly says in his book, *100 Wimbledons: A Celebration*, inspired decisions which have stood the test of time.

Wingfield's hourglass was also straightened out, being replaced by a rectangular playing area, 23.77 metres (78 feet) by 8.23 metres (27 feet), and the position of the server was moved outside the playing area instead of astride the baseline. Finally, five years after Jones had appointed himself referee to the first ever Lawn Tennis Championships to be played at Wimbledon in 1877, the height of the net at the posts was reduced to 107 cm (3 feet 6 inches). Since that date, 1882, nothing pertaining to the measurement of the playing area has been changed.

By then the MCC had happily relinquished control of the game to the All England Club. This left Julian Marshall, as the new All England Club secretary, in a very powerful position.

Birth of the LTA

According to John Olliff, the celebrated lawn tennis correspondent of the *Daily Telegraph*, Marshall was an imposing presence and something of a *bon viveur* whose colourful personality 'earned him many friends and likewise many enemies'. It could be said, in fact, that Marshall's lack of tact led to the formation, in 1888, of the Lawn Tennis Association. Doubtless such a body would have evolved in due course (although there is no reason why the All England Club should not have grown into a world-governing body similar to the MCC), but Marshall certainly seems to have hastened the LTA's arrival.

H. S. Scrivener, a Wimbledon quarter-finalist in 1888 and 1890, and G. W. Hillyard, who ironically would become one of Marshall's successors in 1907, were the two young players who led a growing revolt against the secretary's attitude.

When the LTA eventually came into being in 1888, the All England Club handed over its

Below: Herbert Lawford won the men's singles at Wimbledon in 1887. The holder, William Renshaw, was not defending, and Lawford beat his twin brother, Ernest Renshaw, in the all-comers' final.

Opposite: William Renshaw holds the record of the most wins in the men's singles. He took the title six years running, 1881 to 1886, and for a seventh time in 1889.

legislative authority to the new body. But Julian Marshall, who had done much to enhance the financial stability of the club, resigned in 1888, following a court action brought against the club by its gardener, whom Marshall had mistakenly accused of theft. However, before resigning, Marshall did appoint Thomas Coleman to take the place of the wrongly accused gardener. Coleman held the post for the next 40 years, setting the standard of near perfection that has become accepted as the norm for Wimbledon's grass lawns ever since.

Early champions

Quite suddenly the new game was creating its own champions and its own folklore. Spencer Gore, serving underhand, won the first Wimbledon title in 1877. An ex-pupil of Harrow, Gore followed the natural style of things in those days and took time off in the middle of the tournament to attend the Eton and Harrow cricket match at Lords. Having started the championship on Monday 9th July, it was not until Thursday the 19th that Gore, having played his way through a 22-man field, defeated W. C. Marshall, thus claiming the silver trophy, donated by *The Field*. It was valued at 25 guineas, which was not a bad sum of money in those days.

The following year another Harrovian, Frank Hadow, returned from his coffee plantation in Ceylon, lobbed Gore to death in the final, winning 9-7 in the third set, and promptly disappeared back across the Indian Ocean. He was not seen again at Wimbledon until the Jubilee Championships of 1926.

The Reverend J. T. Hartley did not have to travel quite as far as Hadow but the journeys which led him to the title in 1879 were probably more taxing on the nerves. Not having expected to get as far as the semi-final, the Reverend had made no provision for anyone to cover for him at his parish church in Yorkshire. There was nothing for it but to return home, give his Sunday sermon and head south again as fast as Victorian transport could carry him. He managed it by driving his horse and buggy ten miles to the nearest station at the crack of dawn on Monday; arriving in London by 2 pm and getting across town to Wimbledon in time for his semi-final against a certain Mr Parr. Hartley was, by his own admission, tired and famished but a welcome rain shower allowed him to wolf down what he described as 'a nourishing tea'. Feeling much better, he won the match. The next day Hartley met V. St Leger Gould in the all-comers' final and won in straight sets.

With no word from Hadow in Ceylon, Hartley won the challenge round by default and, the following year, defended his title successfully against the great baseline specialist H. F. Lawford.

Arrival of the smash

However, in 1881, with the hand-stitched Ayres ball being used for the first time, Hartley found himself defending against an immaculately turned-out blond young man with a neat moustache who dealt with his lobs in preposterous fashion, belting them into the newly built stands with what could only be described as a smash. William Renshaw was, in fact, the inventor of the smash and his arrival on the scene, along with his brother Ernest, heralded the game's first golden age.

Apart from an impertinent interruption by Lawford in 1887 when Willie was forced to withdraw with the first recorded case of tennis elbow, the Renshaw twins totally dominated Wimbledon for a decade, winning eight singles titles (just one, in 1888, for Ernie) and five doubles titles. They became the game's first stars — the first to develop a

real following among the spectators, and the first to be besieged for their autographs.

From all accounts Willie Renshaw was the first great practitioner of the art of lawn tennis. No one before him had taken the ball on the rise and attacked the net behind such aggressive volleys. He served overhand and frightened the life out of opponents with his smash. Extrovert and handsome, he was obviously the dominant twin; but observers of the day were quick to point out that comparing his record with Ernie's was unfair because the quieter of the two hated playing his brother and rarely tried to win. Nevertheless, two of the three Wimbledon finals they played against each other went to five sets.

Their celebrity was all lawn tennis needed

Below: The Renshaw twins contested three singles challenge rounds against each other and won the men's doubles five times. The Renshaw Cup is one of the three trophies presented to the winner of the men's singles at Wimbledon.

to establish itself once and for all as an integral part of the British sporting scene. The Renshaws' fame spread overseas, too, helped by their regular visits to the Côte d'Azur, where they set up a winter training camp in Cannes, and to Dublin where, for three years, the prestigious new Irish Championships trophy bore no other name but Renshaw.

Beginnings of a circuit

By the end of the 1880s the first stirrings of a fledgling circuit were taking shape. The Scottish Championships had started on the Dyvons Club courts in Edinburgh and one of the earliest winners, J. G. Horn, threw the ball so high on his service toss that he had to wait motionless for it to come down. Tournaments were also being played at Devonshire Park in Eastbourne, where the grass was considered as near perfect as it is today.

Crossing the Atlantic

Inevitably the game was starting to spread far beyond the confines of the English Channel and the Irish Sea. Back in 1874 one of Major Wingfield's boxes, complete with all the Sphairistike equipment, had been taken to the United States by Clarence and Joseph Clark, who, nine years later, were to play the first recorded international match — against the Renshaws, in England. The Clark brothers lost but by that time the game had already taken a foothold in the US, thanks largely to a holiday the Clarks had enjoyed in Bermuda in 1874. While officers from the English garrison joined in the game the Clarks had set up, a young lady named Mary Outerbridge stood riveted near the playing area. When she returned to the family home in New York, the game went with her.

The Outerbridges, being a family of influence, quickly gained permission to lay out a court at the Staten Island Cricket and Baseball Club and, by the end of the decade, O. E. Woodhouse, the first English tennis player to compete in America, had won a tournament there.

Meanwhile at Nahant in Massachusetts, another of Wingfield's boxes arrived at the summer home of William Appleton, who had a games-crazy nephew called James Dwight. Although Dwight took to the game as if he himself had invented it, Mary Outerbridge's brother Emilius beat him to the punch in organizing the first major tennis event in the United States. Dwight, accompanied by Richard Sears — who was destined to win the first seven United States singles titles once the official Championships was inaugurated at the Newport Casino the following year — travelled down to the Staten Island club in a less than generous frame of mind and found fault with just about everything. Their humour was not improved when, having refused to play in the singles competition, the title went to the tall, lanky Englishman Woodhouse.

Although Dwight would ultimately do most to promote American tennis in the world game, Outerbridge continued to lay the framework. In 1881, seven years before the English thought of doing the same, Outerbridge organized the formation of the United States National Lawn Tennis Association. Sidestepping the rivalry that existed between Outerbridge and Dwight, a compromise president was elected in the person of General R. S. Oliver of Albany. Together with Clarence Clark, who had the backing of a dozen clubs in Pennsylvania, Outerbridge and Dwight sat on the executive committee and set about rewriting the rules which, up to that point, had been implemented in chaotic fashion.

Back in England, public interest in the game began to wane with the end of the Renshaw era. In 1895 the Wimbledon Championships, which had attracted 3,500 spectators ten years before, actually lost money — not much, but a deficit of £33 looked bad on the books in those days. The club's solution was to readmit its croquet members, who had been unceremoniously ejected in 1883. By 1896 the name was changed once again, to the All England Lawn Tennis and Croquet Club.

The Dohertys to the rescue

But almost before the hoops reappeared on the lawns, the bigger, faster game provided a solution of its own. It was called Doherty.

Once again a pair of brothers came to the rescue. Reggie and Laurie Doherty, who were introduced to the game by an elder brother, the Rev. W. V. Doherty, were destined to dominate Wimbledon to an even greater extent than the Renshaws. Reggie, nicknamed 'Big Do', won the singles four times in succession before 'Little Do' took over after a one-year interruption to win five successive titles. As a doubles team they were champions eight times in ten years.

In their youth the Dohertys breathed fire and flair into the summer game, heightening its prestige with their charm and chivalry. Unbuttoned cuffs fluttering at the ends of his long-sleeved shirt, the tall Reggie was all elegance as he used the half volley to get himself to the net much as Cochet did two decades later. Laurie, shorter and less audacious, had the perfect balance of a Rosewall and played the kind of game that writers of tennis textbooks dream about.

When Laurie died while serving at the Air Ministry during the First World War, *The Times* obituary said of the two brothers, 'They played an English game in the spirit in which Englishmen think that games should be played.' It was a fitting epitaph.

The appeal of the Dohertys ensured that the All England Club would never be financially embarrassed again. By 1904, the croquet members were struggling once more to justify their existence, their meeting

Above: A real tennis court at Queen's Club, London. This famous venue is a mecca for all racket sports players, with facilities for real tennis, lawn tennis (on four different surfaces), rackets and squash.

producing a loss of £6 while the Lawn Tennis Championships of that year recorded a staggering profit of £1,300.

The Davis Cup challenge

By the time the Dohertys were in full flower, new challenges were arriving from across the Atlantic. The one that was to leave a lasting imprint on the world game began as a seed of an idea in the mind of a young player at Harvard called Dwight F. Davis. In 1899, Davis, in the company of three other players — Holcombe Ward, Malcolm Whitman and Beals Wright — along with their mentor George Wright, Beals's father, had gone West, not in search of gold but in an attempt to extend the frontiers of the game of lawn tennis.

A few months after their return from San Francisco and British Columbia, Davis wrote to the LTA in London: 'I call your attention to an experiment that we are making which will, I hope, increase the interest in Lawn Tennis. One of our players here has offered a Cup, to be a sort of International Championship Cup. I enclose the conditions in rough form. I trust that we shall both take a deep interest in them for many years to come . . .'

The player donating the Cup — 6.2 kg (217 ounces) of silver costing £1,000 — was, of course, Davis himself. Almost immediately, the unwieldy title he had so modestly suggested was discarded. The competition became known as the Davis Cup.

With amazing speed, the challenge was accepted by the British, and the first match, to be played at the Longwood Cricket Club, was arranged for August that same year. This might well have surprised Davis, who had added in his invitation that he hoped some of the English players would be able to come over and compete for the trophy 'in spite of the Boer War'. In fact, the entire success of the venture took Davis by surprise.

Far from remaining an exclusive Anglo-American affair, Davis's challenge attracted the immediate interest of nations across the world. Britain not only accepted the challenge but designated Australia and New Zealand, British South Africa, Canada and India as other countries prepared to take part. Within two years Austria, Belgium, France, Germany, Holland, Sweden, Norway and Switzerland joined in.

Dwight Davis went on to become Secretary of War in 1925 and, later, Governor General of the Philippines, but friends felt that nothing gave him greater satisfaction than that idea he had at Harvard, inspired by a desire to help foster international understanding.

The first Davis Cup tie

Under the circumstances it was hardly surprising that the conditions and organization of the first Davis Cup tie in history left something to be desired, especially from the visitors' point of view. Despite the absence of

Right: Play on an outside court at Worple Road, Wimbledon, in 1895. Note the decorous attire of the spectators: the tournament was very much an important social event in those days.

the Dohertys, who felt they could not make the journey, the British team — consisting of A. W. Gore, who sneaked a Wimbledon title in the middle of the Doherty reign the following year, Herbert Roper Barrett and Ernest Black — were given an amazing send off. Thousands lined the streets around the railway station, raising their hats and shouting 'Good luck' to the small party as it boarded the boat train. This contrasted rather sharply with the welcome they received in New York. When they stepped off their steamship on the morning of 14 August they were met by a solitary servant sent down from Boston.

To make matters worse, Longwood in 1900 did not measure up to the standards that players had already become accustomed to at Wimbledon. And the British team, which lost, did not allow diplomacy to get in the way of saying so. Roper Barrett wrote: 'The ground was abominable. The grass was long. The net was a disgrace to civilized Lawn Tennis and was held up by guy ropes that were continually sagging. As for the balls, I hardly like to mention them. They were awful — soft and mothery-looking and when served with the American twist came at you like an animated egg. Our team was altogether at a disadvantage. We had never experienced this kind of service before and it quite nonplussed us.' But Roper Barrett could not resist an additional comment which suggested that the

after all, made many visits as a player to Britain and the South of France during the 1890s and was well aware of the standards that were being set.

Facing the twist serve

The first Davis Cup rubber due to be played between Dwight Davis and Ernest Black was delayed because of rain. When it did finally start the Scotsman took the first set 6-4 but soon started to be troubled by the twist serve that Davis had learned from his Harvard team-mate Holcombe Ward. It had, in fact, been Dr Dwight who had originated it, and now a younger man, aided by the virtue of being left-handed, was putting it to very effective use. Davis, appropriately, won the first match to be played for the Cup bearing his name, 6-4 in the fourth, and the Americans never relinquished their grip on the tie, winning 3-0 for the loss of only the one set.

Ignoring any problems that might have existed over the playing conditions, there was no doubt that the American players of that era had discovered a major weapon in the twist serve, more generally known as the kick serve today. When Laurie Doherty first found himself facing it at Wimbledon he took every possible opportunity to get used to the feel of the swerving delivery by hitting back every serve whether or not it was a fault.

The greatest test of just how well 'Little Do' could handle the twist serve probably came in the Davis Cup challenge round of 1905 when Ward, the most aggressive player of his day, attacked the net relentlessly on the Centre Court at Wimbledon and led by two sets to love. But, as Olliff describes it, 'Laurie Doherty did not turn a hair but went on playing orthodox tennis, gradually working his man back from the net until at last he gained complete control of the match and lost only three games in the last three sets.'

Britain were the holders of the Davis Cup by this time, having avenged their humiliating debut by beating the United States in 1903 in Boston, and having kept the Cup in 1904. Coming just a few weeks after his Wimbledon challenge round triumph over the brilliant Australian Norman Brookes, Doherty's defeat of Ward helped Britain retain the Cup and ensured that 1905 would see him reach the pinnacle of his great career.

Tennis goes down under

But by 1907, the Doherty era would be over and, for the first time, tennis would be dominated by talents from a part of the world that would have such a major impact on the game in later years — Australasia. In founding the Australasian LTA in 1904 Norman Brookes struck a canny blow for the future success of his Davis Cup teams because, by including New Zealand, he included Anthony Wilding. Between them these two champions of such contrasting styles and personality dominated the post-Doherty years right up to the beginning of the

British might have fared better had they kept their eyes wholly on that egg-shaped ball: 'The spectators were most impartial,' wrote Barrett, 'and the female portion thereof not at all unpleasant to gaze upon.'

Black, the taciturn Scottish champion, was the only member of the British team to hold his peace at the time. But when asked for his comments many years later, he wrote from his home in Canada, 'Conditions at Longwood were very bad. The courts were bumpy, full of worm holes, I think, but the chief factor of our defeat was the soft ball which you could squash flat in your hand.'

One of the peculiarities of the rules under which this first Davis Cup was played was the seven-minute rest between each set. Black felt this was also an advantage to the Americans. 'They played themselves right out in each set and the rest fixed them up. The effect was quite the opposite for us.' This is an intriguing observation because it suggests a very different level of fitness than we have become used to today.

And what of the American viewpoint? George Wright said some time later that it was a matter of regret that the court fixtures were not better. However, people who knew Dr Dwight found it difficult to believe that a man of such martial bearing and demanding standards would have allowed conditions to be as bad as the British made out. Dr Dwight had,

Right: Norman Brookes was the first overseas player to win the men's singles at Wimbledon. The Australian left-hander triumphed in 1907 and 1914, and won the doubles with Anthony Wilding in the same years.

First World War. Brookes won the Wimbledon singles title in both the remaining years that he played, 1907 and 1914, while Wilding's achievement of winning four consecutive times between 1910 and 1913 was not bettered until Bjorn Borg broke the record in 1980.

It was strange that the styles of these two men did not match their personalities. Brookes, nicknamed 'The Wizard', was the mercurially talented games player with a dashingly aggressive game. Yet off court he was an introvert, an austere aristocrat who was later knighted. Although Wilding could volley, he preferred the back court from where he could wear down his opponents with his superior fitness. Yet Tony Wilding was one of the matinée idols of the age — a ruggedly handsome heart-throb who came down from Cambridge to cut a swathe through the bright young things of the Edwardian era. Heaven knows how many riderless horses he left in his wake as he roared through the hedgerows of Europe on his motor bicycle to compete in tournaments as far apart as Paris and Hamburg.

Forming a partnership with Brookes that seems incongruous in the light of today's great sporting rivalry between Australia and New Zealand, Wilding helped take big-time tennis 'down under' for the first time by ensuring that four consecutive Davis Cup challenge rounds were played on home turf following the initial defeat of Britain at Wimbledon in 1907. Two were played in Melbourne, one in Sydney and, in special deference to Wilding, one, in 1911, at Christchurch, New Zealand. Tony's father, Frederick Wilding, had emigrated to New

Zealand in 1875 and settled at Fownhope, not far from Christchurch; he went on to play cricket for his adopted country. When Wilding helped Australasia to a 5-0 rout of the United States at Christchurch, the uniqueness of the occasion is difficult to envisage. It remains the only time a challenge round or final of the Davis Cup has been played in New Zealand.

Wilding conquers Wimbledon

By the time Brookes returned to Wimbledon to challenge his Davis Cup colleague after a seven-year absence, Wilding had been involved in some memorable matches there. He was called upon to defend his crown twice against the remarkable Arthur W. Gore, a three-time former champion who went on competing at Wimbledon until 1927, having missed only one Championship in the previous 36. In 1912, Gore was 44 years old yet still managed to beat Andre Gobert, a player half his age who had just won the tennis Gold Medal at the Stockholm Olympics, in the all-comers' final. Even against the powerful New Zealander in the challenge round, Gore still managed to win a set.

The next year the queues that have become so much part of the Wimbledon tradition were the longest anyone had known. Ticket touts discovered there was money to be made in tennis and were asking as much as £10 a seat for the challenge round. It was 4 July 1913. The great Tony Wilding was defending his crown for the third time, but it was an American, Maurice McLoughlin, who was causing much of the excitement on American Independence Day. People started talking about a cannonball serve for the first time when they saw this ginger-headed young man pound his first serve into court. Even more so than today, tennis players of that era were given names that seemed more appropriate for boxers. With Brookes, 'The Wizard', absent, McLoughlin became known as the 'Californian Comet'. But the trail he blazed through the fortnight was wrenched from the sky by Wilding, who surprised everyone by standing further in than anyone had thought possible to handle the Comet's explosive serve.

This cut the amount of angle he had to deal with, and when a brilliant blocked winner off a first serve deprived McLoughlin of a set point at 5-4 in the first set, the turning point of what came to be recognized as one of the best duels seen at Worple Road had arrived. Wilding went on to win 10-8 in the third.

Against Brookes the following year, Wilding, boosted by the faith of his supporters, might have been guilty of taking The Wizard too lightly. Having played Davis Cup with him so many times, he should have known better. For once he had not trained as assiduously as usual and, on a particularly hot day, fell prey to the Australian's consummate court craft.

After the match Wilding stretched out on a grass verge to sip a cup of tea with his friend Arthur Balfour. Despite the queues and the ticket touts it was still possible in that calmer age for a Wimbledon champion to take tea undisturbed with a Prime Minister. But the calm was not to last for long.

With pitiful irony, Wilding and Brookes were playing a Davis Cup tie against Germany at the Allegheny Hills Country Club near Pittsburgh two days before war was officially declared. A short time before, both teams had been joking with each other about the ab-

Below: The men's doubles final at Wimbledon in 1908. Anthony Wilding and M.J.G. Ritchie (left) are on their way to victory over Arthur Gore and Herbert Roper Barrett.

surdity of going to war. Now as the matches ended, they shook hands coldly, and Otto Froitzheim and Oscar Kreuzer set off for home. They never got that far because their ship was impounded and they were interned. Pleas from Froitzheim to the All England Club secretary, Commander G. W. Hillyard, to intervene on their behalf with the King fell on deaf ears.

Before a year had passed, on 9 May 1915, a messenger hurried into the chamber of the House of Commons with a telegram for Mr Balfour. With a sadness that was felt throughout the sporting world, Balfour rose to tell the House that Captain Anthony Wilding had fallen at Neuve Chappelle.

Move to Church Road

In 1919, as a war-weary generation turned gratefully back to tennis, it quickly became evident that Worple Road was no longer big enough to hold the burgeoning number of spectators demanding tickets. Once efforts to buy adjoining land had failed, it took only three years for Stanley Peach to design the great cathedral of sport which stands alongside Church Road to this day.

But the interest could hardly have been maintained had it not been for stars of exceptional brilliance. The game was fortunate that three, in particular, arrived out of the scarred horizon to grip the imagination of the sporting public. Suzanne Lenglen, the first and still the only Frenchwoman to win Wimbledon, which she did for the first time in 1919; Bill Tilden, the first American men's winner in 1920; and Jean Borotra, the first Frenchman in 1924, all became attractions of the first magnitude. As John Olliff wrote: 'If Wimbledon had been purely a commercial business enterprise then the names of these three would have been blazoned in giant lights as large as those of Charlie Chaplin and Greta Garbo.'

Of these Miss Lenglen stood alone as a winner and an innovator in both style of play and style of dress. But to understand this woman's role in the history of tennis, it will help to trace the development of the women's game that produced her.

The women's game

In 1884, seven years after the inaugural Championships, it was the ever enterprising Henry Jones who proposed that the club should institute a Ladies' Championships. For the first two years it was won by Maud Watson, but in 1887 the incredibly gifted Lottie Dod won the first of her five titles at the age of 15 years and 285 days. Even in this age of teenage triumph no one has come close to rivalling Miss Dod as the youngest winner of all time.

Max Robertson, in his book *Wimbledon 1877–1977*, even goes so far as to suggest that she might have been the greatest all-round woman athlete of all time. Comparisons are, of course, impossible but there certainly

seems to be no doubt at all that the tall, fleet-footed young woman had all the necessary attributes, as well as a sporting record to go with it. She never lost at Wimbledon, dropping only one set in her five appearances, which were interrupted only because she set sail on a yachting expedition. Having been beaten less than half a dozen times in her entire tennis career, she retired at 21, took up golf and became English champion. She also played international hockey.

No one benefited more from Lottie Dod's defection to golf than Blanche Hillyard, wife of the future club secretary, who had lost to Lottie in all five challenge rounds. Mrs Hillyard had sneaked in to grab one title in 1889 when Lottie was off yachting. But she soon established herself as a champion in her own right by winning five more singles

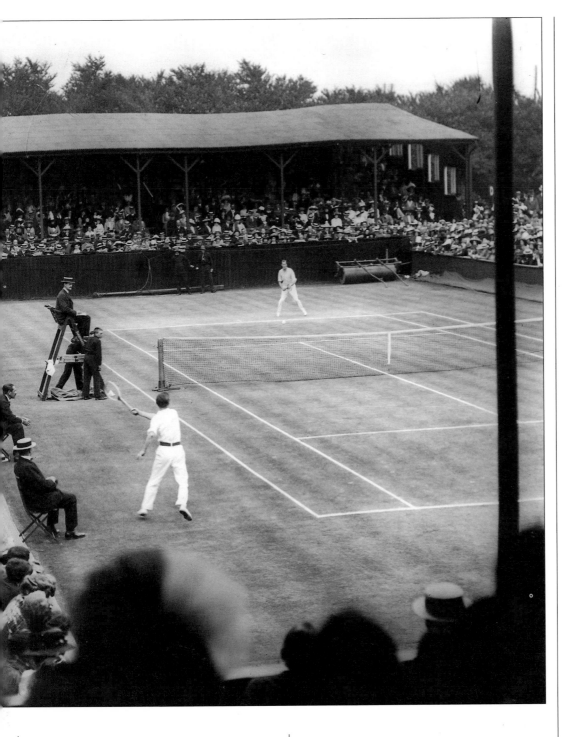

Left: A packed crowd witnesses the 1912 men's singles challenge round between Anthony Wilding and Arthur Gore. Wilding retained his title with a four set victory.

titles at Wimbledon and more tournaments throughout the country than any other player of her era.

Dorothea (Dolly) Douglass, who became Mrs Lambert Chambers, was the next woman to dominate the Wimbledon scene, winning seven times in twelve years. Her most interesting rivalry sprang up in 1905 when the 18-year-old Californian May Sutton, who had already won her own national title two years before, appeared at Wimbledon for the first time. Sutton immediately made history by becoming the first player to carry any of the All England Club titles back overseas.

Employing a big forehand, backed up when necessary by a sound volley developed on the cement courts of Pasadena, May Sutton defeated Dolly Douglass 6-3, 6-4 in the final. She lost to her the following year but reclaimed the crown for the United States in 1907 by beating the newly married Mrs Lambert Chambers 6-1, 6-4. The English-woman resumed her winning ways to such effect that she won four of the five Championships leading up to the First World War, the last when she was almost 36.

Even though she faced the much heralded Suzanne Lenglen in 1919, Mrs Lambert Chambers came within a point of retaining her crown as the oldest champion of all time, when she led Suzanne 8-10, 6-4, 6-5, 40-15, in the final. On the first of the two match points, Lenglen reached up in a desperate attempt to return a lob and caught the ball on the frame of her racket, from where it bounced on top of the net and fell into Lambert Chambers's court. The French girl then went on to win an epic struggle that stood as the longest women's final until Margaret Court needed 46 games to beat Billie Jean King 51 years later.

The two women became good friends, and it was with as much objectivity as a defeated champion can muster that Mrs Lambert Chambers wrote some years later: 'I think, perhaps, it was a tragedy for her, as for me, that I did not win that first 1919 match because after that she just could not bear the thought of ever being beaten (which, of course, is absurd — we all have our off days). Consequently, her nerves went to pieces and in the end she did not enjoy her tennis at all.'

Empress of the courts

Throwing off the corsets that had so restricted the movement of her predecessors, Suzanne Lenglen became the symbol of an era. The female body and the flowing, graceful, athletic movement of which it was capable was no longer something to be hidden behind Victorian trusses. The gay young things were out to enjoy themselves and prove a point. No one helped them more than the new Empress of the Courts, and nowhere was it more obvious than on the French Riviera. As Ted Tinling recalls in his book *Sixty Years in Tennis*: 'Tennis, dancing and gambling were the catalysts of the high-fashion winter calendar, and Suzanne Lenglen, the unquestioned Queen of Art Deco, was the Pied Piper who had only to appear on a peal of laughter to have crowds flocking to see her play tennis between the cocktail hour and the *thés dansants*.'

From his perch in the umpire's chair for over 100 of her matches, Tinling was able to watch Lenglen grow into the most successful woman player of all time. Between 1919 and 1926, when she turned professional, she won Wimbledon singles and doubles (with Elizabeth Ryan) six times and only missed out in 1924 because of ill health. As in 1926, when she withdrew midway through the Championships after her infamous row with the referee

— her late arrival for a doubles had left Queen Mary staring at an empty court — Britain's lively Kitty McKane Godfree became the beneficiary of the temperamental star's various 'indispositions'.

First as Miss McKane in 1924 and again two years later, Mrs Godfree, who was to continue playing tennis into her 90s, won the Wimbledon singles crown. Even without Suzanne Lenglen's presence, Kitty's achievements were considerable, especially in 1924, when she battled back from the seemingly hopeless position of a set and 1-4 down in the final against no less a player than Helen Wills. Wills was the poker-faced girl from San Francisco who went on to win Wimbledon a record number of eight times between 1927 and 1938.

More extraordinary, perhaps, than her run of success at Wimbledon was the virtual invincibility Suzanne Lenglen established during her reign. Her only defeat came in less than ideal circumstances against Molla Mallory in the 1921 US championships, and 90 per cent of the matches she played were won by crushingly one-sided scores. No matter what the standard of opposition she faced, it required a monumental effort of concentration, fuelled by a champion's pride, to go on winning in that fashion.

There was nothing sub-standard, however, about the opposition Lenglen faced at the Carlton Hotel in Cannes on 16 February 1926. Having won the US title three times, Helen Wills had decided that it was time to challenge Lenglen on her own territory. Not only did the match create a level of international media attention unmatched by any single tennis encounter until Billie Jean King played Bobby Riggs 47 years later, but it turned out to be as dramatic as its pre-match build-up.

At 6-3, 6-5, 40-15 to a nervous and exhausted Lenglen, Wills blazed away with another of her big cross-court forehands, and a cry of 'out' was heard. The umpire called the score; the players shook hands and Suzanne was besieged with flowers and well-wishes as she slumped into her chair. But then a frantic signal was noticed from the linesman, Lord Charles Hope. He insisted he had called Helen Wills's shot 'good' and that the 'out' call had come from the crowd. The referee, Commander Hillyard, ordered that the point be given to the American and that the match should continue. As if in a trance, Suzanne threw off her coat and strode back on to the court.

Although she served a double fault the next time that she reached match point — an almost unheard-of occurrence for a player who was reputed to have served only six in her entire career — Suzanne Lenglen eventually won the match for the second time 6-3, 8-6 and collapsed sobbing with emotion as a seething mass of photographers and admirers engulfed her. She had proved her greatness and reached a peak of acclaim that she would never enjoy again.

The Four Musketeers

Although many tennis clubs in France — especially in that middle-class English playground of the Riviera — were still heavily influenced by British management and custom, the French set about reclaiming the game for themselves in the frenetic days of the 1920s. In addition to La Langlen, four male players burst on to the world scene and quickly became known as the 'Four Musketeers'. Three of them, Jean Borotra, Henri Cochet and Rene Lacoste, shared 18 Grand Slam singles titles over a period of nine years, while the fourth, Jacques 'Toto' Brugnon, collected ten doubles titles at Wimbledon, Paris and Australia with either Borotra or Cochet. Their dominance on clay courts was such that they did not allow the French championships, only started in 1925, to fall into foreign hands until Australia's Jack Crawford won it in 1933.

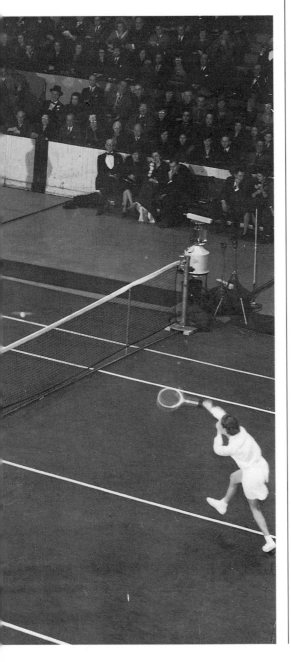

Left: Women's professional action at Madison Square Garden, New York City, in January 1941. Alice Marble (right) makes her pro debut against England's Mary Hardwick, who offered spirited resistance before losing to the former Wimbledon champion, 8-6, 8-6.

Right: William Johnston (1894–1946) was one of the top American players of the 1920s. He and rival Bill Tilden were known as 'Little Bill' and 'Big Bill' respectively. The pair won the Davis Cup for the US from 1920 to 1926, while in individual competition Johnston was Wimbledon champion in 1923 and US champion in 1915 and 1919.

By then the game in France, largely in response to the dashing exploits of the Four Musketeers, had been given a new home on the edge of the Bois de Boulogne. Named after a First World War aviator who became the first man ever to fly across the Mediterranean, it was called Stade Roland Garros.

Ted Tinling umpired the first match ever played on the new Centre Court — a preliminary women's event between France and Britain. But when the championships got under way, the crowds arrived in force, jamming the concrete stadium to its original 12,000 capacity. Two great champions gave the occasion an appropriately international flavour by winning the men's and women's singles — Henri Cochet for France and Helen Wills, now undisputed queen of the amateur game since Miss Lenglen's defection to the professional ranks, for the United States.

Big Bill Tilden

Almost alone, American Bill Tilden provided a challenge to the Four Musketeers. Tilden's compatriot, 'Little Bill' Johnston (who won Wimbledon in 1923) and the Australian Gerald Patterson (who had beaten the 41-year-old Norman Brookes in the first post-war Wimbledon final) were class performers but neither came close to capturing the imagination and affection of the world's sporting public like the arrogantly elegant Bill Tilden.

At home, Tilden was often in trouble with the tennis authorities. When he was suspended and thus ineligible to play for the United States in the 1928 Davis Cup challenge round, the French Federation, desperate to ensure a full house at their new Roland Garros Stadium, used diplomatic channels to petition the President. Eventually the American Ambassador in Paris was instructed to select Tilden over the head of the US Davis Cup captain. The French, justifiably confident, still won 4-1 but the crowds turned out in droves to applaud Big Bill.

Although he won his first tournament at the age of eight, Tilden's comparative lack of success as a teenager made him realize tennis was played in the mind as well as the arm. It was largely as a result of his deeply analytical study of the game's tactics that he turned himself into one of the great champions of all time.

Although Tilden's battles with the Four Musketeers became legend, his greatest challenge, perhaps, lay at home. The problem was 'Little Bill' Johnston. Not only did American tennis audiences prefer the gentlemanly good sportsmanship of Little Bill but, on the evidence of a string of encounters in 1919 — including the US championships which Johnston won in straight sets — Tilden, the flamboyant Philadelphian, was no match for his West Coast rival.

With his confidence boosted after Wimbledon in 1920, Tilden returned to New York prepared for the inevitable showdown. There was no concrete bowl at Forest Hills in those days but the wooden stands set up in front of the clubhouse were packed with 10,000 people for the championship final — and most of them were convinced Johnston would prove his superiority. After a match emblazoned with drama and tinged with tragedy, Big Bill proved them wrong.

The match was poised agonizingly at two sets all — Tilden having lost the fourth set 5-7 after winning the third 7-5 — when an aircraft taking aerial photographs crashed less than a hundred yards from the court. Tilden said he felt the earth shudder. Both occupants were killed but, to forestall panic, the players agreed to continue the match and Big Bill won 6-3 in the fifth.

Incredibly, the two Bills were to contest the next five Forest Hills finals, making a run of seven in all, and Tilden won the last six until the Musketeers thrust their way into the act, with Lacoste beating Borotra in 1926. Nevertheless Tilden tied Richard Sears's record by winning his seventh title in 1929. And although Jimmy Connors holds the distinction of having won the US title on three different surfaces (brought about by court changes at the West Side Tennis Club and the subsequent move to Flushing Meadow), no other player has yet come close to matching Tilden's achievement.

Tilden was virtually forced into the pro ranks because the USLTA decreed that, by signing a contract to make an instructional film, he had surrendered his amateur status. Tilden was not concerned. Although already 37 when he won his last Wimbledon in 1930, he knew he was still fit enough to make a lot of money on the exhibition circuit and proceeded to do so.

Ignoring the tongue-wagging vitriol that poured forth from his enemies, Tilden often used his young protégés in exhibition matches and continued to act in a manner towards them that was incredibly brazen for an age in which homosexuality was hardly considered a polite topic of conversation. In the end Tilden paid dearly for this trait and was twice imprisoned. He died, alone, in a small, shabby apartment he was renting near Hollywood and Vine, the epicentre of the glamorous world which he, more than anyone, had done so much to glamorize.

There are those who maintain to this day that Tilden was the greatest player of all time, but that is an impossible judgement to make. It is better, perhaps, merely to quote another great player of the era who spent no less than five months of non-stop travel around America in the company of Tilden, Don Budge and Mary Hardwick during one of those endless exhibition tours in the early 1940s. In *American Lawn Tennis*, Alice Marble, Wimbledon champion and four-time winner at Forest Hills, wrote, 'We loved Bill . . . temperamental, strange, generous . . . he was the king and always will be to those who love this game of tennis.'

Pride and prejudice

The next great figure of stature and controversy to set the turnstiles clicking was British. The fact that a statue of Fred Perry now greets visitors on arrival at Wimbledon gives some clue as to the achievements of this champion.

Like Tilden, Perry was not a shy or subservient man. In an age when juniors — especially juniors who did not speak the King's English with the accepted accent — were expected to toe the line and speak only when spoken to, Perry was never going to be the establishment's favourite son. But, always, he was going to be a champion.

He began by winning the World Table Tennis Championship and then, with the far-sighted assistance of his father, a Labour MP from Stockport, turned his attention to lawn tennis. He had been born in May 1909, one month before A.W. Gore had won Wimbledon for the last time. No other Englishman was to do so until Perry himself brought the men's title home and kept it there from 1934 to 1936.

Pride and prejudice marked Perry's career. When he survived a throat epidemic at Wimbledon in 1934 and eventually beat the holder Jack Crawford of Australia in straight sets in the final, an All England Club official walked into the dressing room. Laying the club tie that is traditionally awarded to a new champion over the back of the seat where Perry was changing, he turned away without a word. Then, without bothering to lower his voice, he turned to Crawford and said, 'Bad luck, old chap. So sorry the better man couldn't win.'

Thus was Britain's first champion in 25 years welcomed to the club. Perry did not help himself, of course. Although early coaches like his Davis Cup captain Roper Barrett and the BBC's legendary Dan Maskell learned to like and respect this brilliant young athlete, Fred's burning ambition was considered just a little bit too blatant by a generation who still considered the result far less important than the way you played the game. Perry played it hard and ruthlessly. Winning to him meant everything, partially because he had the true champion's inner drive for excellence, partially because of the social chip he carried on his shoulder and perhaps partially because he felt he owed it to his father.

In April 1930, S. F. Perry wrote to Fred's employers asking for a week's leave without wages for his son so that he could play in the British Hardcourt Championships at Bournemouth. His request was refused. That could have been the end but Papa Perry shared his son's love of a challenge.

'I was getting tired of foreign supremacy in sport,' Mr Perry wrote in his son's book published three years later. 'The inferiority complex seemed firmly rooted in British tennis.'

But not for long. Gambling with his son's future, Mr Perry gave Fred 12 months to prove himself. Digging into his modest MP's salary, he would bear the expense of allowing Fred to concentrate solely on his tennis. In the House of Commons, he seemed to gain a great deal more support for this enterprise than Fred himself did among the less democratically minded members of the All England Club. When the Labour MP was afraid to leave the House to watch his son at Wimbledon because his party was governing at the time in a minority situation, Arthur Steel-Maitland, leader of the Opposition, arranged what is termed 'live pairs' for Perry — that is to say, a member of the Opposition who would normally have been voting against the Government in a debate would agree to stay away until his 'pair's' return.

So it was with the blessing of both sides of the House that young Fred set out to conquer the tennis world, and no one could say he did not make a good job of it. Apart from becoming the first man since Wilding to win three consecutive Wimbledons, Perry won the United States singles three times; won the French and Australian once each; and ensured that Britain again reigned supreme in the Davis Cup by winning 45 out of 52 Cup rubbers between 1931 and 1936.

Love affair with Hollywood

Understandably, Perry responded to his popularity in the United States where people were more concerned with his flashing smile, dark good looks and brilliant running forehand than his accent. Hollywood was already in love with tennis and Fred became one of the favourites with the box holders at the Los Angeles Tennis Club. Charlie Chaplin, Gary Cooper, Clark Gable and Marlene Dietrich all thought Fred was wonderful. This love affair between the game and the great stars of the silver screen has continued to this day. Tennis offered good-looking people the chance to socialize and compete in a glamorous setting. In those romantic days between the wars, its lure became irresistible.

Perry turned professional in 1936 and was quickly followed on to the amateur stage by the American red-head he had beaten at Forest Hills that year in one of the greatest of all the US finals — Don Budge. Despite the power of Budge's backhand, Perry won 10-8 in the fifth set. It would have been difficult for Fred to have said goodbye to the great arenas of the tennis world in more fitting style.

Winning the Grand Slam

Budge, of course, was to go on to even greater things. When Don started winning the major titles in increasingly impressive fashion in 1938, Allison Danzig, the great tennis correspondent of the *New York Times*, talked of a 'Grand Slam' of the world's four major championships. Until then no one had won all four in one year, partially perhaps because top players often lacked the time or the inclination to make the long boat trip to Australia.

Left: Bill Tilden was undoubtedly one of the greatest tennis players of all time. He could play every shot to perfection, and his major title haul included seven US and three Wimbledon singles.

Right: Seen here at Wimbledon
in 1938, Donald Budge was the
first man to win the world's
four major tournaments in
one year.

But when Budge returned from Australia with a victory over John Bromwich under his belt and went on to beat Roderick Menzel in the French championships and trounced Bunny Austin at Wimbledon, no one was more aware of the record that lay at his fingertips when he arrived at Forest Hills than Budge himself. Although he was to drop a set in a Grand Slam final for the first time that year, he lost it to his great buddy and doubles partner, Gene Mako, who eventually went down 6-1 in the fourth. It was an emotional climax to one of the great achievements in tennis because, as Budge was to confide later, he felt Mako was the only person in the world who 'really understood what my accomplishment meant to me'.

In fact, it was not until the years rolled on after the war that people started to comprehend the enormity of the task of winning the Grand Slam. Lew Hoad came tantalizingly close in 1956 when, oddly, he too faced his doubles partner in the final at Forest Hills with three titles already won. But Ken Rosewall was a tougher opponent than Mako and won in four sets. So one had to wait for the left-handed genius of Rod Laver in 1962 before anyone managed to join Budge as a true Grand Slam champion. Laver, of course, immortalized himself by doing it again once he was able to return from professional exile in 1969, but no one has since come as close as Hoad did.

Epic encounter

Budge remained unbeaten between July 1937 and September 1938 and promptly joined Perry on the professional tour, earning as much as $100,000 in his first year — an enormous sum in those days. But many feel his greatest match as an amateur was when the United States were playing a Davis Cup semi-final against West Germany at Wimbledon in 1937. A few days before, the great German player Gottfried von Cramm had lost the third of his three consecutive Wimbledon finals to Budge. Now, with the tie poised at two rubbers each, they were destined to meet again.

Ted Tinling, acting in his Wimbledon capacity as the official who accompanied the players on to the Centre Court, was just preparing to escort them out when a long distance phone call was put through to the locker-room for von Cramm. Several times during the conversation that followed von Cramm, standing rigidly to attention, repeated *'Ja, mein Fuhrer'.*

Hitler's good wishes did not do von Cramm much good. He lost one of the greatest matches ever seen on the Centre Court 8-6 in the fifth when Budge, on his fourth match point, slipped on the grass yet still managed to push a drive down the line for a winner. Less than a year later von Cramm's *'Fuhrer'* had him imprisoned on charges of homosexuality. But von Cramm survived, not only the war which saw him making secret trips to Sweden on behalf of anti-Nazi factions in Berlin, but also the devastation of the post-war years in which he was active in helping to rebuild German tennis.

Before the cavalcade was brought to another abrupt and tragic halt in 1939, two Americans, Alice Marble and the irrepressible Bobby Riggs, cleaned up at Wimbledon and Forest Hills. Seven years later the game entered another age.

Percentage tennis

Wimbledon had been bombed by the time the tennis world, depleted once again, congregated for The Championships in 1946. As in 1919, there was a great determination to get on with the show. No one was keener than a crew-cut Californian whose very name was to become a by-word for professional tennis. As well as serving his country in the US Navy,

Jack Kramer had not wasted the war years. Amongst other things he had worked out the possibilities to which an opponent was reduced when faced with a big serve and volley. Budge, for instance, was the only player in the world who could be relied upon to make more than 20 per cent of cross-court passes off the backhand. So, once at the net, Kramer would cover down the line. If he was volleying up to scratch, 80 per cent of the points would be his. It became known as percentage tennis and, in 1946, it was expected to win him Wimbledon. But it didn't.

Percentage tennis does not make allowances for such basic human frailties as blisters on the racket hand and, although Jack refused to use it as an excuse, it was this malady that made him easy prey for a stocky left-hander from Prague called Jaroslav Drobny. Kramer couldn't play again until Forest Hills.

Reshaping the future

So it was that an enormous Frenchman called Yvon Petra became the first post-war Wimbledon winner, an achievement he never came close to repeating, while Kramer, who duly won the US title, revised his well-laid plans not only for his own future but for that of the entire game.

Kramer knew exactly where he was going but before he could progress he needed the Wimbledon title. In 1947 nothing was going to stop him. If Field Marshal Montgomery had parked one of his Eighth Army tanks on the Centre Court, 'Big Jake' would probably have served and volleyed his way right through it. Certainly his opponents were cannon fodder. He dropped one set to Dinny Pails only because, as Pails explained later, Kramer spent a quarter of an hour missing everything by a hair's breadth. In the final, he blitzed the unfortunate American Tom Brown 6-1, 6-3, 6-2.

Then, after retaining his Forest Hills title, he accepted an offer from the promoter Jack Harris and turned professional. His debut was not, personally, an auspicious one because Kramer lost to Bobby Riggs, who had become more accustomed to the fast boards and indoor lighting at Madison Square Garden.

But Jack was not particularly perturbed. What interested him far more was the fact that 15,000 people turned out in thick snow to leave $250,000 at the box office. It only confirmed his gut feeling that professional tennis had a future.

To a very large extent, Kramer became its future. Riggs, whose eye for the dollar has always been unerring, realized that, in the long run, he would make more money managing Kramer than playing him, so for a couple of years Bobby ran the tour. But Kramer's vision, personality and stature had always dominated the tour and it was inevitable that, in 1951, he should eventually take over to form a troupe of touring pros that became indelibly stamped with his own name.

Below: Rod Laver joined the professional ranks at the beginning of 1963, having won the Grand Slam of the four major championships the previous year. He soon established himself as the best of the contract pro's, and when tennis went open in 1968 he returned to the traditional events and completed a second Grand Slam in 1969.

*Left: Jack Kramer, Wimbledon
champion of 1947, turned
professional shortly
afterwards, and within a few
years he took over control of
that area of the game. A great
influence over the development
of modern tennis, he originally
devised the Grand Prix.*

35

Knowing that new blood was needed on a constant basis to maintain interest in players who were virtual outlaws as far as the official game was concerned, banned not only from the major championships but from all arenas that came under the jurisdiction of the ILTF, Kramer began systematically signing up each new Wimbledon champion. It started with Frank Sedgman, the first of Harry Hopman's great Australians, and continued for the next ten years. During that period only Vic Seixas and Jaroslav Drobny resisted his overtures, and it was entirely due to Kramer that, between 1952 and 1962, only Hoad and Laver were repeat champions (before they, too, became Kramer pros).

Kramer was accused of disfiguring the game but he was accused of many things in his time, including a few by his greatest draw card, Pancho Gonzales, with whom he had frequent feuds. But Jack Kramer has always been a big man with a big heart and no one has had such a powerful and lengthy part to play in shaping the destiny of the modern game.

The Hopman era

Ironically, considering how much he was opposed to professional tennis, Hopman spent the 1950s down in Australia sowing the seeds that blossomed into an incredible harvest of champions — and as fast as the fruit ripened, so Kramer plucked them from the amateur tree. After Sedgman came the two teenage wonders, Lew Hoad and Ken Rosewall, who stirred a nation's pride in 1953 by retaining the Davis Cup for Australia against the United States in front of huge crowds at Kooyong. Then, following in rapid succession, came Rex Hartwig, Mervyn Rose, Mal Anderson, Ashley Cooper, Rod Laver, Roy Emerson, Fred Stolle, John Newcombe and Tony Roche.

The next two being cultivated in the Hopman orchard were John Alexander and Phil Dent. But before they blossomed, Hopman, having fallen into financial difficulties, left Australia for the United States. It would be wrong to say that Alexander and Dent died on the vine, but without Hop's doctrinaire approach to training, neither fulfilled his true potential.

Hopman's genius was not as a tactician but as a motivator. It is easy to lead the weak but the weak did not interest Hopman. Pruning his orchard, he took only the strongest saplings and made them bend to his will. As a result, powerful young men with big personalities who liked to party as hard as they played, developed bodies of oak and minds that could withstand the fiercest pressure this game of the mind could create.

At times many of them hated Hop for what he put them through but, just before he died, still in harness at the age of 79 at his tennis camp in Florida, Hopman was able to read the opinion of Fred Stolle in his book *Tennis Down Under*. After chronicling the agonies he underwent in trying to establish himself in Hopman's eyes as a worthy Davis Cup player, Stolle wrote, 'Harry Hopman is the godfather of us all . . . and I have enough respect for what he did for me to put my son, Sandon, in his hands.'

During the Hopman era, Australia won the Davis Cup 15 times in 18 years. When he set up shop in the United States, two of the most irreverent players of the modern generation, Vitas Gerulaitis and John McEnroe, benefited from his teaching.

Ladies' showcase

The tug of war between the amateur establishment and the maverick professionals that was tearing at the fabric of the men's game throughout the 1950s and early 1960s did not affect the women because they did not have the drawing power at the time. Had Maureen Connolly, who won Wimbledon for three consecutive years while achieving the first women's Grand Slam in 1953, not been seriously hurt in a riding accident, it might have been different. But, without a figure of Suzanne Lenglen's magnetic appeal, no promoter was prepared to take such a significant risk.

So Wimbledon remained the ladies' great showcase. With the controversial assistance of Ted Tinling, they showed themselves off with a style and extravagance that the press and the public adored but which the establishment abhorred.

Tinling had been appalled by the unisex look of the first great American champions to dominate Wimbledon after the war. Louise Brough and Margaret Osborne wore clothes that looked like an extension of a wartime uniform. Christian Dior fed women's hunger for a return to femininity with his 'New Look' in 1947. But there was no new look for women as far as sports clothes were concerned. In fact, it was virtually impossible to buy a tennis dress of any design, let alone a fashionable or flattering one.

It was against this background that Tinling and a beautiful American player called Gussy Moran teamed up to create one of the most publicized fashion sensations of all time. Quite simply, Ted designed some lace panties and Gussy wore them. Thirty years on, it is very difficult to comprehend how unsimple it all seemed at the time. Acres of space were taken up on the front pages of the world's newspapers as photographers waited breathlessly for the chance to shoot the tiny strip of lace that was barely visible during Moran's matches.

The excitement this innocent piece of material created was, of course, a reflection of the general drabness of the post-war years, especially in Britain, but it merely inflamed the All England Club committee. Tinling was accused of 'drawing attention to the sexual area', and it led to him severing his connection with a club he had served with unswerving loyalty for the previous 35 years.

Opposite: John Newcombe was the last of the 'amateur' champions — he took the men's singles titles at both Wimbledon and Forest Hills in 1967. The following year tennis went open, and contract professionals became eligible to compete alongside the 'amateurs' in traditional events.

Right: *Ilie Nastase shares a joke with a line judge at Wimbledon. Nastase did much to promote the popularity of tennis in the 1970s, though he was frequently in trouble with officialdom over behaviour that at times became a trifle too exuberant.*

Attracting a wider audience

What the Club refused to acknowledge was the vast world-wide interest Tinling had helped create in the Championships and the game of tennis in general. In this respect, Tinling and Gussy Moran share an important contribution to the sport's overall wellbeing with three other players, Ilie Nastase, Jimmy Connors and John McEnroe. Along with Bjorn Borg, whose majestic bearing and magisterial record acted as a perfect foil to the antics of his three contemporaries, these highly individual personalities have attracted the attention of the general public.

They have drawn them to peer querulously at first, at a game they would never otherwise have dreamed of watching. Many, of course, will have drifted away again. But crowd attendances, which continue to grow year by year, prove that many have turned from sensation seekers to true fans, who now come to enjoy the excitement of a great match rather than to wait for Connors to give someone the finger or for McEnroe to throw a fit.

The All England Club committee were as convinced that Tinling had harmed the game as many people are convinced today that McEnroe is a bad influence on the young. The Nastase-McEnroe phenomenon is a far more complex question — but the simple truth is that, as an arm of the entertainment industry, tennis benefits just as much as a rock concert or a prize fight from publicity which reaches beyond the committed fan. It is the game's consistent ability to produce superstars of this type that has helped it grow in such amazing fashion.

The writing on the wall

The affair of Gussy Moran's panties was the harbinger of further conflicts to come, in which the amateur tennis establishment was in direct confrontation with the increasingly professional world of the players.

Kramer had tried to ensure that every possible obstacle would be taken out of the path of a merger between the professional and amateur games. He resigned his position as boss of the pro tour, handing over to a Professional Players Association, with Tony Trabert, still the last American to win the French title, taking up a dual player-cum-organizational role in Paris.

At the ILTF meeting in Paris in 1960, a groundswell of opinion created a motion for the immediate implementation of some form of open tennis. Pancho Gonzales, Lew Hoad, Ken Rosewall and Alex Olmedo were still at the height of their powers but all were banned from the world's great championships because they were Kramer pros. Under-the-counter payments to amateurs were just starting to become a fact of life at the traditional tournaments around the world and the custom could only grow. Many members of the ILTF hierarchy recognized this and nearly won the day, but the motion failed by five votes. According to Philippe Chatrier, current

President of the ITF, his predecessors in the ILTF hierarchy 'never thought professionalism was here to stay'. It was to be another eight years before open tennis was finally introduced.

And so the erosion continued. After winning Wimbledon twice Laver succumbed to the inevitable and turned pro. So, too, did a few lesser lights such as the British No 1 Mike Davies, Robert Haillet of France, Denmark's Kurt Nielsen and the elegant Spaniard Andres Gimeno. All were fine players that the amateur game could ill afford to lose.

Nevertheless, with the Hopman production line still in operation, there was an abundance of talent around in the early 1960s. The sport was lucky indeed to have such a depth of competitive strength that players of the calibre of America's Chuck McKinley, who bounced through the Wimbledon draw of 1963 as if on a trampoline, and those great Australians Roy Emerson and Fred Stolle were able to maintain the public's interest. And that was just the grass-court line-up.

Over on the continent it was the day of the great clay-court artists. After winning the French title for two consecutive years that imperious Italian Nicola Pietrangeli, displaying one of the most beautiful backhands the game has ever seen, found himself deprived of a hat-trick by a buck-toothed ex-ball boy from Madrid called Manolo Santana. When they played a match to dream about in the 1961 final at Stade Roland Garros, Santana's explosive forehand finally won the day 6-2 in the fifth. Emotional Latin heroes that they were, the two champions stood on the Centre Court with the young Spaniard weeping copiously on the shoulder of the man he had just beaten.

It would be simplistic to maintain that the mere introduction of prize money has rid the sport of such moments. Nor has it eliminated the possibility of fostering new rivalries based on deep-seated friendship and trust, such as those that existed between the dashing American Budge Patty and Jaroslav Drobny, or even later between Emerson and Stolle (who used to cook each other breakfast at their Putney flat before playing in consecutive Wimbledon finals in 1964 and 1965). Of course money has made a difference, but it is society and the world in which we live that have changed sport — not sport that has changed the world.

The players' champions

It was against a background of a world that was becoming economically tougher and more realistic that six men, above all others, wrought changes in tennis that would create as big an upheaval as any major sport has undergone since people first started buying tickets to watch athletes perform.

A former junior player, founder of the highly successful magazine *Tennis de France* and French Davis Cup captain, Philippe

Chatrier took over the French Federation and set in motion the incredible upsurge in popularity of the game in France. With the aid of a $14,000,000 grant from the French government, Chatrier laid the foundation for the modernization of Stade Roland Garros and for the nationwide network of coaches and training centres that eventually started producing players of the calibre of Henri Leconte, Thierry Tulasne, Guy Forget and, particularly, Yannick Noah. In 1977 Chatrier became President of the International Federation. Previously the office rotated every two years. Chatrier, unchallenged, is now entering his second decade of power.

Like Chatrier, the American Donald Dell became his country's Davis Cup captain in the late 1960s. But, having led the United States to crushing victories over Australia, Romania (suddenly a force with the emergence of Ion Tiriac and Ilie Nastase) and West Germany, this dynamic, abrasive lawyer immediately saw the commercial possibilities that would soon exist in a game that was suddenly being discovered by television. While Chatrier, believing deeply in the game's traditions, viewed sponsorship as a necessary evil, Dell not only welcomed the devil into the Washington office he quickly set up with two partners, but virtually shaped the role that devil would play in the brave but desperately naive new world of open tennis. Signing up the stars of his Davis Cup teams, Dell became the game's first agent and wheeler-dealer. With Kramer, he was instrumental in forming the Association of Tennis Professionals.

Right: Three generations of Wimbledon champions are seen together at a tournament at La Quinta, California, in the early 1980s. Tony Trabert (left) was champion in 1955, Jack Kramer (centre) in 1947, and Ellsworth Vines (right) in 1932.

Another lawyer, Mark McCormack was on the golf course making money as the first real sports agent for Arnold Palmer and Jack Nicklaus when he noticed what was happening in pro tennis. Rod Laver became his first tennis client and, by operating in healthy competition with Dell through his company IMG, McCormack ensured that money would continue to flow into the game. The concept of the sponsorship village as a corporate entertainment centre at major tournaments, including Wimbledon, has been one of the most important innovations seen in the game in recent years, and McCormack's staff must take much of the credit.

Lamar Hunt, too, was an entrepreneur already involved in another pro sport. An oil millionaire, and owner of the Kansas City Chiefs grid-iron football team, Hunt joined a promoter called Dave Dixon in a venture to sign up a group of the top amateurs and form a new professional tour. World Championship Tennis was the result, and the original tour set the standard for the professional tournaments that were to proliferate around the world in the years that followed. The second great WCT Dallas final in which Rosewall retained his title by beating Laver in the fifth set tiebreak did more than any other match to fire the imagination of the American television audience in 1972 and give another major boost to the tennis boom that was already on the launching pad. However, Chatrier and Kramer, for a variety of reasons, opposed Hunt at every turn, and WCT's role in the game is now drastically reduced.

In fact, Jack Kramer's influence actually became greater as he moved into middle age. Encouraged by the emerging Chatrier, Kramer started to put his fertile mind to use on behalf of the establishment side of the game once open tennis arrived in 1968. He promptly devised the concept of the Grand Prix, a worldwide network of tournaments, linked by a points system that would award the leaders at year's end with bonus money from a sponsorship pool. Pepsi-Cola became the first overall sponsor and it was in a cold, old stadium in Tokyo in 1970 that Stan Smith won the first ever Masters and a first prize of $15,000. Kramer's offspring, after a peripatetic youth and a variety of foster-parents ranging from Commercial Union to Colgate and Volvo, settled into a permanent home at New York's Madison Square Garden in the mid 1970s. It is administered by the Men's International Professional Tennis Council (MIPTC), which emerged as the game's governing body during the 1970s.

In the meantime, Kramer had been sought out by the new generation of players to act as the Executive Director of the Association of Tennis Professionals which was formed at Forest Hills in 1972. Cliff Drysdale was elected the ATP's first President and was instrumental in leading the fledgling association into a showdown with the amateur establishment that resulted in the 1973 Wimbledon boycott and changed the face of the game forever. But it was Kramer who was made to carry the burden of that momentous decision. Nikki Pilic, a Yugoslav who had refused to play Davis Cup for his country, became the catalyst for the boycott but he was peripheral to the central issue — the insistence of professional athletes that amateur officials should no longer control their destiny. Kramer stood full-square behind the militant players in 1973 and so completed the revolution he had helped to start with his own tour after the Second World War.

It was sad and ironic that the players found themselves hurting the Championships run by the man who had made the whole thing possible. In 1967 Herman David, a volatile Welshman, had finally grown sick of the hypocrisy of 'shamateurism' and had announced to a startled tennis world that, no matter what the ILTF thought about it, he was going to open up Wimbledon to every category of player the following year. Wimbledon's power and influence was such in those days that the anti-open tennis factions inside the ILTF knew that further resistance would be useless.

David's courage was rewarded when Rod Laver returned to Wimbledon in 1968 to reclaim the crown he had been forced to relinquish when he had turned pro after the 1962 final. Beginning with a first-round victory over the Estonian Tomas Lejus in 1961, Laver was to go on to play 31 singles without defeat at Wimbledon until Roger Taylor beat him in

the fourth round in 1970. Bjorn Borg was to have a longer unbeaten run (41) a few years later; but without David's intervention Laver might never have had the opportunity to prove that he, too, was one of Wimbledon's greatest champions.

Even some of his closest friends were saddened by David's attitude towards the players' stand in 1973. The ATP made it plain that the last thing they wanted to do was to hurt Wimbledon and that if David were to defy the ILTF ban on Pilic, the boycott could be avoided. But David, who had championed the professional cause six years before, now chose to side with the ILTF and, partially as a result of the emotional confrontation, died shortly afterwards an embittered man.

Battle of the sexes

If six men had strongly influenced the evolution of the men's game, two women and a man were soon to shape the destiny of women's tennis in similar fashion. Once again, however, it is difficult to keep Kramer out of the story. It was at the Pacific South West in 1970 — a tournament run by Kramer — that Billie Jean King and Rosie Casals became infuriated at the way they were treated as a second-class act by the great macho figure. That year the men's prize money at the tournament was actually ten times as much as the women's, which was the final straw. They got on the phone to Gladys Heldman, publisher of *World Tennis* magazine, and said, in essence, 'Gladys, we can't take this anymore. Get us our own tour.' To cut an extremely long story short, she did.

However, among a million others, it took one more phone call in particular to put the show on the road. That was to the Chairman of the Board of Philip Morris in New York. Joe Cullman, a long-time friend and admirer of Heldman, had a brand of cigarettes, specially marketed for women, called Virginia Slims. With Billie Jean, an increasingly prominent voice in the women's movement in America, ready to front the publicity campaign, Cullman and Heldman came to an immediate agreement. Heldman signed up nine players for a token dollar and became an even longer, sharper thorn in the side of the USLTA than Kramer had ever been.

It is difficult to over-estimate the impact Gladys Heldman had on the growth and development of tennis, particularly in America, during the formative years of the newly structured professional game in the early 1970s. Her editorials in *World Tennis* were radical but reasoned; the causes she espoused controversial but sound. Few people imagined that crowds of any size, let alone television, could be persuaded to take notice of tournaments for women only but, with the pioneering help of Billie Jean King, Rosie Casals, Ann Jones and her own daughter Julie, Heldman took the battle to the barricades and won.

The whole movement was helped to a

Opposite: Nobody has done more to further women's professional tennis than Billie Jean King. She campaigned tirelessly during the 1970s to get the fledgling women's circuit on the road after the players decided to break away from the men's tour.

remarkable degree by a sporting phenomenon that occurred in 1973. The outrageous and indefatigable Bobby Riggs, then a sprightly 55-year-old, challenged the top women players to a match. Margaret Court, the supreme women's champion of the era who ended up with more Grand Slam titles than any woman in history, was the first to accept. But the great Australian was not a leader in the women's movement and, apart from a tendency to be undone by nerves in difficult situations, Margaret never quite understood what it was all about.

No one needed to tell Billie Jean that it was about a great deal more than a tennis match. One of the great feminists of her day and a show-woman to her fingertips, Mrs King grabbed the moment and with the help of a very willing Riggs, turned it into one of the most bizarre showbiz spectaculars of the decade. Wearing a dress sparkling with thousands of sequins hand-sewn by Ted Tinling, Billie Jean was borne into the vast Houston Astrodome like some Egyptian queen, to be greeted by easily the largest crowd — 30,500 — ever to watch a single tennis match. The event, coming towards the end of the Vietnam War and the beginning of the first oil crisis, offered precisely the kind of harmless distraction that people craved. The

Right: Centre Court at the West Hants Club, Bournemouth, England — venue for the world's first open tournament in April, 1968. The British Hard Court Championships, which were played here for many years, ceased to be held after 1982 for lack of a sponsor.

worldwide interest in this self-syled Battle of the Sexes was extraordinary and in America the media went crazy. Even a serious journal like the *Los Angeles Times* led its front page with the story when Billie Jean proved her point brilliantly by beating Riggs.

Not since Suzanne Lenglen defeated Helen Wills at the Carlton in Cannes all those years before had a tennis match involving a woman attracted so much attention. But it went further than that. Never before or since has a game of tennis been the subject of such intense discussion and interest. It was a sociological as well as a sporting phenomenon that may never be repeated.

Soaring popularity

Meanwhile, even the traditional game was undergoing radical change. Under the all-seeing eye of television, pro tournaments were sprouting like mushrooms and the middle-class were stopping only at the pro shop to grab some Fila gear before rushing for the tennis courts. It had become a fad sport and, although many lost interest when they discovered just how difficult it was to play in contrast to how easy the pros made it look on TV, the game's base was broadened and its appeal more deeply rooted among the young and active.

While John Newcombe and Stan Smith

Above: Whitney Reed is seen as a spectator at the US Pro Indoor Championships in Philadelphia. He won a tape recorder as first prize when competing in the tournament in the late 1960s.

themselves acting as the corporate tools of the real-estate developers. Cliff Drysdale won a WCT title among the dust and scaffolding of a new resort site in north Miami that today is known as Turnberry Isle. Other events became almost as nomadic as the players themselves.

Typically, many get-rich-quick merchants were jumping on and falling off the new gravy train when they discovered they couldn't discuss the difference between a top-spin backhand and Bjorn Borg's headband. But, happily for the longterm health of the game, there were others like Marilyn and Ed Fernberger who recognized the possibilities, did their homework, and built tournaments that became pillars of the open-tennis concept.

The Fernbergers began in a school gymnasium in Philadelphia in the late 1960s, and when Whitney Reed, an eccentric and rare talent from San Francisco, won one of the early tournaments he received a tape recorder as first prize. Now crowds of 80,000 pour into the Spectrum one week every winter to watch the likes of John McEnroe or Ivan Lendl pick up purses of over $50,000.

Big earners

By the mid 1970s the wealth in the game had become quite staggering. In 1971 a top pro like Marty Riessen set his sights on a goal of $100,000 in prize money for the year and, despite being the eighth-ranked player in the world, just missed. By 1977, Jaime Fillol, the 29th-highest earner on the circuit, collected $102,000. And the growth has never stopped. In 1982, a somewhat artificial year in that WCT were fighting back against the Grand Prix and offering a series of tournaments with a $100,000 top prize, Lendl raked in $2,028,000 while a total of 54 pros on the men's tour passed the magic $100,000 mark. By the end of 1987 over 60 male pros had earned more than a million dollars in career prize money — but the biggest earner of all was Martina Navratilova.

The Czech-born left-hander who had waited a few years before realizing her full potential spent most of the 1980s locked in a highly lucrative but aesthetically superb duel with Chris Evert. At the time of writing these two great champions had met 74 times in official matches and Martina's prize money total stood at £11,000,000. Chris was not exactly poor, either. After winning 'La Trophee de la Femme' at the Pierre Barthes Club in Cap d'Agde in 1987, Chris thought the Cartier-designed silver leopard and gold ball she had received was something Martina would particularly like so she gave it to her. It was valued at £20,000. It was not just that Chris, with career earnings of £8,000,000, could afford to give away a trinket of such value, but that these two great rivals had defied the trend among the top players of the day and become genuinely close friends.

Spawning an entire generation that would

played the upstanding champions to Ilie Nastase's talented clown and the dour Czech Jan Kodes strong-armed his way to two consecutive French titles and a Wimbledon crown in the boycott year of 1973, the very nature of the tournaments in which they played was undergoing drastic change. In Europe it was a question of modernizing old established events like the Count Godo Cup at the Real Club de Barcelona and the Italian championships at the Foro Italico and streamlining them for the new professional age.

To an extent this was also true in America, where Dwight Davis's home patch at the Longwood Cricket Club in Boston quickly updated itself and became the US Pro Championships. For much of the time on the American tour, however, tennis players found

dominate the tour by sheer weight of numbers in the 1980s, Bjorn Borg carried the Swedish flag out on to the new professional circuit in 1974, winning the French and Italian Opens and the US Pro Championship in Boston as a teenager of precocious skills and narrow-eyed determination.

The sudden emergence of World Team Tennis, an inter-city league devised largely by Billie Jean King and her husband Larry, interrupted Borg's domination of Stade Roland Garros because WTT cut right across the European clay-court circuit. But once he returned there in 1978, he added four more titles to the two he had already won. Bjorn, with his two-handed backhand and superbly grooved ground-strokes, was expected to win on clay. What dumbfounded his fellow players as much as the critics was his unbroken five-year reign as champion of Wimbledon.

Although fortunate that, for most of those years, there was no really topnotch serve-and-volley expert to oppose him, Borg's feat, achieved as it was with a volley that was never of the highest calibre, elevated him to a pantheon reserved for the game's greatest champions.

Tactical victory

It was in 1975, the year before Borg began his run, that Arthur Ashe became the first black male ever to win the Wimbledon singles crown. Following in Althea Gibson's footsteps would have ensured Ashe a special niche in history in any case; but with his victory over Jimmy Connors, who went into the final as one of the hottest favourites for years, Ashe achieved something very difficult and virtually unique. He went out to play the most important match of his life on the world's most awe-inspiring stage and proceeded to play in a style that was totally alien to his character.

On a fast grass court, Ashe slow-balled Connors to defeat. Even when a bewildered Connors clawed his way back into the match by winning the third set, Ashe stuck resolutely to a style he had never adopted before and never tried again. Dinking and lobbing and denying Connors the pace he could feed off so effectively, Ashe completed one of the most intriguing tactical victories ever seen on the Centre Court. Appropriately, perhaps, it was a thinking man's triumph.

Role models

Although Ashe and Borg were very different personalities they both exhibited a court demeanour that made them perfect role models for the young. It was ironic that they both played in an era that, increasingly, saw the game's image plummet. Three players — Nastase, Connors and McEnroe — were largely responsible for it and although some of the younger Americans, often pushed to extremes by fanatically ambitious parents, started to ape the three super-stars, the image become a distortion of the true facts.

Because of the shape and size of the playing area, with spectators near enough to hear a player's whispered oath, tennis players are forced to maintain a far higher level of self-control than their counterparts in other major sports. Also, it still took the public at large a long time to realize that, far from being a game for sissies, tennis was a brutal mental and physical battle. Exploiting this misconception, the media seized upon any outburst, emblazoning the names of Nastase and McEnroe across the front pages of tabloid newspapers as if they were criminals.

Laying down the laws

Although it did indeed create enormous publicity for the sport, the trend needed to be checked before it got out of hand. With the appointment in 1982 of Marshall Happer, a

Above: Arthur Ashe in contemplative mood. The popular and cerebral American was the first black winner of major men's titles in tennis, and one of the game's most articulate spokesmen.

conscientious lawyer from North Carolina, as Chief Administrator of the MIPTC, the game at last had a full-time official to implement the laws laid down by the Council, which consisted of nine unpaid members who met but four times a year. Had a Happer-type figure been appointed soon after the Council came into being some five years before, much of the sloppy officiating which allowed McEnroe and others to get away with their frequently appalling antics could have been avoided.

But that tardiness was, to an extent, a throwback to the chaotic way tennis exploded into the television era as a multi-million dollar business before anyone was properly prepared to deal with it. Making rules, appointing officials and drawing up tournament schedules to cover a circuit that runs non-stop across five continents throughout the year is a task of mind-bending complexity, and the administrative inefficiency that marred the early years of open tennis was virtually unavoidable. Now, with a highly trained group of young umpires — epitomized by the Australian Richard Ings, who first took the chair at the age of 21 — settling into a well-structured routine, the behaviour problem is fading.

Although McEnroe will stand out as the great genius of the age, an incomparable talent who offered the world a new concept in the art of controlling a ball with a racket, he remains the exception to the current trend. The Gores and Scriveners and Hillyards of long ago might find it a hard fact to stomach, but the one word that dominates tennis today is professionalism.

Striving for perfection

If evidence is required, one need look no further than the examples set by the two players who have been nominated by the ITF as the No 1 player in the world more times than any others during the 1980s — Martina Navratilova and Ivan Lendl. Driven, perhaps, by their restricted beginnings in Czechoslovakia, both these great champions have taken whatever talent they were born with and honed it into athletic machines of unrivalled perfection. Using every means at their disposal, from rigidly followed diets to electronic training devices, Martina and Ivan have forced their way to the top of a fiercely competitive game and dominated it by sheer willpower.

Even at this stage in their careers, there are signs that the end of the rainbow might just have appeared on the horizon for both. But it seems certain now that they have set the standards of fitness and commitment that will be required, not merely to reach the top, but to stay there for more than one fleeting moment of glory.

Tennis correspondents lose count of the number of times they tell each other on the circuit, at some distant pit stop in Tokyo, Sydney or Prague, how much the game has changed. They reminisce about how, for example, Lew Hoad stayed up all night before winning the French championship, or how players on the WCT tour, bereft of coaches, agents and psychologists, used to eat together every night and worry about each other's problems.

As Slobodan Zivojinovic was saying only last year after beating his good friend Boris Becker in an unusually acrimonious match in the Seiko Classic, 'It is almost impossible to have friends on the circuit now. There is too much money; too much pressure.'

That, of course, is a sadly ironic sign of success. Too much money; too much at stake. Who ever thought it would come to that? Not Major Wingfield, nor even that remarkable lady who is now entering her 90s, Kitty Godfree. She has had a look at what it is like today and has sat between Ivan and Martina at the ITF gala dinner to honour the world champions which is held in Paris every year during the French Open. They and all future champions, while striving for excellence, could also do well to read some words Kitty wrote back in 1925, just after she had won Wimbledon for the first time.

'Lawn Tennis is one of the good things in the world; one of the things that help and are really worth while.

'A strenuous hour on the tennis court in the fresh air and sunshine is magnificent medicine for a pessimist. Sport, exhilaration, pleasure and good exercise are all realized more quickly and conveniently at lawn tennis than any other way I know and that is, perhaps, why I love it and believe in it.'

At the age of 90 Kitty Godfree was still playing it, loving it and believing in it. Perhaps no more needs to be said.

Opposite: Love match: Jimmy Connors and Chris Evert were engaged to each other when each won the singles at Wimbledon for the first time in 1974. The marriage never took place, and both players found different spouses.

Left: Kitty Godfree, who won the women's singles at Wimbledon in 1924 and 1926, only gave up playing social games at the All England Club when she had passed her 90th birthday.

The Great Players

Any list of the 100 greatest players in the history of tennis has to be subjective. There are well over 100 names on the honours rolls of the four great singles championships for men and women, and many of those players would not figure in the all-time pantheon because their titles were won from modest fields. Conversely, there have been players who can claim a place in the list even though they did not win any of the major singles titles.

In this chapter, players of the modern era take preference over the stars of the early years, because overall standards of play are indisputably higher now than they were before the Second World War. Since the advent of open tennis in 1968, the strength of the international game has risen immeasurably. Proof of this lies in the fact that whereas British players of county standard would once have been accepted direct into the Wimbledon draw, they would now not even gain a place in the qualifying rounds. When computer rankings were introduced in the mid 1970s, a few hundred names were included; now the lists run into thousands.

Unlike sports such as athletics and swimming, where achievement can be tangibly measured, greatness in tennis can only be determined by seeing players in action — and that can only be a rough estimate of ability. Over the years, experts have delighted in speculating whether, say, Bill Tilden at his best would have beaten Bjorn Borg, and chains of results have been compiled to prove that he could, or could not. But such hypotheses are futile, and nothing can be proved beyond doubt.

The 52 men and 48 women selected here are all players who have made their mark in the game to varying degrees. Those who have not found a place are, of course, mentioned in the records section at the end of this book.

Left: Bjorn Borg takes a backhand volley at Wimbledon. The great Swedish player achieved the unique record of winning the title five years in a row — the only male player to do so since the challenge round was abolished in 1922. But Martina Navratilova has won the women's singles for six consecutive years.

Arthur ASHE
b 1943

Arthur Ashe is, to date, the only black player to have won major men's singles titles in tennis. Born in Richmond, Virginia, his background was humble, and his rise to the top flight of the game more difficult than most. His father, a policeman, was able to provide him with a decent education, and he attended UCLA, during which time he became, in 1963, the first black player to be selected for the US Davis Cup team.

National service delayed his entry into the game full-time, and he was twice runner-up for the Australian Championship (1966 and 1967) before he was free to play on an uninterrupted basis. In 1968, the year tennis went open, Ashe retained amateur status to lead the US to their first Davis Cup victory for five years, and he took both the US National (at Boston) and the Open (at Forest Hills) titles — the first American champion for 13 years.

A semi-finalist at Wimbledon in 1968/9, his next big success was the Australian Open of 1970. He also took the WCT (World Championship Tennis) title that year. Ashe applied for a visa to play in South Africa, but was turned down. The South African authorities relented three years later, however, and he was runner-up at Johannesburg in 1973.

His finest year did not come until 1975, when he regained the WCT title and then caused a stunning upset to beat holder and hot favourite Jimmy Connors in the Wimbledon final. This was one of the most famous triumphs ever of brain over brawn — comparable only perhaps with Jack Crawford's defeat of Ellsworth Vines in 1933.

Ashe began 1976 as world No 1, but Achilles heel trouble set in and he missed most of the 1977 season, at which time he married photographer Jeanne Moutoussammy. Then came a remarkable comeback in 1978, culminating in his reaching the final of the Masters in 1979 and missing a match point against Connors. But shortly after Wimbledon, 1979, Ashe suffered a heart attack and underwent triple bypass surgery — which terminated his playing career at the age of 37.

He remained active in a non-playing capacity, however. A former president of the ATP, and always one of the most articulate and outspoken of players, he served as US Davis Cup captain from 1980 to 1985, and has become a TV commentator and journalist.

Ashe was always a fast-court specialist, and all his major successes were on grass or indoors. He was one of the most cerebral of tennis players. During his famous Wimbledon final against Connors, Ashe used the changeovers to meditate rather than simply towel down.

Cilli AUSSEM
b 1909 – d 1963

Until Steffi Graf's 1988 win, Cilli Aussem was the only German woman to have won the women's singles at Wimbledon — a feat she achieved in 1931, beating her compatriot, Hilde Krahwinkel (later Mrs Sperling).

Aussem, who married an Italian nobleman and became the Contessa della Corta Brae, suffered from poor health, and her career at the top was comparatively brief. She made her debut at Wimbledon in 1928, and the following year she reached the quarter-finals before losing to the brilliant but erratic Spaniard, Lili de Alvarez. In 1930 she was 4-all in the final set of the semi-finals against the veteran American, Elizabeth Ryan, then fell and sprained her ankle and had to be carried off the court on a stretcher.

In 1931 Aussem won the French Championship and then was top seed at Wimbledon in the absence of the holder, Helen Wills Moody. She dropped two sets on her way to the final, which was played a day early because one of the men's singles finalists had withdrawn. Although both she and Hilde Krahwinkel were suffering from blistered feet, Aussem won comfortably, 6-2, 7-5.

She did not defend the title, and apart from a quarter-final showing in 1934, her major exploits were confined to her own German championship, where she was the winner in 1927, 1930 and 1931, and runner-up in 1934 and 1935.

A baseliner, Aussem had no outstanding shots and did not hit the ball hard, but she had superb, ballet-like footwork and she rarely made errors.

Tracy AUSTIN
b 1962

Were it not for chronic back trouble which effectively finished her career when she was only 20, Tracy Austin might have earned herself a place as one of the all-time greats of tennis. She had already won two US Open singles titles — the youngest player ever to do so — two Women's International Series championships, the Italian Open and the mixed doubles at Wimbledon. For three months in 1980 she was ranked No 1 in the world.

Austin had an outstanding career as a junior, winning a record 25 US national junior titles. Youngest of a large family of tennis players from Rolling Hills, California, she was featured on the cover of *World Tennis* magazine at the age of four, and in 1977 she

Left: Arthur Ashe pounds
down a serve at the US Open.
He was the first winner of the
title, inaugurated in 1968, and
the first American winner of
the US National men's singles
for 13 years.

became the youngest player for 70 years to compete at Wimbledon.

As a precocious 14-year-old, with ponytails, braces on her teeth and pinafore dresses that became her trademark, she stunned older and more experienced opponents on the professional circuit. Her debut at Wimbledon caused fever-pitch media attention, and her third round Centre Court match against holder Chris Evert (which she lost 1-6, 1-6) made front page news.

Although her service never developed beyond a pat-ball delivery, Austin's strength from the baseline and her unflappable temperament gave her an advantage over stronger and more enterprising players. In due course, she beat every leading player in the game, and her many titles included two on grass, her least favourite surface, with back-to-back wins at Eastbourne in 1980 and 1981.

She never progressed beyond the semifinals at Wimbledon, but she won the US Open in 1979 and 1981, the Italian in 1979 and the Women's Series finals in 1980 and 1981. Her Wimbledon mixed doubles triumph of 1980 with her brother John was the only time that a brother-sister partnership has won a Grand Slam title.

Austin had career head-to-head leads against both her main rivals, Chris Evert Lloyd and Martina Navratilova, but the sciatic back trouble began in early 1981 and forced three lengthy rests before her second, and final, withdrawal from Wimbledon in 1983. After a few tournaments in early 1984, she did not compete until she took part in a few doubles events in late 1988, reaching the US Open mixed doubles semi-finals.

Sue
BARKER
b 1956

From Devon, England, Sue Barker enjoyed a brief spell near the top of the game in the late 1970s. Winner of all her country's national junior titles, she gained a number of major European clay court titles at a time when most of the leading players were competing in World Team Tennis in the US.

Barker's main weapon was a forehand drive of formidable strength. Blonde and vivacious, she had excellent mobility, but her game was erratic, and when she was off form she suffered ignominious defeats, including a number of first round losses at Wimbledon, where British players are always under pressure.

Barker won the Swedish and Swiss titles in 1975, then came her best year, 1976, when she won the French and German Opens and was runner-up in the British Hard Court Championships. In 1977 she proved she could measure up with the best, winning back-to-back titles on the Virginia Slims tour at San Francisco and Dallas, and beating Martina Navratilova before losing a three-set title match against Chris Evert in the Slims finals.

At Wimbledon that year she was poised to join Virginia Wade in an all-British final, but lost her chance in an erratic semi-final against Betty Stove. After that, Barker was never a serious contender for the top slot, although she enjoyed occasional resurgences, including a win over Tracy Austin to help Britain score a rare Wightman Cup victory in 1978. She again defeated Austin on the way to victory in the Brighton women's tournament of 1981.

From a high point of fourth in 1977, Barker slid steadily down the rankings, and eventually retired from competitive play at the end of 1985.

Boris BECKER

b 1967

Boris Becker's sensational first victory at Wimbledon in 1985 set three extraordinary records. He became the youngest winner of the men's singles, the first unseeded player to do so, and the first German. He retained the title in 1986, but in 1987 lost in a stunning second-round upset to an unheralded Australian, Peter Doohan.

Becker's first notable achievement in professional tennis came in the 1984 Australian Open, when he reached the quarter-finals. In early 1985 he won the inaugural World Young Masters, an event for men aged under 21 in Birmingham, England, defeating Sweden's Stefan Edberg in the final.

In the French Open that year he was roundly beaten by Mats Wilander, but at Wimbledon, where his terrific serve was at its most lethal on the grass, he came through a series of tough matches to defeat Kevin Curren in a four-set final. At the end of the year he led West Germany to the final of the Davis Cup in Munich, where he won both his singles, although Sweden took the trophy.

Becker lost to Mikael Schapers of the Netherlands in the Australian Open of 1985, to Milan Srejber of Czechoslovakia at the Lipton Open in Florida of 1986 and to Mikael Pernfors in the 1985 Paris semi-final. But at Wimbledon that year he dropped only two sets on his way to the final, where he routed Ivan Lendl.

Since then, although solidly in the top five, Becker has failed to win a major title. A much-publicized split with his coach, Gunter Bosch, in Australia in early 1987 was followed by some shock losses, culminating with the Wimbledon defeat by Doohan. However, the following year he was hot favourite to regain the title, but was unexpectedly beaten in the final by Stefan Edberg.

Pauline BETZ

b 1919

Pauline Betz led a formidable team of American players that took Wimbledon by storm when the championships resumed after the Second World War in 1946. From Dayton, Ohio, Betz had just emerged when the curtain came down on international competition in 1939. During the war years she was a top player in the US (where tournament play continued), winning the National title in 1942, 1943 and 1944. Coached by Eleanor 'Teach' Tennant, the mentor of Alice Marble and Maureen Connolly, Betz was a baseliner, unlike the other great players of her day. She was also a champion at table tennis.

In 1945 Betz surprisingly lost her US title to veteran Sarah Palfrey Cooke, but in 1946, her only year on the international circuit, she ruled the roost. Her solid, enterprising game shook the British as she led the US to a

Opposite: Tracy Austin gets set for a double-handed backhand drive on the Centre Court at Wimbledon. She never got further than the semi-finals of the singles there, though she did win the mixed doubles — with her brother John — in 1980.

Above: Boris Becker dives into a retrieval on the Centre Court. He threw himself around so much during his 1985 final against Kevin Curren that his shirt and shorts were covered in dust by the end.

Below: Bjorn Borg in action at Stade Roland Garros. He won the French men's singles six times — more than any other player since the tournament was thrown open to all nationalities in 1925.

whitewash victory in the pre-Wimbledon Wightman Cup. Then at Wimbledon she breezed through the field, taming rival Louise Brough 6-2, 6-4 in the final. In the French championships, which followed Wimbledon that year, Betz lost to Margaret Osborne after holding two match points in the final, but she regained her pre-eminence by defeating Doris Hart for the US title at Forest Hills.

Late in that year Betz was deprived of her amateur status by the US Lawn Tennis Association because she had enquired about the possibility of turning professional — though she had not yet firmly decided to do so. Forced into a new career, she became a contract professional for some years before marrying Robert Addie and retiring. It is highly probable that she would have won many more titles, and joined the all-time elite, had she continued in the amateur game.

Bjorn
BORG
b 1956

There are just a handful of players through the course of the history of tennis that have made a lasting impression, and Bjorn Borg is one of them. He has inspired a whole generation of Swedish players, who have made their country the leading nation in international tennis.

From Sodertlage, a suburb of Stockholm, Borg first came to prominence in 1972, when as a 15-year-old he was selected to play in the Swedish Davis Cup team, and also won the boys' singles at Wimbledon. He reached the quarter-finals of the main event the following year, and became the object of 'Borgomania' — a following of thousands of teenage girls who treated him with the sort of adulation normally reserved for pop stars.

Borg's cool temperament and vicious top-spin ground-strokes — double-handed on the backhand, which was rare among men at that time — earned him precocious victories over far more experienced opponents. By the age of 17 he had already won his first major titles: the Italian and French Opens of 1974. Two years later, he won the first of five successive Wimbledon men's singles titles, a unique record in modern times. In 1975 he led Sweden to their first-ever victory in the Davis Cup.

In addition to his five Wimbledon titles, Borg also won the French singles a total of six times between 1974 and 1981, and the Grand Prix Masters twice. He never won the US Open, however, despite reaching the final four times. He always claimed that he could not cope with the floodlights — the match is played in the evening — and he could not master the bounce of the concrete-based courts at Flushing Meadow.

Borg was virtually invincible on European clay. And, though not a natural fast-court player, he adapted his baseline style successfully for Wimbledon's grass. Of his six consecutive Wimbledon finals, the most memorable was in 1980 against John McEnroe, and it was McEnroe who ended Borg's reign in the title match of 1981.

Married to Romanian player Mariana Simionescu for several years in the early 1980s, Borg had left his native country to live in Monte Carlo for tax reasons and in 1982 wanted a rest from tennis. But the rules of the game required him to play a minimum number of events, or be obliged to play in the qualifying rounds. He fulfilled contractual obligations by playing in the Monte Carlo qualifying rounds of 1982 but decided against repeating the exercise for Wimbledon. Apart from another appearance at Monte Carlo in 1984, Borg has since avoided conventional tournaments, devoting his energies to business interests. His skills, and his impeccable sportsmanship, have guaranteed him a perpetual niche among the all-time greats.

Jean
BOROTRA
b 1898

If durability be the only hallmark of a great player, Jean Borotra is the greatest of them all. He first played at Wimbledon in 1922, and was last entered in an open event, the mixed doubles, in 1964. For several years after that he continued to appear in the veterans' doubles. Borotra has played more matches at Wimbledon than any other man — 221, winning 152 — and his Davis Cup record lasted from 1922 to 1947. Perhaps the event with which he is identified more than any other is the annual match between the International Clubs of France and Great Britain. He played *singles* in this fixture on every occasion on which it was held between 1929 and 1985, and he won his match, at the age of 86, against Gus Holden in 1984.

Borotra was one of a quartet of Frenchmen, nicknamed the 'Four Musketeers', that dominated world tennis during the 1920s and 1930s. Borotra, Rene Lacoste, Henri Cochet and Jacques Brugnon, a doubles specialist, won the Davis Cup for France every year from 1927 to 1932, and between them took every Wimbledon men's singles title between 1924 and 1929.

The four had greatly differing personalities and styles. Borotra, the second oldest, was the most extrovert, and a great favourite with the crowd. Nicknamed 'The Bounding Basque' (he was from Arbonne, Basses-Pyrenees), Borotra always wore a black beret to play. His sense of showmanship, with light-hearted pranks and humour strong in his repertoire, can only be compared in modern times with those of Ilie Nastase — but Borotra was never offensive.

Despite his charm and *joie de vivre*, he was a dedicated athlete, and his passion for fitness is the reason for his remarkable durability. He could play any stroke to perfection, and he was an astute match player.

Of the 'Four Musketeers', Borotra had the most successful record, winning singles titles at Wimbledon in 1924 and 1926, the French in

1924 and 1931, and the Australian in 1928. He also won a large number of doubles titles and, with Brugnon, was runner-up for the French title as late as 1939 — at 10-8 in the fifth set!

Spectators at Wimbledon were delighted to see Borotra present Boris Becker with the men's singles trophy in 1986 — an honour usually reserved for members of the British Royal Family, but on this occasion marking the 100th championship.

John
BROMWICH
b 1918

John Bromwich was a fine Australian player whose career spanned either side of the Second World War, and who might have scaled greater heights in the game, but for the halt in competition during his early 20s.

He was ambidextrous, but used both hands on the forehand — a very rare technique at any time in the history of the game. He preferred to have his rackets strung loosely, and at a light weight in order to control the ball, although all his major successes were on grass. He won the Australian singles in 1939 and 1946, but his most famous match was the Wimbledon final of 1948, which he lost to the American Bob Falkenburg after leading 5-2 in the final set and holding three match points. At 5-3 and 40-15 on his service, he turned to the nearest ballboy and said, 'Give me the winning ball.' Sadly for him, he played too safely, and his lanky opponent, who was

Above: Jean Borotra on his backhand volley. He was always a great crowd-pleaser, not only because of the flair and enterprise of his game, but for his sense of showmanship and humorous gestures.

renowned for 'throwing' sets in order to conserve energy, was able to scramble out of trouble.

Bromwich's greatest feats were in doubles. He won eight consecutive Australian titles with compatriot Adrian Quist from 1938 to 1950; three US titles, with Quist, Oliver Sidwell and Frank Sedgman; and two Wimbledons, with Sedgman (1948) and Quist (1950). He also took the 1948 Wimbledon mixed doubles with Louise Brough, and played in 53 Davis Cup rubbers between 1937 and 1950.

Louise
BROUGH
b 1923

Althea Louise Brough was a great player at a time when great players were in some abundance. She was one of the Amazonian team of Americans that ruled women's tennis in the late 1940s and early 1950s, and the intensity of competition between these players provided many classic matches in major events over the years.

Originally from Oklahoma, she was a disciple of the last pre-war champion, Alice Marble, in that she adopted the 'man's game' of serve-volley tactics, with strength and

aggression to the fore instead of touch play from the baseline. She won almost every major title in the game, whether singles, doubles or mixed, though she will perhaps be best remembered for her doubles partnership with her close friend, Margaret Osborne (later Mrs du Pont). They were one of the three great women's doubles pairings of all time, ranking alongside Suzanne Lenglen and Elizabeth Ryan (in the 1920s) and the current team of Martina Navratilova and Pam Shriver. They won the US title every year between 1942 and 1950, then three more times, 1955 to 1957. They also won five times at Wimbledon, and three times in Paris.

Brough was twice triple-champion at Wimbledon, and would have created a unique record of winning all three titles for three years running, had she and John Bromwich won a marathon 1949 mixed doubles against the South Africans, Eric Sturgess and Sheila Summers. In fact, Brough set a record that day by playing three finals over five hours and 20 minutes, involving eight sets and 117 games. In those days, all Wimbledon finals except the men's singles were contested in a single afternoon. Brough won the women's singles against du Pont 10-8, 1-6, 10-8; won the women's doubles with du Pont against Gussy Moran and Pat Todd 8-6, 7-5; and lost the mixed doubles 7-9, 11-9, 5-7.

She won the Wimbledon singles four times, the US once and the Australian once. Her last Wimbledon triumph, in 1955, came after the three-year reign of Maureen Connolly, who beat her in the 1952 and 1954 finals. Brough was never beaten in 22 Wightman Cup rubbers. After she retired in 1957 she married and became Mrs A. T. Clapp.

Donald
BUDGE
b 1915

This formidable Californian had the distinction of becoming the first player to win all four Grand Slam singles titles in the same year — a feat achieved by only one other man, Rod Laver. He was also the first man to win the triple crown at Wimbledon, and he did it for two years running.

Budge was stepping hard upon the heels of the great Englishman, Fred Perry, who had dominated the game in the mid 1930s, when Perry turned professional in 1936. He held two match points against Perry in the 1936 US final, and with the field clear in 1937 he took over a domination which would no doubt have extended several more years had Budge himself not signed a professional contract after completing the Grand Slam in 1938.

He had learnt from Perry to adopt a mentality of sustained aggression. In terms of stroke equipment, his topspin backhand drive

Below: Louise Brough executes a perfect low forehand volley. She was one of the best of a remarkable group of leading Americans that dominated women's tennis during the decade after the Second World War.

was a deadly weapon — particularly on the return of service. In the 1937 Wimbledon final he scored an emphatic straight set win against the elegant German Gottfried von Cramm, though at Forest Hills later that summer, the same opponent stretched their final to the full distance.

Budge's four victims in his Grand Slam finals of 1938 were all different — John Bromwich in Australia, Roderick Menzel of Czechoslovakia in France, Britain's 'Bunny' Austin at Wimbledon, and compatriot Gene Mako at Forest Hills. He won the 1937 and 1938 Wimbledon men's doubles with Mako, and the mixed with Alice Marble. Budge is still seen today as an honoured spectator at Grand Slam events, and for some years he served on the committee that elects the official World Champions.

Maria
BUENO
b 1939

Maria Bueno is the only South American woman to have won Wimbledon and — apart from Chile's Anita Lizana, who won Forest Hills in 1937, and the young Argentine Gabriela Sabatini, who may achieve great things in the future — the only one to have made a significant mark in the game.

Born in São Paulo, Brazil, Maria Esther Bueno was probably the most graceful and artistic player ever to step on to a tennis court. At her best, she was stupendously good, with a balletic, almost effortless, all-court game. But she was erratic and had no margin of safe shots. If she was off form, she was beaten by vastly less talented opponents. She had a regal bearing and always looked majestic and glamorous. She was also an intensely private person, and her apparent aloofness, mistaken by many as arrogance, was really because she was shy, and embarrassed by the adulation she received, particularly in her homeland.

She made her first overseas tour in 1958, winning the Italian singles and the Wimbledon doubles with Althea Gibson. When Gibson turned professional in early 1959, Bueno looked set to rule the game. She won both Wimbledon and the US singles that year, but although she retained Wimbledon in 1960, the emergence of a new star, Margaret Smith, threatened her supremacy. Smith, as a comparatively unknown 17-year-old, upset the Brazilian in the quarter-finals of the 1960 Australian championship, and their rivalry during the early 1960s was the principal feature of the women's game at that time.

Bueno always suffered from ill health, and hepatitis forced her out of competition for most of the 1961 season. At Wimbledon in 1962 she was not the force she had been, and the controversy over her 'shocking pink' panties, designed for her by couturier Ted

Tinling (who dressed her in stunning outfits for most of her career), did not help; she lost to the unseeded Czech Vera Sukova. However, she made a triumphant comeback by winning the 1964 championship, overcoming Smith in a classic final, and she won three more US singles — 1963, 1964 and 1966. In addition, there were five Wimbledon doubles titles, with Gibson (1958), Darlene Hard (1960, 1963), Billie Jean Moffitt (1965) and Nancy Richey (1966); four US doubles (with Hard, 1960, 1962, Richey, 1966, and Margaret Court, 1968); one French doubles (with Hard, 1960); one Australian doubles (with Christine Truman, 1960) and just one mixed doubles, the French of 1960, with Bob Howe.

Bueno's career as a top-flight player ended on the Caribbean circuit in early 1969. She had been suffering from tennis elbow for some time, and it eventually became too

Above: Donald Budge demonstrates considerable power as he hits a high volley on the forehand. He was the first player to score a Grand Slam of the world's four biggest titles in the same year.

It was in the doubles game that Casals excelled, winning five women's and two mixed Wimbledon titles, and five US titles, including one mixed. She formed a partnership with Billie Jean King — so often her nemesis in singles — that will go down as one of the greatest in history, while in later years she was paired almost as effectively with Wendy Turnbull. Her exciting reflexes, extraordinary net-play and determination ensured that, despite her lack of height, she was always a stalwart partner.

In singles, she promised much early on by reaching the semi-finals of the US championships of 1966 and Wimbledon 1967 as an 18-year-old. But in 1969 psychological problems were manifest as she surrendered 6-1, 6-0 to King in the Wimbledon semi-finals, and she was never able to emerge from her older fellow-Californian's shadow. She reached the final at Forest Hills in both 1970 and 1971, and two more semi-finals at Wimbledon (1970 and 1972), but after this she never got past the quarter-finals of a major event.

Casals remained a top-flight doubles performer well into the 1980s, by which time her singles status was mediocre, and her last major title (with Turnbull) was the US Open of 1982. One of four women contract professionals in 1968, she returned to representative play for the US in the Federation and Wightman Cups of 1976 after a nine-year gap, and continued in the teams until 1982.

Pat
CASH
b 1965

Australia's first men's singles champion at Wimbledon since 1971, Pat Cash excitingly took the title in 1987. This followed a year in which he had climbed right back into the top level after a period in the wilderness.

He emerged as his country's best young prospect as a 17-year-old in 1982 when he won the Wimbledon and US junior championships. With a forceful, attacking game and a formidable service, he quickly broke through into the senior game by winning his home town Melbourne Grand Prix title that year. In 1983 he reached the last 16 at Wimbledon, and in 1984 the progress continued with semi-final showings at both Wimbledon and Flushing Meadow, where he missed a matchpoint against Ivan Lendl.

Then disaster struck. He was out of competition for almost the whole of 1985 with a back injury, and his world ranking plummeted from eighth to below 400th. Attempting a comeback in the summer of 1986, he seemed doomed to fail when forced to have an appendectomy just three weeks before Wimbledon. Defying medical advice,

Above: Maria Bueno is poised like a ballerina as she takes this high backhand volley. Bueno was one of the most graceful players ever to step onto a tennis court.
Opposite: Pat Cash is more at home on the Centre Court at Wimbledon than most other players. His exemplary grass court technique proved too good for anyone else in the 1987 tournament. A customary gesture at the end of his matches is to throw his headband and wrist-bands into the crowd.

severe for her to continue. But she made occasional appearances through the 1970s, winning the Japanese Open in 1974 and returning to Wimbledon for some nostalgic Centre Court matches in 1976 and 1977.

She remains active in tennis as a coach and consultant to the International Tennis Federation.

Rosemary
CASALS
b 1948

A multi-talented bundle of energy who burst upon the international scene in 1966, Casals promised to be a champion of the 1970s, but as time unfolded she was fated to be always the bridesmaid in major competition. She had every shot in the book — and that was probably too many. A natural serve-volleyer, she lacked the patience to succeed on slow surfaces, and a wide repertoire of strokes proved to be a handicap, as, in singles, she would select the wrong shot to play in a crisis.

he took part in the tournament on a wild-card, and beat second-seeded Mats Wilander on his way to the quarter-finals. At the end of the year he led Australia to victory over Sweden in the Davis Cup for the second time in three years, beating both Stefan Edberg and Mikael Pernfors, and joining John Fitzgerald to notch up the three points in an heroic effort.

Cash subsequently reached his first major singles final in the Australian Open, but here submitted to Edberg in five sets. However, he was ready for Wimbledon, and in taking the title for the loss of just two sets — overwhelming Lendl 7-6, 6-2, 7-5 in the final with an immaculate display of grass-court tennis — he ended a long drought for the Australian game.

His best showing in Grand Slam events in 1988 was at the Australian Open, where he lost a close five-set final to Mats Wilander. At Wimbledon he was beaten in straight sets in the quarter-finals by Boris Becker.

Henri
COCHET
b 1901 – d 1987

One of the all-conquering 'Four Musketeers' from France, Henri Cochet was perhaps the most gifted and the most enigmatic of the quartet. Cochet, from Lyon, was capable of superb play, but sometimes his form deserted him and he suffered puzzling losses. One such occasion was at Wimbledon in 1932, when as the top seed he lost in four sets in the second round to Ian Collins, a comparatively humble British player. Undismayed, he entered — and won — the All England Plate, a consolation event for early-round losers. He is the only player in history to win this title subsequent to holding the Championship.

A master of the volley and half-volley, Cochet won the Wimbledon singles in 1927 and 1929 and the doubles (with Jacques Brugnon) in 1926 and 1928; the US singles in 1928; the French singles in 1922, 1926, 1928, 1930 and 1932; and the French doubles (with Brugnon) in 1927, 1930 and 1932. He turned professional in 1933 but was reinstated as an amateur after the war, and he regularly attended the tennis at Stade Roland Garros until his death, aged 86, in 1987.

Maureen
CONNOLLY
b 1934 – d 1969

Maureen Connolly would almost certainly have had the greatest record of any player in the history of tennis had she not had her career abruptly terminated before her 20th

birthday. Even as a teenage champion, she is considered by experts to have been one of the four finest women players of all time.

She was never beaten in a Grand Slam singles event. Born in San Diego, California, she won the first of three consecutive US titles in 1951 when still 16 and the third of a hat-trick of Wimbledon titles in 1954. During that stretch she was beaten just four times in singles — twice by Doris Hart, notably in the Italian final of 1953, once by Shirley Fry, and once by Beverley Baker. She took on, and dismissed, the established stars of the era — Hart, Fry, Louise Brough and Margaret du Pont — and the only time she nearly failed in a big tournament was when she had to save a match point against Britain's Susan Partridge in the fourth round of the 1952 Wimbledon.

Connolly was utterly single-minded and ruthless. Injured on the eve of her first Wimbledon, she went against the advice of her coach, Eleanor 'Teach' Tennant, and played — ending an association with one of the best teachers in the US. Her game was founded upon hard, relentless ground-strokes. She rarely volleyed, but did not need to, as her strength and accuracy were too formidable for her all-court opponents to overcome. Her doubles ability, however, was not as effective. Although she won two major titles — the Australian with Julie Sampson in 1953 and the French with Nell Hopman in 1954 — she also suffered the indignity of losing the 1953 Wimbledon doubles final with Sampson against Fry and Hart 0-6, 0-6.

Connolly became the first woman to win the Grand Slam, in 1953, and she won a further French singles in 1954. Her 1953 Wimbledon singles final against Hart, which she won 8-6, 7-5, is regarded as one of the finest women's matches ever played.

Opposite: Jimmy Connors at full speed on the baseline as he dashes to take a wide forehand. The exuberant American prefers to slug it out from the back of the court, although this is physically very demanding for a player of his age.

Right: Maureen Connolly pauses for reflection. She was callous and determined in anything to do with her tennis, but away from it she is remembered as a charming and friendly young woman who died tragically young.

A few weeks before she was due to defend her US title, in July 1954, she broke her leg in a riding accident, and never played again competitively. Soon afterwards, she married an Olympic equestrian, Norman Brinker, and retired to have two daughters. She remained active in tennis as a coach and TV commentator, but in June 1969, the day before the start of Wimbledon, she died of cancer at just 34 years of age.

The Maureen Connolly Brinker Foundation, a project for helping young and underprivileged players in the Dallas area, where she lived during her married life, was set up in her memory by a friend, Nancy Jeffett. A memorial team match between young women players from the US and Great Britain for the Maureen Connolly Trophy is played each autumn.

Jimmy CONNORS
b 1952

One of the great fighters of tennis, Connors has endeared himself to millions over a long career by his dogged, never-say-die attitude, his intense determination, and the way he keeps bouncing back.

From Belleville, Illinois, he is the only great male player to have been coached by a woman — his mother, Gloria. He has a solid, all-court game, but prefers to slug out long, hard-hitting rallies from the baseline — and his double-handed backhand is a potent weapon. Connors is unusual in that he prefers to hit a flat ball, though he will slice on approach shots, and for most of his career he has used an outdated, small-head steel racket that has not been in production for many years.

Connors's personality is volatile. He can vary from being an entertainer, who injects humour into the game and plays to the gallery, to a boor who offends with obscene gestures and bad language, although these traits have become less manifest in recent years. He snubbed Wimbledon's Centennial Parade of Champions in 1977, and for years refused to play in the Davis Cup. In defeat, he has been known to hurry away without waiting for presentations or press conferences. He has, however, shown a more professional attitude since marriage and fatherhood.

After three years of steady progress on the circuit, Connors became a brash and ruthless winner of the Australian, Wimbledon and US Open in 1974. In the latter two finals, he handed crushing defeats to the veteran Ken Rosewall, who was nearly 20 years his elder. The following year he lost all three titles in the finals, and his defeat at Wimbledon by Arthur Ashe paralleled the fate of Ellsworth Vines against Jack Crawford in 1933.

But whereas Vines withered, Connors kept going, and until 1986 he was never out of the top three. His great rivals were Bjorn Borg and John McEnroe, against whom he won and lost many memorable matches. He has the distinction of being the only player to win the US Open on three different surfaces — grass (1974), clay (1976) and cement (1978, 1982, 1983). He went without a major title for four years, but came back strongly to beat McEnroe in the Wimbledon final of 1982, and Ivan Lendl in the US Opens of 1982 and 1983. In addition, he was runner-up at Wimbledon in 1975, 1977, 1978 and 1984, and losing finalist in the US Open in 1975 and 1977. He was losing semi-finalist in both events on most other occasions, although his proud record was spoilt in 1986 when he lost in the first round at Wimbledon and in the third at Flushing Meadow. But he caused the greatest excitement at Wimbledon in 1987 by reaching the last four once again, after fighting back from a seemingly impossible position against Mikael Pernfors, whom he trailed 1-6, 1-6, 1-4 before pulling the match round.

Connors stopped playing doubles early in his career after winning the 1973 Wimbledon and 1975 US titles with Ilie Nastase. But in 1984, with Chris Evert (to whom he had been engaged ten years before), he won the World Mixed Doubles Championship.

Ashley COOPER
b 1936

Throughout the years between the resumption of international competition after the First World War and the institution of open tennis in 1968, the game was constantly drained of its top players by the professional game. In those days, entry to all tournaments under the control of national associations was restricted to 'amateurs' — ie those players who had not signed professional contracts, and who ostensibly played for expenses only, although it was no secret that the big stars were paid unofficial appearance money.

There were very few outstanding male players who did not turn professional during this time, which inevitably meant that they had far shorter careers in traditional tournament play than their counterparts do today. Accordingly, the records of the great events do not always show who the greatest players were at that time, because they were so frequently barred.

A classic example of a fine player who succeeded to the game's highest prizes when better colleagues before him became ineligible was Ashley Cooper, a young Australian who, in due course, himself turned professional. There were many good Australians around at that time. Two of the best, Ken

Rosewall and Lew Hoad, dominated the scene in the mid-1950s. Hoad won three out of the four Grand Slam titles in 1956, and stayed amateur for another year, although Rosewall deserted the amateur ranks at the end of the season.

In the Australian semi-finals of 1957 Hoad went down to Neale Fraser, another Australian, who lost in the final to Cooper. At Wimbledon, however, Hoad was in merciless form, and he routed Cooper 6-2, 6-1, 6-2 in one of the shortest ever finals. Hoad then promptly turned pro before the US Championships, where Cooper lost the final to Mal Anderson.

Cooper's great year was 1958. He won the Australian, Wimbledon and US singles — plus the Australian, French and US doubles — to make his own case for a worthwhile financial guarantee. He signed on the dotted line at the end of 1958.

Margaret COURT
b 1942

As a winner of major titles in international tennis, Margaret Smith Court's record is superlative. In her time, the championships of

Australia, France, Wimbledon, the US, Italy, Germany and South Africa were the most important. She won the singles, doubles and mixed doubles of all seven at least once — and most of them several times over. She won Grand Slams in singles (1970), and, uniquely, mixed doubles (1963). She led her country, Australia, to victory in the Federation Cup four times. Her career spanned 16 years, with three years off for marriage and motherhood.

Although Court won twice as many titles as anyone else in history, she is not regarded as one of the very best players of all time. Tall, athletic and very strong, she had a crunching serve and excellent volleys — benefiting from her long reach — and was equally good on all surfaces. Yet she was prone to nerves and suffered some calamitous losses. The occasional lack of self-confidence was never more tellingly apparent than when she agreed to play the 1939 Wimbledon men's singles champion, Bobby Riggs, in a 'battle of the sexes' in California in May 1973. She allowed him to intimidate her, and was humiliated. A few months later, her great rival Billie Jean King took Riggs on and won triumphantly.

Her record is so impressive that the titles are worth listing in full. Australian: singles 1960, 1961, 1962, 1963, 1964, 1965, 1966, 1969, 1970, 1971, 1973, doubles 1961, 1962, 1963, 1965, 1969, 1970, 1971, 1973, mixed 1963, 1964, 1965 (shared), 1969 (shared).

French: singles 1962, 1964, 1969, 1970, 1973, doubles 1964, 1965, 1966, 1973, mixed 1963, 1964, 1965, 1969. Wimbledon: singles 1963, 1965, 1970, doubles 1964, 1969, mixed 1963, 1965, 1968, 1975. US: singles 1962, 1965, 1968 (amateur), 1969 (amateur), 1969 (open), 1970, 1973, doubles 1963, 1968 (amateur), 1968 (open), 1969 (amateur), 1970, 1973, 1975, mixed 1961, 1962, 1963, 1964, 1965, 1969, 1970, 1972. Italian: singles 1962, 1963, 1964, doubles 1963, 1964, 1968, mixed 1961, 1964, 1968. German: singles 1964, 1965, 1966, doubles 1964, 1965, 1966, mixed 1965, 1966. South African: singles 1968, 1970, 1971, doubles 1966, 1971, mixed 1966, 1970, 1971.

That makes a grand total of 92, of which 67 were in Grand Slam events. There were a good many more finishes as runner-up or losing semi-finalist. She ranks as the most assiduous competitor of post-war years, and the only title of any consequence she failed to win was the Virginia Slims finals. (The Women's International Series did not begin until after her final retirement.)

Her first major success was as a 17-year-old in 1960, when she won the first of 11 Australian singles titles. She signalled her intentions on her first overseas tour in 1961 without taking a major crown, and in 1962, as reigning Australian and French champion, she was top-seeded at Wimbledon. She lost her opening match to Billie Jean Moffitt, but she was back on top for the US title, and in 1963 Wimbledon was hers, as the first Australian women's champion.

She carried on piling up the titles, and generally getting the better of Moffitt and her other chief early rival, Maria Bueno. But in 1966, after surrendering her title to Moffitt (by now Mrs King) in a tame semi-final, she announced she was quitting the game. She spent most of 1967 at home in Perth, running a clothing boutique, then married Barry Court, son of a Western Australia government minister. At the end of 1967, she returned to the circuit.

It took some time to regain her pre-eminence, and she won no major singles title in 1968. But by 1969 Court was back at the top, winning the Australian and French titles. She surprisingly lost to Britain's Ann Jones at Wimbledon, but that was her last failure in a Grand Slam event until May 1971, when she was defeated in the third round at Paris by France's Gail Chanfreau. She also lost, decisively, in the Wimbledon final to her young compatriot, Evonne Goolagong, then announced she was pregnant.

She was out of tennis for over a year, but returned to the circuit in the summer of 1972, and the following year won three of the four Grand Slams. Another baby caused her to miss 1974, and in 1975 she was, at the age of 33, clearly past her best. She retired again, but announced another comeback at the beginning of 1977, until she discovered she was expecting her third child. And that was it.

Court was perhaps least at ease at Wim-

Left: Margaret Court concentrates grimly during her marathon 14-12, 11-9 victory over Billie Jean King in the 1970 women's singles final at Wimbledon. Court, for whom the title gave three-quarters of the Grand Slam she was to take that year, was suffering from an ankle injury at the time and had to scratch from the other events.

bledon. Her record there is less impressive than elsewhere, although her magnificent final against King in 1970, the longest on record, was a triumph of courage and strength.

Deeply religious, Court claimed to have had a vision of the Virgin Mary at her home. She always remained detached from political activity in tennis, but has been involved in the development of young players in Perth.

Jack CRAWFORD
b 1908

Crawford was one of the great eccentrics of tennis. By the 1930s, when he was at his peak, players were using oval-shaped rackets of the same construction as those in favour up to the late 1970s; but Crawford used old-fashioned, flat-topped equipment. His appearance was also anachronistic, with his hair parted in the middle and shirts buttoned at the wrist. In a long match he liked to have a pot of tea, complete with milk and sugar, at the umpire's chair — and he would relax with a cigarette during the interval after the third set.

He won the Australian singles in 1931 and 1933, the French in 1933, and, most notably, Wimbledon the same year. In one of the greatest ever finals he tamed the explosive cannonball serve of Ellsworth Vines, who had won the title so emphatically the year before. His wife fainted with excitement at the end of this triumph.

A great stylist, Crawford played mainly from the baseline. He won the Australian doubles in 1929, 1930, 1932 and 1935, the French in 1933 and Wimbledon in 1935. He also took the Australian mixed doubles three times with his wife.

Unlike his main rivals, Crawford did not turn professional. He continued to play in the Australian championships until 1940, and was still good enough to reach the semi-finals of the singles in 1939.

Lottie DOD
b 1871 – d 1960

In the early years of lawn tennis it was not unusual for the top players to excel in other sports as well. Because tennis was then mainly a summer sport — covered courts were few, and the Europeans and North Americans rarely travelled to the southern hemisphere — an alternative was sought by many for the winter months. Tennis champions have also reached the top of other sports like table tennis, but none has been as great an all-rounder as the English girl, Lottie Dod.

Right: Lottie Dod was not only the youngest player to win a Wimbledon title, but possibly the greatest ever all-round sportswoman. She excelled in golf, hockey, skating and archery as well as lawn tennis.

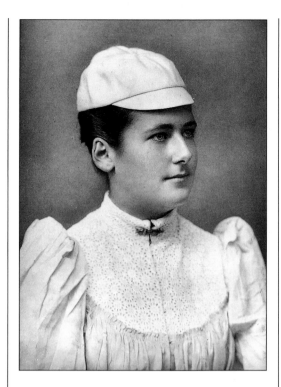

The youngest player ever to win the Wimbledon singles, Dod won first at the age of 15, in 1887. Her precosity had already been in evidence for some years. She won the women's doubles at Manchester when she was only 11, and at 14 she beat the reigning Wimbledon champion, Maud Watson, at Bath. In her first Wimbledon final she beat Blanche Bingley (later Mrs Hillyard), who herself was to win the title six times. Dod was so athletic and had such good ball sense that the older woman was outclassed, 6-2, 6-0. In fact, nobody ever beat the 'Little Wonder', as she was known, at Wimbledon. She won four more times, then retired from tennis at the ripe old age of 21 to seek new challenges.

Dod went on to conquer several other sporting fields. She won the Ladies' Open Golf Championship in 1904, and she played hockey for England in 1899 and 1900. She was a first-class skater who passed the tests for both men and women at St Moritz, competed on the Cresta Run, *and* won a silver medal for archery at the 1908 Olympics. It is probably safe to say that this compulsive sportswoman would have reached the top at whatever she tried.

Jaroslav DROBNY
b 1921

Few victories at Wimbledon have been more popular than that of Jaroslav Drobny, who won at his eleventh attempt, at the age of 33, in 1954. Not only was he the oldest post-war champion, but he was also the only man to play under four different nationalities.

Drobny was born in Prague, and was

classified as Czech at his first Wimbledon entry in 1938. Following Hitler's invasion of his homeland, he was down as representing 'Bohemia-Moravia' the following year. From 1946 his nationality reverted to 'Czech', but in 1949 he left his homeland and became a naturalized Egyptian. In 1960, having lived in England for many years, he was given British citizenship, and he continued to play in the veterans' doubles as a Briton until 1972.

Drobny was a burly man who always played in dark glasses. A left-hander, he had delicate touch as well as a tremendous service and overhead. He became a great favourite with the crowd because he made a habit of becoming involved in long, thrilling matches. The most famous of these was at Wimbledon in 1953, when he beat Budge Patty 8-6, 16-18, 3-6, 8-6, 12-10 — which was, until the Gonzales-Pasarell classic of 1969, the longest on record.

For many years Drobny seemed doomed to disappointment. At Wimbledon, after heroic exploits, he would perennially fail against men he should have beaten. This happened in 1946, when he beat the hot favourite, Jack Kramer, but lost to Geoff Brown. In 1947 he lost to Patty in a tough five-setter. 1948 saw a shock second-round exit against Italy's C. Cucelli. In 1949, after trouncing John Bromwich in the semi-finals, he lost to Ted Schroeder. In 1950, again in five sets, he lost to Frank Sedgman, after winning the first two. In 1951, at 8-6 in the fifth, he was beaten by Tony Mottram. In 1952 he lost to Sedgman in the final. And in 1953, having struggled through to the semi-finals after his exhausting fourth-round win against Patty, Drobny succumbed to Kurt Nielsen.

Time seemed to be running out. At Wimbledon 1954 he was seeded no higher than 11th, and a new generation was taking over. But Drobny beat the second seed, Lew Hoad, in the quarter-finals; went on to beat his old adversary, Patty, in the semis; and then, in the final with the highest number of games (58), beat Ken Rosewall 13-11, 4-6, 6-2, 9-7. There were other major titles after many failures: the French in 1951 and 1952, the Italian in 1950, 1951 and 1953, and the German in 1950. He continued playing open events until he was over 40, and won the veterans' doubles several times in the 1960s. He now owns a sports equipment store in London's smart Kensington district.

Margaret
DU PONT
b 1918

One of the most successful and durable performers of the pre-war era, Margaret Osborne du Pont, who came from Oregon, won her first major title in 1941 and her last, at the age of 44, in 1962. She was a marvellous

volleyer, which accounts for her huge stack of doubles wins, and she had a difficult twist serve and a chopped forehand. She won more US national titles — 24 — than any other player, to which she added seven Wimbledons and five French titles.

She married a member of the wealthy Du Pont Industries family in 1948, and she played tennis for the sheer love of it. Cheerful and generous, she formed with Louise Brough one of the great doubles partnerships of all time, and she was still good enough to be selected for the US Wightman Cup when other members of the team were young enough to be her daughters.

In singles, her first major title was the French of 1946, when she spoiled the seemingly invincible record of Pauline Betz. She regained the title in 1949, and won the doubles three times with Brough. She won the Wimbledon singles once, in 1947, and was runner-up twice, including a memorable 8-10, 6-1, 8-10 loss to Brough in 1949. In doubles, she and Brough triumphed in 1946, 1948, 1949, 1950 and 1954. She did not find victory in mixed doubles at Wimbledon until 1962, when her win with Neale Fraser made her the oldest champion ever.

But it was in the US nationals where du Pont was pre-eminent, including the triple crown in 1950. Her titles were: singles 1948, 1949, 1950 (plus runner-up 1944, 1947); doubles 1941 (with Sarah Cooke), every year from 1942 to 1950, and again 1955, 1956, 1957 (all with Brough), plus runner-up 1953, 1954; and mixed doubles 1943, 1944, 1945, 1946 (with Bill Talbert), 1950 (with Ken McGregor), 1956 (with Ken Rosewall), and 1958, 1959, 1960 (with Fraser). She won every mixed doubles final in which she played. In

Below: Burly and bespectacled, Jaroslav Drobny runs for a wide forehand on the Centre Court. Originally from Czechoslovakia, he won Wimbledon as an Egyptian before acquiring British nationality.

the Wightman Cup, she played and won 18 rubbers in the years from 1946 to 1950, 1954, 1955, 1957 and 1962 and was also down to play the final doubles of 1961, which was conceded.

Françoise DURR

b 1942

Nobody would hold up Françoise Durr, born in Algiers but a French national, as a text-book tennis player. She had a style all her own, with a Western-grip forehand, an awkward backhand with her forefinger pointed down the grip, and the weakest of serves. But she was a fine tactician and was a leading doubles player for many years. She was a crowd favourite, as much for her volatile

Gallic temperament as for her unorthodoxy.

Durr became the first Frenchwoman to win the singles at Roland Garros for 19 years when she beat in successive rounds Maria Bueno, Ann Jones and Lesley Turner, to the delight of an audience that usually regarded women's tennis with indifference. The same year, 1967, she won the German singles and became a semi-finalist at Forest Hills. She did not win a major singles title after this, although she reached the semi-finals at Wimbledon in 1970 and at Paris in 1972 and 1973.

In doubles, Durr won the French title for five years running — with Gail Sherriff in 1967, 1970 and 1971, and with Ann Jones in 1968 and 1969. She reached the Wimbledon final six times without ever winning — with compatriot Janine Lieffrig (1965), Jones (1968), Virginia Wade (1970), Judy Dalton (1972) and Betty Stove (1973, 1975). On three occasions it was only at 7-5 in the final set. The bitterest defeat was in 1975, when having beaten the favourites, Rosemary Casals and Billie Jean King, Durr and Stove lost to the US-Japanese pair, Ann Kiyomura and Kazuko Sawamatsu, after actually winning more games than their opponents in the 5-7, 6-1, 5-7 scoreline. The following year Durr gained some consolation by winning the mixed doubles with Tony Roche after saving a match point against Casals and Dick Stockton.

She won the US doubles twice, with Darlene Hard (1969) and Stove (1972). And the French mixed doubles was hers three times with Jean Claude Barclay (1968, 1971, 1973).

She married an American, Boyd Browning, towards the end of her career, but continued to play under her maiden name. She retired in 1980 and lives in Phoenix, Arizona.

Stefan EDBERG

b 1966

The first Swede to win the Wimbledon men's singles title since Bjorn Borg — a feat he excitingly achieved in 1988, Stefan Edberg is exceptional in that he does not hit his backhand with two grips, and he is at his best on grass and other fast surfaces. Modest and undemonstrative, he may yet prove to be the best of all the current generation of Swedes, and time is on his side. He lives in London, and is coached by a former British Davis Cup player, Tony Pickard.

Edberg had an outstanding junior career, winning the Grand Slam of under-18 events at Melbourne, Paris, Wimbledon and Flushing Meadow. Only one previous player, Earl Buchholz, has achieved the feat. As an 18-year-old he won his first Grand Prix title in Milan in 1984, and played doubles with

Below: Françoise Durr shows her unorthodox forehand drive technique at Roland Garros, where she won a total of nine titles. The Virginia Slims cigarette motif on her dress reflects Durr's staunch support of the breakaway women's professional circuit in the early 1970s.

Anders Jarryd in Sweden's Davis Cup victory over the US at Gothenberg. By the end of 1985 Edberg was ranked fifth in the world, having upset Ivan Lendl at the Lipton tournament in Florida, reaching the quarter-finals at Paris and then taking his first big title, the Australian Open, with back-to-back wins over Lendl and Mats Wilander.

His form in 1986 was patchy, with early exits at Paris and Melbourne, but he won through to the last four at Flushing Meadow, and retained his Australian title early in 1987 over Pat Cash, who had beaten him in the Davis Cup a few weeks before. There was another early loss in Paris, then at Wimbledon he got through to the semi-finals before losing to Lendl in four close sets. He reached the same stage at Flushing Meadow before losing to Wilander. Edberg also has a good doubles record, having won the 1985 Masters and 1987 US Open titles with fellow-Swede Anders Jarryd.

Left: Roy Emerson means business with this backhand drive at Wimbledon. He won more major titles than any other male player.
Below: Stefan Edberg is one of the best of an almost unlimited current supply of world-class Swedish players. Unlike most of his compatriots, he has an aggressive game more suited to fast courts.

Roy EMERSON

b 1936

Emerson has won more major titles than any other man in tennis. His career spanned the closing years of the pre-open era, fading out just when the rewards were becoming really huge. In the mid 1960s he was No 1 in the world, but when the likes of Rod Laver and Ken Rosewall returned to traditional competition after their years as contract professionals, he was obliged to play a more supporting role.

Son of a Queensland farmer, he is said to have developed his exceptionally strong wrists by milking cows. This may or may not be so, but he was certainly a dedicated athlete, at one time being described as 'lean, keen and trained to the last ounce'. His service had an unusual wind-up, but when it was unleashed, it was fearsome. He backed this up with sure volleys and sound ground-strokes, and unlike many Australians he was equally good on grass and clay.

Emerson won the Australian six times, including five times in sequence from 1963 to 1967. He was Wimbledon champion in 1964 and 1965, but was denied a hat-trick in 1966 when, in the quarter-finals against Owen Davidson, he slipped and skidded into the umpire's chair, the injury ruining his chances. A similar misfortune befell him the following year at Forest Hills, again in the quarter-finals, when he tried to leap the net after running for a drop shot, caught his leg in the net cord and somersaulted to the ground. This helped Clark Graebner to win the match.

Emerson won the US singles in 1961 and 1964, and the French in 1963 and 1967. He was Italian champion three times (1959, 1961, 1966), South African once (1966), and

German once (1967). He also won the doubles championships in all seven major tournaments: Australia (1960, 1966, 1969); France (1960, 1961, 1962, 1963, 1964, 1965, with five different partners); Wimbledon (1959, 1961, 1971); US (1959, 1960, 1965, 1966); Italy (1959, 1960, 1961, 1966); Germany (1960); and South Africa (1966). The grand total is 39, although only two were in the open game.

Chris
EVERT
b 1954

There are just a handful of players in the history of tennis who have changed the course of the game. Bjorn Borg, who made topspin indispensable and galvanized a whole nation, was one; Alice Marble, who proved that women could play like men, was another; and Billie Jean King, whose tireless efforts enabled women to earn like men, was a third.

Christine Marie Evert, from Fort Lauderdale, Florida, also influenced a generation. Neat, feminine and professional to her fingertips, she revived the classic virtues of baseline play, and millions copied her double-handed backhand — though only Tracy Austin came close to emulating it.

As her long and splendid career draws to a close, it is worth reflecting that nobody in tennis has played to such a level of consistency over so many years. In 16 years of competition, without break, she has only twice failed to reach the semi-finals of a Grand Slam event — and once was when she was ill. She won at least one Grand Slam title every year from 1974 to 1986, was never beaten in a Wightman Cup singles, and lost only twice in the Federation Cup. She has won nearly 150 professional titles, and was unbeaten on clay for six years.

Evert was still 15 when she beat the reigning Grand Slam champion, Margaret Court, at a tournament in Charlotte, North Carolina, in September 1970. The following year, as a surprise selection, she won both her Wightman Cup rubbers against vastly more experienced players, and she reached the semi-finals of the US Open at her first attempt. She quickly established herself as one of the top four players in the world, and her Wimbledon debut was greeted with more media attention than anyone since Maureen Connolly, with whom she was inevitably compared.

Like Connolly, Evert played almost entirely from the baseline, pounding the ball back in long rallies and thwarting would-be volleyers with deadly accurate lobs and passing shots. She also scored effectively with deceptive drop-shots. She hardly varied her game throughout her career, although in later years she made herself fitter in order to keep up with her greatest rival, Martina

Navratilova. And, though she was reluctant to go to the net, she knew how to volley.

Evert lost a classic semi-final to Evonne Goolagong at Wimbledon 1972, then was beaten at the same stage at Forest Hills by another Australian, Kerry Melville. In 1973 she reached the finals at Paris and Wimbledon, losing a great encounter to Court in the former, then, after avenging that loss, failing against King in the latter. Court stopped her at Forest Hills, but Evert took the South African title over Goolagong.

Her victory parade began in 1974, when she was unbeaten for 10 tournaments from March to September. That took in Rome, Paris and Wimbledon, and she beat the only Russian woman to reach a Grand Slam final, Olga Morozova, in the latter two. She lost to Goolagong at Forest Hills, but that was her last defeat in the US Open until 1979.

She was ranked No 1 in the world for four straight years from 1975 to 1978, and her titles were at the French (1975), Wimbledon (1976) and the US Open (1975 to 1978). Navratilova beat her in the Wimbledon finals of 1978 and 1979, and Tracy Austin, who had ended her six-year clay-court streak in Rome, dethroned her at Flushing Meadow. Evert decided to take a break after a poor showing in the Women's Series Championships, but she was back with a vengeance in the spring of 1980. She won the Italian and French titles, lost the Wimbledon final to Goolagong Cawley, but regained the US Open.

In 1981 Evert lost the French to Hana Mandlikova but took her revenge in the Wimbledon final. She lost to Navratilova in the semi-finals at Flushing Meadow, then in 1982/3 she held three out of the four Grand Slam titles with the US Open, Australian and French. But disaster struck at Wimbledon, where she suffered a stomach upset and lost to Kathy Jordan in the third round. In 1984 she once again took the Australian, and she beat Navratilova in two classic French finals in 1985 and 1986. But the emergence of Steffi Graf in 1987 meant that, for the first time in 13 years, she failed to win a Grand Slam, and the era of her shared dominance of the women's game with Navratilova drew to a close.

Evert was runner-up in the 1988 Australian Open and a semi-finalist at Wimbledon and Flushing Meadow. Her rivalry with Navratilova has been the greatest in women's tennis, yet the two are firm friends. Apart from her 18 Grand Slam titles, bettered only by Margaret Court and Helen Wills Moody, she has won three major doubles events — the French of 1974 (with Morozova) and 1975 (with Navratilova), and the Wimbledon of 1976 (with Navratilova). She also won the World Mixed Doubles in 1984 with her erstwhile fiancé, Jimmy Connors.

An icon among Americans, she has been married twice: to the British player John Lloyd from 1979 to 1987, and to American skier Andy Mill from July 1988.

Opposite: Chris Evert has been the most consistently successful player in the history of tennis. Nobody else can match her record of at least one major singles title for each of 13 consecutive years, and only three failures to reach the semi-finals in 54 Grand Slam singles events.

Neale
FRASER
b 1933

Of all the great Australian players of the 1950s and 1960s, immediately prior to the arrival of open tennis, only Neale Fraser resisted the temptation to turn professional. (Roy Emerson signed a contract in the spring of 1968, just before the revolution took effect.) He had a long career in the amateur ranks, and was a doubles finalist at Wimbledon as late as 1973, when he was 40.

Fraser, from Melbourne, was a copybook player, left-handed, with a no-frills serve and volley game. He first got into Wimbledon via the qualifying event and was a semi-finalist in 1957 and runner-up in 1958 before winning the title in 1960, beating Rod Laver. In 1961 he sensationally lost to the British player, Bobby Wilson in the fourth round, but in 1962 he was back in the semi-finals with his younger brother John (neither won). He won the doubles with Emerson in 1959 and 1961, and the mixed with Margaret du Pont in 1962.

He also won the French doubles in 1958, 1960 and 1962, the US singles in 1959 and 1960, the US doubles in 1957, 1959 and 1960, and the US mixed doubles in 1958, 1959 and 1960. He never won his native Australian title, although he was runner-up in 1957, 1959 and 1960. He took the doubles in 1957, 1958 and 1962, and the mixed in 1956.

Fraser was one of the luckiest Wimbledon champions; in his winning year he had to save five match points against Earl Buchholz — who retired with cramp when leading two sets to one and 15 games all. Fraser was in the winning Australian Davis Cup teams of 1959, 1960, 1961 and 1962, the greatest triumph being in 1959 at Forest Hills, when he beat the reigning Wimbledon champion, Alex Olmedo, in the opening rubber and clinched the trophy in the fifth by defeating Barry McKay (on McKay's birthday). He was also non-playing captain for Australia's wins in 1973, 1977, 1983 and 1986.

He reached the Wimbledon doubles semi-finals of 1972 and final of 1973 with John Cooper, younger brother of 1958 champion Ashley Cooper.

Shirley
FRY
b 1927

Shirley Fry had to wait a long time before she attained the highest honours in the game. If patience and persistence be worth a special prize, she would deserve it. After she first broke into the top flight, she had watched her peers win the titles for 12 years before she finally secured the most glittering crowns.

Fry, from Akron, Ohio, was a good player with all the strokes, but she was rarely good enough to upset the best players of her era, like Louise Brough, Doris Hart and Maureen Connolly. At seven Wimbledons from 1948, she was always in the last 16 or better. Her one major triumph in singles before 1956 was in the 1951 French, when she beat Hart in three sets in the final. But Hart exacted a crushing revenge at 6-1, 6-0 in the Wimbledon final two weeks later.

In 1956 she had her great chance. The players that had thwarted her were missing, and she won Wimbledon, beating Britain's Angela Buxton in the final; the US Nationals, defeating Althea Gibson; and then the Australian of 1957, again over Gibson. Then, at the age of 30, she called it a day and retired to become Mrs Irvin.

In doubles, the story was different. She formed a tremendous partnership with Hart that claimed 12 major titles: Wimbledon (1951, 1952, 1953), US (1951, 1952, 1953, 1954), France (1950, 1951, 1952, 1953) and Italy (1951). She also took the Australian in 1957 with Gibson, the mixed doubles at Wimbledon in 1956 (with Vic Seixas) and the mixed in Italy in 1951 (with Felicissimo

Below: Neale Fraser with the men's singles trophy at Wimbledon in 1960. He was one of a very small number of eventual champions who were required to qualify the first time they entered.

Ampon of the Philippines). Fry and Hart's Wimbledon win of 1953 was uniquely devastating in that they won both their semi-final and their final by 6-0, 6-0, and lost only four games throughout the event.

Vitas
GERULAITIS
b 1954

Gerulaitis was one of the great talents of tennis, who never quite fulfilled the promise he displayed in the early part of his career. A New Yorker, he produced some of his best form in his home city, reaching the finals of the US Open in 1979 and the Masters in 1980 and 1982.

He had a strong all-round game, and was capable of electrifying play, although he went through periods of uncertainty and loss of motivation. Involvement in a drugs scandal did not help his career, and a love of night life harmed his progress; but he did buckle down and work hard under the supervision of Fred Stolle, to produce his best results in 1979.

He won three major titles — the Italian of 1977 and 1979 and the Australian in December 1977. Also in 1977, he played one of Wimbledon's best-remembered matches when he forced Bjorn Borg to five pulsating sets in the semi-finals. In addition, he took the Wimbledon doubles in 1975 (with Sandy Mayer), the WCT Finals in 1978 and the South African Open in 1982. In 1981 bad behaviour caused him to be suspended twice.

One of his last appearances was a 'battle of the sexes' exhibition doubles in Atlantic City in 1985, when he and Bobby Riggs were beaten by Martina Navratilova and Pam Shriver.

Althea
GIBSON
b 1927

The first black player of either sex to win major titles in tennis, Gibson had to endure years of prejudice before she was able to make her mark. Her tough Harlem background and her race appeared to be insurmountable obstacles. Were it not for a campaign by former champion Alice Marble to get her accepted by the authorities that issued invitations to the main US circuit tournaments, Althea might never have made it. Even as a champion herself, she felt an outsider and had a chip on her shoulder.

Tall, strong and athletic, she had a formidable serve-volley game and won the American Tennis Association (for coloured players) title ten years running. In 1950 she was finally allowed to play the Eastern grass-

court circuit, and then the US Nationals at Forest Hills, where she nearly defeated Louise Brough. She played at Wimbledon in 1951 and lost in the third round, but did not return until 1956 because she was studying for a university degree in Tallahassee.

In 1956, aged 29, she made her move. She won the French singles, beating holder Angela Mortimer in the final, and won the doubles with another Briton, Angela Buxton. They also won the doubles at Wimbledon, where Gibson lost a close singles quarter-final against Shirley Fry. Fry beat her in the 1956 US and 1957 Australian finals as well, by identical 6-3, 6-4 scores. But having won the 1956 Italian singles, Gibson had lifted herself to No 2 in the world.

The following two years she was un-assailably at the top. Those years gained her two Wimbledon singles, two US singles, two Wimbledon doubles, and the US mixed doubles of 1957. In the four singles finals, against Darlene Hard (Wimbledon 1957),

Above: Vitas Gerulaitis was one of the most exciting and flamboyant players of the 1970s. He will be best remembered for a magnificent semi-final against Bjorn Borg at Wimbledon in 1977.

Louise Brough (US 1957), Mortimer (Wimbledon 1958) and Hard (US 1958), she dropped just one set. In 1957 she had the honour of being one of only three winners ever to receive the Wimbledon trophy from the Queen of England.

At the end of 1958 Gibson turned professional, and played a series of curtain-raisers for the Harlem Globetrotters against glamour-girl Karol Fageros. She later turned to golf, and became Mrs Darbon.

Andres GIMENO
b 1937

A tall Spaniard with a powerful but skilful game, Andres Gimeno denied himself the chance of more major success by turning professional at the age of 23. His only notable victory up till then had been the London Grass Court Championships of 1960. At that time the most important professional tournament was the London Pro Championship at Wembley, where he was runner-up in 1965. By 1967 he was one of the top four pros, and reached the semi-finals of the one-off pro tournament on the Centre Court at Wimbledon in August of that year.

He was able to return to the traditional events in 1968, the year tennis went open, and he was a semi-finalist at Bournemouth, Paris and Wembley, and runner-up in the US doubles with Arthur Ashe. In 1969 he was runner-up to Rod Laver in the Australian Open, and in 1970 a semi-finalist at Wimbledon. In 1971 he won the German Open and was runner-up with Roger Taylor in the Italian doubles.

In 1972, when he was nearly 35, came the greatest success of his career when he won the French Open, albeit in a field shorn of many of the top players because of a dispute between the International Federation and World Championship Tennis, which had most of them under contract. Gimeno defeated Stan Smith, Alex Metreveli and Patrick Proisy in the last three rounds, and although a home player was losing finalist, the Spaniard's was a popular and sentimental victory. At Wimbledon soon afterwards he was seeded 4th but lost in the second round to New Zealand's Onny Parun, whilst at the US Open he was beaten by Smith in the last 16. He faded from the scene in due course, leaving Spain to muse on what might have been had he been eligible to partner Manuel Santana in the Davis Cup during the latter's great years.

Spain has now entered a new era of strength in world class tennis with the emergence of Emilio Sanchez and Sergio Casal. Sanchez was runner-up in the 1986 Italian Open, while with Casal he reached the 1987 men's doubles final at Wimbledon.

Kitty GODFREE
b 1897

One of only two British women to win Wimbledon between the wars, Kathleen McKane (who married British player Leslie Godfree in 1926) was an all-round sportswoman. A fine hockey player and a champion at badminton, she had an excellent tennis game and was a superb match player, with a determination to win that enabled her to snatch victory from the jaws of defeat.

Her career overlapped those of the two great between-the-wars champions, Suzanne Lenglen and Helen Wills. Lenglen beat her in the 1923 Wimbledon final, but the following year, while recovering from jaundice, Lenglen scratched from their semi-final, giving the British player a free passage to the title match. In this she faced the 18-year-old Wills. Although McKane had easily won their Wightman Cup rubber two weeks before, Wills was in commanding mood, and she led by a set and 4-1. But McKane staged an extraordinary recovery and won five successive games, levelling the score and closing out the match 6-4 in the third.

In 1925 Lenglen was back at her devastating best, and having beaten McKane 6-1, 6-2 in the final at Paris, she crushed her 6-0, 6-0 in the Wimbledon semi-finals. But in 1926 Lenglen had sensationally pulled out of

the tournament, Wills was absent, and Mrs Godfree, as she now was, regained the title with a three-set win over the Spanish star, Lili de Alvarez. She went on to win the mixed doubles with her husband — the only time the feat has been achieved by a married couple.

Elsewhere, Godfree was runner-up to Wills in the 1925 US Nationals, and she was on the winning British teams in the Wightman Cup of 1924, 1925 and 1930. She continued to play intermittently until the mid 1930s, but by now she was a mother, and her family duties came first.

Sixty years on, she remains a tennis personality. She carried on playing tennis socially at the All England club until she was 89, and accepted invitations to present the women's singles trophies at Paris and Wimbledon in 1986. The previous year she took part in a mixed doubles in the annual International Club match against France, competing against her contemporary, Jean Borotra.

Pancho
GONZALES
b 1928

By common consent, the two greatest players in the history of tennis that never won the men's singles at Wimbledon have been Pancho Gonzales and Ken Rosewall. Both

turned professional before their talent had fully flowered, and both returned to the traditional events with the advent of open tennis — by which time it was too late.

Gonzales, a southern Californian of Hispanic origin, was a spectacular performer whose matches were often enhanced by drama and emotion. He hit the ball powerfully — at its best, his service was almost unreturnable — but he also had exceptional touch, and his strength was tempered with artistry. He burst on to the international scene in 1948, winning the US singles with a straight-sets victory over the South African, Eric Sturgess. Making his only overseas tour as an amateur in 1949, he reached the semi-finals in Paris, losing to Budge Patty, and won the doubles with Frank Parker. At Wimbledon, seeded second, he surprisingly lost in the fourth round to Australia's Geoff Brown, but he won the doubles with Parker. At Forest Hills he retained the singles with a titanic 16-18, 2-6, 6-1, 6-2, 6-4 recovery against Ted Schroeder, and lost another marathon mixed doubles semi-final with Gussie Moran against Sturgess and Louise Brough, 6-8, 6-3, 15-13.

Then Gonzales was lured into professionalism, perhaps unwisely as he was only 21, and the major circuit was denied his presence for 19 years. During the 1950s he soon established himself as the dominant player on the pro tour, winning the London title in 1950, 1951, 1952 and 1956, and the US pro title every year from 1953 to 1959, and again in 1961.

By 1968, when he was able to return to Wimbledon and the other Grand Slam events, Gonzales was 40 — but still a force to be reckoned with. He had the dubious distinction of being the first pro to lose to an amateur in an open tournament, failing against Britain's Mark Cox at Bournemouth, but he reached the quarter-finals of the French and US singles. At Wimbledon, seeded 8th, he lost in the third round to the USSR's Alex Metreveli, but the following year he defied the years and a far younger opponent and won the longest match ever played at the Championships.

In the first round, appealing angrily about poor light, he lost the first two sets against Charlie Pasarell 22-24, 1-6, before the match was halted overnight. On resumption the following day, Gonzales fought off five match points to triumph 16-14, 6-3, 11-9. Overall, it lasted for 5 hours 12 minutes, and took 112 games — shattering the previous record (Jaroslav Drobny vs Budge Patty, 1953, which took 93 games). Remarkably, the 41-year-old winner won both his next two matches in straight sets before surrendering in the fourth round against Arthur Ashe.

He did not play much more competitive tennis after that, but he appeared, as himself, in a 1979 film, *Players*, in which he emerged with more acting honours than most other members of the cast.

Left: Pancho Gonzales pictured during his heyday as the world's top contract professional — a position he held throughout the 1950s. He was one of the very few players in history that continued to play at the highest level after the age of 40.

Evonne GOOLAGONG
b 1951

At her best, Evonne Goolagong was a sheer delight. The part-Aboriginal from the New South Wales outback was a totally instinctive player, and the daintiest and most graceful champion since Maria Bueno. Her tennis was effortless and beautiful to behold. She did not hit the ball hard, but she could put it away with breathtaking angles, and her volleying skills made her particularly effective on grass. Never demonstrative in her emotions, she did not seem to be at all perturbed whatever was happening. On her bad days (the press called her occasional lapses of concentration her 'walkabouts') she appeared to be as unconcerned as when she was playing well.

Right: Evonne Goolagong, later Mrs Cawley, was a delightful player who enchanted the Centre Court crowd at Wimbledon, where she won the singles twice, nine years apart. She is the only part-Aboriginal ever to make any impact in tennis.

Goolagong was taken from her remote home as a teenager and trained by Vic Edwards, one of Australia's foremost coaches. On her first overseas tour in 1970 she won a string of minor British tournaments but flopped spectacularly on the Centre Court against the US Wightman Cup player, Jane 'Peaches' Bartkowicz. She matured rapidly from a good player to a great one during the Australian season of 1970/1, helping her team win the Federation Cup and then beating fellow Australian, Margaret Court, for the first time in the Victoria Open final at Melbourne. She narrowly lost to Court in the Australian National final, but she won the French Open, beating her compatriot Helen Gourlay. She went on to win Wimbledon at only her second attempt, crushing Court 6-4, 6-1 in a stunning final.

The remaining years of the 1970s, however, were comparatively disappointing,

as her only Grand Slam titles were in Australia (1974, 1975, 1976, 1978), when the opposition was less strong than in the other majors. She lost both her French and Wimbledon titles in the finals of 1972 against Billie Jean King, and she was runner-up twice more at Wimbledon — in 1975 (just after she married an Englishman, Roger Cawley) and 1976. She never won the US Open, and was runner-up for four years running (1973, 1974, 1975, 1976), though she won the Virginia Slims championship twice, in 1974 and 1976. Her other major singles titles were the South African in 1972 and the Italian in 1973. She won the Wimbledon doubles in 1974 with Peggy Michel of the US, and took four Australian doubles titles (1971, with Court; 1974 and 1975, with Michel; and 1976, with another Mrs Cawley, the former Helen Gourlay).

She missed the 1977 season to have her first child, and by 1980, when she was nearly 29, it was assumed that her best years were behind her. But Wimbledon that year rejoiced in a women's singles final between two highly popular foreign players with English husbands — 'the Merry Wives of Wimbledon' — with Evonne Cawley coming through to play Chris Evert Lloyd. Although Evonne had won their first encounter, a classic semi-final in 1972, Evert Lloyd had had by far the better of their meetings through the years, and was expected to win. But the graceful Australian took a rain-interrupted final 6-1, 7-6, and became not only the first woman to regain the title after a nine-year interval, but the first mother to triumph since 1914.

She missed 1981 to have another baby, and by 1982, when she was humiliated in her opening match by the young American, Zina Garrison, she was no longer able to keep up with the sharply rising standards of the international game. She played little more after this. But she was a much-loved competitor whose carefree attitude was a throwback to the more light-hearted amateur days of many years before.

Steffi GRAF
b 1969

In 1988 Steffi Graf earned the unique distinction of becoming the only tennis player of either sex to win a 'Gold Slam' — the four Grand Slam singles titles of Australia, France, Wimbledon and the US, plus the gold medal in Seoul, as tennis returned to the Olympic Games for the first time in 64 years.

From Bruehl, West Germany, she is coached by her father, Peter. Strong and athletic, she has a venomous serve and bullet-like ground-strokes — her forehand in particular is hit with such pace that few opponents can withstand it. Of her contemporaries, only her Argentine doubles partner, Gabriela Sabatini, looks capable of rivalling her — though Sabatini will have to improve significantly to achieve it.

Graf became the youngest player ever, at 13, to secure a place on the Women's Tennis Association computer ranking list in 1982. In 1984, at the age of 15, she reached the last 16 at Wimbledon and won the Olympic Games demonstration event at Los Angeles (restricted to players aged 20 and under). In 1985 she reached the fourth round at Paris and Wimbledon, and the semi-finals at the Lipton tournament and Flushing Meadow. In 1986 she began seriously to challenge the top players. Having lost to Evert in the Lipton final, Graf beat her at Hilton Head, and then defeated Navratilova in the German Open final. She missed a match point and lost to Hana Mandlikova in the quarter-finals at Paris, and was unable to play at Wimbledon because of illness. A freak injury put her out of the Federation Cup, but she reached the last four at the US Open and lost a third set tie-break to Navratilova after holding match points. During the year she won eight of 11 tournaments played.

Graf's watershed year was 1987. She was unbeaten through to Wimbledon, taking the Lipton title (routing both Navratilova and Evert in the last two rounds), retaining the German Open and capturing the French with a thrilling win over Navratilova.

At Wimbledon she breezed through to the final, dropping only one set (to Sabatini), but found Navratilova too strong on the grass, and suffered her first loss after 45 consecutive wins. Graf played a significant role in West Germany's first ever triumph in the Federation Cup at Vancouver, defeating Evert and then joining Claudia Kohde-Kilsch to stage an astonishing recovery against Evert and Pam Shriver in the decisive doubles. She then attained the No 1 ranking at Los Angeles by again beating Evert, who had overcome Navratilova in the semi-finals. However, at the US Open Navratilova once more checked her progress by retaining the title with a 7-6, 6-1 victory.

Darlene
HARD
b 1936

Certainly a contender for the best woman that never won the Wimbledon singles, Hard, from Los Angeles, was among the top players in the world from 1955, when she first competed on the international circuit, until 1964, when she turned professional. Strong and athletic, she had an excellent serve-volley game and was particularly good in doubles, in which she amassed a bagful of major trophies.

An 18-year-old semi-finalist at Forest Hills in 1954, she reached the same stage at Wimbledon the following year. In 1956 she was runner-up in the Italian doubles with Angela Buxton, and in the French doubles with Dorothy Knode, but lost in the third round of the singles at Wimbledon to Angela Mortimer. At Forest Hills she was runner-up in the mixed doubles with Lew Hoad. In 1957 she won the French doubles with Shirley Bloomer, reached the final of the Wimbledon singles and won both doubles, with Althea Gibson and Mervyn Rose. At Forest Hills she was a semi-finalist in the singles, runner-up in the doubles (with Gibson) and runner-up in the mixed (with Bob Howe).

Hard missed most of the 1958 season because she was graduating from Pomona, although she became the first winner of the US Intercollegiate title. At Forest Hills she was runner-up in the singles, and she won the doubles (with Jeanne Arth).

Above: Steffi Graf is set to rule women's tennis for the foreseeable future. Already the Women's Series and French Open champion at the age of 18, she ended the domination of Martina Navratilova, which had lasted since the early 1980s.

She once again reached all three finals at Wimbledon in 1959, losing the singles to Maria Bueno, but winning the doubles (with Arth) and the mixed (with Rod Laver). At Forest Hills she was a semi-finalist in the singles and retained the doubles with Arth.

Hard's best year was 1960. She won the French singles, beating Bueno in the semi-finals, and beating Mexico's Yola Ramirez in the final, and winning the doubles (with Bueno). She lost to Sandra Reynolds in the quarter-finals at Wimbledon, but won both doubles, with Bueno and Rod Laver.

The mixed doubles final was notable in that Howe and Bueno, having lost the first set 11-13, but won the second 6-3, were poised to win, with Bueno to serve at 5-2 in the third. Suddenly without a word to anyone, Hard dashed from the court and was missing for ten minutes. In an extraordinary and unprecedented hiatus, the other three players were kept waiting on court. But Hard dealt with the emergency, returned to play and with her partner saved three match points to take the final set 8-6.

It was unfortunate for Bueno, who would otherwise have won the triple crown. But this did not affect the women's friendship. After Hard had won the 1960 US singles, beating Bueno in a marathon final, and the two had won the doubles, Bueno fell ill with hepatitis, and returned home from Europe in the spring of 1961. Hard cancelled her own plans and stayed with Bueno to nurse her.

Back at Forest Hills, Hard retained the singles and took the doubles with Lesley Turner. In 1962 she won the Italian doubles with Bueno, but lost in the quarter-finals at Wimbledon to Vera Sukova. With Bueno, she lost in the semi-finals of the doubles to Sandra Price and Renee Schuurman. At Forest Hills she lost her singles title to Margaret Smith in the final, but regained the doubles with Bueno.

Her last full year on the circuit was 1963. She was a singles semi-finalist at Wimbledon, regained the doubles with Bueno, and was runner-up in the mixed with Bob Hewitt. She and Bueno lost the US doubles final. She was triple-champion in the South African championships of 1964, then turned professional. Five years later, she returned briefly to competition, and won the US doubles with Françoise Durr. That extended her tally of US doubles titles to six, having won five years running from 1958 to 1962.

where she never competed and which did not enjoy a strong entry in her day, she won the singles, doubles and mixed at least once in the four Grand Slam tournaments, the Italian and the South African.

Hart was also remarkable in that she overcame a major disability to reach the top. As a child in St Louis, Missouri, she suffered an illness that damaged her right leg and was feared at one time to be polio. This leg was shorter than the other, so she looked slightly awkward, but rigorous exercise enabled her to avoid lack of mobility, and she was able to run with the best of them. She had a formidable armoury of shots, and was a fine stylist in a golden era of women's tennis.

Hart figured in either the semi-finals or finals of every US championship from 1944 to 1955, and during that time took two singles (1954, 1955), four doubles (1951, 1952, 1953, 1954) and five mixed doubles titles (1951, 1952, 1953, 1954, 1955), thereby being triple champion for two years running. Most of these titles came late in her career because the early years were dominated by Louise Brough, Margaret du Pont and Maureen Connolly. She was a great rival of these three, beating them all at various times, but her successes at Forest Hills and Boston (where the doubles were played) came after they faded out.

At Wimbledon she was twice runner-up (1947, 1948) before winning the triple crown in 1951, and she was runner-up in the singles for a third time in 1953. She first won the doubles in 1947 with Pat Todd, and in 1951, 1952, 1953 with Shirley Fry. She won the mixed five years running, with Frank Sedgman (1951, 1952) and Vic Seixas (1953, 1954, 1955).

Hart won the Australian singles and mixed in 1949, and the doubles (with Brough) and mixed (for the second time with Sedgman) in 1950. She won the French singles in 1950 and 1952; the doubles in 1948 (with Todd) and 1950, 1951, 1952, and 1953 (with Fry); and the mixed in 1951 (with Sedgman — a fourth triple crown), 1952 (with Sedgman) and 1953 (with Seixas). Her Italian laurels were the singles of 1951 and 1953, the doubles of 1951 and the mixed of 1953. She won the South African singles and doubles in 1952 and the mixed in 1950.

She turned professional in 1955 after a glorious career that also included ten successive appearances in the Wightman Cup.

Doris
HART
b 1925

There are only a handful of players who have won all three titles at all the major championships, and Doris Hart is one of them. Except for the German championship,

---

Lew
HOAD
b 1934

One of the best of a fine batch of Australians that dominated the game in the 1950s and 1960s, Lew Hoad was a power player *par excellence*, able to hit the ball with terrific strength and little apparent effort. He had a superb serve-volley game, and his topspin backhand drive, which he acquired in time to win his first Wimbledon, was much admired.

Hoad's great rival was Ken Rosewall, who was just three weeks older. They burst upon the international scene in 1953 and together won the Wimbledon doubles, plus the Australian and French doubles titles. Hoad, who had been a semi-finalist at Forest Hills, won both his singles rubbers in the Davis Cup challenge round to help Australia retain the trophy against the United States. The 'Twins', as they were known, lost their doubles titles in 1954, but regained the Wimbledon crown in 1955. The following year saw Hoad's big breakthrough. He won the Australian, French, Italian and Wimbledon singles, and was only deprived of the Grand Slam by Rosewall in the final at Forest Hills.

In 1957 Neale Fraser beat him in the Australian semi-finals, but together they won the doubles that year — Hoad having also won it the year before with Rosewall. At the 1957 Wimbledon he was all-conquering, losing only one set in seven matches and annihilating Ashley Cooper 6-2, 6-1, 6-2 in the final.

Hoad then turned professional, but chronic back trouble prevented him from reaching the top of that field. He competed in traditional events for a few years after the institution of open tennis without notable success. In the mid 1960s he bought land in southern Spain and established a successful tennis centre there.

Helen
JACOBS
b 1908

The major motif of the women's game in the 1930s was the rivalry of the 'two Helens' — Helen Wills Moody and Helen Jacobs, who both came from Berkeley, California, and who detested each other. They had many notable duels over the years, and the differences between them made for much drama and media attention. Moody, who was cold, beautiful and ruthless, contrasted with Jacobs, who was warm and friendly. They played four Wimbledon finals and two American finals against each other — and Moody won them all except the 1933 title match at Forest Hills.

On that occasion Moody retired when trailing 0-3 in the final set. In one of the most famous snubs in the history of tennis, she ignored a sporting gesture by her opponent. Moody was suffering from a back injury, and when she told the umpire she was defaulting the other Helen put her hand on her shoulder and said, 'Won't you rest awhile, Helen?' 'Take your hand off my shoulder,' Moody coldly replied, and left the court.

There was more drama at Wimbledon. In the 1935 final, Jacobs had a match point but fluffed an easy volley. Reprieved, Moody took the next five games. And in 1938, the situation was reversed from the US 1933 sensation. Jacobs had strained her Achilles tendon, and came on court with her foot bandaged. It was causing her difficulty, and at 4-5 in the first set she asked her opponent if they could stop while she took it off. Moody made no reply. Some time later Jacobs did take it off, while Moody paid no attention. But the pain was even worse, and Jacobs, who refused to retire, limped through the rest of the match, which she lost 4-6, 0-6.

Jacobs did win a number of titles in her rival's absence. She was a highly popular winner at Wimbledon in 1936, when she beat Hilde Sperling in the final, and apart from her US singles win of 1933 she won the title in 1932, 1934 and 1935. She was runner-up at Wimbledon a total of five times (1929, 1932,

Above: Lew Hoad is perfectly balanced for this volley on Court Two at Wimbledon. He was unlucky not to take the Grand Slam in 1956 — having won the Australian, French and Wimbledon titles, he was thwarted by his doubles partner, Ken Rosewall, in the US final at Forest Hills.

Above: Ann Jones suffered many disappointments at Wimbledon before she finally took the title at her 13th attempt. One of the shrewdest and most consistent of British players, she was a losing semi-finalist six times and runner-up once.

finals. Later that year she reached the semi-finals at Flushing Meadow, and by then had beaten most of the top players.

Jaeger was not an exciting player to watch. A baseliner, with a double-handed backhand, she was a shrewd tactician, but there was little aesthetic appeal in her game. She maintained steady progress in 1981, reaching the semi-finals at Paris (and winning the mixed doubles with Jimmy Arias). By the autumn of that year she was No 2 on the WTA computer ranking list. In 1982 she beat Chris Evert to reach the Paris final, and was a semi-finalist at Flushing Meadow and Melbourne. Then in 1983 she was runner-up at Wimbledon, although her defeat by Martina Navratilova was one of the most one-sided on record.

In 1984 Jaeger lost interest in competitive tennis, although she was earning vast sums in prize money. She decided to go to college, and since then has made only spasmodic appearances on the circuit. A native of Chicago, she now lives in Florida.

Ann JONES
b 1938

Born Ann Haydon in Birmingham, England, she was one of Britain's most consistent and successful players over a long career that lasted from the mid 1950s to the early 1970s. The first left-hander to win the women's singles at Wimbledon, she was also a top table tennis player who was runner-up in the World Championships of 1957. An instinctive baseliner, she turned herself into a Wimbledon champion by improving her volleying — and she would have been unlikely to have achieved this without turning professional in 1968 and practising with the top men.

One of a bright crop of young British stars that emerged in the late 1950s, she reached her first Wimbledon semi-final in 1958, and appeared at that stage five more times before getting to the final in 1967. In 1968 she was in a winning position in the semi-finals against Billie Jean King before faltering, but in 1969 she scored victories over the two best players in the world, Margaret Court and King, to win the title. She did not defend it in 1970, and competed only once more — in the doubles of the Centennial championships in 1977.

Most of her early success was on clay. She won the French singles in 1961 and 1966 (and was runner-up in 1963, 1968 and 1969). She reached the final of the US championships in 1961 and 1967, and won the Italian singles in 1966. In doubles, she won the French (with Françoise Durr) in 1968/9, and the Italian (with Durr) in 1969, and she took the Wimbledon mixed with Fred Stolle in 1969. She represented Great Britain in the Wightman Cup 12 times between 1957 and

1934, 1935, 1938), and at Forest Hills four times (1928, 1936, 1939, 1940). In the French singles she was runner-up in 1930 and 1934. In 1934 she won both the Italian singles and the doubles (with Elizabeth Ryan). She had success in the US doubles in 1932, 1934, and 1935 with Sarah Palfrey Fabyan, and she took the mixed in 1934 with George Lott.

Andrea JAEGER
b 1965

Few high-ranking players in tennis have had as short careers, at such an early age, and then voluntarily retired, as did Andrea Jaeger. Her time as one of the world's top players lasted four years, from the age of 15 to 19. An outstanding junior, she won the Orange Bowl (the unofficial world junior championship, for players aged 18 and under) at only 13, and she began playing pro tournaments, with remarkable success, when still 14. At her first Wimbledon, in 1980, she beat the former holder, Virginia Wade, to reach the quarter-

1975, and was in the Federation Cup team from 1963 to 1967 and 1971.

Married to Pip Jones since 1962, she has four children and remains active in tennis as a TV commentator and member of the Women's Pro Council.

Billie Jean
KING
b 1943

Billie Jean King was one of the finest tennis players in history, and one of its most influential reformers. Largely through her efforts, women's tennis has been transformed from a second-class sideshow, inferior in attention and in prize money to men's events, into a major sport in its own right, enjoying complete parity with the men.

King, who comes from Long Beach, California, had the longest top-class career of any player of modern times. She was among the best players in the world from 1961 to 1983, she won a record number of Wimbledon titles, and she took the singles, doubles and mixed of every major championship.

It was at Wimbledon that she derived her greatest inspiration. A natural serve-volley player, she had every stroke and was a superb competitor, although for most of her career she was more adept on fast surfaces like grass. She also endured much injury, and had a number of operations on both knees. Of her 20 Wimbledon titles, six were in singles, ten in doubles and four in mixed. She was runner-up on a further nine occasions, and was a quarter-finalist in the singles 20 times in 22 years, the only exceptions being 1976 and 1981, when she did not compete. She played a total of 265 matches at Wimbledon (Elizabeth Ryan is second on the list, with 189), and such was her affinity with the Centre Court that it was referred to as 'The

Left: Billie Jean King keeps her eyes fixedly on the ball as she is challenged at the net on the Centre Court. Despite the fact that she wore spectacles, King was reckoned by many to possess the best eye for the ball in tennis.

Old Lady's House'. (King was already known as 'The Old Lady' by the time she was 29.)

She was triple champion twice — in 1967 and 1973. She was 18 when she won her first title (as Billie Jean Moffitt), the doubles of 1961 with Karen Hantze (later Mrs Susman), and she was 40 when she reached the singles semi-finals for the 14th time in 1983. She was singles champion in 1966, 1967, 1968, 1972, 1973 and 1975, and runner-up in 1963, 1969, 1970. Her doubles titles were in 1961, 1962 (with Susman), 1965 (with Maria Bueno), 1967, 1968, 1970, 1971 (with Rosemary Casals), 1972 (with Betty Stove), 1973 (with Casals), and 1979 (with Martina Navratilova). All four mixed titles (1967, 1971, 1973, 1974) were with Owen Davidson.

Overall King won 39 Grand Slam titles, bettered by only two other players. She won the US singles in 1967, 1971, 1972 and 1974, the doubles in 1964 (with Susman), 1967, 1974 (with Casals), 1978 and 1980 (with Navratilova), and the mixed in 1967, 1971, 1973 (with Davidson) and 1976 (with Phil Dent). Her French titles were: singles 1972, doubles 1972 (with Stove) and mixed 1967 (with Davidson) and 1970 (with Bob Hewitt). She won the Australian singles in 1968 and shared the mixed with Dick Crealy. The Italian singles and doubles (with Casals) were hers in 1970, and the German singles in 1971. She won the South African singles in 1966, 1967 and 1969, the doubles (with Casals) in 1967 and 1970, and the mixed (with Davidson) in 1967. She played in the Federation Cup nine times and was on seven winning teams, and was in the Wightman Cup 10 times, on the winning side nine times.

An ardent feminist — indeed, one of the most notable in any walk of life — King campaigned tirelessly for women's equality in tennis, and was instrumental in setting up the successful women's pro circuit. She herself signed a professional contract in 1968, and led the boycott of the Pacific South West Championships of 1970 (when the men's prize money was 10 times greater than the women's) to form the Virginia Slims tour.

Two notable matches were inspired by the need to give this new movement credibility. In 1971, in the semi-finals at Forest Hills, she brought to an end the winning run of the 16-year-old Chris Evert (who at that time represented the 'establishment') in a match she felt had to be won for political reasons. And in 1973, having accepted a 'battle of the sexes' challenge from Bobby Riggs, who had earlier trounced Court, King struck another blow for her cause by winning — in a match which holds the record for the biggest worldwide audience for a tennis event in history.

Twice President of the Women's Tennis Association, she was also involved in the establishment of the World Team Tennis League in 1974 with her husband Larry, whom she had married in 1965. Her extrovert personality and unbounded enthusiasm

helped to get this project off the ground, and she is currently commissioner for the league in its present format.

Her private life was painfully brought out into the open in 1981 when her former lover, Marilyn Barnett, unsuccessfully sued her for 'palimony'.

Jan
KODES
b 1946

Jan Kodes is the only player to have won Wimbledon representing Czechoslovakia. (Jaroslav Drobny was playing under Egyptian colours at the time of his victory, Martina Navratilova was listed as American and Ivan Lendl had yet to take the title at the time of writing.) Resourceful and persistent, Kodes at one time disliked playing on grass, but eventually he came to like the surface and even installed a grass court in the garden of his home in Prague.

He first achieved international fame in 1966 when he led Czechoslovakia to victory in the Galea Cup, the unofficial men's world team championship for players aged 20 and under. For several years one of the best clay court players in the world, he was a semi-finalist in Rome in 1969 and runner-up for the next three years. He took the French title in 1970 and 1971, then was a shock unseeded finalist in the 1971 US Open, beating top-seeded John Newcombe in the first round and Arthur Ashe in the semi-finals before submitting to Stan Smith. In 1972 Kodes reached the semi-finals at Wimbledon and finished fourth in the Grand Prix.

He won Wimbledon in 1973 — the year all but three members of the Association of Tennis Professionals boycotted the tournament over the 'Pilic Affair'. He almost went out in the semi-finals, when Britain's Roger Taylor served for the match at 5-4 in the final set, but he overcame Alex Metreveli in straight sets for the title. He proved that he was a worthy champion by once again reaching the US Open final the same year — with all the top players taking part.

Kodes appeared in two Davis Cup finals — in 1975, when the Czechs were runners-up to Sweden, and in 1980, when they won the trophy. He is now in tennis administration.

Jack
KRAMER
b 1921

Kramer was a tennis player of the tough breed. Strong and athletic, he looked every inch the all-American boy, with his crew cut and T-shirts. He appeared in the last pre-war

Davis Cup final, aged 18, and had it not been for the war he would probably have figured more prominently in the world game than he did. A master of the serve-volley technique, he had height, reach and a sturdy physique. He was a fine match player — and a great sportsman.

Born in Las Vegas, Nevada, he grew up on Californian cement. In the US Nationals, which continued through the war, he was a semi-finalist in the singles in 1940, runner-up in 1943 and winner in 1946 and 1947. He won the doubles in 1940 and 1941 with Ted Schroeder and in 1943 with Frank Parker, then again in 1947 with Schroeder. He did not play every year, because he spent some time in service with the US Navy.

At Wimbledon in 1946 Kramer was the hot favourite, but he had developed a blister on his playing hand, and he lost in the fourth round to Jaroslav Drobny. He was back the following year, however, and won the title with impressive ease, dropping only one set in seven rounds — to Australia's Dinny Pails in the semi-finals — and he routed compatriot Tom Brown 6-1, 6-3, 6-2 in the final in an astounding 45 minutes. He won the men's doubles in 1946 with Brown, and in 1947 with Bob Falkenburg, then after retaining his US titles he turned professional.

It was in this sphere of the game that Kramer was most influential. He transformed the pro game from a haphazard, poorly organized entity into a proper circuit, and it was he who offered contracts to the succeeding generations of top players until the early 1960s. In 1948 he won the US Pro title. He became a respected TV commentator, and was executive director of the ATP from 1972 to 1975.

Rene
LACOSTE
b 1904

The youngest of the famous 'Four Musketeers', Lacoste, who came from Paris, was a serious and diligent tennis player who studied his strokes and tactics more than any of his three great compatriots. The crocodile, which he adopted as his mascot and had sewn on to his tennis clothes, was said to symbolize his determination to keep hanging on and devour his opponents in the end. He was the best ground-stroke player of his time, and possibly the most astute. Had it not been for poor health, which eventually forced him to retire when still in his early 20s, Lacoste might have carved for himself the greatest career of any Frenchman.

As it was, he enjoyed exceptional success in the major championships. He was three times singles winner in the French, beating Jean Borotra in two finals (1925 and 1929) and Bill Tilden in 1927. In the latter final he

Left: Rene Lacoste smiles winningly for the camera before a Centre Court match. But he was extremely serious about his tennis, and it was a great pity that illness forced him to stop playing competitively before his 25th birthday.

saved two match points in the final set and secured it 11-9, and in the 1929 match against Borotra he only took the final set at 8-6. He also took the doubles with Borotra in 1925 and 1929. He won Wimbledon in 1925 against Borotra, and in 1928 against Henri Cochet; and he took the doubles with Borotra in 1925. He won the US singles in 1926, over Borotra, and in 1927 over Tilden.

The Davis Cup was always regarded as the most important event in those days, and Lacoste became the French hero when, by defeating both Tilden and Bill Johnston in the 1927 challenge round, he enabled his country to win the trophy for the first time. Overall, he played 51 rubbers in the competition between 1923 and 1928.

He was forced by illness to retire midway through the 1929 season when not yet 25. However, the name Lacoste has been perpetuated by his highly successful sports and leisure clothing company, with its crocodile logo, which even today is regarded as one of the world's leaders of tennis fashion.

Above: An early picture of Rod Laver, aged 17, on his first trip to Britain in 1955. He was to become the only player in the history of tennis to win two singles Grand Slams — as an amateur in 1962 and as a professional in 1969.

Dorothea
LAMBERT CHAMBERS
b 1878 – d 1960

A formidable figure — tall, dour and lantern-jawed — Dorothea Lambert Chambers (née Douglass) was the outstanding woman player before the First World War. She took her tennis seriously, and rejected the notion that sport was a garden-party pastime, purely for enjoyment, and never mind the result. She played to win, and she was the forerunner of today's dedicated professionals.

Ironically, Lambert Chambers's pugnacious attitude belied the fact that she had a conventional background for a tennis player of her time. A clergyman's daughter (like her modern counterpart, Virginia Wade), she came from the genteel London suburb of Ealing. She reached her first Wimbledon challenge round in 1903, when she succeeded to the title by default as the holder, Muriel Robb, was not defending. She retained the title against Charlotte Sterry, but lost it in 1905 to May Sutton of the US. The following year she had her revenge, but lost to Sutton again in 1907.

Lambert Chambers did not return to Wimbledon until 1910, after having a baby. She then won the title four times in the next five years, making a total of seven Wimbledon titles. Her 1911 success over Dora Boothby was by 6-0, 6-0 — the only time that awesome score has been inflicted in a Wimbledon singles final.

Like the other women of her day she was a baseliner, and like them her movement was restricted by long skirts and petticoats. She was only freed from these encumbrances when her career resumed after the First World War in 1919.

She defended her title in the first post-war championship and, as holder, was not required to play until the challenge round, where she faced the brilliant young Frenchwoman, Suzanne Lenglen. This was probably the most exciting of all women's finals at Wimbledon — even more than the 1970 classic between Margaret Court and Billie Jean King — because the outcome was in doubt right up to the last shot. Lambert Chambers was then 40 years old, but she so nearly won. She had two match points at 6-5 in the final set, and Lenglen, close to exhaustion, only just saved one of them with a dead netcord. The final score was 10-8, 4-6, 9-7. The following year, Lambert Chambers came through the all-comers' competition to challenge the French girl, but this time she was crushed 6-3, 6-0.

However, the Englishwoman was not finished yet. In 1925, when she was aged 46, she was selected to play for Great Britain in the Wightman Cup at Forest Hills. On the first day, she took part in a doubles rubber with Ermyntrude Harvey against Molla Mallory and May Sutton (now Mrs Bundy). The British pair won, 10-8, 6-1. The next day, Lambert Chambers was back on court for a singles against Eleanor Goss, a woman half her age. In searing heat, the veteran won 7-5, 3-6, 6-1, with, in the words of the British team manager J. Arthur Batley, 'the brainiest display of lawn tennis one could wish to see'. The victory helped Great Britain take the trophy on American soil for the first time, and it would be 50 years before they did it again. Lambert Chambers also played in the 1926 tie at Wimbledon, though this time she lost her one doubles rubber. She became a coach in 1928.

Rod
LAVER
b 1938

In most people's opinion, Rod 'Rocket' Laver, from Rockhampton, Queensland, was the finest tennis player of all time. He is the only player in history to win two separate singles Grand Slams — seven years apart — and he dominated the game both as an amateur then as a contract professional, who was able to return to the traditional events with the arrival of open tennis.

A left-hander, Laver was supreme in every department. He had a vicious, swinging serve, crisp, decisive volleys, an unreturnable smash and deadly accurate ground-strokes, heavy with spin. Lightly built, he was agile and speedy around the court, and mentally he was so tough that he was likely to outlast any opponent through sheer willpower. Quiet and unassuming, he displayed no histrionics, and he was so ruthlessly efficient that some found the sheer predictability of his winning ways rather dull. But he was the consummate sportsman, and he took defeat with dignity and professionalism.

Laver appeared in four successive Wimbledon finals, losing to Alex Olmedo in 1959 and Neale Fraser in 1960 before winning against Chuck McKinley in 1961 and Martin Mulligan in 1962. He was in three consecutive US finals, losing to Fraser in 1960 and Roy Emerson in 1961 before taking the 1962 title, to clinch his first Grand Slam, against Emerson. He had his toughest section of the Slam in Paris, where he had to save a match point against Mulligan in the quarter-finals, then came back from losing the first two sets to beat Emerson in the final. He was in three successive Australian finals, beating Fraser in 1960, losing to Emerson in 1961 and beating Emerson in 1962. He won the Australian doubles three years running with Bob Mark (1959 to 1961) and the French doubles with Emerson in 1961, while in mixed doubles he won the 1961 French and the 1959 and 1960 Wimbledon titles with Darlene Hard. His 1962 Grand Slam year was enhanced by victories in the Italian and German singles.

On signing a contract in 1962 he soon established a dominance in the professional game. He won the US Pro title five times and the London title four times, plus the 1967 Wimbledon Centre Court tournament. When open tennis materialized in 1968, Laver was indisputably the best player in the world.

He did not have things all his own way in 1968. Ken Rosewall beat him in the final of the first ever open tournament, at Bournemouth, and did so again in the French final. Laver triumphed at Wimbledon, over Tony Roche, but in the US Open he was knocked out in the fourth round by South Africa's Cliff Drysdale. However, in 1969 Laver made it clear that he was after another Grand Slam. He took the Australian title in January, over Andres Gimeno; the French in June, against Rosewall; Wimbledon in July, over John Newcombe; and the US Open in September, over Roche.

It must have taken more out of him than seemed apparent at the time, because he never won another Grand Slam singles title after that. He did not defend his Australian and French titles in 1970, and at Wimbledon he went out in the fourth round against Roger Taylor. He lost at the same stage at Forest Hills to Dennis Ralston. It was a similar story in 1971, when he was beaten by Mark Cox in the third round of the Australian and by Tom Gorman in the quarter-finals at Wimbledon. However, he did win a title there that he had never got before by succeeding in the doubles with Emerson. His last notable achievement was joining Newcombe, at the age of 35, to beat the US in the 1973 Davis Cup final at Cleveland.

Ivan
LENDL
b 1960

Ranked No. 1 1985 to 1988, Ivan Lendl is the greatest Czech tennis star of all time and one of the hardest-ever hitters of the ball, though he has yet to learn to adapt his power game to the requirements of grass, and remains without a major tournament win on that surface.

He was an outstanding junior, winning the 18-and-under titles at Wimbledon, Paris and Rome in 1978. He quickly made his mark in the senior game, and was in the top ten by 1980. He won seven Grand Prix titles that year, and reached the final of the Masters in

Above: Ivan Lendl is alert and ready for anything in this picture taken on Court One at Wimbledon. Despite having won the US, French and Masters titles many times over, he remained without a Wimbledon victory at the end of 1987.

Right: A typical pose from Suzanne Lenglen, who was as much a leader of fashion as an invincible tennis player. Apart from one retirement, when she was ill, Lenglen did not lose a singles match after 1914.

At Wimbledon Lendl has yet to reproduce the devastating form that other audiences have come to expect from him. In 1983 he lost in the semi-finals to McEnroe, and in 1984 to Connors. In 1985 he submitted in the fourth round to Henri Leconte. In 1986 he was runner-up to Boris Becker, and in 1987 to Pat Cash. In 1988 he fell at the semi-final hurdle to Becker, and ended the year without a Grand Slam title to his credit. When he yielded his US Open crown to Wilander, he also lost the world No. 1 ranking he had for three years.

He has also failed to win the Australian title, losing the 1983 final to Wilander and the 1985 semi-finals to Stefan Edberg. In 1987 he lost in the semi-finals to Cash. On indoor carpet he has a marvellous record, having taken the Masters four times.

Lendl is coached by the former Australian star, Tony Roche. Like several of his compatriots, he has turned his back on Czechoslovakia; he now lives in Greenwich, Connecticut. He no longer plays for his country in the Davis Cup (he was in the team that took the trophy in 1980) and has applied for US citizenship.

Suzanne LENGLEN
b 1899–d 1938

Those who are old enough to have seen the great Lenglen play are usually quite certain that she was the best woman tennis player ever. Although her competition was far less formidable than that faced by more recent champions, she appears to have possessed a unique brilliance which would probably have enabled her to win the game's highest honours at any time. We are able to see flickering early film of her in action, to be sure, but we must rely on the memories of her contemporaries to appreciate the full wonder of this Frenchwoman's skills.

She had extraordinary control over the ball, and could hit it exactly how she liked, where she liked. (Legend has it that her accuracy was developed and honed by exercises set by her father, in which she was required to hit handkerchiefs placed at various positions on the other side of the net.) She hardly ever made mistakes, her anticipation was uncanny, and her footwork perfect. She was a mistress of all the strokes, and volleyed much more than other women of her day; and she was so good that she did not lose a singles (except for one occasion when she retired ill halfway through a match) between 1919 and 1926, when she turned professional.

In appearance Lenglen was striking rather than attractive. She was a fashion-setter, introducing loose-fitting one-piece dresses at a time when women still wore collars, cuffs,

New York in January 1981, losing to Bjorn Borg in four sets. For a time, however, he seemed to be doomed to be runner-up in Grand Slam events, losing four finals (US Open 1982 and 1983, French 1981 and Australian 1983) before defeating John McEnroe after losing the first two sets at Paris in 1984. He lost the 1985 French final to Mats Wilander, but triumphed there over Mikael Pernfors in 1986 and over Wilander in 1987. He has been in the last seven finals at Flushing Meadow, losing to Jimmy Connors in 1982 and 1983, to McEnroe in 1984 and to Wilander in 1988, but he won three straight years 1985–87 against McEnroe, fellow-Czech Miloslav Mecir, and Wilander.

stays and petticoats to play. She wore brightly coloured bandeaux around her head, and usually made her entrances on court in glamorous fur coats, whatever the weather. She was as great a star as the goddesses of the silver screen, and her following was stupendous. Lenglen revelled in her fame, but she had a prima donna's temperament and her career was punctuated with tantrums and bouts of hysterics.

At the age of 15 she won the World Hard Court championship at St Cloud, but as this was in 1914 she had to wait until the end of the First World War before she could continue. She arrived at Wimbledon in 1919 with a reputation for precosity, but no one gave the French girl much of a chance. In fact, she swept through the all-comers' event, and then defeated the holder, Dorothea Lambert Chambers, in a sensational challenge round, in which she was match-point down for the only time in her postwar career.

After that, Lenglen piled up the titles. She was triple champion at Wimbledon three times — in 1920, 1922 and 1925 — and in all she amassed a total of six singles, six doubles (all with Elizabeth Ryan), and three mixed (with Gerald Patterson, Pat O'Hara Wood and Jean Borotra). She had to retire from the tournament in 1924 while suffering from the after-effects of jaundice, having been stretched to the limit in a gruelling quarter-final against Ryan, who took the only singles set Lenglen lost at Wimbledon after 1919.

In her native France Lenglen was equally overwhelming. She took the World Hard Court title in 1921, 1922 and 1923, and the Olympic Games (in Antwerp) gold medal in 1920. She also won the French championships every year between 1920 and 1923 (when it was restricted to members of French clubs) and in 1925 and 1926, on both occasions as triple champion (winning the doubles with Didi Vlasto and Jacques Brugnon).

She ruled the Cote d'Azur circuit for many years, and on at least five occasions she went right through a singles event without losing any games at all. In 1926 she won a highly publicized 'match of the century' at Cannes against the other great player of her era, Helen Wills; this was their only meeting.

The only arena Lenglen failed to conquer was the US championship at Forest Hills. The long sea journey had aggravated her chronic asthma, and she was unfit when required to play her first match. Her opponent was persuaded to scratch, but in the next round, with seeding not yet introduced, she was drawn to play the holder, Molla Mallory. The American was leading 6-2, 2-0 when Lenglen, in tears, retired. This was in 1921, and proved to be her only amateur appearance in the US.

In 1926 at Wimbledon, due to a misunderstanding, she failed to show up for a Centre Court match in front of one of her greatest fans, Queen Mary. After a series of arguments with the referee she scratched from the tournament and never played amateur tennis

again. She became a touring professional and then set up a tennis school in Paris. She was only 39 when in 1938 she died of leukemia.

Molla
MALLORY
b 1892 – d 1959

Originally from Norway, Molla Bjurstedt (who became Mrs Franklin Mallory in 1919) won more women's singles titles in the US championships than any other player. One of them, in 1917, was regarded as a 'national patriotic tournament', however, and if this is discounted she is tied on seven titles with Helen Wills Moody, one ahead of Chris Evert.

By present standards, she was a player with glaring weaknesses. She had the weakest of serves, she had a backhand that was largely defensive, and she never went to the net unless drawn by a drop-shot. But she had a fearsome forehand drive, her mobility was excellent, and she never gave up.

All her major titles were won in the US championships. She took the singles in 1915, 1916, 1917, 1918, 1920, 1921, 1922 and 1926. Every year between 1915 and 1929 she either won or lost in the quarter-finals, semi-finals or final. She won the doubles in 1916 and 1917 with Eleanora Sears, and she won the mixed in 1917 with Ian Wright and in 1922 and 1923 with Bill Tilden.

At Wimbledon Mallory was runner-up in 1922, when Lenglen avenged that blemish with an overwhelming 6-2, 6-0 victory; and she was a semi-finalist in 1920 and 1923. She represented the US five times in the Wightman Cup, and was runner-up to Lenglen in the 1921 World Hard Court Championship. She died in 1959 while on a visit to her native Norway, the year after she was enshrined in the International Hall of Fame at Newport, Rhode Island.

Hana
MANDLIKOVA
b 1962

Only fleetingly has Mandlikova shown signs of translating her undoubted genius into solid fulfilment. Brilliant but inconsistent, she has always threatened to reach the very top of the women's game, yet her career has so far been a series of peaks and troughs, and there is no sign yet that the pattern will be altered.

A delightful stroke-player, she can produce bursts of form that make her virtually unplayable. These have rewarded her with four major singles titles — the Australian in 1980 and 1987, the French in 1981 and the US Open in 1985. But there have been many bad defeats, when her concentration has faltered, she has lost her temper, and she has given up trying.

From Czechoslovakia, Mandlikova was runner-up to Tracy Austin in the 1978 Wimbledon junior event, then swiftly broke into the top 20 in the senior game and won five tournaments in 1979. In 1980 she reached the US Open final, losing to Chris Evert after taking the first set. She won the Australian Open at the end of 1980, beating Wendy Turnbull after the favourites, Martina Navratilova and Evonne Cawley, had been removed from her path. She defeated Chris Evert in the semi-finals of the 1981 French Open, and went on to beat Sylvia Hanika in the final, then at Wimbledon she overcame Navratilova in the semis before losing a one-sided final against Evert in which she had no apparent match-plan.

The rollercoaster of ups and downs continued, with the next 'up' occurring at the US Open of 1982, as she overcame Austin and Shriver before throwing away a lacklustre final against Evert. It was two years before she reached another Grand Slam final, when she played the best tennis of her life to beat both Evert and Navratilova and win the 1985 US Open. She had, however, led Czechoslovakia to three successive wins in the Federation Cup, in Zurich, 1983, São Paulo, 1984, and Nagoya, 1985. In 1986 she was a semi-finalist in Paris, beating Steffi Graf before being trounced by Evert. But she had her revenge in the semi-finals at Wimbledon, and mounted a lively challenge against Navratilova before losing 7-6, 6-3.

During the 1986 Federation Cup in Prague, she suddenly and unexpectedly married a Czech expatriate who had settled in Australia, Jan Sedlak. Celebrating her move to a new homeland (she has been granted Australian citizenship), she won the singles there in 1987 at the expense of Navratilova. But her hitherto erratic form subsequently took a consistently downward turn. She suffered a series of shock defeats throughout the rest of 1987 and 1988, and ceased to be a leading contender.

She has yet to win a Grand Slam doubles title, though she took the Virginia Slims championship with Wendy Turnbull in 1985 and 1986. They were runners-up at Wimbledon and Flushing Meadow in 1986.

the air whenever she could. She created a trend that was followed by her successors to the major titles — Brough, du Pont and Hart — and she developed a power game that, when it matured, was too formidable for anyone else to overcome.

Her origins were humble. She came from a large family in San Francisco, and money was scarce after her father died. She was only able to make her first tour when financial support came from an unknown benefactor. Other obstacles had to be overcome, too. In 1933, in the US Wightman Cup trials, she had to play almost continuously for nearly nine hours in scorching heat. That evening she collapsed from sunstroke and anaemia, but the ordeal had more far-reaching effects. In the French championships the following spring she fainted on court and was rushed to hospital. Doctors later diagnosed tuberculosis, and told her she would never play tennis again.

But Marble was determined to get back. Helped by her coach, 'Teach' Tennant, she spent a while in a sanatorium in southern California. The recovery process was slow, but two years later she was sufficiently fit to play at Forest Hills, where she beat Helen Jacobs in the final. This was the first of four US singles titles — she won again in 1938, 1939, and 1940. She also took the doubles with Sarah Palfrey Fabyan for four successive years, 1937 to 1940, and the mixed four times — with Gene Mako (1936), Don Budge (1938), Harry Hopman (1939) and Bobby Riggs (1940). This gave her the triple crown for three years running, a feat no other player had achieved since Hazel Hotchkiss and Mary K. Browne did it before the First World War.

At Wimbledon Marble was a losing semi-finalist in 1937 and 1938, but she took the triple crown in 1939, a unique occasion as Riggs took all the men's events. She also won the women's doubles with Fabyan in 1938 and the mixed with Budge in 1937 and 1938. She did not win any French titles, or compete in Australia, but she was in the Wightman Cup team in 1933, 1937, 1938 and 1939. She turned professional in 1941.

Tragically, her husband died during the war after only three years of marriage. In recent years she has undergone major surgery, but she remains full of zest, and is regularly seen at the major championships.

Alice
MARBLE
b 1913

Alice Marble blazed a trail for women in tennis. She was the first complete, all-round woman player to base her game on aggression, and to win from the net. Women before her had volleyed when required, but she got herself into position to take the ball in

Simone
MATHIEU
b 1908 – d 1980

Mlle Simone Passemard became Mme Mathieu very early. She was already married when she won the French junior championship at the age of 18, and she is the only married woman on the roll of any major tennis nation's junior titles. She succeeded

Lenglen as France's principal contender for international honours, continuing in this role up to the Second World War.

A baseliner, she had most success in women's doubles, at which event she was champion of France six times — with Elizabeth Ryan in 1933 and 1934, Billie Yorke of Great Britain in 1936 to 1938, and Jadwiga Jedrejowska in 1939. She also took the mixed in 1937 with Damien Mitic and in 1938 with Yvon Petra, thereby securing the triple crown. And she took three Wimbledon doubles, with Ryan (1933, 1934) and Yorke (1937).

In singles, Mathieu had to wait until she was 30 before winning the French title. She did so in 1938 and 1939 after having been runner-up no less than six times (1929, 1932, 1933, 1935, 1936, 1937), losing on each of the last three occasions to Hilde Sperling. She was also six times a semi-finalist at Wimbledon between 1930 and 1937 without getting further, and was runner-up in the US doubles with Jedrejowska in 1938. She played again at Wimbledon in 1946, losing 8-6 in the final set to another veteran, Betty Nuthall.

John McENROE

b 1959

McEnroe is the most brilliant and most temperamental player of our time. At his best, he has elevated tennis to an art form, with near perfect displays of stroke skill and tactics. But his whole career has been marred by outbursts of arrogance, rudeness and sullenness which have severely harmed the professional image of the game and reduced its disciplinary powers to farce.

He made a spectacular and thrilling debut on the international scene at the age of 18, when he won the French mixed doubles title with fellow New Yorker Mary Carillo and became the first qualifier ever to reach the semi-finals at Wimbledon. That was in 1977, and, ever since, his record has been a heady combination of awesome feats on court and outrageous tantrums both on and off it. Perennially dubbed by the world's press with such nicknames as 'Superbrat' and 'McEnrow', he appears to suffer from a form of paranoia that makes him believe that the whole world is against him. His own excuses have ranged from the alleged ineptitude of court officials to an assertion that he has been afflicted by temporary insanity — a condition he claimed was brought about at the 1987 US Open when his wife was expecting their second child.

The fault lies not only with McEnroe himself, but the pusillanimity of the officials, who have continually let him escape with the slightest of fines and, at worst, the odd suspension. His catalogue of misdemeanours is far too lengthy to list here, but suffice to say

that his commercial value to the game has allowed him to bring it into disrepute. McEnroe means big box-office and TV interest — so those in control of the game baulk at banning him permanently.

Yet McEnroe has brought pleasure to millions from his sheer genius. Although slight of build and not particularly athletic, he has such good control that he can overwhelm bigger and stronger players by keeping the ball out of their reach. A left-hander, his service has such slice that it swings right out of court, and he can vary it with lightning-fast aces down the middle. He has magnificent touch and expert disguise, enabling him to punch or caress the ball at will. His dexterity at the net — which has also made him one of the world's great doubles players — allows him to direct the ball at stupendous angles, and demoralize an opponent into mental submission.

In the early years of his career McEnroe was a reliable representative for the US in the Davis Cup, helping them to win it in 1978, 1979, 1981 and 1982. Then arguments set in with the US captain, Arthur Ashe and, after 1984, when he was sensationally defeated in the final tie at Stockholm by Sweden's Henrik Sundstrom, he was only occasionally available.

In singles tournament play he scored his first big triumph in 1979, when he won the first of three successive US Open titles. He regained the trophy in 1984, but that has been his last major victory to date. He has taken the Masters title three times — 1979, 1983 and 1984 — and the WCT singles in the same three years.

At Wimbledon he followed his 1977 semi-final showing with a first-round exit in 1978, and a fourth-round loss in 1979. In 1980 he lost a classic final to Bjorn Borg, but he gained revenge the following year, thus bringing about the Swede's first reversal in the Championship for six years. In 1982 he lost a marathon and temperamental final against Jimmy Connors, but he scored two easy wins there in both 1983 and 1984. In 1985 he was out of sorts, and his straight-set defeat by Kevin Curren in the quarter-finals marked the end of his reign as world No 1 — a position he had held since toppling Borg four years earlier.

Not long afterwards he took a long break from competitive tennis, during which time he had a child with actress Tatum O'Neal, whom he later married. He was missing from January to August 1986, and his comeback was less than successful, so by the end of the year his ranking had dropped to 15th. He suffered first-round losses at Flushing Meadow in 1986 and Paris in 1987, then missed Wimbledon again. At Flushing in 1987 he reached the quarter-finals, but early round losses were to be his fate in all major tournaments of 1988, and his great days appeared to be well over.

McEnroe has never prospered on slower surfaces. The nearest he got to winning the French singles was in 1984, when he led Lendl 2-0 in sets in the final before losing his way, and he has also failed in several attempts to win the Australian. He has amassed a vast number of doubles titles with Peter Fleming, including Wimbledon in 1979, 1981, 1983 and 1984; the US Open in 1979, 1981 and 1983; the Masters every year from 1978 to 1984, and the World Doubles in 1979.

Chuck McKINLEY
b 1941 – d 1986

Bouncy and athletic, McKinley was a good grass-court player whose career in the top flight was brief, although he touched the heights. An efficient serve-volleyer, he came from St Louis, Missouri. He was extremely quick about the court, retrieving seemingly impossible shots, and his entertainment value made him a great favourite with the crowd.

At Wimbledon in 1961 he destroyed the hopes of two late British survivors, Bobby Wilson and Mike Sangster, and reached the final, where he was no match for Rod Laver. In 1962 he was beaten by another Briton, Mike Hann, in the second round, but in 1963 he won the title without having to play another seed in any round. In a rain-afflicted tournament he benefited from the shock defeats of both favourites, Roy Emerson and Manuel Santana, to come through to the final against Fred Stolle, whom he tamed in straight sets. Not only did he win every round without dropping a set, but upsets were so numerous that no seed played a match against another — a unique occurrence in the history of the event. He lost in the quarter-finals to Stolle the following year, and that was his last appearance.

In the US championships McKinley was a quarter-finalist in 1960 and a semi-finalist in 1962, 1963 and 1964. He won the doubles three times with Dennis Ralston (1961, 1963, 1964), and played for the US in the Davis Cup 16 times between 1960 and 1965, appearing in the winning team of 1963.

McKinley retired when still only 24 years old and died tragically young, of cancer, in 1986.

Kerry MELVILLE
b 1947

Kerry Melville was one of a group of fine Australian players that made their country a leading power in women's tennis during the 1960s and 1970s. Melville (who married US player 'Raz' Reid in 1975 and moved to South

Carolina) promised much as a teenager but later had to settle for a long career in the top ten without ever scaling the highest peaks. Her finest hour was in the US Open of 1972, when she beat Chris Evert to reach the final, and her most important titles were the Australian singles in January 1977 and the Wimbledon doubles (with Wendy Turnbull) in 1978.

A natural baseliner, she developed her volleying sufficiently to become a solid all-round performer, and she had a good brain for match-play. Australian junior champion in 1965, she made an exciting senior debut in 1966 by reaching the semi-finals of both the Australian and US singles (beating Wimbledon champion Billie Jean King). In 1967 she defeated holder Ann Jones to reach the semi-finals in Paris, and she was in the winning Federation Cup team in the same city in 1968. In 1969 she was runner-up in the Italian Open, but, at Wimbledon, as sixth seed, she lost in the third round to Rosemary Casals.

In doubles, apart from her Wimbledon triumph with Turnbull, Melville was twice in the semi-finals with the late Karen Krantzcke, champion of Australia in 1970 with the same partner, and runner-up in 1973 and 1974 with Kerry Harris. She lost in the 1978 US final with Turnbull. After many years as one of the most regular players on the tour, she retired in 1980 to have her first child.

Angela
MORTIMER
b 1932

One of a strong batch of British players to achieve prominence in the late 1950s and early 1960s, Angela Mortimer had little natural ability at tennis but made herself a re-doubtable player through sheer hard work. She was frail of physique and suffered more than her fair share of ill-health, including a serious illness contracted in Egypt in 1957 which threatened her career. Unglamorous at a time when the dresses designed by Ted Tinling showed off many of the players at their most feminine, Mortimer always played in functional shirts and shorts. She had a very weak service, but she had reliable ground-strokes and her volleying was adequate. A native of Devon, she was taught by Arthur Roberts, who was the most notable British coach of his day.

She won three out of the four Grand Slam titles: the French in 1955, the Australian in 1958, and Wimbledon in 1961. She also took the Wimbledon doubles with fellow-Briton Anne Shilcock in 1955 — the only all-British pair to do so since the war. She was runner-up at Wimbledon in 1958, and three years later she reached the same stage to face her compatriot, Christine Truman. In a dramatic

Above: An elegant forehand from Angela Mortimer, who was the first British player to win the Wimbledon singles for 24 years when she beat her compatriot, Christine Truman, in the 1961 final. Mortimer preferred to wear functional tennis clothes in an era when designs for dresses reached extravagant proportions.

final, interrupted by rain, she recovered from a losing position to become the first native winner of the title for 24 years. The following year she lost in the fourth round to Vera Sukova, and she played little top-class tennis after that. In 1967 she married the former Davis Cup player, John Barrett, and retired to have a family, although she continued in a non-playing capacity as Wightman Cup captain until 1970.

Ilie
NASTASE
b 1946

Below: A head-on confrontation for Ilie Nastase in Paris. The highly talented Romanian won the French singles in 1973, the year he was hot favourite at Wimbledon in the aftermath of the boycott of the tournament by 79 of 82 ATP members. He lost to unseeded Sandy Mayer in the fourth round.

Ilie Nastase was undoubtedly the best player to emerge from the Balkans, and perhaps the third best never to win Wimbledon (after Rosewall and Gonzales). He was a brilliant performer whose immense skill was marred by a temperamental record exceeded only by McEnroe, against whom he lost a notorious match at Flushing Meadow in 1979, when the umpire was removed by the referee.

But whereas McEnroe's excesses have been angry and abrasive, Nastase's antics were to some extent mitigated by charm and good humour, which meant that he rarely antagonized the crowd. There were numerous occasions when he should have been more severely punished. He was disqualified several times during his career, and he was banned from the Davis Cup for a year after a particularly acrimonious tie against the British in 1977. Intriguingly, whereas Bjorn Borg inspired a whole generation of Swedish men, Nastase's influence on the game in his native Romania provided more of a catalyst for Romanian women players. Three — Virginia Ruzici, Florenza Mihai and Mariana Simionescu — reached the higher levels of international tennis during the late 1970s.

Nastase's tennis was highly entertaining. He could perform equally well on all surfaces — proved by major titles in all conditions — and he was a successful doubles player as well. Like so many Europeans of his time, he relied on touch rather than power, but he was prone to lapses of concentration that allowed lesser opponents to wriggle off the hook and get the better of him.

There were two notable occasions when he failed to clinch the highest honours just as they appeared to be easily within his grasp. The first was in 1972, when Romania never had a better chance of winning the Davis Cup. As runners-up to the USA in the last ever challenge round of 1971, they were allowed a home tie in Bucharest for the 1972 final against the same country. Although he had lost a memorable five-set final to Stan Smith at Wimbledon earlier that year, Nastase was expected to gain revenge on his home ground in the opening rubber. But Smith won, and that proved crucial to the overall result. Then at Wimbledon the following year, Nastase was one of only three ATP members to defy the boycott, and in the weakened field he was the overwhelming favourite. Here he frittered away his great chance by losing to Sandy Mayer in the fourth round, and he never had another opportunity, although he reached the final once again in 1976.

On the plus side, he won the US Open title in 1972 and the French in 1973, as well as two Italian titles (1970, 1973). He also took the Grand Prix Masters four times (1971, 1972, 1973, 1975) and two Wimbledon mixed doubles titles with Rosemary Casals (1970, 1972). In men's doubles he was successful at Wimbledon with Jimmy Connors in 1973, in Paris with Ion Tiriac (1970), at Forest Hills with Connors (1975) and at Rome with Tiriac (1970, 1972). At Wimbledon he was runner-up twice, to Smith (1972) and Borg (1976). He lost the 1971 French final to Jan Kodes, and the 1974 Italian final to Borg. In the Davis Cup he led Romania to the title round in 1969, 1971 and 1972.

Nastase carried on playing the pro circuit well after his peak years of the early 1970s, though towards the end he rarely survived the early rounds of any tournament. As his skills

faded, he relied increasingly on gamesmanship and outrageous behaviour, and other players on the thriving over-35 tour were opposed to his competing. Since retirement he has written a couple of novels based on tennis and has recorded a pop song. In 1986 he was engaged as coach to the young Swedish player, Henrik Sundstrom.

Martina
NAVRATILOVA
b 1956

The highest-earning tennis player of all time, Navratilova has stated that it is her ambition to be regarded as the greatest of all. In some ways she has achieved it. She has won 48 Grand Slam titles in singles, doubles and mixed — a feat bettered only by Margaret Court. She has held simultaneous Grand Slams in singles and doubles, and at the 1987 US Open she became the first holder of all three titles at a Grand Slam championship since Billie Jean King in 1973. As a player, she has systematically and scientifically worked for total perfection through exercise, training and diet, achieved with the aid of computer programming. Her use of technology has broken new ground, and she has developed her skills through means unheard of by the triumvirate of great stars she seeks to surpass — Suzanne Lenglen, Helen Wills Moody and Maureen Connolly.

Supreme in all departments of the game, she has had to overcome major social obstacles to reach this position. Having taken the decision to defect from her native Czechoslovakia at the age of 19, she enthusiastically embraced the American lifestyle. Adapting to it, however, temporarily damaged her form. Then a series of much-publicized relationships with other women, some of them celebrities in their own right, made for heavy pressures in a world only just beginning to accept unconventional sexual attitudes.

Always supported by an entourage of coaches, advisers, friends and family, Navratilova has triumphed over these obstacles and won a devoted following. Although her successes were usually ignored by the Czech media, her sentimental return to Prague for the 1986 Federation Cup, after an absence of 11 years, was rapturously greeted by her former compatriots.

Her early career was a switchback of triumphs and disasters. She burst upon the international scene as a highly promising 16-year-old in 1973, and within two years she was rated No 2 in the world, behind her career-long rival, Chris Evert. Then came her defection at the end of the 1975 US Open, and a discovery of hamburgers, ice cream, expensive jewellery and other luxuries associated with the new lifestyle. Her weight

ballooned and her form sank, culminating in a 1976 US Open first-round exit in tears at the hands of a steady US Wightman Cup player, Janet Newberry. There were more shock defeats in 1977, but she picked herself up and, under the guidance of golf pro Sandra Heynie, she blossomed in 1978, winning Wimbledon for the first time over Evert. She repeated the victory in 1979, then her career stood still as she was overtaken by the remarkable Tracy Austin and her one-time fellow-Czech Hana Mandlikova.

In 1982 Navratilova returned to the top with the first of a record sequence of six winning Wimbledons, and she began to pile up other major titles as well. She drew ahead of Evert and the rest of the field, and after her sole 1983 loss — to Kathleen Horvath in Paris — she was unbeaten in a Grand Slam event for nearly two years. The advent of Steffi Graf brought her reign to an end in 1987, and she did not win a singles title until July of that year when she beat Graf in the Wimbledon final, then did so again at Flushing Meadow. But Graf had now replaced her at No. 1 on the

Above: Martina Navratilova in action at Wimbledon, where she won the singles in 1978 and 1979, then six years running from 1982 to 1987. She was only the second left-hander to win the title, the first being Ann Jones.

WTA computer, and beat her in the 1988 Wimbledon final. Navratilova lost in the Australian Open to Evert, the French to Zvereva, and the US Open to Garrison.

In addition to her extraordinary singles record (which included a 74-match unbeaten sequence between January and December 1984), Navratilova formed an even more formidable doubles partnership with Pam Shriver. They did not lose anywhere between April 1983 and July 1985, which gave them a 109-match streak.

Her catalogue of major titles runs as follows: French: singles winner 1982, 1984, runner-up 1975, 1985, 1986, 1987; doubles 1975 (Evert), 1982, 1984, 1985 (Shriver), 1986 (Andrea Temesvari), 1987 (Shriver); mixed 1974 (Ivan Molina), 1985 (Heinz Guenthardt). Wimbledon: singles winner 1978, 1979, 1982, 1983, 1984, 1985, 1986, 1987; doubles 1976 (Evert), 1979 (King), 1981, 1982, 1983, 1984, 1986 (Shriver); mixed 1985 (Paul McNamee). US Open: singles winner 1983, 1984, 1986, 1987; runner-up 1981, 1985; doubles 1977 (Betty Stove), 1978, 1980 (King), 1983, 1984, 1986, 1987 (Shriver); mixed 1985 (Guenthardt), 1987 (Emilio Sanchez). Australian: singles winner 1981, 1983, 1985; runner-up 1975, 1982, 1987; doubles 1980 (Betsy Nagelsen), 1982, 1983, 1984, 1985, 1987 (Shriver). Women's World Series: 1979, 1982, 1983, 1984, 1985, 1986.

Navratilova is the only player to have played on winning Federation Cup teams of different nations — for Czechoslovakia in 1975, and for the USA in 1982 and 1986. She was also in the winning US Wightman Cup side of 1983.

John NEWCOMBE
b 1944

John Newcombe was the last of the amateur champions at Wimbledon, and the last of a great line of Australian champions, trained and nurtured by the late Harry Hopman, who dominated the game throughout the 1950s and 1960s. His career spanned the old and new eras on either side of the introduction of open tennis in 1968 — he first played in the Davis Cup in 1963 and he appeared for the last time in 1976. He also won major titles on either side of 1968 as an amateur and as a contract professional.

Rugged and personable, Newcombe was a no-frills player with a solidly efficient serve-volley game. The majority of his successes were on grass, although he did win the German Open in 1968 and the Italian Open on clay in 1969. He won the Wimbledon singles three times — in 1967 with an easy victory over Germany's Wilhelm Bungert, dropping only five games; in 1970, when most of the crowd were behind his opponent, the veteran Ken Rosewall; and in 1971, when he narrowly outvolleyed the tall American, Stan Smith. He was runner-up to Rod Laver in 1969 and competed in singles at Wimbledon for the last time in 1978. He was US champion in 1967 and 1973, and Australian champion in 1973 and 1975.

With Tony Roche, Newcombe formed one of the finest doubles partnerships in history. They won Wimbledon in 1965, 1968, 1969, 1970 and 1974; the US title in 1967; the French in 1967 and 1969, and the Australian in 1965, 1967, 1971 and 1976. Newcombe also won Wimbledon in 1966 with Ken Fletcher, the US Open with Roger Taylor in 1971 and with Owen Davidson in 1973, the French with Tom Okker in 1973, and the Australian with Mal Anderson in 1973. He took the 1964 US mixed doubles with Margaret Smith and they also shared the 1965 Australian title.

Newcombe continued to compete occasionally in doubles in major events after he retired from singles. In 1979 he reached the Wimbledon mixed semi-finals with Evonne Cawley. In 1981, in partnership with Fred Stolle, he battled through to the semi-finals at Flushing Meadow, and only lost to John McEnroe and Peter Fleming in a final-set tie break. At Wimbledon in 1985 the 40-year-old Newcombe and Andrea Leand missed a handful of match points against holders John Lloyd and Wendy Turnbull.

Below: John Newcombe launches into a crunching serve on the Centre Court. The last of the amateur champions, he won two more Wimbledon singles titles in the open era, and had a powerful serve-volley game entirely suited to the grass.

Through astute business deals, Newcombe has amassed a substantial fortune since retiring, including a line of tennis clothes featuring a moustache logo after his own facial trademark. He also set up a successful tennis camp in Texas.

Yannick
NOAH
b 1960

French men's tennis has enjoyed a considerable renaissance during the 1980s, with the successes of Yannick Noah, Henri Leconte, Thierry Tulasne and Guy Forget making for their best decade since the era of the 'Four Musketeers'. Of this talented quartet, Noah is perhaps the most gifted — and the least predictable.

Noah was born in Sedan, eastern France, but spent much of his early life in the Cameroons, where he was 'discovered' by Arthur Ashe. He was French Open junior champion in 1977, and within a year he was in the Top 50 in the senior game. Experts predicted a fine future for this stylish performer, whose powerful hitting complemented a great delicacy of touch. In 1979 he won three Grand Prix tournaments, and in 1980 he was runner-up in the Italian Open.

After a steady rise in the rankings, Noah enjoyed his best year to date in 1983 when he became the first Frenchman to triumph in Paris since Marcel Bernard in 1946, defeating holder Mats Wilander in the final. He also won the German Open and reached the quarter-finals at Flushing Meadow. But the adulation of his compatriots took its toll, and the burden of expectation had a severe effect upon his mental wellbeing. His results in 1984 were very disappointing, but his depression lifted late in the year when he married and had a son. He had a much better year in 1985, winning the Italian Open, but a series of injuries frustrated his chances of further success in major events.

He was in the French team that reached the final of the Davis Cup in 1982, and in doubles he won the French Open in 1984 with Leconte. He was runner-up in the 1985 US Open doubles (with Leconte) and in the 1986 Masters doubles and 1987 French Open doubles (with Forget).

Noah has yet to make any impression at Wimbledon, where he has competed infrequently, but he has reached the quarter-finals in Paris four times (1981, 1982, 1984, 1987). With his striking appearance — he wears his hair in dreadlocks — and athletic play, Noah has always been a great crowd pleaser.

Betty
NUTHALL
b 1911

Prodigies in tennis have not always gone on to achieve great things. But Lottie Dod, Tracy Austin and Chris Evert, all top players while still in their teens, are among the handful that did — as is Betty Nuthall. Now Mrs Shoemaker, Nuthall was the outstanding juvenile star of the 1930s. Remarkably, she was a British player that never shone at Wimbledon, as she failed to get beyond the quarter-finals, but she is one of only two British women to win the US singles — the other being Virginia Wade.

She was only 13 when she won her first British Junior Championship in 1924, and she won a total of seven titles in this tournament over the next three years. In 1925 she electrified the domestic scene by winning the women's singles in the Westgate-on-Sea tournament, and in 1927 she beat the reigning US champion, Molla Mallory, at Wimbledon and reached the final at Forest Hills.

The British thought that they had another Suzanne Lenglen on their hands. Like Lenglen, Nuthall was trained intensively by her father. She had an aggressive, enterprising game, and she was pretty to boot, which made her a great crowd favourite. Following her appearance in the US final at 16, when she

Left: Yannick Noah is an exciting player to watch, with acrobatic feats and seemingly impossible shots as regular parts of his repertoire. The first French winner of the men's singles in Paris for 37 years, he later had to overcome bouts of injury and depression.

lost to Helen Wills, she took advantage of Wills's absence in 1930 and won both the singles (beating Anna Harper in the final) and the doubles, with Sarah Palfrey. She won the US doubles twice more, with compatriots Eileen Whittingstall (1931) and Freda James (1933), and also took the mixed with George Lott in 1929 and 1931.

She was runner-up in the French singles in 1931, the same year she won the doubles with Whittingstall, and she won the mixed in 1931 with Phil Spence and in 1932 with Fred Perry. Her comparative lack of success at Wimbledon — where she was four times a singles quarter-finalist, four times a doubles semi-finalist between 1927 and 1939, and three times a mixed semi-finalist — was a remarkable jinx, especially as she came from the nearby Surrey suburb of Surbiton. Her appearances at Wimbledon spanned 20 years, and at her final attempt, in 1946 (aged 35) she reached the last 16 of the singles.

Alex OLMEDO
b 1936

Although he won Wimbledon in 1959 as an American, Olmedo was a Peruvian by origin. His victory, coupled with that of Brazil's Maria Bueno in the women's singles, meant that South American players won the game's highest honours for the first time in the same year.

Olmedo had probably the briefest career in top-class amateur play of anyone in the history of tennis. A superb athlete and a dominating power player, he went to university in California and won the Intercollegiate title in 1956 and 1958. In the latter year he was selected for the US Davis Cup team, and almost single-handedly regained the trophy for them in the challenge round at Brisbane. He won both his singles rubbers, beating Mal Anderson and the reigning Wimbledon champion, Ashley Cooper, and he joined Ham Richardson to take the doubles. Soon afterwards he won the Australian singles over Neale Fraser, and he went on to capture Wimbledon at his second attempt, beating Rod Laver in the final in straight sets.

He did not succeed at Forest Hills, where he was a quarter-finalist in 1958 (although he won the doubles with Richardson), and runner-up in 1959. He was disappointing in the US defence of the Davis Cup, losing to Fraser despite defeating Laver, and the Cup went back to Australia. Immediately afterwards he turned professional and had a good few years, winning the US Pro title in 1960. He returned to Wimbledon for the first open championship in 1968, reaching the third round of the singles before losing to Roy Emerson. In the doubles he joined fellow South American, Pancho Segura, to win the

longest set recorded in the history of the event — a 32-30, 5-7, 6-4, 6-4 win in the second round over South Africa's Gordon Forbes and Abe Segal.

Manuel ORANTES
b 1949

The successor as Spanish No 1 to Manuel Santana, Orantes was one of the best European clay court players of the 1970s. He had a beautiful style and excellent control, and had exemplary manners as well. Winner of the Wimbledon junior title in 1967, he was selected to play for Spain in the challenge round of the Davis Cup the same year, and in 1968/9 he led his country to successive victories in the Galea Cup. His greatest triumph was in the 1975 US Open — the first year it was held on clay — when he recovered from one set to two and 0-5 against Guillermo Vilas to reach the final, where he easily overcame Jimmy Connors only 15 hours later.

Orantes won the Italian Open in 1972, and was runner-up in 1973 and 1975, and he was four times in the final of the German Open, winning in 1972 and 1975 and losing in 1976/7. He also won the doubles there in 1975 with compatriot Jose Gisbert. He was runner-up in the French Open in 1974, and won the British Hard Court Championship in 1975 and 1982. The latter triumph was a remarkable comeback because he suffered from tennis elbow and had an operation on his arm in 1980. He won the US Clay Court title in 1975 and 1977, while his greatest triumph indoors was the Masters in 1976.

Rafael OSUNA
b 1938 – d 1969

Mexican tennis was cruelly robbed of its greatest player in June 1969 when a plane en route from Mexico City to Los Angeles crashed near Monterrey, killing all its occupants. One of them was Rafael Osuna, fresh from helping Mexico upset Australia in the Davis Cup. He had won all three of his rubbers, in the latest of a series of heroic exploits that made him one of the outstanding performers in the competition.

He first played for Mexico in 1958. That year, challenging in the European Zone, Mexico beat Finland before losing to Poland. Osuna was not selected for 1959, when they lost their first outing against Australia, but in 1960 he was one of a team that only failed against the US by the narrowest of margins. In 1961 they trounced Morocco before once again losing to the US by a narrow margin,

Left: Rafael Osuna gets down to a delicate half-volley on the Centre Court. The finest player to come out of Mexico, he won the US singles in 1963 and had just led his country to victory over Australia in the Davis Cup when he died in a plane crash in 1969.

and in 1962 they finally did beat the US en route to the challenge round — the first Latin American country ever to reach this stage — where they lost 5-0 to Australia in Brisbane.

The US turned the tables on them in 1963 at Los Angeles, and it was Australia's turn to defeat them in 1964. In 1965 they lost to the US in Dallas, and in 1966 the same thing happened in Cleveland. In 1967, with the tie at home, they thought they had a good chance of getting revenge, but although Osuna beat Cliff Richey in the opening rubber, he later went down to Arthur Ashe, and Mexico lost 1-4. In 1968 the usual confrontation took place at Berkeley, and the Americans did not drop a rubber.

Osuna took part in all these matches, and it was fitting, if tragic, that he died just after one of their greatest triumphs. He was a mercurially fast, energetic player, and he and his long-time partner, Antonio Palafox, were known as the 'Mexican jumping beans'. Unusually for a player brought up on slow clay courts, Osuna volleyed well and was a fine grass-court player, proved by his victory in the US singles of 1963. He was four times a losing semi-finalist at Forest Hills (1961, 1962, 1964, 1965) and won the doubles in 1962. He was twice men's doubles champion at Wimbledon — in 1960 with Dennis Ralston,

and 1963 with Palafox — and he was three times a quarter-finalist in the singles.

Adriano PANATTA
b 1950

The best Italian player since Nicola Pietrangeli, Panatta enjoyed a fantastic year in 1976 when he won the Italian and French Opens and led his country to their only victory in the Davis Cup — although they were runners-up on three other occasions with Panatta in the team. Handsome and charismatic, he was a popular pin-up star and had tremendous natural flair, but he was prone to laziness and could have done even better had he been prepared to work really hard. His victories in the two major clay court events of 1976 were remarkable in that he survived 11 match points against Kim Warwick in the first round in Rome and one against Pavel Hutka in the first round in Paris.

He was to reach the Italian final again in 1978, when he lost a five-set classic to Bjorn Borg, and his other notable feats in Europe

Above: Intent concentration from Adriano Panatta, whose best year was 1976, when he won the Italian and French titles and led his country to their sole victory in the Davis Cup. A big man, Panatta enjoyed la dolce vita, *and consequently had problems with his weight.*

stages in any subsequent years, but he was Australian champion in 1927, after losing the finals of 1922 and 1925. He was four times Australian doubles champion — in 1922 (with John Hawkes), 1925 (with O'Hara Wood), and 1926 and 1927 (with Hawkes). He never won the doubles at Wimbledon, but he took the mixed in 1920 with Suzanne Lenglen.

A nephew of Dame Nellie Melba, Patterson represented Australia in the Davis Cup between 1919 and 1928 and was on the winning team in 1919.

Budge
PATTY
b 1924

An American in Paris, where he lived and developed his game, Patty was elegant and sophisticated — a polar opposite to compatriots like Jack Kramer and Ted Schroeder. He had one of the greatest forehand volleys of all time, and an excellent match temperament. His topspin lobs were a vital part of a court armoury that blossomed in 1950, when he won both the French championship and Wimbledon.

Originally from Arkansas, he was three times a losing semi-finalist at Wimbledon (1947, when he beat the holder, Yvon Petra, 1954 and 1955), and he won the men's doubles in 1957 with 43-year-old Gardner Mulloy. He was three times a quarter-finalist at Forest Hills (1951, 1953, 1957), and runner-up at Paris in 1949. His back-to-back triumphs of 1950 were at the expense of Jaroslav Drobny in Paris and Frank Sedgman at Wimbledon. Against Drobny he lost Wimbledon's second longest match in the third round in 1953, and their rivalry over the years — they played a number of marathons — is the reason why he is best remembered today.

were a final at Hamburg in 1972 and two semi-finals in Paris, 1973 and 1975. He won the British Hard Court title in 1973 and was a quarter-finalist at Wimbledon in 1979.

In Davis Cup play, he took part in 100 rubbers between 1970 and 1982, winning 64, and his appearances in the final were in 1976, when Italy beat Chile in Santiago; in 1977, when they lost to Australia in Sydney; in 1979, when the US beat them in San Francisco; and in 1980, when they were beaten by the Czechs in Prague.

Gerald
PATTERSON
b 1895 – d 1967

One of a group of Australian players that were prominent immediately after the First World War, Patterson had a stupendous service, modelled on the 'cannonball' delivery of the American player, Maurice McLoughlin, and was one of the earliest exponents of the serve-volley power game.

Patterson was runner-up to compatriot Pat O'Hara Wood in the 1914 Australian championship, then became the first post-war Wimbledon winner by defeating yet another Australian, Norman Brookes. He lost the title to Bill Tilden in 1920, and did not compete in 1921; but in 1922, the year the All England Club moved to its present Church Road ground and the challenge round was abolished, he regained the title, beating Randolph Lycett. He did not reach the later

Fred
PERRY
b 1909

Britain's best ever player, he was the first man to take all four Grand Slam singles titles, though he did not hold them all simultaneously. Son of a Labour Member of Parliament, he was grammar-school educated in an era when other leading British players were from public schools. (Grammar schools were secondary schools run by the State, while public schools were private fee-paying establishments.) A former table tennis champion, he was immensely fit, determined and confident. Because Perry is the only Briton to win major singles titles since the First World War, he is the standard with which his compatriots are compared — and have always fallen short. His most notable shot was a running forehand, played with a Continental grip, and such was his willpower that few opponents ever gained a psychological advantage over him.

He did not attain a degree of invincibility over his peers, but he was the dominant player of the mid 1930s, winning eight of the 13 Grand Slam titles contested between September 1933 and September 1936. In the years before his golden period he was a Wimbledon semi-finalist in 1931 and quarter-finalist in 1932, a US semi-finalist in 1931, and a French quarter-finalist in 1932, 1933 and 1934.

Perry lost to Norman Farquharson of Australia in the second round at Wimbledon in 1933, but after that he was unbeaten in the tournament. He won the singles for three years running, 1934 to 1936, becoming the first man to do so since the challenge round was abolished, and the only one until Bjorn Borg broke his record in the late 1970s. He did not win the Wimbledon doubles — he was runner-up in 1932 with Pat Hughes — but he took the mixed in 1935 and 1936 with Dorothy Round. In 1984 the All England Club commemorated the 50th anniversary of his first title by erecting a statue of him just inside the south-eastern entry to the ground, which was renamed the Fred Perry Gate.

He won the US singles three times, in 1933, 1934 and 1936, his only blemish being a semi-final loss to Wilmer Allison in 1935. He won the US mixed with Sarah Palfrey in 1932. He took the Australian singles and doubles (with Hughes) in 1934, and the French singles in 1935 and doubles (with Hughes) in 1933. And he led Great Britain to four successive victories in the Davis Cup, 1933 to 1936.

Perry turned professional at the end of 1936 and won the US Pro title in 1938 and 1941. He later became a US citizen and a radio commentator. His name is given to a sportswear company that is still one of the leading brands in tennis.

Nicola
PIETRANGELI
b 1933

Born in Tunis of a French father and Russian mother, Pietrangeli can claim to be the finest Italian player of all time. He played more Davis Cup rubbers than anyone else, and between 1954 and 1972 he won 120 rubbers out of a total of 163. He led Italy to two challenge rounds against Australia in 1960 and 1961. He has continued his involvement with the competition as non-playing captain.

A consummate clay court player, he had superb touch but was prone to inconsistency. His best tournament results were in the three great European championships, and his peak

years were 1959 and 1960, when he won the French singles with victories over Ian Vermaak and Luis Ayala. He was runner-up to Manuel Santana in 1961 and 1964, and he won the doubles in 1959 with compatriot Orlando Sirola. In 1957 and 1961 he won the Italian singles, and was runner-up in 1958 and 1966. With Sirola, he won the Rome doubles once (1960) and was runner-up six times between 1955 and 1963, and he also reached the final in 1966 with Cliff Drysdale. He was German champion in 1960, the same year he reached the semi-finals at Wimbledon, and he was runner-up in the Wimbledon doubles with Sirola in 1956. In mixed doubles, he was champion of France in 1958 with Shirley Bloomer.

Nancy
RICHEY
b 1942

Unusually for American players of the late 1960s, Richey was a baseliner, and with her dour attitude and poker face, plus her peaked cap and shorts, she was reminiscent of Helen Wills Moody. A Texan, she was a leading player in the women's game at the same time as her younger brother Cliff occupied a similar status among the men. She was resolute rather than stylish, seldom came to the net, and rarely made unforced errors.

Richey won two Grand Slam singles titles — the Australian of 1967 and the French of 1968. She was doubles champion at Wimbledon in 1966 (with Maria Bueno), and at the US championships in 1965 and the Australian in 1967 (with Carole Graebner). She ruled the US Clay Court Championships at Indianapolis from 1963 to 1968 — a six-year winning sequence — and was runner-up as late as 1977, while in 1975 she missed two match points in the semi-finals against Chris Evert, having led 7-5, 5-0.

She was runner-up twice at Forest Hills, in 1966 and 1969, and lost the 1966 French final to Ann Jones, against whom she was avenged two years later. At Wimbledon she was seven times a quarter-finalist between 1964 and 1972, but progressed to the last four only in 1968. She played in the Wightman Cup for nine successive years, 1962 to 1970, and in the Federation Cup of 1964, 1968 and 1969.

Bobby
RIGGS
b 1918

Probably the most notable hustler in the history of tennis, Bobby Riggs is famous on two counts: as a triple champion on his only appearance at Wimbledon in 1939, and as an

Above: Fred Perry had an attitude towards tennis that no other Briton has been able to reproduce in the last half century. An exuberant competitor, Perry became the first man to have won all four Grand Slam titles (though not holding them simultaneously).

'anti-feminist' who played 'battle-of-the-sexes' matches against Margaret Court and Billie Jean King in 1973, then a doubles exhibition with Vitas Gerulaitis against Martina Navratilova and Pam Shriver in 1985.

Born in Los Angeles, Riggs was interested primarily in money, and he backed himself with a bookmaker to win all three titles at Wimbledon. The odds were lengthened when he was beaten 6-0, 6-1 by Gottfried von Cramm in the London Grass Court Championships at Queen's Club immediately prior to Wimbledon, and he was widely thought to have deliberately 'thrown' it. Shrewd on court as well as off, he was confident and aggressive, and but for the Second World War he might have added significantly to his title haul.

Following the departure of Donald Budge to the professional ranks, Riggs established himself as world No 1 by adding the US singles to his Wimbledon titles in 1939. He was also runner-up in Paris that year to compatriot Don McNeill. In the US championships of 1940 he lost his singles title in the final to McNeill, but he regained it in 1941 against Frank Kovacs. He won the mixed doubles in 1940 with Alice Marble.

Turning professional in 1941, Riggs was three times winner of the US Pro title (1946, 1947, 1949), but perhaps his biggest moment in the spotlight was the much-hyped match against King in 1973 (which he lost), watched by a record 30,500 spectators at the Houston Astrodome and a TV audience of nearly 50 million.

Tony ROCHE
b 1945

But for chronic tennis elbow, Tony Roche might have won greater honours in the game than those he did achieve, and his one Grand Slam singles title — the French of 1966 — was secured early on in his career. Powerful and an expert serve-volleyer in the tradition of top-class Australians trained by Harry Hopman, he excelled particularly in doubles, winning a total of 14 men's and two mixed doubles in Grand Slam events.

From Wagga Wagga, New South Wales, Roche's Davis Cup appearances spanned the years 1964 to 1978. He won the French singles in 1966 over Istvan Gulyas of Hungary, having been runner-up the previous year to Fred Stolle. The following year he lost the final to Roy Emerson, whom he had beaten in the semi-finals of 1965. He won the French doubles in 1967 and 1969 with John Newcombe.

At Wimbledon he was runner-up in 1969 to Rod Laver, and he won the doubles five times with Newcombe — in 1965, 1968, 1969,

1970 and 1974. He took the mixed in 1976 with Françoise Durr. He was also runner-up in 1965 and 1969 with Judy Tegart. In the US singles he was runner-up in 1969 and 1970, and won the doubles with Newcombe in 1967. Although he never reached the final of the Australian singles, he won the doubles five times — with Newcombe in 1965, 1967, 1971 and 1976 and with Arthur Ashe in January 1977. He won the mixed with Tegart in 1966. In Rome he was three times a singles finalist, winning in 1966 and runner-up in 1967 and 1969. With Newcombe he shared the Italian doubles twice and won it outright in 1971.

Despairing of a surgical cure for his tennis elbow, Roche went to the Philippines for a cure by a faith healer, and it was partially successful. But his career was interrupted on several occasions by the problem, and he never really fulfilled his potential. In recent years he has become conspicuous as coach to Ivan Lendl, against whom he played a singles quarter-final as a substitute in the Scottish Grass Court Championships of 1987.

Ken ROSEWALL
b 1934

Short in stature but big in heart, 'Muscles' Rosewall had one of the most extraordinary careers of any player. His time in international competitive tennis lasted 25 years, and he played in Wimbledon singles finals 20 years apart.

This amazing Australian was unusual among his countrymen in that he relied on finesse rather than power. His service was not particularly impressive, but he had one of the best backhands ever, and he could cover the court with deadly speed. He was perhaps at his best on slow courts, although he established a formidable record on other surfaces.

His career falls into three distinct phases: as one of the leading amateurs from 1952 to 1956; as a contract professional from 1956 to 1968; and as a top player during the first decade after tennis went open. He started winning major titles while he was still in his teens, and he was still winning them when he was past 40.

Rosewall burst upon the scene in 1952 along with another 17-year-old prodigy, Lew Hoad. Although it was Hoad that later won two Wimbledon singles — the one major title Rosewall never captured — it was the slightly older Rosewall who enjoyed more early success, winning both the Australian and French titles as an 18-year-old in 1953. In 1954 he was runner-up at Wimbledon to Jaroslav Drobny, and in 1955 he regained the Australian singles and was runner-up at Forest Hills. In 1956 he was runner-up to Hoad in the Australian and Wimbledon finals, but he got his revenge at Forest Hills,

Dorothy
ROUND
b 1909–d 1982

There were two British winners of the women's singles at Wimbledon between the wars, Kitty Godfree and Dorothy Round. Not only did they both win twice, but they both did so in the years when the leading players of their time — Suzanne Lenglen and Helen Wills Moody — were not in contention. Round (later Mrs Little) was very fit and determined, and she was formidably powerful and accurate off the ground — particularly on the forehand. She was also a woman of strong religious principles, and caused some consternation by refusing to play on a Sunday in the French and US championships.

She had an excellent record at Wimbledon, where she was a quarter-finalist in 1931, 1932, 1935, 1936, runner-up in 1933 and winner in 1934 and 1937. Both of her winning finals were hard-fought and memorable.

In 1934, against Helen Jacobs, she was so tired at 4-3 in the final set that she abandoned the baseline and mounted a volleying attack, which paid off. And in 1937 she trailed 2-4 in the final set against the Pole, Jadwiga Jedrejowska, before pulling it round. She also won the mixed doubles three times — with Miki of Japan in 1934, and with Fred Perry in 1935 and 1936.

Round was the first foreign player to win the Australian women's singles in 1935, but the only final she reached in other Grand Slam events was the US women's doubles of 1931. She played in every Wightman Cup match from 1931 to 1936, though the British did not win the trophy on any of these occasions.

Elizabeth
RYAN
b 1892–d 1979

Born in Los Angeles, Elizabeth 'Bunny' Ryan was an Anglophile who lived in England for most of her life. Until 1979 she held the record of the greatest number of Wimbledon titles — all of them in doubles — and she was probably the most enthusiastic competitor of all time, winning at least 659 titles during 19 playing years between 1912 and 1934. She was a fine volleyer, her approach shot being a heavily chopped forehand, and with Suzanne Lenglen she established one of the best doubles partnerships of all time. She was no mean singles player, but her career overlapped those of Lenglen and Helen Wills Moody, and she probably ranks as the best woman never to win a major singles title (though she did take the championship of Imperial Russia in 1914).

Left: Ken Rosewall sports an orange shirt in the 1972 US Open at Forest Hills. He could not have done this at Wimbledon, where a strict 'predominantly white' rule applies.

---

depriving Hoad of the Grand Slam. He then turned professional, where he eventually succeeded Pancho Gonzales as winner of the US Pro title in 1963 and 1965, and as London Pro Champion in 1957 and 1960, 1961, 1962 and 1963.

He won the world's first open tournament at Bournemouth, England in 1968, and took his second French title — 15 years after his first — the same year. In 1970 he regained the US Open, and the Australian title came his way again in 1971 and 1972. He was runner-up at Wimbledon for the third time in 1970, and for the fourth in 1974, when he was overwhelmed by Jimmy Connors, who was 18 years younger. Connors also beat him in the 1974 US Open final by the huge margin of 6-1, 6-0, 6-1, which was a sad sight indeed.

In doubles, Rosewall won a number of Grand Slam titles: Wimbledon 1953, 1956 (with Hoad); US 1956 (Hoad), 1969 (Fred Stolle), mixed 1956 (Margaret du Pont); French 1953 (Hoad), 1968 (Stolle); Australian 1953, 1956 (Hoad), 1972 (Owen Davidson).

Always quiet and unassuming, he was temperamentally very similar to his great compatriot, Rod Laver, against whom he played many great matches over the years. Curiously, they only met in two Grand Slam finals — the French of 1968 and 1969, winning one apiece.

Ryan won a total of 19 Wimbledon titles, a record bettered only by Billie Jean King, who included six singles in her tally. Ryan took the women's doubles in 1914 (with Agnes Morton), 1919, 1920, 1921, 1922, 1923, 1925 (with Lenglen), 1926 (with Mary K. Browne, the year the French Federation insisted that Lenglen should play with fellow Frenchwoman, Didi Vlasto, and whom the Americans beat in the first round), 1927, 1930 (with Moody), and 1933 and 1934 (with Simone Mathieu). She was also runner-up with Helen Jacobs in 1932. Her mixed doubles titles were in 1919, 1921, 1923 (with Randolph Lycett), 1927 (with Frank Hunter), 1928 (with Phil Spence), 1930 (with Jack Crawford) and 1932 (with Enrique Maier). She was runner-up in 1920 and 1922 with Lycett and in 1925 with Hugo de Morpurgo. She was runner-up in the all-comers' singles final in 1914 and 1920, in the challenge round in 1921, and in the final in 1930. She was a semi-finalist on four other occasions. Her greatest disappointment was in 1924, when in the quarter-finals she became the only player since 1919 to wrest a set from the great Lenglen; had she won, she would have probably taken the title. Ironically, Lenglen promptly scratched from the tournament.

Ryan was less successful in the US championships, where she won the women's doubles in 1926 with Eleanor Goss and the mixed in 1926 with Jean Borotra and 1933 with Ellsworth Vines. She was runner-up in the singles in 1926, missing a match point against Molla Mallory at 7-6 in the final set. She won four French women's doubles, with Moody (1930 and 1932) and Mathieu (1933 and 1934), and she took part in just one Wightman Cup contest, winning two rubbers out of three in 1926.

A regular spectator at Wimbledon right up to her death, she did not live to see King surpass the record of 19 titles they had jointly held for the previous four years. She died at Wimbledon the day before King notched up her 20th title in the women's doubles of 1979.

Manuel SANTANA
b 1938

The only Spaniard to win the men's singles at Wimbledon, Manuel Santana had a unique style, involving heavy topspin on both forehand and backhand, and he was able to produce passing shots from seemingly impossible angles. He was a superb clay court player who also enjoyed considerable success on grass, and he was one of the most amiable of players, which made him extremely popular. His rivalry with Roy Emerson was a classic contrast of power vs subtlety, while two winning French finals against Nicola Pietrangeli were particularly memorable for the good spirit in which they were played.

Santana won the French title in 1961 and 1964, and was a semi-finalist in 1962 and 1963. He won Wimbledon in 1966, and was a semi-finalist in 1963; and he won the US singles in 1965, reaching the last four the following year. He was runner-up in the Italian singles in 1965 and in the German singles in 1962 and 1967, and he won the South African singles in 1967. In doubles play his one major title was the French of 1963, with Emerson.

He twice took Spain to the challenge round of the Davis Cup (1965, 1967), but with his great compatriot Andres Gimeno ineligible to take part as a contract professional, there was no Spaniard good enough to help him wrest the trophy from Australia. His career faded out almost exactly with the advent of open tennis, though he won the last of eight Spanish titles against Rod Laver in 1969. He is the only Wimbledon champion to lose in the first round the following year — beaten in 1967 by Charlie Pasarell.

Frank SEDGMAN
b 1927

The first of the great Australian champions trained by Harry Hopman, Sedgman was a textbook player, with a brilliant forehand, deadly volleying skills and superb anticipation. He was equally good at singles and doubles, and he was the last man to win the triple crown at Wimbledon. He was also the first Australian to win the US singles. Of the 12 Grand Slam events the only one he failed to take was the French singles, recording victories in the singles, doubles and mixed of all the others.

Sedgman won all four Grand Slam doubles titles with Ken McGregor in 1951, and he also won three out of the four mixed championships that year. At Wimbledon he was runner-up in the singles in 1950 and winner in 1952; he won the doubles in 1951 and 1952 with McGregor, and the mixed in 1951 and 1952 with Doris Hart. He won the US singles in 1951 and 1952, the doubles in 1950 (with John Bromwich) and 1951 (with McGregor) and the mixed in 1951 and 1952 with Hart, thereby having triple-crown success in 1951. In 1952 he was runner-up in the French singles, and took the doubles in 1951 and 1952 with McGregor and the mixed in 1951 and 1952 with Hart. He was Australian champion at singles in 1949 and 1950, in doubles in 1951 and 1952 with McGregor, and in mixed in 1949 and 1950 with Hart.

He played in the Davis Cup from 1949 to 1952, and he never lost a doubles rubber at any time, while in three winning challenge rounds, 1950, 1951 and 1952, he was unbeaten in singles.

favourite, Australian and French champion Ken Rosewall. Despite the rigours of the previous two rounds, Seixas was fitter, stronger and more determined than his opponent, and he won fairly comfortably, 9-7, 6-3, 6-4, in a mere 80 minutes.

The following year he won the US singles, defeating Ham Richardson and Rex Hartwig in the last two rounds. These were his only major singles titles. In doubles he was twice runner-up at Wimbledon, with Eric Sturgess in 1953 and with Tony Trabert in 1955. With Trabert he won the US title in 1955, the French in 1954 and 1955, and the Australian in 1955. He took the Wimbledon mixed title four years running, with Doris Hart in 1953, 1954, 1955 and with Shirley Fry in 1956. With Hart, he took a hat-trick of US titles in 1953, 1954, 1955, and the French in 1953. They took the South African title in 1950 and the Italian in 1953, where Seixas also succeeded in 1954 with Maureen Connolly.

More than a decade after his peak, Seixas established a world record at the 1966 Pennsylvania Grass Court Championships, when he beat Bill Bowrey 32-34, 6-4, 10-8. This was then the longest set in singles ever played, and it has been surpassed only once. He was 43 years old at the time.

Pam
SHRIVER
b 1962

A prodigy who promised to be a far better player than she has so far achieved, Pam Shriver, from Baltimore, has formed with Martina Navratilova one of the strongest women's doubles partnerships of all time, but she has yet to win a major singles title.

One of the wittiest and most extrovert of current players, Shriver has an awkward, rather ungainly style, and she is prone to be erratic. But she is a strong serve-volleyer, with an avowed dislike of clay courts, which she usually avoids. In singles, her best results have been on grass, where she has thrice been a semi-finalist at Wimbledon (1981, 1987, 1988), and she has won a string of English pre-Wimbledon grass court titles at Beckenham and Edgbaston.

Renowned for wearing her heart on her sleeve, Shriver has yelled and wept her way to many shock defeats, and has only very occasionally beaten regular opponents like Navratilova and Chris Evert. But she is popular among her fellow players and the media, whom she has entertained with many a lively press conference. Related to the former Democratic candidate for Vice President, Sargent Shriver, she is herself a staunch Republican who was active in Ronald Reagan's 1984 election campaign.

As a 16-year-old in 1978, Shriver stunned the tennis world by defeating Navratilova to

Left: Manuel Santana is the only Spaniard to have won the men's singles at Wimbledon. He is pictured here on his way to victory over Owen Davidson, whom he beat in the semi-finals of his title year — 1966.

Sedgman turned professional at the beginning of 1953, and his most notable match in this segment of his career was the London Pro final of 1956. He lost to Pancho Gonzales 4-6, 11-9, 11-9, 9-7 in just under three hours, and it was perhaps the most enthralling professional encounter ever seen.

Vic
SEIXAS
b 1923

Not a great stylist, Seixas (pronounced 'Sayshus') holds the record for the greatest number of Davis Cup rubbers played by an American (55, between 1951 and 1957). He was most successful in tournament play at mixed doubles, at which event he won a total of eight Grand Slam titles (four Wimbledon, three US and one Australian). A native of Philadelphia, he was a tough, determined competitor with matinee-idol looks, who resisted the temptation to turn professional.

He won Wimbledon in 1953. Frank Sedgman had vacated the title, but the field was extremely strong, and Seixas had to survive two exceptionally hard matches, against Lew Hoad (5-7, 6-4, 6-3, 1-6, 9-7) and Mervyn Rose (6-4, 10-12, 9-11, 6-4, 6-3) to reach the final. Here he met the unseeded Dane, Kurt Neilsen, who had eliminated the

become the youngest ever finalist at the US Open, but this remains her only appearance in a Grand Slam singles final. The following year she suffered a nasty shoulder injury and languished in the lower part of the top 50 before regaining a consistent top ten place from 1980.

Her doubles record with Navratilova is superlative. They won the Grand Slam in 1984 and were completely invincible for over two years, between April 1983 and July 1985. They have five Wimbledon titles (1981, 1982, 1983, 1984, 1986), four US titles (1983, 1984, 1986, 1987), six Australian (1982 to 1988 inclusive), four French (1984–85, 1987–88) and six Women's Series championships (1981, 1982, 1983, 1984, 1986, 1987).

Shriver also took the 1987 French mixed doubles with Emilio Sanchez. She made her Wightman Cup debut in 1978, losing both her singles (against Michele Tyler) and doubles (with Evert against Sue Barker and Virginia Wade), but was on the winning side in 1981, 1983, 1985 and 1987. She played in the Federation Cup in 1986 and 1987.

Below: Pam Shriver is always likely to see the funny side of a situation on the tennis court. One of the most talkative of current players, she is a leading doubles exponent, but has yet to fulfil her early promise in singles.

Stan
SMITH
b 1946

There have been more exciting champions than Stan Smith, but he was a fine ambassador for American tennis, with an impressive Davis Cup record, faultless sportsmanship and a highly effective serve-volley game. He will be best remembered for two notable victories over Ilie Nastase in 1972 — a magnificent five-set Wimbledon final (the first ever to be played on a Sunday) and the opening rubber of the Davis Cup final in Bucharest, which was his greatest performance on clay.

Smith won the US National championship in 1969 — the second of two years that a tournament which was denied to contract professionals was held in Boston before the US Open at Forest Hills. In 1970 he won the inaugural Grand Prix Masters in Tokyo, beating both Rod Laver and Ken Rosewall, and in 1971 he was runner-up to John Newcombe in the Wimbledon final and won the US Open against Jan Kodes.

His Wimbledon victory came in a year when players contracted to the World Championship Tennis group did not compete because of political differences between that body and the International Tennis Federation; but the final against Nastase more than made amends for the thin field.

The Davis Cup triumph in the face of hostile crowds, partisan court officials and bizarre gamesmanship on the part of the Romanians, was one of the major sporting achievements of the decade. Smith was, in fact, a member of five consecutive winning Davis Cup teams from 1968 to 1972, and was in the side that lost the trophy to Australia in the 1973 final at Cleveland.

With Bob Lutz he formed a notable doubles partnership that uniquely won US National titles on all four surfaces — grass, clay, cement and indoors — including four US Open championships in 1968, 1974, 1978 and 1980. They were also runners-up in 1979, while at Wimbledon they reached the final in 1974 (the same year that they were runners-up in Paris), 1980 and 1981. They won the Australian title in 1970. With Erik van Dillen, Smith was runner-up at Forest Hills in 1971 and Wimbledon in 1972. Lutz and Smith were the US Davis Cup doubles pair every year from 1968 to 1979, winning final rubbers against Great Britain in 1978 and Italy in 1979.

Hilde
SPERLING
b 1908

Tall and uncompromising, Hilde Krahwinkel was German by birth but adopted her husband's Danish nationality on marriage in 1934. She was a leading player throughout the 1930s, and her stonewalling tactics and remarkable powers of retrieval made her a formidable opponent. She lost an all-German Wimbledon women's singles final in 1931 to Cilli Aussem, and although she never took the title, she had a longer and more successful career than her more delicate compatriot.

Sperling won the French singles three years running, in 1935, 1936 and 1937, and was a semi-finalist in 1931 and 1932; in the doubles she was runner-up in 1935 with Isabelle Adamoff.

At Wimbledon she was runner-up in 1931 and 1936 (to Helen Jacobs, at 7-5 in the final set), and she was a semi-finalist in 1933, 1935, 1938 and 1939, although on the last occasion she was devastated by Alice Marble, 6-0, 6-0. She was runner-up in the doubles in 1935 with Simone Mathieu, while in the mixed she was losing finalist in 1930 with Daniel Prenn and winner in 1933 with Gottfried von Cramm — the last German woman to take a Wimbledon title until Claudia Kohde-Kilsch shared the doubles with Helena Sukova in 1987.

She won the Italian singles in 1935, and won a total of 11 German titles, more than any other woman — singles every year from 1933 to 1939 (there was no competition in 1936 because of the Berlin Olympics), the doubles in 1932 and 1939, and the mixed in 1932, 1933 and 1934.

Although the Second World War interrupted her career when she was 31, she resumed afterwards, and took the last of five Scandinavian singles titles as late as 1950.

Fred
STOLLE
b 1938

A leading Australian player of the 1960s, Fred Stolle was primarily a great doubles exponent, as in singles he tended to be overshadowed by compatriots like Rod Laver, Roy Emerson, Tony Roche and John Newcombe. A former bank clerk, he was an efficient grass court player with a particularly good backhand, but he was not outstandingly mobile.

He was runner-up at Wimbledon three years in a row, in 1963, 1964 and 1965, and never reached the Australian singles final, but he was French champion in 1965 and US (unseeded) and German champion in 1966. In doubles play, he won Wimbledon in 1962 and 1964 with Bob Hewitt, was runner-up with Ken Rosewall in 1968 and 1970, and won the mixed with Lesley Turner in 1961 and 1964 and with Ann Jones in 1969. He was US champion with Emerson in 1965 and 1966 and Rosewall in 1969, and took the mixed with Margaret Smith in 1962 and 1965. French titles came with Emerson in 1965 and Rosewall in 1968, and Australian with Hewitt in 1963 and 1964 and Emerson in 1966, plus the mixed with Turner in 1962. He was in the winning Australian Davis Cup teams of 1964, 1965 and 1966.

Stolle signed a professional contract at the beginning of 1967, but with open tennis arriving in 1968 he was only out of traditional competition for one season. Apart from a few successes, he did not make much impact on the open game, but in doubles he was a US Open semi-finalist as late as 1981 (with Newcombe).

Helena
SUKOVA
b 1965

Daughter of the late Vera Sukova, who was runner-up at Wimbledon in 1962, and Cyril Suk, President of the Czech Tennis Federation, Helena Sukova had yet to win a major singles title at the time of writing, but she has appeared in two Grand Slam singles finals and won two Grand Slam doubles crowns. Tall and athletic, she is a product of the progressive national coaching scheme and follows Martina Navratilova and Hana Mandlikova in a generation that has made Czechoslovakia one of the strongest nations in women's tennis. Like them, she has an all-court game, though her best results have usually come in indoor tournaments.

In 1984 Sukova became the first player to defeat Navratilova in 11 months en route to the Australian final, where she lost to Chris Evert. In 1986 she reached the final at Flushing Meadow, but her results against these two players were reversed as she beat Evert for the first time in 15 meetings only to lose to Navratilova. She was a quarter-finalist at Wimbledon in 1985 and 1987, on both occasions losing to opponents she was expected to beat — Kathy Rinaldi and Pam Shriver. Ironically, she was among the frontrunners for Wimbledon in 1987, having won the Eastbourne title the week before the Championships with back-to-back wins over Evert and Navratilova. She was runner-up in the Virginia Slims finals of 1985 and 1986.

In doubles, she has formed an effective

partnership with Germany's Claudia Kohde-Kilsch. They won the US Open in 1985 and Wimbledon in 1987, and they were runners-up in Paris in 1985 and Melbourne in 1984. She supported Mandlikova in their three Federation Cup victories of 1983, 1984, 1985, and she has been in the team every year since 1981.

May SUTTON
b 1887–d 1975

Although she was actually born in Plymouth, England, the American May Sutton (later Mrs Bundy) was the first overseas challenger to win a Wimbledon title, taking the women's singles in 1905. She was short but sturdy, and she had a very powerful forehand drive, which made up for a certain lack of mobility. She was only 16 when she won the US singles in 1904, the youngest ever champion until Tracy Austin beat the record in 1979 — but she was still playing at the age of 43, when she reached the quarter-finals at Wimbledon as late as 1929.

She took the US title only once, although she was a semi-finalist years later in 1921 and 1922, while at Wimbledon she played three challenge rounds against Dorothea Lambert Chambers, winning in 1905 and 1907. She won the US doubles in 1904 and was runner-up in 1925 with Elizabeth Ryan, and she was runner-up in the mixed in 1904. It seems that she did not compete much, if at all, during the decade from 1910 to 1920, but she was a regular participant at both Wimbledon and the US championships throughout the 1920s. She took part in the Wightman Cup of 1925, losing a doubles rubber to her old foe, Lambert Chambers.

Her daughter Dorothy Bundy Cheney (born 1916) also had a notable tennis career, becoming the first American woman to win the Australian singles (1938) and playing in the Wightman Cup 12 years after her mother. Both women hold achievement records in tennis. May won her first American tournament, the Pacific Coast singles, in 1901, and her last, the Pacific South West singles, in 1928, while Dorothy holds a record number of US National titles, mainly in veterans' events. She had notched up 116 championships by 1982.

Bill TILDEN
b 1893–d 1953

Not only one of the greatest ever tennis players, but also one of the most fascinating characters of the game, Bill Tilden was a very complex personality indeed. Although he adopted an intellectual approach to tennis and sought to improve his game by careful analysis and preparation, his real ambition was actually to be a great actor. He appeared on the stage and even in the odd movie, but by common consent he had no exceptional ability in this field. His tennis, however, was of the finest quality, and many connoisseurs believe that this American ranks as the greatest in the all-time Valhalla of champions.

He had an extremely powerful service — once clocked at 151 mph — and although his volleying was consummate, he preferred to stay on the baseline and outmanoeuvre his opponents with variations of pace and length with his excellent ground-strokes. Topspin, slice, spin and cut — he had them all, plus footwork and physique. His delight in chesslike strategy and tactics is reflected in the various books and articles he wrote about the game, though his newspaper work conflicted with his amateur status, and he was more than once in trouble with the US Lawn Tennis Association over this. He spent a whole winter remodelling his backhand, and when he returned to competition in the spring of 1920 he was a world-beater. The loss of part of a finger in 1922 proved to be no obstacle, because he simply modified his grip.

Born in Philadelphia, Tilden was a fairly late developer, and had most of his success in his late 20s and 30s. Early on, he was a leading exponent of mixed doubles. He was

Below: Bill Tilden in action whilst at his peak. He never stopped playing competitive tennis, and died of a heart attack in 1953 (aged 60) while preparing to travel to play in a professional tournament.

runner-up in the US mixed championship of 1910 and 1911 with Miss E. Wildey, won the title in 1913 and 1914 with Mary K. Browne, and was runner-up in 1916 and 1917 with Miss F. Ballin. He was runner-up with Molla Mallory in 1921 and 1924, and they won in 1922 and 1923. He won the men's doubles five times — with Vivian Richards in 1918, 1921 and 1922, with Brian Norton in 1923, and Frank Hunter in 1927. After losing the singles final in 1918 to R. L. Murray and in 1919 to Bill Johnston, he returned with his re-modelled backhand and was invincible in the championship for six years, beating Johnston in every final but one. In 1927 he lost to Rene Lacoste (the only member of the 'Four Musketeers' that usually got the better of him), but he took the title for a record-equalling seventh time in 1929. Indeed, with his 16 US National titles, he leads the all-time list of male winners.

He won the Wimbledon singles in 1920 and 1921, then stayed away for five years. He was a losing semi-finalist three years running — to Henri Cochet (1927 and 1929) and Lacoste (1928) — but in 1930 he won for a third time, nine years after his last success, with an extraordinary 0-6, 6-4, 4-6, 6-0, 7-5 semi-final against Jean Borotra and a straight set final over Wilmer Allison. He won the doubles in 1927 with Hunter, but never featured in the later stages of the mixed. Two of his Wimbledon titles — the singles against Norton in 1921 and the doubles of 1927 — were won from match point down in the final.

He did not win the French singles, although he had two match points against Lacoste in the 1927 final, and he was runner-up again, to Cochet, in 1930. Also in 1930, he won the mixed doubles with Cilli Aussem. His Davis Cup record was superb, with 13 successive singles wins in the challenge round from 1920 to 1926. He had two rare wins over Lacoste in the 1925 and 1926 matches on his home ground at Philadelphia, but the French turned the tables in 1927 as he lost to Lacoste after beating Cochet. He failed to bring the trophy back to America in three successive challenge rounds in Paris, 1928, 1929 and 1930, and the following year, at the age of 38, he turned professional.

Tilden won the US Pro title in 1931 and 1935, but his later years were blighted by indiscretions in his private life. A homosexual, he was twice jailed for indecency offences, and as a result of these he was largely ostracized by his former friends. An eccentric in many ways, it has been claimed that he rarely bathed, and never went naked in the locker rooms. He formed close relationships with a series of young men players, though it is doubtful whether he actually committed sexual acts with them; and he was also a close friend and mentor of several women players, including Mallory, Aussem and Helen Jacobs (but he detested both Suzanne Lenglen and Helen Wills Moody).

Pat TODD
b 1922

Attractive, graceful and statuesque, Pat Todd (née Canning) was prevented from reaching the very top of the game because she was a contemporary of the great players of American woman's tennis immediately following the Second World War. She was a tremendous competitor, and relished a battle, but the standard of opposition in her peak years was too strong for her to register more than the occasional big victory, and she usually had to be content as a perennial quarter-finalist or semi-finalist in the major events. She never reached the singles final at either Wimbledon or Forest Hills, but she scored her one Grand Slam success at Paris in 1947, when she beat Margaret Osborne in the semi-finals and Doris Hart in the final. She also reached the final in 1950, losing to Hart.

Todd was four times in the last four at Wimbledon (1948, 1949, 1950, 1952), the most notable occasion being the last, when she defeated Hart, the top seed, in a terrific match, 6-8, 7-5, 6-4. She was a semi-finalist at Forest Hills in 1946 and 1948, but she was never selected for a singles rubber in the Wightman Cup in five years in the team (1947 to 1951). She had three Grand Slam doubles titles — Wimbledon in 1947 and the French of 1948 (both with Hart), plus the French mixed of 1948 with Jaroslav Drobny. She was runner-up in the Wimbledon mixed of 1950 with Geoff Brown and the French mixed the same year with Bill Talbert.

Her Wimbledon title with Hart was her most exciting, and the final was regarded as one of the most memorable in the history of the event. Trailing Margaret Osborne and Louise Brough 3-5 and 0-40, on Brough's serve in the final set, Todd brought off a series of spectacular winners, and, swept along by the vociferous support of the crowd, she and Hart fought their way back to victory.

After a few years off for motherhood, Todd made a temporary comeback in 1957 and reached the semi-finals of both doubles events at Forest Hills.

Tony TRABERT
b 1930

One of the strangest jinxes in modern tennis has been the inability of American players to capture the French men's singles. Between 1938 and 1950 Donald Budge, Don McNeill and Budge Patty won it once, and Frank Parker twice; but none has succeeded since Tony Trabert, who took the title for the second time in 1955.

Trabert, from Cincinnati, had a short but spectacular amateur career. Strong and aggressive, his main strength was a trenchant backhand, and he was a prime exponent of the net-rushing power game. He displayed early promise at Wimbledon and Forest Hills in 1950, reaching the doubles semi-finals at both tournaments, and he was a US singles quarter-finalist in 1951. He missed the following year because of service in the US forces, but in 1953 he won the US singles, beating Vic Seixas in the final. During the next two years he established himself as No 1 in the world. He took the French in 1954 and three out of the four Grand Slam singles titles in 1955, failing only in Australia where he lost to Ken Rosewall in the semi-finals. He retained his French title over Sweden's Sven Davidson, and took both Wimbledon and Forest Hills without dropping a set.

Trabert also took five major doubles titles — the French of 1950 (with Bill Talbert), 1954 and 1955 (with Seixas), the US of 1954 and the Australian of 1955 (both with Seixas). They were runners-up at Wimbledon in 1954. He also won the Italian doubles of 1950 with Talbert. From 1951 to 1955 he represented the US in the Davis Cup, beating Lew Hoad and winning the doubles with Seixas at Sydney in 1954, when the US won the trophy for the only time during those years.

Trabert turned professional in 1955 but did not reach the top at this level, as the pro game throughout the late 1950s was dominated by Pancho Gonzales.

Christine
TRUMAN
b 1941

The quintessential English heroine, Christine Truman was a role model for a whole generation of schoolgirls; her teenage feats at Wimbledon were the stuff of juvenile fiction. Adored by a nation, Truman (a housewives' choice who became a conventional housewife and mother as Mrs Gerald Janes from 1967) did not quite play out the story, as she missed winning Wimbledon by a whisker, but she was so charming and sporting that, in a way, it would have been inappropriate for her to have done so.

After languishing in the shadow of the all-conquering Americans for 20 years, Britain suddenly produced a crop of champions in the late 1950s of which Truman was the youngest and most naturally talented. Angela Buxton, Angela Mortimer, Shirley Bloomer (later Mrs Brasher) and Pat Ward had all made their mark by the time Truman burst upon the scene in 1957. The bouncy 16-year-old romped through the first three rounds at her first Wimbledon, then stunned the pundits by trouncing third-seeded Bloomer, the reigning French champion, to reach the

quarter-finals. She then survived a gruelling three-set match against a second-rank American, Betty Pratt, to line up in the semi-finals against the favourite Althea Gibson.

In 1958 the Wightman Cup was played at Wimbledon just before the Championships, and it was Truman who scored three out of the four points needed to wrest the famous trophy away from the US for the first time in 28 years. Not only did she beat the US No 2, Dorothy Knode, and win her doubles with Bloomer, but she defeated Gibson 2-6, 6-3, 6-4 on the second day — the first time that the reigning Wimbledon champion had been beaten in the Wightman Cup. Ann Haydon scored the other vital point for Britain against Mimi Arnold, and the whole nation went crazy. Sadly, however, it was the same Mimi Arnold that rained on Christine's parade a week later, beating the second-seeded English girl in the fourth round of the championships.

This set the pattern for a rollercoaster of triumphs and disasters that marked the rest of Truman's career as a top-flight player. In 1959 she won both the Italian and French titles, and became the first British player to be seeded No 1 at Wimbledon for 20 years. Then a Mexican, Yola Ramirez, caught her on an off-day in the fourth round. She bounced back to reach the US final and ended the year ranked No 2 in the world while still only 18. In 1960 she was a semi-finalist in both the Australian championships and Wimbledon, and won the Australian doubles with Maria Bueno. There was another Wightman Cup victory, in which she clinched the decisive doubles rubber with Shirley Brasher, and a semi-final showing at Forest Hills.

Then came her big chance at Wimbledon in 1961. The two leading players, Bueno and Darlene Hard, were both missing, and Truman survived a tough quarter-final against the new young star, Margaret Smith. To patriotic delight, she and Mortimer both came through to the final, overcoming South African opposition. Nobody can tell whether or not Truman would have won had she not sustained a heavy fall on the damp grass when leading 6-4, 4-3, 40-30. But it undoubtedly affected her chances, and amid almost unbearable excitement it was the steadier, less flamboyant Mortimer who eventually prevailed, 4-6, 6-4, 7-5.

Truman was still only 20, but she never again had a real shot at the top. She was out of tennis for most of 1962 after putting her foot through a rotten floorboard on court in Jamaica, and the best she did in major championships after that were semi-final showings at Paris in 1963 and Wimbledon in 1965. But in the Wightman Cup — a competition that might have been designed with her in mind — she still had heroic parts to play.

In the 1961 fixture at Chicago she was the only British winner in a disastrous defence by a roster of British champions against a team

of inexperienced US teenagers. In 1963 she lost a dour struggle against Billie Jean Moffitt 4-6, 17-19, which involved the longest singles set ever played by women. In 1967 she was once again the only British winner, recovering to beat the new sensation, Rosemary Casals, and in 1968 she clinched a third British victory in eight years by winning the final doubles with her younger sister Nell (herself a notable player for several years). Mrs Janes, as she now was, appeared for the last time in 1971, which was the year Chris Evert made her awesome debut.

She carried on playing domestic tournaments for a few more years (she was Martina Navratilova's first Wimbledon opponent in 1973), in between giving birth to four children, and finally called it a day in 1975.

Wendy *TURNBULL*

b 1952

A reliable and consistent competitor who lifted herself from second to top-rank status at the relatively late age of 25, Turnbull has never won a major singles title, but she has taken the women's and mixed doubles championships of all the Grand Slam events except, ironically, her native Australia.

Nicknamed 'Rabbit' because of her willingness to run, she lacks an outstanding killer shot, but her volleying skills have characterized her many successes in doubles. Her notable singles showing was beating Rosemary Casals, Virginia Wade and Martina Navratilova to reach the US Open final of 1977, where she lost to Chris Evert, and heralded a consistent place in the top ten for the next eight years. She was also runner-up to Evert in the 1979 French Open, and she reached the semi-finals at Flushing Meadow in 1978 and 1984, and Melbourne in 1981 and 1984. At Wimbledon she has not progressed beyond the last eight, where she had the indignity of losing 6-0, 6-0 to Hana Mandlikova in 1981.

She won the Wimbledon doubles in 1978 with Kerry Reid, saving a match point against Mima Jausovec and Virginia Ruzici, and she was runner-up in 1979, 1980 and 1983 with Casals, and in 1986 with Mandlikova. She was a mixed doubles finalist with John Lloyd three years in a row, winning in 1983 and 1984. She won the US Open doubles in 1979 and 1982 and was runner-up in 1981 with Casals, runner-up in 1984 with Anne Hobbs, and in 1986 with Mandlikova. In 1980 she won the mixed with Marty Riessen. She won the French doubles in 1979 with Betty Stove and was runner-up in 1982 with Casals, and won the mixed in 1979 with Bob Hewitt and in 1982 with Lloyd. She was runner-up in the 1983 Australian Open with Hobbs. Other major titles include the 1979 Italian with

Above: Christine Truman came from a respectable middle-class suburban background, and was one of a large family of good tennis players. Her game was boisterous, uninhibited and intuitive, and her main strength was a booming forehand drive — although she was not afraid to attack the net.

Above: Guillermo Vilas glides aggressively into a backhand volley at Stade Roland Garros. He won the title there in 1977, dropping only three games in the final against Brian Gottfried.

She was a good doubles player, winning Wimbledon in 1964 with Smith; Forest Hills in 1961 with Darlene Hard; Paris in 1964 and 1965 with Smith; the Australian in 1964 and 1967 with Judy Tegart and in 1965 with Smith; the Italian in 1961 with Jan Lehane, 1964 with Smith and 1967 with Rosemary Casals; and the German in 1962 (Lehane), 1964 and 1965 (Smith) and 1967 (Tegart). In mixed doubles, she took the Wimbledon title in 1961 and 1964 with Fred Stolle; the Australian in 1962 (Stolle) and 1967 (Owen Davidson); the Italian in 1962 (Stolle) and 1967 (Bowrey); and the German in 1962 (Ken Fletcher) and 1963 (Stolle).

She missed the 1966 season through illness and 1970 through pregnancy, but she was a French quarter-finalist in 1971. In 1978, some years after retirement, she made a sentimental return to Paris and Wimbledon, and narrowly failed to regain the French doubles — she and Gail Lovera were beaten 5-7, 6-4, 8-6 in the final by Mima Jausovec and Virginia Ruzici. Her daughter Michele is a leading Australian junior.

Guillermo VILAS

b 1952

The best and most consistent male player to come out of South America, this reflective Argentinian (who has published books of poetry) has influenced and inspired players of both sexes in his country, and indeed led a major upsurge in strong players from South America in the late 1970s. Although his game is based on heavily topspun ground-strokes, Vilas has enjoyed considerable success on grass, and has won all major titles in the game except Wimbledon, where he only twice got as far as the quarter-finals.

Vilas made his breakthrough to the top flight in 1974, winning six Grand Prix titles in the second half of the year and finishing off with the Masters title on grass at Melbourne. His best year was 1977, when he won the French, US Open and South African titles and set a record for invincibility in the open era by winning 50 consecutive matches. His other major titles were the Australian in 1978 and 1979, the German in 1978 and the Italian in 1980. He was runner-up in the French in 1975, 1978 and 1982, the Australian in January 1977, the Italian in 1976 and 1979, the German in 1980 and the South African in 1982.

He led Argentina to the Davis Cup final in 1981, and was in their winning Nations Cup team of 1980. He rarely played doubles, but when required to for team events he formed an effective partnership with Jose Luis Clerc. In the 1981 Davis Cup final they extended Peter Fleming and John McEnroe to an 11-9 final set. He also had the satisfaction of

Casals and the Women's Series of 1980 (Casals) and 1985 and 1986 (Mandlikova).

She has represented Australia in the Federation Cup every year since 1977. In 1987 she won the US Open over-35 doubles with Sharon Walsh-Pete.

Lesley TURNER

b 1942

Perhaps the only high-ranking Australian woman who was better on clay courts than on grass, Turner (who married fellow-player Bill Bowrey in 1968) was a resolute baseliner with beautifully grooved ground-strokes and excellent footwork. Petite and pretty, she was also fit and clever, and in 1963 she was ranked as high as No 2 in the world, behind her compatriot Margaret Smith.

Turner achieved her best results on European clay, winning the French singles in 1963 and 1965, and the Italian in 1967 and 1968. She was also runner-up in the French in 1962 and 1967; in the Italian in 1961, 1963 and 1964; in the German in 1967; and in the Australian (her only major grass court final) in 1964 and 1967. She was a semi-finalist at Wimbledon in 1964, and in the US in 1967.

clinching Argentine wins over the US at Buenos Aires in the 1977, 1980 and 1983 competitions. His career slumped in 1983 when he was under threat of suspension for allegedly accepting a guarantee to play in a tournament in Rotterdam, but he made something of a comeback in 1986 by reaching the final of the WCT Tournament of Champions at Forest Hills and the quarter-finals of the French Open.

Ellsworth
VINES
b 1911

In his peak year of 1932, American Ellsworth Vines was possibly the most devastating player the game has ever known. He won Wimbledon with almost contemptuous ease, taking his last three matches with an overwhelming display of lightning forehands and cannonball serves. Tall and gangling, he hit the ball flat and tremendously hard, and in this one great year he was so powerful and so accurate that nobody could get close to him. In the final against Britain's 'Bunny' Austin he projected 30 clean aces. The final point is the best remembered: both his opponent and the spectators saw him winding up to serve, and heard the ball ricochet off the back canvas, but nobody actually saw it.

Vines also won the US singles in 1931 and 1932 — though not with the same degree of dominance — and the US doubles with Keith Gledhill in 1932. But in 1933 he was not the same player. He failed to reach the semi-finals of the Australian singles, and at Wimbledon he dropped sets in four of six matches to reach the final. Here he faced the unorthodox Australian, Jack Crawford, and in a triumph of brain over brawn he was beaten in a thrilling five-set encounter. Vines also lost his US singles, although he won the mixed with Elizabeth Ryan. Somewhat chastened, he turned professional at the end of the year. He won the US Pro title in 1939, but then left tennis for golf, in which game he also became a leading player.

He represented the US in the Davis Cup in 1932 and 1933, winning 13 of 16 rubbers.

Gottfried
von CRAMM
b 1909 – d 1976

Cool, elegant and impeccably courteous, Baron von Cramm was a superb stylist and stroke-maker who perhaps lacked the iron determination necessary for a great champion. As it was, he won the French singles twice and his own German title six times, and he was unlucky in that political pressures

Left: Gottfried von Cramm's great days were in the 1930s, but he continued to play at a high level well after the Second World War. This trophy was won at Hamburg in 1949, when he was 40 years old.

interrupted his career at a time when he might have succeeded to even greater honours.

He was runner-up three years in a row at Wimbledon, losing in straight sets all three times. Fred Perry beat him in 1935 and 1936 — on the latter occasion von Cramm pulled a leg muscle in the second game and could offer only token resistance as he was overwhelmed 6-1, 6-1, 6-0 in Wimbledon's shortest ever singles final. The following year he was similarly outplayed by Donald Budge, who also beat him in the final at Forest Hills.

Von Cramm's classic purity of style reached its full flower in Paris. He was a finalist here too for three consecutive years, beating Jack Crawford in 1934, losing to Perry in 1935 and gaining sweet revenge over the Briton in 1936. He won the German singles four years running, from 1932 to 1935. There was no tournament in 1936, and he did not play again until after the war. His most memorable match was in the Inter-Zone final of the Davis Cup in 1937. Germany and the US were tied at two rubbers each as von Cramm went into the final rubber with Budge on the grass at Wimbledon. The German led 5-2 in the final set, but Budge somehow hung on and clinched a victory at 8-6 after an encounter of almost unsurpassed brilliance and excitement.

But there were unpleasant repercussions for von Cramm. Under intense political pressure from the Nazi regime, which he opposed, he was abruptly summoned home and imprisoned by the Gestapo for alleged homosexual offences. He was released in time to play in the London Grass Court Championships in June 1939, which he won, but his entry for Wimbledon was not accepted. He was thus denied the best chance he ever had of winning the title, as Perry and Budge had both departed to the professional ranks, and he had beaten the ultimate winner, Bobby Riggs, 6-0, 6-1 at Queen's.

Von Cramm had to be content with just one Wimbledon title — the mixed of 1933, with Hilde Krahwinkel. He won the US and French doubles titles with Henner Henkel in 1937, plus five men's and three mixed German titles. After the war he won the German singles in 1948 and 1949. He was in Germany's Davis Cup team first in 1932 and last in 1953. His five German men's doubles titles all came after the war — with Jeff Harper of Australia in 1948 and 1949, and with Budge Patty in 1953, 1954 and 1955, by which time he was 46. The three mixed were all with Krahwinkel, from 1932 to 1934.

For a while during the 1950s he was married to the Woolworth heiress, Barbara Hutton. He died in a car crash near Cairo in 1976.

Virginia
WADE
b 1945

The most internationally famous of any British woman player, Virginia Wade had a long and extraordinary tennis career that spanned nearly a quarter of a century. She won three of the four Grand Slam titles in both singles and doubles, competed at Wimbledon 26 times, and holds the record for appearances in both the Federation and Wightman Cups.

In her early years she was temperamental and volatile, but she eventually matured as a consistent and successful match player. In Wimbledon's Centennial year she won the singles at her 16th attempt, at almost 32, after a complete reappraisal of her technical and mental approach. She had a formidable armoury of shots that needed honing into a cohesive unit before she could transform herself from a spasmodically brilliant performer into a reliable one.

Strong and athletic, Wade had a powerful service, though it was not a fluid stroke. A sliced backhand, adequate forehand, good overhead and crisp volleys became much better once she learned not to snatch them. Prone to petulant outbursts and occasional tears early on, she developed a mental toughness playing Team Tennis in the USA, and this was the key to her later successes.

Daughter of the Archdeacon of Durban, she was born in England but spent much of her childhood in South Africa. She returned to Britain at the age of 15, though never won the British Junior Championship. Combining university studies with competitive tennis, she actually took her degree while competing in the 1966 Wightman Cup at Wimbledon (quite literally, as she had a special exam room set up at the All England Club, where she sat her finals).

Wade's first major title was the inaugural US Open at Forest Hills in 1968. She had already gone through a frustratingly erratic season, winning all three of her Wightman Cup rubbers to help the British win the trophy for the first time in eight years, but crashing out of Wimbledon in the first round. Playing with intuitive dash, she blazed through the field at Forest Hills after a nervous start, and did not drop a set in overwhelming Rosemary Casals, Judy Tegart, Ann Jones and Billie Jean King in the last four rounds.

Instead of building on this early triumph, she stumbled through several years of disappointing results before taking her next big title, the Australian Open of 1972. In this final she beat Evonne Goolagong, a player who, unwittingly, enjoyed a greater psychological superiority over her than any other. Wade also won the Italian title of 1971, albeit in a small field, against another regular tormentor, Germany's Helga Masthoff.

At Wimbledon, where patriotic expectation was an unbearable burden for many years, Wade failed to justify her seeding from 1967, when she was a quarter-finalist, until 1972. She then reached the last eight or better every year until 1980. In 1974 she was a semi-finalist for the first time, and frittered away a winning lead against Russia's Olga Morozova, and she was well beaten by Goolagong in the semi-finals of 1976.

But in 1977, after years as the only serious British contender, another home player, Sue

Right: Virginia Wade's tennis career became such a long-standing feature of British sport that a play running for years in the West End included the line: 'I hear Virginia is doing well at Wimbledon this year.' Wade, whose tempestuous persona belied the fact that she was a clergyman's daughter, kept a nation on the edge of its seat for nearly a quarter of a century.

Barker, had emerged to challenge her position. They both reached the last four, but whereas Barker flopped against the Dutch girl, Betty Stove, Wade gloriously defeated the holder, Chris Evert; then after an inhibited first set, she conquered her nerves — and Stove — to take the title. It was a magnificent patriotic occasion, in front of the Queen in her Silver Jubilee year, and the British went wild with delight. For the first and only time in Wimbledon's history, the normally restrained Centre Court crowd sang 'For She's a Jolly Good Fellow' — and nobody who was there will ever forget it.

In addition to her four major singles titles, Wade won the US Open doubles with Margaret Court in 1973 and 1975; the French doubles with Court in 1973; the Australian doubles with Court in 1973; the Italian doubles with Court in 1968, with Masthoff in 1971 and with Morozova in 1973; and 10 British Hard Court Championships in singles, doubles and mixed between 1967 and 1974. She took part in every Wightman Cup contest from 1965 to 1985 — a record 21 ties — was captain from 1973 and was on the winning side four times (1968, 1974, 1975, 1978). In the Federation Cup she represented Great Britain for 17 consecutive years, playing a record 100 rubbers and winning 66 of them. She was in each of the four British teams to reach the final — in 1967, 1971, 1972 and 1981 — and as captain she stood down in 1984 although she was still one of the country's top three players.

She finally retired from singles at the end of 1985 after coming within two points of beating Anne Hobbs in a dramatic and marathon British National final. She was still playing doubles at Wimbledon, at the age of 42, in 1987.

During her later years on the circuit and since retirement she has remained captain of the British teams, and become a coach, TV commentator and member of the Wimbledon Committee of Management — the first woman to occupy such a role.

Hazel
WIGHTMAN
b 1886 – d 1974

Hazel Wightman is best remembered as donor of the Wightman Cup, the international team trophy competed for by the top women players of the United States and Great Britain, but she was a fine player in her own right and won 16 US National grass court titles — more than any other woman except Margaret du Pont, Margaret Court and Louise Brough.

Born Hazel Hotchkiss in Healdsburg, California, she was an excellent volleyer and was very fast about the court. She was triple US champion for three years running, 1909 to

1911, and she took the singles for a fourth time in 1919. She won the doubles in 1909 and 1910 with Edith Rotch, in 1911 with Eleanora Sears, and in 1924 and 1928 with Helen Wills. Her mixed titles came in 1909, 1911, 1915 and 1920 (with Bill Johnston), in 1910 with John Carpenter, and in 1918 with Ian Wright. She won the Wimbledon doubles with Wills in 1924, and was a quarter-finalist in the US singles as late as 1928, the year she won the doubles for the last time, with Wills. An indomitable competitor, she won the US Indoor doubles ten times between 1919 and 1943, the last time at the age of 57.

She captained the US Wightman Cup team 13 times between 1923 and 1948, and played five times between 1923 and 1931. She had a compelling personality, and continued to influence American women's tennis for many years. The 50th anniversary Wightman Cup match of 1973 was held near her home in Boston, and she received an honorary MBE.

Mats
WILANDER
b 1964

The second most successful Swede in tennis after Bjorn Borg, Wilander became the youngest ever winner of a Grand Slam title (the record has since been beaten by Boris

Above: Mats Wilander is as cool and phlegmatic as most Swedish players, but his iron determination is evident in this picture taken at Stade Roland Garros, where he has appeared in the final five times.

Right: Anthony Wilding, the only New Zealander to win major tennis titles. He was killed in action during the First World War, and it would be 69 years before another Kiwi, Chris Lewis, reached the final at Wimbledon.

Becker) when he took the French singles at the age of 17¾ in 1982. He is a player of great determination and discipline, and is also impeccably sporting, like most of his compatriots. He plays chiefly from the baseline, and bases his game on remorseless topspun driving, though he has more recently shown that he can volley as well.

That sensational win in Paris — his first Grand Prix title — included wins over Ivan Lendl, Vitas Gerulaitis, Jose Luis Clerc and Guillermo Vilas. He won a Grand Slam title each year for four years — the French in 1982, the Australian in 1983 and 1984, and the French again in 1985. In 1986, although he did not win a Grand Slam singles, he took the Wimbledon doubles with Joakim Nystrom. He was also runner-up in Paris in 1983 (to Yannick Noah) and 1987 (to Lendl), in the 1985 Australian Open (to Stefan Edberg) and in the 1987 US Open (to Lendl). In 1988 he became the best player in the world by winning three of the four Grand Slam titles, missing out only at Wimbledon, where he has only twice reached as far as the quarter-finals.

Anthony WILDING
b 1883 – d 1915

Anthony Wilding was the first tennis heart-throb, idolized for his good looks and sporting behaviour, and the only New Zealander to win Wimbledon. (The only other to reach the final, Chris Lewis, did so in the 100th anniversary year of Wilding's birth.)

After winning the championships of Canterbury, New Zealand at 17, Wilding went to Cambridge University, playing for them in 1904/5. He was a quarter-finalist at Wimbledon in 1905 and 1908 and a semi-finalist in 1909, then he won the title four years in a row, 1910 to 1913. The following year he was beaten in the challenge round by his Australasian Davis Cup team-mate, Norman Brookes.

He won the Wimbledon doubles with Brookes in 1907 and 1914, and with Malcolm Ritchie in 1908 and 1910. He was Australian singles champion in 1906 and 1909, and took the doubles in 1906 with Rodney Heath. He was in the winning Australasian Davis Cup teams (Australia and New Zealand competed together until 1923) in 1907, 1908, 1909, 1911 and 1914, winning 21 of 30 rubbers.

During the First World War Wilding was killed in action at Neuve Chapelle, France, in 1915, aged 31.

Helen WILLS MOODY
b 1905

The American, Helen Wills (later Mrs Moody, later Mrs Roark), had a career in top-class tennis that spanned the years 1922 to 1938, and she was unquestionably the leading player for more than a decade after Suzanne Lenglen turned professional. For many years she held the record for the most Wimbledon singles titles. (Her total of eight was matched by Martina Navratilova in 1987.) The most ruthlessly efficient of all players, she never displayed any emotion on court and was considered to be cold and insensitive. She had poor footwork and did less running than most great players, but her driving was so powerful and accurate that it did not matter. She was a noted beauty and an accomplished artist, and her social circle was one of intellectuals and celebrities. She did not mix with other tennis players.

She was beaten only once at Wimbledon — in the 1924 final, after leading by a set and 4-1 against Kitty McKane. On all her subsequent appearances she was the champion — in 1927, 1928, 1929, 1930, 1932, 1933, 1935 and 1938. Two of her finals were

Left: Helen Wills Moody (left) and Hilde Sperling walk out onto the Centre Court for their Wimbledon semi-final in 1938. Moody won the match, 12-10, 6-4, and went on to defeat Helen Jacobs for a record eighth singles title.

very close: she dropped a set to Dorothy Round in 1933, and in 1935 she had to save a match point against her great rival, Helen Jacobs. Jacobs was, in fact, her victim in four of the finals, and the manner of Moody's last win in 1938, when she paid no attention to the fact that her opponent was in great pain, was coolly received by the crowd.

In fact, Moody had total concentration. Nothing, not even the score, was allowed to distract her. She played each point with equal effort, and that was the reason she was so difficult to beat. Inscrutable under her white eye-shade, machine-like in her skill, it is no wonder that she does not rank among the more popular champions.

In addition to her eight singles, she won three doubles titles at Wimbledon — with Hazel Wightman in 1924 and 1927, and with Elizabeth Ryan in 1930. She also took the mixed in 1929 with Frank Hunter.

She won the US singles seven times in nine years between 1923 and 1931, the exceptions being 1926 and 1930, when she did not compete. She was runner-up at the age of 16 to Molla Mallory in 1922, and also to Jacobs in 1933, when she retired in the third set because of an injured back. In her seven winning finals she dropped only one set — to

McKane in 1925. She won the US doubles four times — with Marion Jessup in 1922, with Wightman in 1924 and 1928, and with Mary K. Browne in 1925. She also took the mixed in 1924 with Vivian Richards and in 1928 with John Hawkes. This meant she was triple champion in 1924 and 1928 — a feat she never achieved at Wimbledon.

She won the French singles four times (1928, 1929, 1930, 1932), and the doubles in 1930 and 1932 (with Ryan), but failed to win the mixed despite three appearances in the final. Because of differences with the USLTA she did not compete at Forest Hills after 1933, but she did agree to one last appearance in the Wightman Cup in 1938, six years after her previous involvement. She played in it nine times, and was only twice beaten in singles — by both Phyllis Covell and McKane in 1924. She did not lose a set anywhere in singles between 1927 and 1932, a record bettered only by Lenglen, to whom she lost in their only meeting, at Cannes in 1926.

A native of Berkeley, California, Mrs Roark, as she has been since 1938, has lived quietly in retirement and was one of the few former champions who decided not to attend the Centennial celebrations at Wimbledon in 1977 and the US Open in 1981.

The Grand Slam Events

Tennis has borrowed the phrase 'Grand Slam' from golf, in which it refers to the feat of winning the four major championships — the British Open, US Open, US PGA and US Masters — all in the same season. In tennis, the tournaments counting for the Grand Slam are The Championships (Wimbledon), the US Open, French Open and Australian Open. In order to take the Grand Slam it used to be necessary to win all four titles (in whichever event) in the same calendar year. This has now been modified slightly to holding them all simultaneously, so the Slam can be won by, say, winning Wimbledon and the US Open one year and the Australian and French titles the next.

These are the four championships that count most in tennis. There are other big titles, most notably the Grand Prix Masters for men, and the Women's Series finals, currently sponsored by Nabisco and Virginia Slims cigarettes respectively. These are both events with limited fields, and only the top few finishers from the year-long circuits can qualify for them by aggregating the most points.

The Grand Slam events are the most historic and have among the biggest entries. It is the long histories of the Big Four that give them their prestige and universal recognition.

In recent years, the International Tennis Federation has sought to maintain the pre-eminence of the Big Four by securing sponsorship for a major bonus prize in the event of a player capturing the Grand Slam. When Martina Navratilova achieved the feat in 1984 she was rewarded with a cheque for one million dollars, presented by the International Tennis Federation.

Left: Aerial view of the All England Club, Wimbledon — venue for the world's most famous tennis tournament. The area to the left of the main stadium — the Centre Court — has been developed to provide extra courts and spectator facilities during the last ten years.

Above: Three outside courts at the original All England Club ground in Worple Road, Wimbledon. It lay beside a main railway line, which provided a noisy distraction for players and spectators.

WIMBLEDON

The oldest and most prestigious of all tennis tournaments is held during the last week of June and the first week of July each year at the All England Club, Wimbledon — a leafy suburb southwest of London. Its official title is 'The Lawn Tennis Championships'. (Another title sometimes given to it, the 'All England Championships', is not correct.) Universally known as 'Wimbledon', it is the most popular and most highly publicized of a string of great English summer sporting festivals that also includes the Royal Ascot race meeting, the Test Matches in cricket, and the boating regatta at Henley.

Sense of occasion

Wimbledon is so much synonymous with the sport that many people are unaware that tennis is an all-year game with a large number of important events. The British public flock to Wimbledon as much for the sense of occasion as a wish actually to watch top-class tennis; and Centre Court tickets are so coveted that they change hands for stupendous sums of money. Wimbledon 'fortnight' has always been associated with Royalty and other celebrities, with fashion, glamour and gossip. In media terms, it is possibly the most hyped sporting event of all, enjoying continuous coverage on British television (and considerable air-time in most overseas countries) and an extraordinary invasion by the world's press, both specialist and news-oriented.

Jointly managed by the All England Club and the British Lawn Tennis Association, the tournament is unique in that it has no direct commercial sponsorship. Whereas almost all other professional events have a sponsor's name in their title (the US Open does not overall, but each event does), The Championships remain free of such adornment. The organizers are anxious to preserve this quality, and there is no need for it to be otherwise. Each year the tournament generates huge profits in television rights (the single greatest form of income), ticket sales, suppliers' fees, hospitality marquees and marketing revenue. Profitability is guaranteed before a ball is struck, because each meeting is heavily invested in beforehand. After the accounting, all profits not retained for improvements to the facility are handed over by the All England Club to the LTA for the benefit of British tennis.

Ironically, Wimbledon could make even more money (the profits run into several million pounds) if spectator-space were not so comparatively limited. The ground capacity is about 31,000, though in 1987 the gates were closed once 28,000 people were inside, in order to ease congestion. The famous Centre Court seats 12,433 and has standing room for about 2,000, and the other stadia in the ground can cope with about 15,000 between them. Not all of these spectators are paying, and the demand for tickets outnumbers availability by around ten to one. Each year a ballot is held to determine

which of the ticket applicants are successful.

Apart from all the running costs, Wimbledon pays out an enormous sum to the competitors as prize money. The figure for 1987 was £2,470,020. If the tournament were to be sponsored (and there would be no shortage of companies interested), the profits could be even greater. But Wimbledon has a mystique; and direct sponsorship, essential for most other events, is neither needed nor wanted. Indeed, such is the tradition of the event that a sponsor's name would never become popularly associated with it. And in the words of leading entrepreneur Mark McCormack, 'You couldn't sponsor Wimbledon, anymore than you could sponsor the Coronation.'

First tournament

It was believed until recently that The Championships was the very first lawn tennis tournament ever held. But research has unearthed a tournament that took place in Nahant, Massachusetts, in August 1876 — nearly a year before the first Wimbledon meeting of 1877. Played on a round-robin basis (all played all) between a group of friends in the small New England town, it used scoring borrowed from the Victorian game of rackets (from which squash has evolved) and was won by James Dwight. However, Wimbledon held the first Championship open to all-comers, upon the lawns of the All England Croquet and Lawn Tennis Club.

The original ground of the club was in Worple Road, near the main London-to-Portsmouth railway line. It was founded, at first for croquet only, in 1870. The club agreed to include two other popular new pastimes, lawn tennis and badminton, in 1875. Two years later, they decided 'That a public meeting be held on July 10th and following days to compete for the Championships in Lawn Tennis'.

The inaugural tournament was for men's singles only. Women's singles and men's doubles were introduced in 1884, and women's and mixed doubles in 1913. However, an event known as the All England Ladies' Doubles Championship was held at Buxton, Derbyshire, from 1884 to 1953, and an All England Mixed Doubles alternated between Manchester and Liverpool from 1888 to 1938. Unofficial (ie non-championship) women's and mixed doubles were held at Wimbledon from 1899.

The new ground

The All England Club moved from Worple Road to its present site between Church Road and Somerset Road in 1922. Growth had not been steady — indeed, during the 1890s the tournament actually went into a decline — but as competition gathered momentum in the years immediately following the First World War, the Worple Road ground became inadequate to hold the number of people that wanted to attend. The most significant single factor in this upsurge of interest was the great French player Suzanne Lenglen, whose matches always had to be held on the 7,000 capacity Centre Court. The crowds adored her, and the queues that formed to watch her play were known by a corruption of

Above: The 1909 women's singles challenge round at Wimbledon: Dora Boothby (left) is on her way to victory over Agnes Morton. At Worple Road the Centre Court actually was in the middle of the club ground.

the wartime song: 'There's a Leng-len trail a-winding'.

Accordingly, a much larger piece of land was acquired in stages. The present site has been much developed and improved over the years, and the club as it appears today bears little resemblance to that which came into use for the first time in June, 1922. The least-changing element has been the courts, which are among the finest lawns in the world. They may not be the best grass courts of all — Devonshire Park, Eastbourne, and Memorial Drive, Adelaide, would both dispute Wimbledon's pre-eminence in this respect — but they are meticulously tended and require a large permanent staff to get them into immaculate condition for the start of each Championship. There was a period in the late 1970s when they fell short of previous standards, but in recent years, despite some of the wettest summers in memory, the courts have returned to a state of perfection that is to be expected for the most famous tournament in the world.

Grass — an anachronism?

However, the fact that Wimbledon continues to be played on grass — and the organizers insist that there will be no change in the foreseeable future — means that it is beginning to become anachronistic. At one time, the majority of the international circuit was played on grass. The Australian Open used the surface until 1987 but has now switched to a hard court. The US Eastern grass-court circuit, culminating in the old Nationals at Forest Hills, has long since given way to varieties of cement. International grass-court play has now shrunk to just seven weeks of the calendar — the two weeks prior to Wimbledon, with men's tournaments at Queen's Club and Bristol, and women's events at Edgbaston and Eastbourne; the Championships fortnight; the last remaining American professional grass-court tournament at Newport; and two weeks in Australia.

The name of the game, once known as 'lawn tennis', no longer obtains except in England and India (where they also have grass courts), and even in England many clubs are replacing their grass courts with all-weather surfaces. Grass is simply too expensive to maintain, and the use that can be got out of it, particularly in a bad summer, is too limited. It is only at facilities like the All England Club, where there are abundant financial resources, that grass can be retained.

Keeping pace

Wimbledon has, over the years, made every effort to keep pace with the ever-increasing demands of a top-class sporting event. The biggest changes have come about during the last decade. In 1977 the Championships celebrated their centenary, marked by the opening of the Wimbledon Museum and the Kenneth Ritchie Wimbledon Library. The Museum — the first of its kind in Europe,

Right: René Lacoste and Suzanne Lenglen at Wimbledon in 1925. Each won their respective singles event that year — in Lenglen's case for the loss of only five games in five rounds.

although the Hall of Fame at Newport, Rhode Island, was already in existence — is open throughout the year and holds a fascinating collection of memorabilia.

In 1979 the roof of the Centre Court was raised to provide extra seating, and in 1980 four new courts were brought into use to bring the total to 18 — six of which include grandstands for important matches. In 1981 the buildings at each end of the second-best court, No 1, were replaced, giving vastly better facilities for the players and officials as well as more room for spectators. The following year a huge area at the north end of the ground was opened up to accommodate bigger and better catering facilities for the spectators. Further rebuilding took place on one side of the Centre Court in 1985, with more seats and a new press tower. It is generally agreed that Wimbledon now offers the best arrangements for the media of any tennis tournament in the world.

The twelve events

The Championships now comprise 12 events, and the total programme for the 13 days of

Wimbledon has always been regarded as the most prestigious of all tournaments, although the US and French championships would take issue with that claim. There was a time in the 1970s and early 1980s when some prominent clay-court specialists stayed away because their computer rankings were likely to be adversely affected by poor performances on the grass. Ivan Lendl, most notably, did not enter in 1982 for this reason, but he now states that to win Wimbledon is his dearest wish. It is a fact that winning a Wimbledon title holds the same value for a tennis player as an Oscar does for an actor — it increases his earning potential and ensures him immortality in the annals of the game.

Men's singles

The men's singles is, of course, the oldest of the events. The winner, in addition to a handsome cheque (the 1987 first prize was £155,000) is presented with three cups, of which he retains replicas. The more than 100 names inscribed on the main Challenge Cup, which is the one presented to the champion on court, make an impressive catalogue of the history of men's tennis. (Yet there are a number of great players missing from the list — outstanding players like Gottfried von Cramm, Pancho Gonzales, Ken Rosewall and Ilie Nastase — who never actually won the Wimbledon singles title.)

The greatest number of titles won was seven, by Britain's William Renshaw between 1881 and 1889 (his brother Ernest also won in 1888). Other multiple winners have been Laurie Doherty (Great Britain, five titles 1902 to 1906), Bjorn Borg (Sweden, 1976 to 1980), Reggie Doherty (Great Britain, four titles 1897 to 1900), Anthony Wilding (New Zea-

Below: The Renshaw twins, Ernest and William, dominated The Championships throughout the 1880s. They are pictured here contesting the 1882 men's singles challenge round, won by William in five sets.

play involves some 668 matches. The five main events, with the number of players or pairs in the draw, are: Men's Singles (128), Women's Singles (128), Men's Doubles (64), Women's Doubles (64), and Mixed Doubles (64). The All England Ladies' Plate, for players beaten in the first two rounds of the women's singles, or those accepted for doubles events only, has a draw of 48. There is an invitation men's 35-and-over singles (16 players) and doubles (8 pairs). And there are international junior events, comprising boys' singles (64), girls' singles (64), boys' doubles (16) and girls' doubles (16).

From 1896 to 1981 there was a plate event for men, but this was discontinued through lack of support. From 1964 to 1981 there was a doubles event for veterans aged 45 or over, then this was replaced by over-35 singles and doubles. In accordance with all other tournaments in the Nabisco Grand Prix and Virginia Slims Women's Series, entries are accepted on the basis of computer rankings, with provision for wild cards and qualifiers. The qualifying rounds take place at nearby Roehampton the week before the Championships.

land, 1910 to 1913), and Rod Laver (Australia, 1961, 1962, 1968, 1969). Just 10 nations have provided the winners: Australia (10), Czechoslovakia (1), Egypt (1), France (4), Great Britain (14), New Zealand (1), Spain (1), Sweden (2), United States (19), and West Germany (1).

The size of the men's singles draw has remained constant at 128 since 1924. This requires all players to play seven rounds to win the title. Given good weather, they can expect a day off between most rounds. And as the matches have always been the best of five sets, with the tie-break operating in all except the fifth since 1971, the programme is not as demanding as, say, the US Open, where the last two rounds are played on successive days.

Women's singles

The women's singles championship was not instituted until seven years after the men's, in 1884. It is not the oldest women's tournament in tennis — that distinction goes to the Irish Championships, where women had an event from 1879. The first final at Wimbledon was contested between two sisters — Maud and Lillian Watson, with the former winning. She received a silver trophy which was replaced in 1886 by the magnificent silver salver that is in use today. Maud Watson's trophy is now presented to the winner of the grass court tournament at Edgbaston.

Only six nationalities have so far claimed the title (seven if you count Martina Navratilova's country of origin, Czechoslovakia, in 1978). There have been two winners from Australia, one from Brazil, one from France, two from Germany, 18 from Great Britain and 15 from the United States. Two players have won it eight times: Helen Wills Moody (1927 to 1930, 1932, 1933, 1935, 1938) and Navratilova (1978, 1979, 1982 to 1987). Dorothea Douglass (later Mrs Lambert Chambers) won seven times (1903, 1904, 1906, 1910, 1911, 1913, 1914). Six-time winners were Blanche Bingley Hillyard (1886, 1889, 1894, 1897, 1899, 1900), Suzanne Lenglen (1919 to 1923, 1925) and Billie Jean King (1966 to 1968, 1972, 1973, 1975).

The size of the draw was smaller than the men's singles until 1983. The number of entries varied: 1890 saw an all-time low of just four, while in 1922 a limit on acceptances was fixed at 64. This number was increased to 80 in 1927 and 96 in 1929, which remained the limit until in 1983 the Women's International Tennis Association secured a parity with the men at 128.

The doubles

The winners of the men's doubles each receive identical cups donated by Oxford University in 1883 and by Sir Herbert Wilberforce in 1937. This event has had a draw of 64 pairs since 1921, and the most prolific winners were the Doherty brothers, who took the title eight times between 1897 and 1905. Other multiple winners were Ernest and William Renshaw (seven times between 1880 and 1889), Herbert and Wilfred Baddeley (four times between 1888 and 1896), John Newcombe and Tony Roche (five times between 1965 and 1974) and Peter Fleming and John McEnroe (four times between 1979 and 1984). The event has always been scheduled to be played throughout as the best of five sets, though there have been occasions when, because of the weather, some rounds have had to be curtailed to the best of three.

Identical cups for the women's and mixed doubles were presented by Princess Marina and the family of an early champion, Sidney Smith, in 1949. The women's doubles draw was increased to 64 in 1985, whereas the mixed has been increased, reduced and increased again. There was a draw of 80 pairs from 1931 to 1975, when it was cut to 64. In 1977 it was reduced to 48 pairs, then increased again to 56 in 1984 and 64 in 1986. Elizabeth Ryan has won the most titles in each event, with various partners — 12 women's doubles between 1914 and 1934, and seven mixed between 1919 and 1932. Three men have each won four mixed titles: Vic Seixas, Ken Fletcher and Owen Davidson.

The challenge round was abolished in all events in 1922, and seeding was introduced in 1927. The only unseeded player to win a singles title was Boris Becker in 1985, though there have been many occasions when unseeded pairs have won doubles titles. Since 1986 all five events have included sixteen seeds in the draw.

Wimbledon has always run like clockwork, and the smooth organization is a credit to year-long planning for each tournament. Every last detail is carefully scrutinized, and no other tournament can match it for efficiency and consideration towards players and public alike.

Royal patronage

Continual patronage by the British Royal Family has done much to lend it prestige and media attention. King George V and Queen Mary were regular visitors, and their second son, who later became King George VI, actually took part in the men's doubles in 1926. (He and Sir Louis Grieg were current Royal Air Force tennis champions and thus in those days eligible to compete, though they were beaten in the first round.)

Princess Marina, wife of the Duke of Kent, was President of the All England Club for some years and in this capacity presented the trophies; after her death in 1968, she was succeeded as President by her son, the present Duke, who always attends the finals with the Duchess, herself a tennis player. Queen Elizabeth visited the Championships in 1957, 1962 and 1977, while the Princess of Wales and the Duchess of York are regular visitors in the 1980s. The Royal Box, which commands the Centre Court, is always filled with distinguished guests from the worlds of politics, show business and industry.

The courts

There is always plenty to see at Wimbledon. All 18 courts are kept busy with the early rounds of the principal five events during the first week, then the later rounds occupy the show courts, while the Ladies' Plate, junior events and men's 35-and-over competitions are played on the outside courts during the second week.

The Centre Court, the most famous arena in tennis, has changed little in its interior appearance since it was built. Octagonal in shape, it is roofed all the way round, and painted entirely dark green to blend with the lawn in the centre. The stands are reached via a labyrinth of corridors and staircases, and the atmosphere inside is unique.

It is usually full, except late in the evening, and the sense of history is undeniable. There have been so many great occasions enacted within this stadium that to replace it for a bigger arena would be unthinkable. It has the solemnity of a cathedral, but on major

Above: Elizabeth Ryan at Wimbledon in 1954. She won more doubles titles than anyone else in the history of The Championships, and until 1979 (when she was overtaken by Billie Jean King) she held the record of most titles overall.

Opposite: Billie Jean King won the women's singles for the second time in 1967. She is seen displaying the silver salver that has been presented to every winner of the title since 1886.

occasions for celebration it erupts into a vibrancy that is hard to match. There are no sponsors' banners, as in other sporting arenas, and what advertising there is, such as the Rolex name on the electronic scoreboards, the Slazenger logo on the fixtures, and the Coca-Cola logo on the umpire's chair, is discreet.

Players find the Centre Court intimidating on their first appearance — there is a large area of grass between the court and the barriers — but once used to it, they derive incomparable inspiration. One of the grandest occasions on the Centre Court was in 1977, when all living singles champions went on parade and were presented with commemorative medals by the Duke and Duchess of Kent.

Court No 1, alongside, is also impressive and atmospheric. There are covered stands at

Below: While doubles partner Jimmy Connors fixes himself a drink between games, Ilie Nastase turns the tables on photographers at Wimbledon in 1973. Connors and Nastase won the men's doubles title that year — in more recent years, Connors has confined himself to the singles.

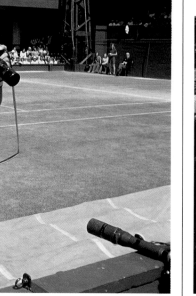

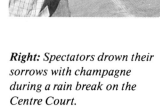
Right: Spectators drown their sorrows with champagne during a rain break on the Centre Court.
Far right: A staircase leading up to the Centre Court is turned into a waterfall during a torrential downpour at Wimbledon in 1985.
Above right: No play until further notice: when it rains at Wimbledon, a tent-like tarpaulin is hoisted over the Centre Court to allow the grass to 'breathe'.

surroundings are the dark green concrete buildings added during the past few years. Court 14 has a temporary stand.

Beyond this row lies Aorangi Park, with a large Food Village, concession-holders' marquees, a waitress-service public restaurant, shops, and a set of practice courts. Even if rain has stopped play, there is plenty to occupy the visitor.

Attendance records

Over 400,000 people attend the tournament during its 13 days. This official total has, in recent years, been surpassed by the US Open, but that meeting holds two separate sessions per day. Wimbledon's programme each day begins at 12.30 and continues until dusk — around 9 pm. Admission charges are remarkably low considering the amount of entertainment that is to be enjoyed. There is no refund in the event of no play — but there have only been 25 days without any play whatsoever in the 100 years of the Championships. And there have been only nine occasions when the programme has overrun into an extra day. Uniquely among grass-court tournaments, every event — major and minor — has always been finished.

In 1982, for example, there was so much rain during the fortnight that all sorts of contingency arrangements were made. On the final day, the first round of the mixed doubles was still unfinished, yet the referee managed to get the final played before dusk. However, there remained one final unplayed — that of the boys' doubles — and this was solemnly held the following day, for the sake of the players involved.

Unlike the other Grand Slam championships, it is rare for home players to figure in the later stages these days. No Briton has won the men's singles or doubles since 1936, the women's doubles since 1956 or the women's singles since 1977. But there has been a measure of British success in the mixed doubles, with John Lloyd twice sharing the title with Australia's Wendy Turnbull in 1983/4 and an all-British partnership, Jeremy Bates and Jo Durie, triumphing in 1987. In the singles, however, no Briton has survived the quarter-finals since 1978, and it is in the minor events like the Ladies' Plate and the juniors that they have their best hopes of picking up a title.

Tennis as a sideline

The first Wimbledon Championship of 1877 had an entry of 22, most of the competitors players of real tennis and rackets. The title was won by Spencer W. Gore, a 27-year-old surveyor and former pupil of Harrow (the famous school where many great men, including Winston Churchill, were educated). The final, in which Gore beat William Marshall, a former Cambridge University tennis 'blue', 6-1, 6-2, 6-4, was actually delayed a day as most people involved in various ways wanted to see the Eton vs

Left: The 'Old Contemptibles' at Wimbledon. Seats are always reserved for veterans of the First World War who live in London's famous Chelsea Barracks.

either end, and a huge open stand on one side which is higher than any bank of seats on the Centre Court. Finals take place here only if the programme has been telescoped by bad weather, but this court has been used for many Davis Cup and Wightman Cup ties in the past. Centre and No 1 are the two courts where matches have full television coverage, though cameras are positioned to show action from some of the other main courts as well.

On the other side of the main concourse, across from the two principal stadia, are courts 2 to 5. Court 2 has grandstands on both sides, while Court 3 has one. The next row of courts, numbers 6 to 10, includes small stands between Courts 6 and 7, then the third row of courts, 11 to 13, includes a large temporary stand beside Court 13. On the other side of the Centre and No. 1 Courts is the row of four new courts, brought into use in 1980. Here, the ambience is rather different — there is no view of the main entrance to the club, surrounded by Virginia creeper, and the

Harrow cricket match, which always took place on the second Saturday of July.

Gore himself was sceptical about the future of lawn tennis as a major sport. Fifteen years later, in 1892, he wrote, 'That anyone who has really played well at cricket, [real] tennis, or even rackets, will ever seriously give his attention to lawn tennis, beyond showing himself to be a promising player, is extremely doubtful, for in all probability the monotony of the game as compared with others would choke him off before he had time to excel in it.'

The following year, as champion, Gore was not required to play through the tournament, and a 23-year-old coffee planter on leave from Ceylon, Frank Hadow, came through to challenge him for the trophy. Hadow won, 7-5, 6-1, 9-7 — and never played tennis at Wimbledon again. In fact, he did not return until 1926, when he was persuaded to attend the 50th anniversary celebrations.

Hadow was succeeded in 1879 by John Hartley, a 33-year-old clergyman from North Yorkshire. He had to travel home in the middle of the tournament to take Sunday services, then returned to play the all-comers' final against Vere St Leger Gould, younger son of an Irish baronet. Gould, who was beaten 6-2, 6-4, 6-2, attained notoriety in later life as a convicted murderer and died on Devil's Island in 1909. Hartley retained his title in 1880, beating Herbert Lawford. But

this was the end of lawn tennis being played by competitors who preferred other racket sports.

The pioneering twins

1881 saw the beginning of the Renshaw era, in which twin brothers dominated the tournament throughout the decade. Instead of playing the game in the style of real tennis or rackets, they pioneered a technique that was wholly appropriate for the outdoor, grass-court game. William Renshaw ousted Hartley as champion in 1881 and took the title six more times, while Ernest took it once. Following the Renshaws, the youngest champion for 80 years to come, Wilfred Baddeley — who was 19 when he took his first title in 1891 — won three times.

There were three winners from Ireland — Willoughby Hamilton, Joshua Pim and Harold Mahoney. In fact, the Irish achieved domination of the tournament in 1890, with all three titles going to players from the Emerald Isle — Hamilton, Lena Rice in the women's singles, and Pim and Frederick Stoker in the doubles. However, their pre-eminence coincided with a slump, as entries and attendance declined.

Taking on the world

It was the arrival of two more brothers — Laurie and Reggie Doherty — that revived the tournament's sagging fortunes towards the end of the century. This pair ruled the courts from 1897 to 1906. They not only revitalized Wimbledon but took on the world as well, being instrumental in winning the Davis Cup for the British Isles.

Apart from Ireland, which was then part of the United Kingdom, overseas players appeared first in 1884, with three American challengers — James Dwight, Richard Sears (the US champion) and A. L. Rives. The first American woman at Wimbledon, Marion Jones, took part in 1900. But it was not until 1905 that a foreign player actually took a title, in the person of May Sutton, who hailed from California. Two years later, an Australian, Norman Brookes, took the men's singles for the first time. Apart from Arthur Wentworth Gore — who was the oldest champion at 41 when he took the title in 1909 — Brookes and his Australasian Davis Cup team-mate, Anthony Wilding, owned the trophy up until the outbreak of the First World War.

Championships of the World

From 1913 to 1923 the tournament was officially known as the Championships of the World on Grass. This was at the behest of the International Lawn Tennis Federation, which was established in 1913. They also had a World Championship on Hard Courts in Paris during those years, and a World Covered Court meeting that moved around Europe, being held at such venues as Stockholm, Paris, London, Copenhagen, St Moritz and Barcelona. But all these titles were

Below: Alice Marble gets ready for a forehand drive at Beckenham. This has always been one of a series of grass court tournaments in June leading up to Wimbledon.

Left: When The Championships celebrated their Golden Jubilee in 1926, the King and Queen of England met all former singles champions in a special ceremony on the Centre Court. Queen Mary, who was a great supporter of tennis, is seen here with 1926 champion Jean Borotra.

scrapped in 1923 at the insistence of the US Lawn Tennis Association, who objected to Wimbledon having this extra kudos. Since then, there have been no World Championships as such in tennis, although there has been a circuit called WCT (World Championship Tennis) since 1971. In addition, the ITF now annually elect World Champions in men's and women's play.

Wimbledon resumed in 1919 with a new men's champion from Australia, Gerald Patterson, and the best challenge round ever in the women's singles, in which 19-year-old Suzanne Lenglen defeated Dorothea Lambert Chambers after saving two match points. Apart from one year when she was ill, Lenglen dominated the women's events for the next five years, while 1920 and 1921 saw the first two victories of the great American player, Bill Tilden.

In 1922 the All England Club moved from Worple Road to Church Road, and the challenge round was abolished. From 1924 to 1929 the men's singles was won every year by a Frenchman — Jean Borotra, Rene Lacoste and Henri Cochet taking two titles apiece. In 1925 the only non-Gallic winner was America's Elizabeth Ryan, who shared the women's doubles with Lenglen.

The early 1930s saw a spell of US domination, with Tilden, Sidney Wood, Ellsworth Vines and Helen Wills Moody collecting the silverware, although there was a unique all-German women's final in 1931. Then in the middle of the decade the British enjoyed their first years of glory since the early years of the century. Apart from Kitty McKane Godfree, who had taken the women's singles twice in the 1920s, no home player had triumphed since Arthur Gore in 1909. Fred Perry took the men's singles three years running from 1934 to 1936, Dorothy Round the women's in 1934 and 1937, Pat Hughes and Raymond Tuckey the men's doubles in 1936, Freda James and Kay Stammers the women's doubles in 1935 and 1936, and Perry and Round the mixed in 1935 and 1936. After this the Americans regained control, with Don Budge, Bobby Riggs and Alice Marble closing out the last years before the Second World War.

The war years

The club was badly damaged by bombs during this war, and when competition resumed in 1946 part of the Centre Court was unusable. It was remarkable that the first post-war men's singles champion came from France. Yvon Petra, who had been a prisoner of war during the hostilities, was the last man to wear long trousers on the Centre Court until the American player, Trey Waltke, did so in 1983, in a move intended to gain himself a clothing endorsement.

The only country in which competitive tennis had not been interrupted by the war was the United States, and in the women's game this nation was supreme, providing every winner until 1959. Indeed, such was their domination that for the first ten Championships after the war, only one non-American — South Africa's Sheila Summers, in 1947 — penetrated as far as the semi-finals. During this spell, a series of fine, aggressive players — Pauline Betz, Louise Brough (four times), Margaret Osborne du Pont, Doris Hart, Maureen Connolly (three times), Shirley Fry and Althea Gibson (twice) — received the champion's salver from Princess Marina.

Americans took the men's title for most of this period as well. Apart from Frank Sedgman of Australia (1952) and Jaroslav Drobny, representing Egypt (1954), sons of Uncle Sam successively lifted the men's cup in the persons of Jack Kramer, Robert Falkenburg, Ted Schroeder, Budge Patty, Dick Savitt and Tony Trabert.

The late 1950s and 1960s witnessed a shift of strength to the Australians, with Lew Hoad, Ashley Cooper, Neale Fraser, Rod Laver, Roy Emerson, John Newcombe and — in women's play — Margaret Smith coming to the fore. The only non-Australians to triumph during this stage were Alex Olmedo (1959), Chuck McKinley (1963) and Manuel Santana (1966). The women's game entered a period with no particular nation in the ascendancy, with Maria Bueno (three times), Smith (twice) and Angela Mortimer having their share of glory among the wins of Karen Susman and Billie Jean King.

Throwing the game open

The rapid succession of different champions among the men was largely due to the defection of the majority to the professional game, which automatically barred them from

Above: Royalty has always been closely associated with Wimbledon. Princess Marina, who was President of the All England Club for many years, presents the women's singles trophy to Maureen Connolly after the 1954 final, as runner-up Louise Brough looks on.
Right: King George VI attended the 1947 men's singles final, and is pictured presenting the trophy to Jack Kramer. Queen Elizabeth (later the Queen Mother) is seen second from left.

competing at Wimbledon and other events under the control of amateur associations. Throughout the late 1950s and 1960s the British LTA campaigned vigorously for the game to be thrown open, and they finally took the bull between the horns at the end of 1967 and declared that, from 1968, Wimbledon and other major British tournaments would welcome contract professionals as competitors.

As a preliminary exercise, and as a tangible means of throwing down the gauntlet to the ILTF, who were predominantly opposed to open tennis, the All England Club staged a remarkable one-off professional tournament on the Centre Court in August 1967. Sponsored and televised by one of the British TV networks, it featured eight top players and was won by Rod Laver. In due course, the ILTF were forced by a chain of events — including support from the USLTA, which swung the balance — into accepting the revolution and sanctioning a number of major tournaments in 1968 as open to the professionals.

The first open Wimbledon was notable for dreadful weather during the first week, which prevented the meeting from improving on the previous year's record attendance, when it had broken the 300,000 barrier for the first time. Laver, who had last won the title as an amateur in 1962, justified his top seeding by winning the men's singles with a straight-set final victory over Tony Roche.

As in earlier open events at Bournemouth, Paris, Beckenham and Queen's Club, it was proved that the contract pros were not in a different league from the amateurs, with three of the top four — Ken Rosewall, Andres Gimeno and Pancho Gonzales — all losing before the quarter-finals. In fact, among 16 seeds — the highest total since 1950 — Rod

Left: Rod Laver was the first open Wimbledon champion in 1968. For this occasion, the old gold-plated Challenge Cup was revived as the trophy presented on court to the men's singles winner. (There are three trophies in all associated with the title.)

Laver, always a consistent player, was the only one among the top eight to reach his allotted position in the draw.

The women's singles was not affected by the change, as the four current contract pros had all taken part the previous year. Billie Jean King took the title for the third year running over seventh-seeded Judy Tegart of Australia. But the only one of the five major titles that did not go to contract pros was the mixed doubles, regained by Ken Fletcher and Margaret Court over the first ever finalists from the USSR, Alex Metreveli and Olga Morozova.

Longest match ever played

Laver retained his men's title in 1969, but King was deposed in the women's final by the British professional, Ann Jones, who more than any other player had benefited from the rigours of contract play. The year was also noteworthy for the longest match ever played at Wimbledon, with the 41-year-old Gonzales coming from behind to beat 25-year-old Charles Pasarell 22-24, 1-6, 16-14, 6-3, 11-9 in the first round. It is unlikely that a match of that length can ever be played again, as tiebreaks now operate in all tennis events except in the final set.

In 1970, Laver lost his title sensationally to Britain's Roger Taylor in the fourth round, and there were two exceptional finals to round off an otherwise rather dull fortnight. John Newcombe, the last of the amateur champions in 1967, regained the title against the will of the crowd by defeating veteran Ken Rosewall — twice a finalist in the 1950s. Court and King fought out a titanic 14-12, 11-9 women's final, won by the Australian, which beat the 1919 record for the longest final, set by Lenglen and Lambert Chambers.

Newcombe retained his title in 1971, while the women's crown was seized by the enchanting young part-Aboriginal, Evonne Goolagong. This was the year that the tiebreak was introduced, though until 1979 it was to be played at 8-all in a set, instead of 6-all as in the US.

Then came two years in which only a few of the best men took part at Wimbledon. In 1972 there was a major political schism between the ILTF and the new WCT (World Championship Tennis) organization, which controlled all the contract professionals. As a result, none of the contract pros competed at any open tournament in 1972 until the US Open, by which time the breach had been repaired. However, Wimbledon hardly suffered, and the comparative weakness of the draw was more than compensated by a thrilling final won by Stan Smith over Ilie Nastase. Rain had prevented a Saturday finish, and for the first time in the event's history the last round was contested on a Sunday. (Up till then, the British had forbidden sport on the Sabbath, although it was practised in most other parts of the world.)

The women's singles created even more interest, because the most highly publicized debut of any player since Maureen Connolly 20 years earlier was to take place. Chris Evert, whose precocious skills had taken her to the semi-finals at Forest Hills the previous autumn, duly reached the semi-finals and an intriguing first meeting with the reigning champion, Evonne Goolagong. The Australian, who was three years older than Evert, won an absorbing tussle 4-6, 6-3, 6-4, but in the final she was swept aside by a revitalized Billie Jean King.

Player-power

The 1973 event was a milestone regretted by some and hailed by others as a breakthrough for player-power. The fledgling male players' union, the Association of Tennis Professionals, held Wimbledon to ransom by demanding that they accept as a competitor Nikki Pilic, who had been suspended by his national association for declining to represent Yugoslavia in that year's Davis Cup. The All England Club, faced with the alternative of a mass player boycott, refused to yield.

Accordingly, all but three of the 82-strong

Opposite: Pancho Gonzales was 41 years old when he won the longest match ever played at Wimbledon in 1969. He defeated Charlie Pasarell — a man almost half his age — by 22-24, 1-6, 16-14, 6-3, 11-9 over two days.

Left: Evonne Cawley (née Goolagong) won her second Wimbledon singles title nine years after the first one, in 1980. She was also the first mother to win the women's singles since Dorothea Lambert Chambers in 1914.

players' union pulled out of the tournament, the exceptions being Nastase, Taylor and an Australian, Ray Keldie. The deadline fell halfway through the qualifying tournament, which was promptly cancelled, as all the players involved would now get straight in. Both sides claimed a moral victory out of this sad affair: the players proved that they would no longer take orders from the traditional administration, while the establishment declared that Wimbledon was bigger than the players, and proved their point by noting the highest attendance since the game went open.

Top-seeded Nastase missed his best ever chance of winning the singles, and crashed out in the fourth round to an American college player, Sandy Mayer (though Nastase won the doubles with Jimmy Connors, a non-ATP member). Ultimate winner was Jan Kodes, who survived a titanic semi-final against Taylor and defeated Metreveli in a unique all-Eastern bloc final. In a one-sided women's singles final Billie Jean King took the triple crown for the second time in her career, beating Chris Evert.

The 1974 Championships was a very wet fortnight, and so telescoped was the programme that the men's semi-finals and women's final had to be played on the same afternoon. Evert took the women's title for the first time, while Rosewall, at 40 the oldest finalist since Norman Brookes in 1919, and 20 years after his first title match, got through over Newcombe and Smith. But in the final, reality was cruelly imposed as he was hammered off the court by 21-year-old Connors.

Arthur Ashe clinically bludgeoned Con-

nors' fire-power in the 1975 final, while King annihilated Evonne Goolagong, now Mrs Cawley, for her sixth women's title. The following year — the hottest British summer on record — saw the beginning of the Borg era. Bjorn had previously caused 'teeny-bopper' adulation at Wimbledon with his boyish good looks and explosive power, and by now, at 20, he had matured into an invincible grass-court player. He took the 1976 championship without dropping a set, and overcame Nastase in what was to be the Romanian's last serious crack at the title. Evert regained the women's crown with a close three-set decision over Cawley.

Centenary celebrations

The Centenary Wimbledon of 1977 featured tennis worthy of the occasion. There were a number of former champions in the draw, with Bueno, Susman and Jones all making nostalgic reappearances. There was also the debut of 14-year-old Tracy Austin, which caused as much media attention as the arrival of Evert five years earlier. But it was to be a glorious British victory that really set the seal on the tournament, with Virginia Wade, at her 16th attempt, claiming the women's singles before the Queen, who was making a rare visit to mark her own Silver Jubilee. Borg took his second title after two sensational matches in the last two rounds, against Vitas Gerulaitis and Connors.

Borg and Connors once more contested the men's final in 1978, though this time there was an easy victory for the Swede. Martina Navratilova took the first of her record-

Below: Ilie Nastase clowns in typical fashion during a match in which he felt it was raining too hard for play to continue. Nastase never won the Wimbledon singles, although he was runner-up in 1972 and 1976.

Left: *Chris Evert is pictured in 1975. Her overall record in Grand Slam singles events is superior to any other player, inasmuch as she has reached at least the semi-finals of all but two events each time she has entered since 1971. She won at least one Grand Slam singles title each year between 1974 and 1986.*

Right: Bjorn Borg and John McEnroe before their momentous Wimbledon men's singles final of 1981. Borg had won the title for five successive years, but McEnroe was to bring his run to an end with a four-set victory.

equalling eight women's titles, outlasting Evert in a close finish. At the time, Navratilova, having defected from her native Czechoslovakia three years earlier, was officially stateless, but the influence of the Duchess of Kent helped sway the Czech authorities to allow her mother to travel to Wimbledon to see her retain the title the following year.

With Borg and Navratilova triumphing again in 1979, the main interest switched to the doubles, in which King finally beat the record number of Wimbledon titles she had jointly shared with Elizabeth Ryan for the last four years. By winning the women's doubles with Navratilova, King set up an all-time best of 20 championships, which she had begun collecting 18 years earlier. Ryan, by now a frail 87, did not live to see her record surpassed. She died at Wimbledon the previous day.

Thrilling finals

At the 1980 Championships, Borg became the first player to win five consecutive singles titles since the abolition of the challenge round, while Evonne Cawley became the first mother since 1914 to win the women's singles. The men's final featured perhaps the most exciting tiebreak ever, in the fourth set, with the score swinging between what were match-points for Borg and setpoints for John McEnroe. The latter eventually won the set,

but the Swede triumphed at the end of one of the finest finals of all time. The women's final was a joyous occasion between two of the most loved players of the era — particularly for the British fans as both Cawley and Evert Lloyd had British husbands. The Australian set another record in becoming the first woman to regain the title after a nine-year gap.

The Borg era came to an end in 1981, with McEnroe reversing the previous year's final. but he was a controversial champion, and such was his abrasive behaviour (he missed the traditional Champions' Dinner at the close of the meeting) that the All England committee departed from tradition and did not offer him honorary membership of the club, as was customary. This was not rectified until he won for the second time in 1983. Evert Lloyd, meanwhile, took her third title over the young Czech, Hana Mandlikova.

Jimmy Connors bounced back after an eight-year gap to win his second crown in 1982. The Wimbledon fortnight had been bedevilled with appalling weather and a public transport strike, which prevented crowds of the usual size from attending the tournament. This was the first year that it was scheduled to finish on the second Sunday (though the first Sunday remains a day off). In a final marred by tempestuous outbursts from both players, Connors beat McEnroe after a 4 hour 16 minute marathon — in terms

Left: Posing appropriately in front of the Stars and Stripes, 1982 Wimbledon champions Jimmy Connors and Martina Navratilova are seen with the then Chairman of the All England Club, Sir Brian Burnett.

of duration, the longest final on record. McEnroe subsequently took part in the men's doubles final, which because of the lateness of the hour was reduced to the best of three sets for the only time in Wimbledon's history. McEnroe, mentally and physically exhausted, and his partner Peter Fleming were swiftly defeated by the Australians, Peter McNamara and Paul McNamee. The women's title was regained by Navratilova, who began a record-breaking sequence of six successive victories.

In 1983 McEnroe, this time behaving and playing impeccably, routed the first finalist from New Zealand in 69 years, Chris Lewis. Navratilova romped to victory against an 18-year-old finalist, Andrea Jaeger, who had beaten the 40-year-old King in the semi-finals. The same two winners emerged in 1984, with Connors gaining just four games against McEnroe and Evert Lloyd losing to Navratilova for the fourth time in the final.

Three records in one

Boris Becker shot into the record books on three counts in 1985. He was the youngest ever men's champion at 17, the first unseeded winner, and the first German. The event followed an extraordinary course, with Kevin Curren, a South African-born US citizen, routing both McEnroe and Connors by wide margins to reach the final, where he was narrowly defeated by the ferociously serving Becker. Navratilova and Evert Lloyd once again contested the women's final, with the former winning in three sets.

Becker retained his title in 1986 over Ivan Lendl, while Navratilova repulsed the challenge of Mandlikova. At this 100th staging of the Championships, an attempt by Navratilova to win the triple crown was once again thwarted despite her reaching all three finals. In 1985 she had missed out on the women's doubles, and this time she failed in the mixed.

The 1987 meeting brought Wimbledon its first Australian men's singles champion since 1971. Pat Cash, a rugged grass-court expert, frustrated world No 1 Lendl's hopes of winning the title for the second final running, but the real hero of the tournament was the 35-year-old Connors, who recovered from a seemingly impossible deficit of 1-6, 1-6, 1-4 to beat Mikael Pernfors in the fourth round. Becker fell at an early hurdle against an unheralded Australian, Peter Doohan, who subsequently lost to a Yugoslav who regularly distinguished himself at Wimbledon, Slobodan Zivojinovic. In 1988 Stefan Edberg became the first Swede to win since Borg. In 1987, with a change among top entrants, the women's title was expected to go to the 18-year-old West German sensation, Steffi Graf, who had not lost a match all year, but in the end she succumbed to Martina Navratilova, and she had to wait another year before becoming the first German woman to win since Cilli Aussem in 1931.

US OPEN

No major tennis tournament has changed more over the years than the United States Open championships. The second oldest of the Grand Slam events — it dates from 1881, so is four years younger than Wimbledon — has had a complicated history, involving several changes of venue and format, and it has been played on three different surfaces. Until 1988 it was the only one of the four major championships to be held at a public facility as opposed to a private club (the Australian Open has now also moved to a purpose-built venue), and since the introduction of open tennis it has also boasted the greatest prize money.

But the US championships have always suffered from something of an inferiority complex. America has invariably enjoyed the status of the strongest tennis nation, by standard of players and depth of financial resources, yet their national championships have never quite surpassed the pre-eminence of Wimbledon in terms of prestige. The organization of the tournament lacks the smooth efficiency of its British rival, and the French Open is also regarded as a better-run meeting. Currently, the demands of television, which require the climax of the US Open to be squeezed into the last two days, with scheduling that pays no heed to the convenience of the players, make it vulnerable to criticism and ridicule.

No half measures

Even so, there is no denying the fact that the US Open is the most exciting, pulsating and vibrant of the four Grand Slam championships. The location of the tournament, at Flushing Meadow Park, New York City, has much to do with this. Like New York, it is tough and uncompromising, noisy (with the constant roar of jet aircraft overhead), irreverent (the crowds are as voluble and undisciplined as they are quiet and respectful at Wimbledon) and brash (bizarre happenings, unheard of at other major events, frequently occur). There are no half measures about the US Open. You either love it or hate it. The contrasting attitudes of players exemplify this dichotomy. Ivan Lendl, who has won the men's singles for the last three years, describes Flushing Meadow as 'a beautiful place'. But Kevin Curren, in an extraordinary outburst after losing in the first round in 1985, said, 'They should drop an A-bomb on it!'

The National Tennis Centre, constructed on and around the old Louis Armstrong Stadium, site of the 1948 World Fair, is the latest of a string of venues for the US championships. Until the arrival of open tennis in 1968, the events were played at different times and locations. There was an initial fixture called the 'Championship of America', open

Right: The Stadium Court at Flushing Meadow Park, New York, venue for the US Open since 1978. The site was acquired by the US Tennis Association and developed from a complex that included the old Louis Armstrong Stadium. It was used for the World Fair in 1948.

to all-comers, at the Staten Island Cricket and Baseball Club, in September 1880. It used the rackets scoring system, and the winner was an Englishman, O. E. Woodhouse, who beat a Canadian, J. F. Helmuth, in the final.

Then after the formation of the US National Lawn Tennis Association in 1881, the inaugural National Championship, restricted to US residents, was held at Newport Casino, Rhode Island, on grass. Men's singles and doubles were held from the start, while women's singles, women's doubles and mixed doubles were staged separately at the Philadelphia Cricket Club from 1887. This segregation of the sexes in US tennis remained a feature until 1935. The tournament was thrown open to players of all nationalities in 1884.

The women's events stayed at Philadelphia until 1921, and the men's singles remained at Newport until 1915, but the men's doubles moved occasionally to such venues as the Orange LTC, New Jersey, the Staten Island Club, and St George's Club, Chicago. In 1915 both men's events moved to

the West Side Club, Forest Hills, on Long Island. The women's singles and doubles joined them there in 1921, but the mixed doubles took up residence at the Longwood Cricket Club in Boston. The men's and women's singles stayed at Forest Hills right up to 1968, but the doubles events moved to Boston in 1935, where they stayed as a separate tournament, with the mixed transferring to Forest Hills in 1942. It was not until 1935 that the men's and women's events were played at the same time and at the same venues.

End of the Nationals
The introduction of open tennis brought about a duplication of championships. In 1968 and 1969 the USLTA continued the old Nationals, with all five events taking place at Boston, and excluding contract professionals, while the following two weeks they inaugurated the US Open, for all players, at Forest Hills. From 1970, the Nationals were no more, although US Amateur Championships continued elsewhere for a few more years. In 1975 the grass courts at the West Side Club were resurfaced with clay, then in 1978 the

Left: The West Side Club, Forest Hills, was venue for the US championships from 1915 until 1977. The club has continued as a top-class tennis venue by hosting the WCT Tournament of Champions in May each year. Some of the grass courts were resurfaced with clay in 1975.

tournament was resited at Flushing Meadow, where it has remained.

It was the decade between 1968 and 1978 that transformed the US Open from a comparatively obscure sporting event at an exclusive private club into a big, important festival, drawing huge crowds and increasing media interest. Although its status as one of the Big Four championships was assured from the beginning, only the leading foreign players bothered to make the trip across the Atlantic in the amateur days. The huge horseshoe-shaped stadium at the West Side Club was rarely full until the later stages — and not always then — while the organization was sloppy and erratic. Once the game went open, the USLTA made a concentrated effort to build up the tournament as a worthy rival to Wimbledon.

An area in which it was notoriously deficient was the condition of the courts, which were never good. The players complained of bad footing and appalling bounces, and the dominance of service made for generally longer sets than in England.

Sudden death

One way of reducing this problem was the introduction of the tiebreak in 1970, though in its original format it was a lottery. The 'sudden death' expedite scoring called for the first player to win five points to win a set under this system. So if the score reached four points all, even at 6 games all in the final set, it would be match point for either side. Whoever happened to be serving at the time had an obvious advantage, and a bad bounce or netcord was a cruel and unfair way of deciding a match in a major championship. Fortunately, the tiebreak scoring was brought into line with the rest of the world after a few years.

In 1974, the organizers decided to dig up the grass and lay an American clay court patented as 'HarTru'. This made for an improved playing surface, but it gave the European players a better chance, and was not popular with many of the home players, who preferred grass — even if it was sprayed with green paint, as they used to do in the later stages, by which time little natural green remained. But this was only a temporary expedient. It became obvious that the tournament had outgrown the cramped conditions at Forest Hills, and under the direction of Slew Hester, the President of the USTA (they dropped the 'Lawn' in the title in 1975), a huge new facility was constructed at Flushing Meadow.

The new centre

The surface chosen was DecoTurf II, an acrylic cement court which gives a lively bounce and in pace is about halfway between grass and clay. It was ideal for the Americans, who proceeded to dominate the tournament for the first few years after the move. But as the strength in depth of US tennis began to wane in the 1980s, corresponding with a significant resurgence from Europe, the home players took on an increasingly supporting role.

There is plenty of room for spectators to move around at Flushing Meadow, but there are drawbacks which have always been apparent. The most severe problem is the ground's siting beneath the flightpath of jet aircraft leaving from and descending to nearby La Guardia Airport. The overhead screech proved to be an intense irritation, not only for the players, but also for spectators perched high in the vast open tiers around the Stadium Court (which seats 20,000 — far more than the Centre Court at Wimbledon). With planes passing over every 90 seconds, the noise threatened people's eardrums as well as their concentration. In later years, influential USTA members were able to get the number of planes passing over reduced for important matches, but it remains a notorious hazard.

Similarly, the design of the huge stadium did not take into account the need for

spectators to reach their seats quickly. Insufficient gangways and staircases were provided, so that people arriving and leaving during changeovers are still moving all round the stadium long after the players are ready to resume play. In any case, American tennis audiences are less considerate than their European counterparts, and their entrances and exits less strictly controlled by stewards than at European tournaments.

Other problems at the US Open that tax the players' powers of concentration are varieties of odours that often assail the nostrils. The scent of frying hamburgers from the dozens of food stands dotted around the ground frequently pervades the air, and there have been other smells, such as the time the plumbing broke down and a large section of the centre reeked of sewage.

Members of the press, on arriving at Flushing Meadow for the first time in 1978, were appalled to find that their accommodation was situated right at the top of the stadium, reached either by a lift — or when that broke down, by several hundred steps. There is no separate seating and writing room, so they must watch, type and telephone their stories from the same lofty position, from which the players look like ants. When the sun was shining, which was most of the time, the heat was unbearable, and at least one writer was obliged to work lying down under the table. Since the installation of air conditioning, the press area has now turned into a refrigerator.

It is also a far less attractive place than any other major tennis venue. There is concrete everywhere. Because the facility was built so hurriedly, with less than two years between announcement and completion, the building was not of the soundest quality, and cracks in the fabric have begun to appear.

For all that, Flushing Meadow is nonetheless a splendid public tennis centre, open for court bookings all the year round except for the two weeks in early September when the tournament is in progress. There are 27 courts — ten of them covered — and ample seating

Left: Slew Hester was President of the US Tennis Association when it decided to move the US Open from Forest Hills to Flushing Meadow. It was largely through Hester's vision and determination that the great public tennis facility at Flushing Meadow came to fruition.

for all spectators, unlike Wimbledon. The old Louis Armstrong Stadium was actually divided, with the main court surrounded by seating and the adjoining Grandstand Court with seats on three sides. Those perched at the top can watch play on either court, and they also have a magnificent view of the Manhattan skyline across the East River. Road and rail links with downtown New York are good, although the railway station for Flushing Meadow also serves nearby Shea Stadium, which can cause congestion if there is a football game on there as well.

Long and tough

The US Open is the longest and toughest of all Grand Slam championships. Play lasts for 14 days, beginning at 10 am and often continuing well beyond midnight. There are separate daytime and evening sessions. The latter begin at 7.30 under floodlights, and the scheduling pays more heed to the demands of television than the convenience of the players, spectators and media. Sometimes doubles matches take place before singles, which means that an important singles match might not even get on to court until an impossibly late hour. Unlike Wimbledon, where the main show courts are always fully occupied with good matches, there can be long gaps, or unappealing programmes, which scarcely justify the high ticket prices charged. The Labor Day public holiday usually falls on the second Monday, and a good programme is essential, but it is the final three days that cause the greatest criticism.

The men's doubles final is always scheduled for the second Friday, along with the women's singles semi-finals. The following day, they must play the first men's singles semi-final, followed by the women's singles final, followed by the second men's semi-final. This requires a great amount of viewing for the spectators — many would say too much. Sandwiching the women's final between the two men's semis means that the finalists do not know what time their match is to begin, which is a regrettable shortcoming for such an important contest. Then on the last day, the men's singles final begins at the set hour of 4 pm, again to satisfy television. The other finals set for the Stadium are usually well out of the way by then, but should the women's doubles still be in progress, it must be moved on to another court. No wonder the women, who fought so hard for equal prize money and the same size draw as the men at the US Open, still feel hard done by!

Another hazard for the players necessitated by the 4 pm start is that the match, particularly if it is a long one, starts in daylight and ends under artificial illumination. One of the reasons why Bjorn Borg never won any of his four finals there was because he was disturbed by the floodlights. Each year a chorus of protest greets the USTA's insistence on these tiresome arrangements. But the value of

TV coverage is so great that they will not budge. This is because live telecast fees are so lucrative, and because the tournament's many sponsors want prime-time exposure. Each event is supported by a different corporation, and each has a number of placards around the court to catch the cameras.

Because of these various inconveniences, one might wonder why the players still turn out at virtually full strength each year. It's because the US Open is too big to miss. The prize money is better than anywhere else, it has the status of a Grand Slam championship, and the computer ranking and Grand Prix points are accordingly extremely valuable. In marketing terms, a player's earning potential through product endorsement is considerably enhanced if he or she does well in the tournament.

Uniquely among the Grand Slam titles, the US championships have continued uninterrupted through the two World Wars.

Left: John Newcombe gives equal prominence to the trophy and his racket after winning the US Open men's singles in 1973. The racket, of aluminium construction, enjoyed a brief popularity during the early 1970s.

The only year that a meeting was held without championship status was in 1917, when a grandly named 'National Patriotic Tournament' was staged.

For the record

American players dominate the list of winners, with only 26 occasions out of 107 that the men's singles has gone overseas, and 14 out of 102 in the case of the women. There have been nine Australian men champions, including a seven-year sequence from 1956 to 1962, two British, two French, and one from Sweden, Mexico, Romania, Argentina and Czechoslovakia. There have been two British women champions, and one each from Ireland, Chile, Brazil, Australia, Czechoslovakia and West Germany.

The greatest number of titles in singles, doubles and mixed has gone to Margaret du Pont (24), Margaret Court (22, including the National Championships held in addition to the Open in 1968/9), Louise Brough (17), Bill Tilden (16), Hazel Wightman (16), and Sarah Fabyan (15). Record numbers of singles titles went to Richard Sears, the first champion, who was unbeaten for seven years (and retired undefeated), equalled by Tilden, Molla Mallory (who won eight if the unofficial 1917 event is included), Helen Wills Moody, and Court (including the 1968/9 duplication).

There have also been numerous occasions when a player won the triple crown. Recent triple crown winners have been Billie Jean King (1967), Margaret Court (1970) and Martina Navratilova (1987).

Before the First World War, there was a remarkable sequence of six years when two players, Hazel Hotchkiss and Mary K. Browne, were each unbeaten in all three events for three years in a row. Don Budge was triple champion in 1938, the year he also won the Grand Slam in singles, being the first player to do so.

Multiple winners

The US Open, which of course dates as such from 1968, has been dominated by three men and four women. Jimmy Connors has the unique record of having won the men's singles on three different surfaces — on grass in 1974, on clay in 1976, and on cement in 1978, 1982 and 1983. He was also runner-up twice, in 1975 and 1977, and reached the semi-finals for 12 years in a row from 1974 to 1985, then again in 1987. Such is his extraordinary enthusiasm and durability that he has certainly been the most consistent and charismatic competitor of the open era, and with the New York crowds, the most popular as well.

John McEnroe, whose Douglaston home is only a few miles from Flushing Meadow, became the first man to win the US singles three years running (1979 to 1981) since

Right: A busy scene during the US Open at Forest Hills in 1972. In the foreground is a section of the huge horseshoe-shaped stadium that was constructed in 1923. In the background is the Tudor-style clubhouse. The grass courts were not of sufficient quality to stand up to two weeks of tournament play, with bad bounces being the rule rather than the exception.

Below right: Spectators at Flushing Meadow resemble prisoners in a penitentiary as they seek any possible vantage point for an important match.

Tilden, more than 50 years earlier. He took it once again in 1984. Not as popular with the crowd as Connors, McEnroe has nonetheless earned universal admiration for his tremendous skill and tenacity. He has also won the men's doubles three times with Peter Fleming.

Ivan Lendl, who lives within commuting distance at Greenwich, Connecticut, has appeared in each of the last six finals, losing the first three (1982 to 1984) and winning the others. His 1986 final over fellow-Czech, Miloslav Mecir, followed a women's final in which both players were also Czech-born.

Chris Evert reached the women's semi-finals every year from 1971 to 1986 and failed to do so only in 1987, when she lost in the quarter-finals to Lori McNeil. She has always been the darling of the Open spectators. At her first attempt, at the age of 16, she survived match points against Mary Ann Eisel in the second round, and it took the experience of Billie Jean King to bring her down in the last four. That round was her exit until 1975, when she began a four-year reign as champion. She lost the title to Tracy Austin (the youngest ever winner) in 1979, but regained it the following year, and again in 1982. She was losing finalist on three occasions.

Martina Navratilova has appeared in six finals and won four of them. She did not take the title until 1983, but she lost two finals in a third set tiebreak — to Austin in 1981 and to Hana Mandlikova in 1985. The other two multiple winners were Court and King, who each won three Open singles titles.

Like Wimbledon, the Nationals had a challenge round in the early years, but it was abolished in all events by 1918. More notably, the women's singles was played over the best of five sets for six years around the turn of the century. The idea of five sets for women was not revived until 1983, when the final of the Women's International Series championships at Madison Square Garden adopted the practice. To date, however, that is the only time during the year that it happens.

Above: The cement-type courts at Flushing Meadow do not readily absorb rain water, which is why a ballboy has to mop up after a shower.

FRENCH OPEN

There are many among the connoisseurs of tennis who claim that the French championships meeting is the best of all tournaments. Held during the last week of May and the first week of June at the Stade Roland Garros, near the Bois de Boulogne in the west Parisian suburb of Auteuil, it is the most important tournament played on red clay. Whereas the faster surfaces of grass, cement and carpet place a greater emphasis on serve-volley skills, and reduce the chance of interesting rallies, clay is the surface that brings out the artistry and variation of great players who can use the court like a chessboard.

Epicurean's delight

Paris is regarded as more relaxed and civilized than the meticulous regimentation of Wimbledon or the hurly-burly of Flushing Meadow. The atmosphere is friendlier, and everything about the tournament is an epicurean's delight, from the stylish outfits of the court officials to the cuisine and hospitality. Anyone who has visited Paris in the late spring will know that it is one of the pleasantest places to be at that time of year.

The French championships are traditionally the culmination of the European clay court circuit, which takes in the Monte Carlo, German and Italian Opens. In recent years it has been the only one of these great meetings where the men and women still play side-by-side, and since 1983 the five major events have had draws of 128 for both men's and women's singles, and 64 pairs in each doubles field. Like the other three Grand Slam fortnights, there are also international junior events for players aged 18 and under.

A gap of only two weeks separates the French Open from Wimbledon, so many players eliminated in the early rounds of the singles leave for England to play in the grass court tournaments already in progress there as preparation for Wimbledon, rather than stay in Paris. As a result, the French doubles lack as much strength in depth as their other Grand Slam counterparts.

Players who prefer faster surfaces sometimes give European clay a miss, as their computer rankings are likely to suffer. The Europeans and South Americans, who perform best on the *terre battue* as it is known, have ruled the French men's singles since 1969. No American has won the title since 1955, although John McEnroe came very close in 1984. Australians won nine times between 1956 and 1969, though only one — Phil Dent, in 1977 — has reached the semifinals since then.

Stade Roland Garros occupies a much smaller site than any of the other Grand Slam locations. There were plans to rebuild the huge Centre Court in the late 1970s, but sufficient finance could not be raised, so it

Left: Stade Roland Garros, venue for the French Open, occupies a considerably smaller area than those of the other three Grand Slam championships. But it has been beautifully refurbished in recent years, and the large new stadium to the left of the picture has proved to be a valuable site for important matches.

was superbly restored in 1980. Like the stadium at Flushing Meadow, it is an open arena, with high tribunes that allow seating for about 14,000. There are ten other courts, and the whole facility, which is the headquarters of the French Tennis Federation, is beautifully laid out, with many trees and flowers adding to the colour. Due in no small part to Philippe Chatrier, now President of the ITF, the tournament has been much improved during the last decade, with sensible scheduling and excellent provision for players, spectators and media alike.

Early beginnings

As an international tournament, the French championships dates only from 1925. Prior to that it was restricted to members of French clubs (which could include foreigners) and held at the Ile de Puteaux on the River Seine. The first championship, in 1891, was won by an Englishman, J. Briggs, as was the doubles title (F. Warden and Wynes), and in later years the best French player before the first World War, Max Decugis, won the men's singles eight times. The women's championship began in 1897, with Suzanne Lenglen winning four times from 1920.

In 1912 the World Hard Court Championships began at the Stade Français, St Cloud. They continued there in 1913 and 1914, and resumed after the war in 1920 and 1921. In 1922 the tournament was held in Brussels, but it returned to Paris in 1923. The titles then ceased to exist, but a major international event was held in Paris, at the Stade Colombes, in the form of the tennis programme for the 1924 Olympic Games.

Below: Guillermo Vilas, winner of the French men's singles in 1977, shows off the trophy. In his winning final against America's Brian Gottfried he lost only three games in three sets.

The inauguration of the French championships as an open tournament for all nationalities in 1925 had St Cloud as its venue, then the 1926 tournament took place at the Racing Club of France at Auteuil. In 1927 it returned to St Cloud. But now the city needed a large new stadium to accommodate the large number of people that wished to see France defend the Davis Cup, which it had won for the first time in 1927.

Accordingly, the City of Paris gave to the French Federation a site of about three hectares at the Auteuil Gate, and the Stade Français and Racing Club joined forces to build the new venue. It was named after Roland Garros, a famous aviator who was killed in aerial combat in 1918. He had been a member of the Stade Français athletics team.

This has been the tournament's permanent home ever since. There was a break in competition during the Second World War, and the first year after the championships resumed in 1946 they were held after Wimbledon, in late July. There have been some tinkerings with the format, for example in 1972, when a *tableau finale* draw was used, with the best players exempt to the last 32. But it did not catch on, nor did an experiment in

Left: *A view of the outside courts at Roland Garros. The French championships have been held there since 1928 — prior to that, they alternated between clubs at St Cloud and Auteuil.*

the early 1970s to reduce the early rounds of the men's events to best-of-three set matches.

The champions

Players of 13 nationalities have won the French men's singles since 1925. Australians have won most often, with eight champions, including three — Ken Rosewall, Rod Laver and Roy Emerson — who each won twice. France comes second, with five winners, of which Henri Cochet triumphed four times, and Rene Lacoste three times. The United States have also had five winners, with Frank Parker and Tony Trabert succeeding twice. Three Swedes — Bjorn Borg six times, Mats Wilander three, and Sven Davidson — have had their name on the trophy, and two Czechs — Ivan Lendl three times and Jan Kodes twice. Germany's Gottfried von Cramm (twice) and Henner Henkel won in the 1930s, and two winners have come from Spain (Manuel Santana twice and Andres Gimeno) and Italy (Nicola Pietrangeli and Adriano Panatta). Nations with sole winners are Egypt (twice, through Jaroslav Drobny), Great Britain (Fred Perry), Hungary (Joseph Asboth), Romania (Ilie Nastase) and Argentina (Guillermo Vilas).

Players from the United States have had by far the greatest share of the women's singles, which is played for the Coupe Suzanne Lenglen. There have been 12 American winners, led by Chris Evert (seven titles), Helen Wills Moody (four), and two each for Margaret Osborne du Pont, Doris Hart, Maureen Connolly and Martina Navratilova. The other American winners were Pat Todd, Shirley Fry, Althea Gibson, Darlene Hard, Nancy Richey and Billie Jean King. Second in the league is Great Britain, with six winners — Peggy Scriven (twice), Angela Mortimer, Shirley Bloomer, Christine Truman, Ann Haydon Jones (twice) and Sue Barker. There have also been eight Australian victories, divided among three women: Margaret Smith Court (five), Lesley Turner (two), and Evonne Goolagong. France has had four winners: Lenglen (twice), Simone Mathieu (twice), Nellie Landry, and Françoise Durr. Two Germans — Steffi Graf (twice) and Cilli Aussem — have succeeded, and one each from the following nations: Denmark (Hilde Sperling, three times), Hungary (Suzi Kormoczy), Netherlands (Kae Bouman), Yugoslavia (Mima Jausovec), Romania (Virginia Ruzici), and Czechoslovakia (won by Hana Mandlikova).

The greatest number of titles in all events has been won by Court (13), Mathieu (10), Hart (10), Cochet (9), Durr (9), and Evert (9). No man has won the triple crown, but five women — Lenglen (twice), Mathieu, Hart, Connolly and Court — have achieved the feat, though the last occasion was as long ago as 1964.

Early winners

The French dominated the early years of the international championships, with their players winning all five titles in 1925, four in 1926, and three in 1927. Frenchmen took the men's singles each year until 1932, although only twice more thereafter, through Marcel Bernard (1946) and Yannick Noah (1983).

Suzanne Lenglen never played at Roland Garros, and it was Simone Mathieu, who was runner-up six times in the singles before she finally wrested the trophy in 1938/9, who was the host nation's principal contender in the 1930s. The French have been relatively uninterested in women's tennis (albeit not to the same degree as the Italians, who did not even

Right: Yannick Noah became the first French winner of the French Open men's singles for 37 years when he took the title in 1983. Noah was born in Sedan, eastern France, but spent much of his childhood in the Cameroons.

allow the women on to the Centre Court at Rome for their finals until the late 1960s). Home victories in the singles became increasingly rare after the war, so the successes of Françoise Durr (1967) and Noah were rapturously received.

The French had the distinction of staging the world's first open Grand Slam championships in 1968. The circumstances were not auspicious, with Paris crippled by a general strike in the wake of the student riots of that spring. Yet despite the lack of public transport and the restricted petrol, the tournament went ahead and attendances were huge. There were a large number of walkovers in the early rounds, as many entrants were unable to reach the city. But the contract professionals were there in force, and the men's singles went to Ken Rosewall, who had previously won it as an amateur 15 years before.

His defeated opponent in the final, Rod Laver, reversed this result the following year, on the way to his second Grand Slam. Then in 1970 and 1971 the title was won by Jan Kodes, who defeated fellow East Europeans in the final each time. A Frenchman, Patrick Proisy,

Left: Mats Wilander has won the French men's singles title in 1982, 1985 and 1988. On the first occasion he was at the time the youngest man ever to win a Grand Slam singles title — and the first to win the junior and senior events at a major tournament in consecutive years.

Above: Bjorn Borg and Chris Evert Lloyd were honoured in Paris in 1981 as World Champions. These awards were instituted in the late 1970s by the International Tennis Federation and were bestowed by panels of great champions of the past.

Right: Borg holds aloft the French men's singles trophy after winning it in 1980. He took the title six times — more than any other player since the tournament was thrown open to all nationalities in 1925.

was runner-up to Gimeno in 1972, the year when, because of the rift between the ILTF and WCT, the contract professionals were all missing. Ilie Nastase took the title over Nikki Pilic in 1973 as the storm clouds were gathering over Pilic's failure to represent Yugoslavia in the Davis Cup — an issue that was to deprive Wimbledon of 79 ATP members later in the month.

The Borg era

The following year saw the first of six victories for Borg, who was just 18 years old at the time of his first win. He made a remarkable recovery in the final against Spain's Manuel Orantes, losing the first two sets and winning the next three for the loss of only two more games. Borg retained the title in 1975 over Vilas, but in 1976 he was beaten in the quarter-finals by Panatta, who went on to add the French to the Italian crown he had gained a fortnight earlier. Borg missed the 1977 meeting due to commitments with Team Tennis in the US, and Vilas succeeded to the title with a devastating 6-0, 6-3, 6-0 demolition of Brian Gottfried, one of four Americans to reach the final since Trabert was their last winner in 1955. Borg was back in 1978 for the first of four successive titles which, added to the two he had already won, make him the holder of a record number since 1925.

He did not defend the trophy in 1982, when another Swede, Mats Wilander, succeeded to the title. Unseeded, and only 17 years of age, Wilander had the unique distinction of winning the junior and senior titles in consecutive years. He, in turn, lost to Noah in the 1983 final, while in 1984 McEnroe had the title snatched from his grasp by Lendl, who thus took a Grand Slam championship for the first time. Lendl yielded to Wilander in the 1985 final, but the Czech

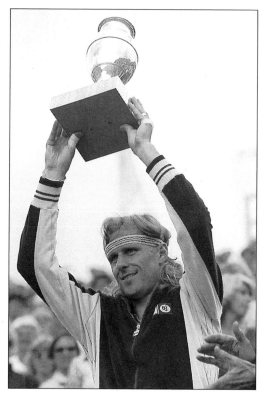

was champion again in 1986, over an unseeded Swede, Mikael Pernfors, who had toppled Stefan Edberg, Boris Becker and Henri Leconte on his way through. Lendl triumphed for the third time in 1987.

Evert's record

The women's singles at Roland Garros has been dominated in the open era by Chris Evert, who holds an all-time record seven titles. She first played there in 1973, when she lost a classic final to Margaret Court, but the following year she was in irresistible form and allowed the Russian, Olga Morozova,

Left: *The favoured courtside position, to see and be seen, is in the 'Loges' on the centre court at Roland Garros.*

only three closely fought games in the final.

Throughout the mid 1970s the women's field was badly affected by the rival demands of Team Tennis, and the overall standard was not comparable to the fields at Wimbledon and Forest Hills. Evert retained the title in 1975 over Martina Navratilova, then she herself stayed away for three years, leaving the way clear for Sue Barker, Mima Jausovec and Virginia Ruzici to grab the trophy. The prize money available was actually reduced for these years, but in 1978 the sum offered for the women's champion was increased from 35,000F to 100,000F. Evert — by now Mrs Lloyd — was back in 1979, and crushed Wendy Turnbull in the most one-sided final for over 50 years. She was similarly ruthless against Ruzici in the 1980 decider.

Evert Lloyd's first defeat in Paris for eight years came in 1981, when she was eliminated in the semi-finals by Hana Mandlikova, who went on to take the title over West Germany's Sylvia Hanika. And in 1982 she lost at the same stage to Andrea Jaeger, who dropped only four games, but was no match for Navratilova in the title round. In 1983 two favourites, Navratilova and Tracy Austin, lost to Kathy Horvath and Jo Durie respectively, and Evert Lloyd sailed serenely through for her fifth title, against Jausovec.

Navratilova and Evert Lloyd contested each of the next three finals. In 1984 Navratilova clinched the Grand Slam with a 6-3, 6-1 victory, but in both 1985 and 1986 it was the older American who came off court the winner. Her 6-3, 6-7, 7-5 victory in 1985 was one of the most exciting, high-quality women's matches ever seen. In 1987, however, when the two met in the semi-finals, Navratilova had a comfortable revenge at 6-2, 6-2, but she lost the final after being within sight of victory against Steffi Graf.

Above: *A brass band entertains the crowd before the start of the men's singles final.*
Left: *Ballboys at major tournaments are meticulously trained. At the French Open, which prides itself on style, they are also eye-catchingly dressed.*

AUSTRALIAN OPEN

Until recent years, the inclusion of the Australian Open as one of the four Grand Slam constituents was more in deference to the calibre of Australian players than the quality of the tournament itself. The country was too remote for its grass-court circuit each December and January to attract more than a token entry of good foreign players. That was a time of year when they preferred to take a couple of months off, enjoy Christmas and recharge their batteries before setting out on another season.

Paris, Wimbledon and Forest Hills were all summer tournaments (in terms of the northern hemisphere). Even the US championships did not have a significant degree of foreign participation until tennis went open, because amateurs had to be sent on official tours by their national associations, and only the wealthier ones could afford the expense. The Australian circuit, comprising state championships for Queensland, New South Wales, Victoria, and South Australia — and to a lesser degree, Western Australia and Tasmania — led up to the Australian championships, which rotated between Melbourne, Sydney, Brisbane, Adelaide and Perth. All the top Australians took part in most of these tournaments, of course, but leading foreign players rarely made the trip more than once or twice.

Potent force

Although the country's geographical isolation meant that around 90 per cent of the competitors were home-grown, logic demanded that in order to win the Grand Slam, you had to go there. Also, despite its small population, Australia's wonderful climate and tremendous sporting tradition made it a powerful force in tennis from the earliest years of the 20th century — particularly in the men's game. It was a regular winner of the Davis Cup, and when the Federation Cup came along it was frequently successful in that competition as well. In terms of individual success, Australia's record is surpassed only by that of the United States, whereas the fortunes of the other two Grand Slam host countries, Great Britain and France, declined steadily from their peak years in the early part of the century.

Competitive tennis in Australia dates from 1879, when the first Victorian Championships were staged at Melbourne. This was before any other tournament for allcomers was held outside the British Isles. (Wimbledon began in 1877, the Scottish Championships in 1878, and the Irish in 1879.) In those days, Victoria was a colony, and Australian National Championships could not begin until 1905, when the various colonies of the continent were grouped together as a commonwealth. In actual fact,

Right: The gleaming facade of the new National Tennis Centre at Flinders Park, Melbourne, Australia.

Right: *Jimmy Connors with the Australian men's singles trophy in 1974. He won three out of the four Grand Slam titles that year, missing only the French Open, from which he was barred. Remarkably, he lost each of his titles — Australia, Wimbledon and the US Open — at the final stage in 1975.*

the tournament was known until 1925 as the Australasian Championships, because the Australasian Lawn Tennis Association included New Zealand, and the tournament was twice held there — at Christchurch in 1906 and Hastings in 1912. (The two nations also competed as one in the Davis Cup until the split.)

Australian tennis has always been well organized, with superb venues. Those used for the Open, all on grass, were Kooyong, Melbourne; White City, Sydney; the Milton Ground, Brisbane; Memorial Drive, Adelaide; and King's Park, Perth. These are all marvellous facilities with perfect grass courts and large, open stadia, rather similar to Test cricket grounds in England. In 1970 the Australian LTA decided that the tournament would from then on alternate between the two biggest cities, Sydney and Melbourne, but since 1972 it has found a permanent home at Melbourne alone.

There have been three significant developments in the history of the tournament since the first Open, for which professionals were eligible, took place at Brisbane in 1969. The first development was in 1977, when the competition took place twice in the same calendar year. Until this date, the championships had always been held in January, the height of the Australian summer. But with the Grand Prix Masters now requiring an early-January slot indoors in New York, it seemed more convenient to move the Australian Open a month forward, to early December. In 1986, however, the Masters itself moved back to December, and the Australian Open accordingly reverted to January, which meant that there was no event during that calendar year.

Segregation of the sexes

The second major development was in 1980, when the LTAA agreed with the Women's Tennis Association that the women's events should be held separately. This followed a policy already adopted by other major tournaments, such as the Italian, German and South African, because the women felt that they had a raw deal in terms of match scheduling and media attention in events where they played alongside the men. At one point, there were only four championships — Wimbledon, Paris, US Open and US Clay Courts — where both sexes stayed together. The mixed doubles in Australia had in any case been discontinued after 1968.

However, this segregation lasted only three years. In 1983, in an effort to upgrade the Australian Open into one of the Big Four international meetings — equal in prestige, size, duration and prize money to the other three Grand Slam championships — the ITF asked the LTAA to restore a mixed tournament. But by holding a separate event, the strength of the women's entry had been promoted to a full international level, with all leading players taking part for the first time in its history. Mixed doubles was restored to the

programme in 1987, making for a full five-event meeting, plus junior events, with 96 in the men's singles, 64 in the women's, 48 in the men's doubles, 32 in the women's doubles, and 32 in the mixed.

Flinders Park

The third, and biggest, change came about in 1988, coinciding with the bicentennial of Australia's discovery by Captain Cook. It had been decided three years earlier that Kooyong, although owning a magnificent stadium court with seating for nearly 20,000, was too small a venue for a tournament of this size. Accordingly, the LTAA (now retitled Tennis Australia) purchased a six-hectare site in Flinders Park, near the Yarra River in Melbourne's city centre. The design incorporated three stadia, the main one having a retractable roof in case of rain and, like the US facility at Flushing Meadow, this National Tennis Centre is available to the public instead of being a private club.

The move did not receive universal approval, but it was a brave gamble that had to be made if Australia was to have a chance of reviving its flagging fortunes as a tennis nation. Instead of grass, the new venue, after considerable debate, laid a cushioned hard-court surface called Synpave Rebound Ace, which is composed of polyurethane and synthetic rubber. The playing characteristics are said to correspond to grass, but without the vagaries of natural turf.

The centre is also Tennis Australia's headquarters for the training of the country's leading juniors. One of the reasons given for Australia's decline as a tennis power since the early 1970s has been the gradual disappearance of grass as a top-class playing surface. Apart from a number of indoor Grand Prix events that are held in Australia in November and December, the main playing surface round the country remained grass, even though the rest of the English-speaking world, particularly the United States, had switched to cement. The Flinders Park facility with its hard-court surface will be a major training asset for young Australians.

Roll of champions

The infrequent participation by foreign nationalities in the Australian championships until 1969 is reflected in the few overseas names that figure on the roll of singles champions. In the men's list, non-Australian winners sometimes appear in years when a visiting team was in the country to challenge for the Davis Cup. The only ones before the Second World War were five Britons — James Parke (1912), Frank Lowe (1915), Algernon Kingscote (1919), John Gregory (1929) and Fred Perry (1934) — plus an American, F. B. Alexander (1908) and a Frenchman, Jean Borotra (1928).

Since the war, foreign winners have been more numerous, with seven Americans — Dick Savitt (1951), Alex Olmedo (1959),

Above: Stefan Edberg won the Australian singles in 1985 and 1987. There was no event held during the calendar year 1986, because it switched from December to January. Edberg's two triumphs were therefore only 13 months apart.

Denton in both of his finals, at a time when the entry reached a low ebb in terms of class, thus has the distinction of being the only South African to have won a Grand Slam singles title, although that country has produced many fine players, particularly in doubles, over the years.

In women's play, only five different nationalities have won the Australian singles. So few foreign players entered before the Second World War that the list of winners provides only two non-Australians for this period — Britain's Dorothy Round in 1935, and America's Dorothy Bundy in 1938. Top Americans began to visit in later years, with Doris Hart (1949), Louise Brough (1950), Maureen Connolly (1953), Shirley Fry (1957), Billie Jean King (1968) and Barbara Jordan (1979) taking the title. There were also British victories for Angela Mortimer (1958) and Virginia Wade (1972).

But as with the men, the standard of entry slumped alarmingly in the late 1970s, allowing Barbara Jordan (the less successful older sister of Kathy Jordan) and an Australian, Chris O'Neil, the chance to grab the silverware. In these years, when the tournament was threatened with losing its Grand Slam status, the prize money was sharply reduced. When the women's events were upgraded and held separately, however, a world-class entry appeared, reflected in the star names of the last few winners — Hana Mandlikova (1980, 1987), Martina Navratilova (1981, 1983, 1985), Chris Evert Lloyd (1982, 1984) and Steffi Graf (1988).

Margaret Court stands as the overall most prolific title winner. She holds 21 titles, including 11 singles, won between 1960 and 1973. Only just behind comes Nancye Bolton, who won 20 titles between 1936 and 1951, and Thelma Long, whose 18 titles spanned the years 1936 to 1958. Australia's best woman player in the 1920s, Daphne Akhurst, won 13 titles, as did the most successful man, Adrian Quist, between 1936 and 1950. The greatest number of men's singles victories is six, held by Roy Emerson (he lost only once between 1961 and 1967), while the oldest champion was Ken Rosewall, who won for the fourth time in 1972 at the age of 37 — 19 years after his first triumph in 1953. It was impossible to become triple champion between 1969 and 1985, when there was no mixed doubles event, and Margart Smith (later Mrs Court) was the last to do it, in 1963.

The future looks bright for this one-time Cinderella of the Grand Slams, with its splendid new venue and its vastly improved player support. Sponsored by the Ford Motor Company, it is now televised around the world and the media are flocking 'down under' in far greater numbers than ever before. Pat Cash's victory at Wimbledon in 1987 has enormously boosted the morale of the Australian players, and vast sums of money are being spent in an effort to revive the nation's golden era.

Arthur Ashe (1970), Jimmy Connors (1974), Roscoe Tanner (January 1977), Vitas Gerulaitis (December 1977) and Brian Teacher (1980). Australians monopolized the title between 1935 and 1950, and again from 1960 to 1969, but none has succeeded since Mark Edmondson was a surprise winner in 1976. Apart from Teacher, each of the last four winners have won the title two years running: Guillermo Vilas (1978/9), Johan Kriek (1981/2), Mats Wilander (1983/4), and Stefan Edberg (1985/7, bearing in mind that only 13 months separated the 1985 and 1987 tournaments). Kriek, who beat America's Steve

Team Spirit

Although tennis is not strictly regarded as a team sport, the majority of competitive tennis played around the world is on a team basis. For any player not ranked on the ATP or WITA computer rankings, competition usually means appearances in league matches against other schools, clubs or geographical divisions.

At world-class level, however, tennis has always been a lonely game. But in recent years, following the example of Team Tennis in the USA — in which major cities are represented by teams in a league system along the lines of those found in other sports — professional leagues have flourished in many parts of the world.

Being part of a team is something that many tennis players relish. A common complaint of professional players is that they cannot become too friendly with someone they will have to oppose on court the next day, so they welcome the chance to sit beside their fellow team members on the bench and cheer for one of their side in a match.

The big international events like the Davis Cup and the Federation Cup are goals for all players to strive towards. In these, tradition and patriotism are more important than the money, though in recent years generous sponsorship has ensured that the best players turn out for them. The return of tennis to the Olympics as a medal sport in 1988 after an absence of 64 years has created a new incentive.

Left: There are few more magnificent indoor venues for tennis than London's Royal Albert Hall. It regularly stages two events: the Wightman Cup match between women's teams from Great Britain and the United States; and the annual Nabisco World Doubles Championships.

Right: *The Davis Cup, donated for men's international team play in 1900, has needed two supporting plinths to be added over the years, in order to accommodate the names of the winning teams and players.*

DAVIS CUP

An enormous silver punchbowl trimmed with gold, resting on a matching double plinth, is the oldest and most prestigious team trophy in tennis. Dwight Filley Davis, a leading American player, offered it to the United States Lawn Tennis Association in 1900 to be competed for by all nations, and the competition officially became the International Lawn Tennis Championship.

The Davis Cup, as the competition has always been known, is really the blue riband event for the sport, comparable to football's Superbowl, sailing's America's Cup and golf's Ryder Cup. In most countries, particularly those that do not hold Grand Slam events, it is regarded as *the* most important competition, because it is often the only time that leading foreign players will visit — and because of the gate receipts and television fees generated by a home tie.

Major changes

Although always played right through the year, beginning early in the spring and finishing late in the year, the actual format of the competition has gone through four distinct phases. From 1900 to 1922 there was an open draw in the all-comers' section, with the winners qualifying to challenge the holders. From 1923 it was divided into European and American Zones, with an Eastern Zone being added in 1952. Then in 1972 the challenge round was abolished, long after it had been discontinued in other major tournaments. The biggest change came about in 1981, when the top 16 nations were put into a non-zonal draw, with a promotion and relegation system operating to give any other nation the chance to qualify for it.

However the format of each match, or tie, as it is also known, has remained unaltered. Each Davis Cup team consists of three to four male players. The two singles players on either team play their opposite numbers on the first day. (Each individual match within a tie is known as a rubber.) The doubles rubber takes place on the second, and the reverse singles are played on the third. There is always a draw beforehand to see whether the first strings play each other on the first day or the third, and to decide the order in which the rubbers take place.

It has sometimes been suggested that, rather than lasting the whole year, the Davis Cup should be played off in one week at one venue, as is the case in the women's equivalent, the Federation Cup. But the idea has never gained much support. The rubbers have always been played over the best of five sets, without a tie break in any set; so confining the event to one, or even two weeks, would be impracticable. The expense of travelling huge distances to play would deter minor nations (this was why zones were introduced), and of course the national associations would miss out on the profits accrued from home ties.

The streamlining of the event since 1981, which requires only four weeks of play for the World Group, has meant that leading players do not have to commit themselves to duty, at the expense of conventional tournament play, for as many weeks as they used to. And sponsorship from the Japanese electronics giant, NEC (which also supports the Federation Cup and the World Youth Cup) has guaranteed that they are not out of pocket.

Unpredictable results

Tennis is one of the most international of sports, and this is borne out by the fact that over 75 nations have participated in the competition since its inception. Until the abolition of the challenge round, only four nations had won the trophy — the United States, Great Britain (originally as the British Isles), Australia (originally as Australasia), and France. But with the holders now required to play through, and not always enjoying home advantage in their defence, the destiny of the Davis Cup is far less predictable. Since 1972, South Africa, Sweden, Italy and Czechoslovakia have all had their teams engraved upon the plinth of the famous trophy.

Since 1973, the final has been scheduled to take place at the end of the year. When it is played off in the northern hemisphere, it has usually been held indoors. The last time it was held outdoors (when not in Australia) was in 1978, when the US defeated Great Britain at Palm Springs, California.

Since 1979, the administration of the competition has been in the hands of the International Tennis Federation. Originally it had been the responsibility of the champion nation, and, at a later date, it fell to the Davis Cup Nations committee, which held its annual general meeting during the Wimbledon Championships.

For the record, the US, the original holders, have been champions 28 times, Australia 26, Great Britain 9, France 6, Sweden 4, and South Africa, Italy and Czechoslovakia once each. Other nations to have reached the challenge round or final have been (in chronological order): Belgium, Japan, Mexico, Spain, India, Romania, West Germany, Chile and Argentina. There has been one occasion when no final has taken place — in 1974, when India refused to play South Africa. The presence of the country with the apartheid regime continually disrupted the Davis Cup throughout the 1970s, and it has not competed since 1978.

Origins of the Cup

The history of the Davis Cup is virtually as long as that of international competition in tennis. Prior to 1900, few players competed abroad, but a series of visits by British players to the US championships in the 1890s, and the introduction of an international match between England and Ireland, prompted Davis to donate his trophy to the US Association. Davis, incidentally, was only 21 years old at the time. He later became US Secretary of State for War and Governor-General of the Philippines, dying in 1946.

Only one nation challenged the US for the trophy in its inaugural year. This was the British Isles. Neither of their two leading players, Laurie and Reggie Doherty, could make the trip, so their team comprised Arthur Gore (who was to win Wimbledon the following year), Herbert Roper Barrett (three times doubles champion) and Ernest Black. The US team consisted of Davis, Holcombe Ward (the reigning National doubles champions) and Malcolm Whitman, who was National singles champion. The match was staged at the Longwood Cricket Club in

Right: Laurie (left) and Reggie Doherty proved too good for the Americans in the Davis Cup of 1903, and kept the trophy in British hands for four years.

Boston on August 8–10, 1900, and the Americans won resoundingly against an ill-prepared British team. The reverse singles were abandoned because of a thunderstorm, so the result was 3-0 to the USA, for the loss of only one set.

The British did not challenge in 1901, but they returned at full strength the following year with both Doherty brothers plus Dr Joshua Pim, a distinguished Irish player who had won Wimbledon in 1893 and 1894. This time, with the match staged in New York, the visitors actually led two rubbers to one before Whitman and William Larned, the current US champion, took the two reverse singles to retain the trophy.

The Doherty brothers won the cup for the British Isles in 1903, so the latter took on the right to stage the competition in 1904. The US could not raise a team prepared to cross the Atlantic, but three European nations were attracted by the prospect of the less expensive journey to London, and Austria, Belgium and France all challenged for the first time. In the event, Austria defaulted, so Belgium defeated France for the right to take on the defenders. The British Isles easily retained the cup, 5-0, and they again retained it in 1905 against the US at Wimbledon.

Enter Australasia

In 1906 Australasia entered for the first time. Norman Brookes and Anthony Wilding readily defeated Austria, but they failed to win a rubber against the US, who in turn lost to the British. The pattern continued in 1907, but in 1908, the British were without the services of the Doherty brothers and were forced to rely on two members of their original team — Gore and Roper Barrett. Australasia's Brookes and Wilding had by now matured into first-class players, and they beat both the US and the British Isles to take the trophy 'down under' for the first time.

In 1908 the matches took place in more than one country for the first time. (Prior to this, the challengers had played off in Britain around the time of the Wimbledon Championships.) The US beat the British Isles in Boston, but they lost a close challenge round to Australasia in Melbourne. The same three nations produced the same results in 1909, but in 1910 there were no challengers, so Australasia retained the trophy by default. In 1911 the Americans defeated the British in New York and the challenge round was held in Christchurch, New Zealand, where Brookes, Rodney Heath and Arthur Dunlop accounted for Larned, Beals Wright and Maurice McLoughlin.

The US did not play in 1912, and the British sprang a surprise by taking the trophy back from Australasia in Melbourne. The return of the cup to Europe meant a considerable influx of new competitors in 1913, with Germany, Canada and South Africa all competing for the first time, along with reappearances by France and Belgium. The US beat Australasia in the first round, Germany in the second and Canada in the all-comers' final, then regained the trophy for the first time in 10 years over the British at Wimbledon. But in 1914 it was the turn of Australasia again, with Brookes and Wilding overcoming the Americans in the challenge round just after the First World War had broken out.

When competition resumed in 1919, there were only four challengers, and the US was not among them. The British Isles defeated South Africa and France to earn the right to travel to Sydney for the challenge round, but they could capture only one rubber from the defending champions.

Below: Anthony Wilding of New Zealand and Norman Brookes of Australia joined forces to win the Davis Cup for Australasia from 1907 to 1909.

Champions from over the Seas.

America's reign

Holland were first-time challengers in 1920. Although they reached the final, they only actually played one match, beating South Africa. They had a walkover from Canada (ie they were the official winners because Canada withdrew without playing), but decided not to travel to the US, giving the latter a free passage through to the challenge round. With two formidable new players in their side in Bill Tilden and Bill Johnston, America swept to victory over Brookes and the current top Australian, Gerald Patterson.

Japan, among a number of new entries in 1921, upset the usual US–Australasia–British Isles control by reaching the challenge round. They had two walkovers, then beat India in the third round and shocked Australasia 4-1 in the final. Although the Americans retained the trophy 5-0, only one of the rubbers was decided in straight sets.

In 1922 the US retained the trophy comfortably against Australasia and the same challenge round occurred in 1923, with Australasia now renamed as Australia. (New Zealand entered separately from then on.) The 1923 competition was the last to be played using an open draw. Walkovers were commonplace when nations in different continents were due to meet, so zoning was introduced to reduce the amount of travel required.

European and American Zones were instituted. Countries outside these continents could opt for which one to play in, and India chose to play in Europe, while Japan competed in America. France defeated Spain in the European Zone final, and Australia beat Japan in the American. Australia then went through to the challenge round, where the US prevailed 4-1.

Events followed a similar course in 1925, but in 1926 it was the French that emerged to challenge the might of America. Johnston and Tilden were still invincible that year, but in 1927 the tables were turned, and the Davis Cup was taken from its homeland after a six-year stay.

The Four Musketeers

France now enjoyed a six-year reign as champion nation. In 1928, 1929 and 1930 they successfully defended against the US. On the clay of Stade Roland Garros, which had been specially built for France's first defence of the Davis Cup in 1928, the so-called 'Four Musketeers' — Jean Borotra, Henri Cochet, Rene Lacoste and Jacques Brugnon — proved too strong for Tilden & Co.

Great Britain now emerged as a force once more, with stars of the calibre of Fred Perry and Herbert 'Bunny' Austin, and they defeated the US in the Inter-Zone final of 1931. Such was the importance of the Davis Cup at this time that one of the American team, Frank Shields, had earlier been obliged to forfeit the Wimbledon final against his fellow team member, Sidney Wood, because

Right: Jean Borotra (in the beret) and Jacques Brugnon were two of the French 'Four Musketeers' that owned the Davis Cup from 1927 to 1932. Borotra and Brugnon actually played doubles together twice in the challenge round.

he had strained a leg muscle in the semi-finals and his captain did not want him to aggravate the injury.

The challenge round was extremely close, with Cochet clinching victory by defeating Perry in the final rubber. In 1932 Great Britain lost to Germany, who lost to the US in the Inter-Zone final. France retained the trophy with one rubber to spare.

Back to Britain

Great Britain brought the trophy back to London for the first time for 20 years when they excitingly beat the French in the 1933 challenge round. The American Zone had by now been divided into North and South sections, while from 1933 the European draw was staggered to give the stronger nations exemption until the later stages. In 1934 and 1935 the British defended the trophy against the US, while in 1936 the Australians came through to challenge. Jack Crawford and Adrian Quist gave the holders a tougher battle than had the Americans, but Perry easily overcame Crawford in the deciding rubber.

Change of ownership

However, the rise of America's Donald Budge to No 1 in the world, following Perry's departure to the professional ranks, brought about a change of ownership in 1937. The US just scraped past Germany in the Inter-Zone final, with Budge recovering from 2-5 in the final set of the final rubber to beat Gottfried von Cramm, then they overcame Great Britain 4-1. In 1938, without any of the players that had held the trophy for four years, Britain lost 0-5 to Yugoslavia in the second round. Germany — albeit without von Cramm — reached the Inter-Zone final for the fourth year running, but lost to Australia. The US retained the trophy 3-2. In 1939 Australia beat Yugoslavia in the Inter-Zone final, and, just as they had done on the eve of the outbreak of the previous World War, dethroned America to take the cup 'down under' for the duration of hostilities.

US/Australian stranglehold

No other country apart from the US and Australia won the cup between 1936 and 1974. Indeed, no other country got even as far as the challenge round until 1960, when Italy finally broke their stranglehold.

The trophy was regained by the Americans in 1946, then it passed back into Australian hands in 1950 for a further four years. The US broke their domination for one year, 1954, then once again in 1958, and once more in 1963. But in the main, a succession of great players trained by the legendary Harry Hopman, who captained the Australian team throughout this period, was too strong — and the advantage of always defending the trophy at home on grass was in their favour.

During the period from 1946 to 1959, with all other nations shut out of the challenge round, these countries' realistic goal was simply to reach the Inter-Zone final. Sweden did it four times (1946, 1950, 1951, 1954), Italy three times (1949, 1955, 1958), Czechoslovakia twice (1947, 1948), Belgium twice (1953, 1957), and India twice (1956, 1959). The introduction of an Eastern Zone in 1952 ultimately made for Inter-Zone finals involving three countries, so the foregoing records show the last country to be eliminated before the challenge round.

Above: Gottfried von Cramm (left) and Donald Budge fought out one of the most thrilling encounters in the history of the Davis Cup in 1937. Germany and the US were level, 2-2, in the Inter Zone Final at Wimbledon, and Budge only took the deciding rubber after von Cramm had led 5-2 in the final set.

Shock defeats

Italy finally broke the US-Australia duopoly in 1960 by defeating the US 3-2 in Perth. They actually recovered after losing both the opening singles, with Nicola Pietrangeli and Orlando Sirola defeating Earl Buchholz and Chuck McKinley in the doubles and then taking both reverse singles rubbers. In the challenge round, however, they did not score until after the Australians had taken a winning 3-0 lead.

The Italians beat the US once again to challenge for the cup in 1961, but this time they were repulsed 5-0. The 1962 competition brought a new set of nations to the final stages. The US were beaten in the American Zone for the first time since 1936 when they lost to Mexico, while the Italians went down to Sweden in the European Zone final. The Mexicans, represented by Rafael Osuna and Antonio Palafox, beat Yugoslavia (who had entered the American Zone), Sweden and India to reach the challenge round, but the

Mexicans too were sent home without a point.

America compensated for their shock defeats of 1960 to 1962 to regain the trophy for the first time in five years in 1963. Chuck McKinley, the reigning Wimbledon champion, beat John Newcombe in the deciding rubber of the challenge round.

The Australians won the cup the next four years running, from 1964 to 1967. They dropped only one rubber — against Mexico — on the way to the challenge round in 1964. It was a close match, with Roy Emerson overcoming McKinley in the deciding rubber. In 1965 the US were defeated by Spain in the Inter-Zone finals, and by eliminating India, the Spaniards reached the challenge round for the first time. But they only took a dead rubber against Australia after the overall result had been decided.

America's decline continued in 1966 with a loss to Brazil, who in turn went down to India. So again Australia faced a new challenger, and they suffered the embarrassment of losing the doubles rubber in the challenge round, but took all four singles. The following year Spain won through for a second time, taking the final Inter-Zone tie against South Africa, but once more Australia handed them a 4-1 defeat. The US had suffered the humiliation of losing to tiny Ecuador.

End of an era

The mid 1960s in fact saw the final years of Australian supremacy. With the departure of Harry Hopman to pastures new — he emigrated to the US, where he became a coach — the well of talent that the country had enjoyed for so long suddenly dried up.

The arrival of open tennis in 1968 caused no immediate change in the Davis Cup. As tournaments that included contract professionals were limited, and only players under the control of their national associations were eligible to be selected, the Davis Cup was not thrown open to all players until 1973. In the meantime, the entire 1967 Australian team — Emerson, Newcombe and Tony Roche — had departed to the professional ranks, and their replacements — Bill Bowrey, Ray Ruffels and John Alexander — were not of sufficient calibre to resist the revitalized American side that had come through. Clark Graebner, Arthur Ashe and Bob Lutz built up a winning lead over the Aussies before Bowrey gained some solace in beating Ashe in a dead rubber.

A new order

This was the beginning of a spell of American domination that lasted until the rules of eligibility were revised. The year 1969 saw a British revival, with the original challengers getting through to the Inter-Zone final for the first time since the war. With the severely weakened Australians having crashed out to Mexico in the American Zone (North) final, and Spain losing to the emerging Romanians, a new order was taking over. Mexico subsequently lost to Brazil (they had lost their star player, Rafael Osuna, in a plane crash), and Brazil went out to Great Britain, who had already eliminated West Germany and South Africa. The Inter-Zone final saw Romania rather unexpectedly oust the British at Wimbledon, so an Eastern European country was in the challenge round for the first time. However, they failed to take a rubber from the Americans in an extremely hard-fought tie.

Such was the fluid nature of the competition at this time that 1970 brought a different set of nations to the final stages. The previous year's Inter-Zone finalists, Romania and Great Britain, lost early to Yugoslavia and Austria respectively, while Australia had no joy against India. It was ultimately West Germany that came through to challenge — a stage they had never reached before, even in their great days of the 1930s. The US took the first four rubbers without losing a set, but in the final (dead) singles Christian Kuhnke extended Ashe to a record-breaking 6-8, 10-12, 9-7, 13-11, 6-4 marathon.

In 1971 Romania came through a second time, and now they lost to the US only by 2-3 at Charlotte, North Carolina. It was in this year that the Davis Cup Nations decided to drop the challenge round format.

Under the revised system, the holders were required to play through in 1972. The winners of the two European Zones (this area having been divided since 1964 by a draw instead of a geographical division) met the winners of the American and Eastern Zones in the semifinals. At this stage, the US overcame Spain, and Romania defeated Australia. Because they had played away in the previous year's challenge round, the Romanians were granted the home advantage for the final, and with Ilie Nastase by then established as the world's leading clay-court player, they were expected to win. Stan Smith beat him in the opening rubber, however, and beat Ion Tiriac in the fourth. Furthermore, by overwhelming the Romanians in the doubles, Smith and Erik van Dillen defied extraordinary partisanship on the part of the officials, the hostility of the crowd and the gamesmanship of their opponents. The US retained the cup 3-2.

Restrictions lifted

In 1973 the restriction on categories of player was lifted, which enabled Australia to call on the services of their two best players, Newcombe and 35-year-old Rod Laver. Using the same three players as the previous year, the US were routed 5-0 in the challenge round at Cleveland, which was the first occasion that the final was played indoors.

The Big Four lose the Cup

In 1974, the growing anti-apartheid lobby against South Africa threatened to throw the competition into disarray. South Africa challenged in the American Zone because so many European nations refused to play them,

but even here they were given a walkover by Argentina. The holders, Australia, were unable to draw on any of their leading players and failed against India, while America, beginning a series of shock defeats in Latin America, collapsed against Colombia at Bogota. Colombia lost in turn to South Africa, who went on to beat Italy in the semifinals. India qualified to play them in the final at the expense of the USSR. There was no final. The Indian government refused to allow their players to meet the South Africans, who thus became the first nation outside the Big Four of Davis Cup history (US, Australia, Great Britain and France) to hold the trophy.

A motion to expel South Africa at the Davis Cup Nations' AGM failed to gain the necessary majority, and they were allowed to enter in 1975. But having been given walkovers by both Mexico and Colombia in the American Zone, they were removed by Chile — much to the organizers' relief. The

Above: Rafael Osuna was Mexico's Davis Cup hero throughout the 1960s. He was tragically killed in an air crash immediately after securing a notable victory over Australia in 1969.

Right: Adriano Panatta spearheaded the Italian effort for many years. They reached the final four times in five years, but took the trophy only once — at Santiago in 1976.

Below: Guillermo Vilas takes refreshment during a gruelling tie. This robust Argentinian led his country to three wins over the US in Buenos Aires, although they lost to the same opponents in the 1981 final at Cincinnati.

Americans suffered another embarrassing loss, to Mexico, and in due course Sweden beat Chile, and Czechoslovakia beat Australia in the semi-finals. Bjorn Borg, in the year before he won the first of his five Wimbledon titles, was the hero of Sweden's historic victory at Stockholm, in the first all-European decider since 1933.

In order to ease the increasingly congested international calendar, the opening rounds of the 1976 competition were begun in the autumn of 1975, before that year's competition had been concluded. The leading nations were exempt until the later rounds. At that stage the Swedes — without the services of Borg, by now a tax exile — went out to Italy, and the Czechs to Hungary. The US lost once again to Mexico, with Raul Ramirez defeating Jimmy Connors in the deciding rubber. For the second year running, Mexico defaulted to South Africa, who in turn lost to Chile. The latter, themselves unacceptable opponents for some nations because of their dreadful human rights record, were given a walkover into the final by the USSR, while Italy eliminated Australia. The Italians, led by reigning French champion Adriano Panatta, won their only Davis Cup competition in what would become four finals appearances in five years.

Bedevilled by politics

Australia, although still lacking a major player, returned the cup to the Antipodes in 1977 after the most politically fraught year in the competition's history. The tournament had become increasingly bedevilled by political interference, and the US proposed that any nation that defaulted on political grounds should be banned. The motion failed, and the US, supported by Great Britain and France, announced that they would take no further part in the Davis Cup. With the whole competition threatened with extinction, these three nations were persuaded to reconsider — and the 1977 event went ahead with all of them competing. The two 'villains', Chile and South Africa, were beaten by Argentina and the US respectively, then Argentina overcame the US in Buenos Aires. Using old-stagers Tony Roche and John Alexander, the Australians toppled Italy in the final on grass at Sydney.

In 1978, after years of disappointment, the US finally survived the perilous American Zone, beating South Africa and Chile, and regained the cup for the first time since 1972. Their unexpected final opponents were Great Britain, who came through after a glorious run against France, Czechoslovakia and Australia. In the last outdoor final to be played in the northern hemisphere, the US won 4-1 at Palm Springs, owing much to the young and talented John McEnroe, who now emerged as the outstanding Davis Cup player of the era. The US retained the cup against Italy in 1979, this being the first year, apart from 1972, that South Africa were not in the draw.

First Eastern European win

But in 1980 America succumbed again to Guillermo Vilas and Jose Luis Clerc — who both defeated McEnroe — at Buenos Aires. Argentina had high hopes of winning the trophy, but despite home advantage, both of their stars lost to Ivan Lendl as Czechoslovakia went through to the final. Italy came through once again, over Australia, but the Czechs prevailed in Prague to become the first Eastern European winners of the competition.

Promotion and relegation

It was at this time that the most radical change in format in the cup's history occurred. From 1981, the top 16 nations were placed in a World Group, involving just four rounds and giving each nation the same number of ties to play regardless of their geographical location. The zone format remained for all other entries. The eight first-round losers in the World Group played a relegation round, the winners surviving for the following year and the losers being relegated and replaced by the winners of the four zones (European A, European B, American and Eastern).

This is the system still in use today, and though admirably fair it can result in dramatic changes from year to year. It is now possible for a nation to win the cup one year, lose in the first round and relegation rounds the next, and be obliged to compete with the 'minnows' the year after. In fact the US, France and Great Britain have all been relegated in recent years.

The 1981 competition was notable for Britain's first victory against Italy for 48 years (they eventually lost to Argentina in the semi-finals), and the second appearance in the ultimate tie of a South American country. The US, given home advantage, readily avenged their 1977 and 1980 defeats by the Argentines. In 1982 it was the turn of France to enjoy a good run in the cup, and they reached the last round for the first time since 1933. Once again, however, McEnroe ensured that the US retained the cup.

But 1983 brought yet another win for Argentina over the US at Buenos Aires,

McEnroe once again losing to both Clerc and Vilas. Another South American country, Paraguay, brought about the biggest shock in the first round by removing Czechoslovakia. For the first time in many years, a tie was played at a neutral venue for reasons of convenience rather than political expediency (Rhodesia had played Sweden at a private club in France in 1968 to avoid anti-apartheid demonstrations in Sweden), with Sweden beating New Zealand (who had choice of ground) at Eastbourne. Sweden beat Argentina in the semi-finals, while Australia overcame France. The final, in Melbourne, marked the first significant performance by Pat Cash, who beat Joakim Nystrom to clinch the tie. Australia did not have a player ranked among the world top 20 at the time.

Unsporting final

Sweden regained the trophy in 1984 after one of the most infamous finals in the Davis Cup's history. Both McEnroe and Connors, appearing together in the US team for the first year, behaved appallingly as Mats Wilander routed Connors for the loss of only seven games, and then Henrik Sundstrom stunned McEnroe with a straight-set defeat. The covered clay court, hurriedly laid in Gothenberg, was greatly disliked by the Americans, but the unsporting manner in which they took defeat would have caused Dwight Davis to turn in his grave. Anders Jarryd and Stefan Edberg clinched the trophy by handing McEnroe and Peter Fleming a four-set beating. The USTA banned both McEnroe and Connors from taking part the following year.

The strength of Swedish tennis allowed them the luxury of having at least half

Below: John McEnroe shares a confidence with the US Davis Cup team captain, Arthur Ashe, during a press conference. Sadly, the two fell out over McEnroe's behaviour in the 1984 final at Stockholm, when the US lost to Sweden.

Opposite: Virginia Wade played more times than any other player in both the Federation Cup and the Wightman Cup. In the former competition she notched up 100 rubbers between 1967 and 1983.

a dozen first-class players to draw on and still have a good chance of beating any opponents. This worked to their advantage in 1985, as with several permutations of team they came through to win for the second time in succession and the third overall. The Americans lost to West Germany who, with Wimbledon champion Boris Becker, clearly posed a threat. But West Germany did not have an adequate player to support him, and though Becker beat both Wilander and Edberg in the final tie in Munich, the Swedes retained the trophy 3-2 (and became the first European nation to do so since Great Britain in the 1930s).

Heroic victory

It seemed as if Sweden would remain invincible for some years, but Australia had different ideas. They overcame a weak US team, still without the services of McEnroe and Connors, in the semi-finals of the 1986 competition. Then Cash played an heroic role, winning all three of his rubbers, to give Australia victory over Sweden at Melbourne in the final. There can be no doubt that the grass surface was the reason for the outcome, but the manner of Cash's singles triumphs (he beat Edberg, the reigning Australian champion, in straight sets, and then Mikael Pernfors after losing the first two sets) gave an enormous fillip to his compatriots. It proved to be no flash in the pan, as Cash won Wimbledon six months later.

An injury which ruled Cash out of the singles proved disastrous to Australia's hopes the following year, and they went down to India at Sydney in the semi-finals. Ramesh Krishnan (who beat both John Fitzgerald and Wally Masur) and Vijay Amritraj (who also

Right: Pat Cash played a leading part in two Australian victories over Sweden at Melbourne, in the finals of 1983 and 1986. On the latter occasion, he was involved in each of his country's three winning rubbers.

overcame Masur) thus put India in the final for the third time in their country's history. For both Indian players it was a remarkable feat. Krishnan's father, Ramanathan, had been in the side that reached the challenge round in 1966, while Amritraj, by now a part-time player, would have turned out for India had they been allowed to meet South Africa in the 1974 final.

For the US, 1987 was a disastrous year. Still lacking fresh new talent to keep them among the leading contenders, they crashed to Paraguay in the first round and then lost the relegation play-off against Germany, who had been defeated by Spain. Sweden defeated Italy, France and Spain to reach the final, where they readily accounted for India 5-0 in Gothenburg.

FEDERATION CUP

Compared with the venerable Davis Cup, the women's equivalent is a fairly young event, having begun in 1963. The much older Wightman Cup, which dates from 1923, has always been a two-way contest between the top women players of the United States and Great Britain, with a format of five singles and two doubles. Until the early 1960s, these were by far the two dominant nations of women's tennis. Stars like Suzanne Lenglen and Maria Bueno were isolated examples of champions of other nationalities that would not have had adequate support from their compatriots.

The rise of Australia in the women's game, with strong players like Margaret Smith, Lesley Turner, Jan Lehane and Robyn Ebbern, prompted the International Lawn Tennis Federation to donate a trophy for international team competition on the occasion of their 50th anniversary in 1963. Unlike the Davis Cup, it was decided that the event would be played at the same venue in one week. The inaugural event was played just before Wimbledon knowing that most of the top players would be present. Since then it has stood as a separate entity. The format has always been a knock-out tournament with a straight draw. Ties consist of two singles and a doubles, with the second strings playing first.

New success

The Federation Cup has become a successful promotion only in recent years. Up to the mid 1970s, few countries were anxious to stage it, and for some years the Americans had difficulty in raising a strong enough team to reflect their customary pre-eminence in the women's game. But the introduction of sponsorship, by Colgate-Palmolive, in 1976 brought back the leading Americans, and the competition increased in prestige and profitability. Sponsored by the Nippon Electric Company since 1980, it is probably

the most successful annual event for women.

The trophy, a large silver flower bowl, has been won 11 times by the US, seven times by Australia, four times by Czechoslovakia, and once each by South Africa and West Germany. The only other countries to reach the final have been Great Britain (four times) and the Netherlands.

Fourteen countries have staged the competition during its 25-year history. It has been held four times in West Germany, three times in Australia (they are due to stage it again in 1988), three times in the USA, twice each in Britain, Italy, France and Japan, and once in Greece, South Africa, Spain, Switzerland, Brazil, Czechoslovakia and Canada. The ITF now have a policy of moving it between Europe, the Americas and Asia or Australasia by rotation. In terms of surface, it has been played 13 times on clay, six times on grass, five times on cement, and once indoors on carpet.

During the 1960s, the number of teams entering varied according to the location. There were only 16 participating nations in the inaugural year, and on the first two occasions the Federation Cup was held in Australia there were only 11 and 12, due to the expense involved. Since sponsorship came in, support has been much better, with a record 42 teams taking part in 1987.

Virginia Wade of Great Britain holds the record by far for the greatest number of appearances. She took part every year from 1967 to 1983, and played 100 rubbers in 57 ties. Next come Wendy Turnbull of Australia (59 rubbers in 42 ties), Billie Jean (Moffitt) King of the US (58 rubbers in 36 ties), Betty Stove of the Netherlands (55 rubbers in 29 ties), and Helga (Niessen) Masthoff of West Germany (53 rubbers in 31 ties).

Modest beginnings

The inaugural Federation Cup competition was played in June 1963 at Queen's Club, London, the week before the Wimbledon Championships. Unfortunately, the matches were played alongside the traditional London Grass Court Championships, so some of the importance of the event was dissipated. And with only 16 nations taking part, it was a modest beginning for the trophy. Notable absentees were Brazil, Mexico, Sweden and Spain, but those countries taking part were all represented by their strongest teams.

The US had a tough first-round struggle against Italy, with Darlene Hard and Billie Jean Moffitt both dropping sets against Lea Pericoli and Sylvana Lazzarino, but they went on to reach the final, beating the Netherlands and Great Britain. Australia came through the other half of the draw at the expense of Belgium, Hungary and South Africa, and the final was as exciting as one could wish for. Hard was heavily defeated by Margaret Smith, then Moffitt squared matters with a three-set win over Lesley Turner. In the deciding doubles, the Americans hovered

perilously on the brink of defeat before eventually overcoming the Australian pair 3-6, 13-11, 6-3.

Australia's revenge

The 1964 competition was held at the Germantown Cricket Club, Philadelphia — scene of several Davis Cup challenge rounds between the wars. The entry increased to 20, and Australia gained revenge over the US in the final with Smith beating Moffitt and Turner overcoming Nancy Richey to establish a

Above: Margaret Court was never beaten in singles in the Federation Cup. She represented Australia six times between 1963 and 1971, and was on the winning team on four occasions.

winning lead. They retained the title the following year at Melbourne, and once again Turner and Smith each won their singles rubbers — against Carole Graebner and Moffitt — to clinch the trophy.

The venue for 1966 was Turin, so the competition went on to clay for the first time. West Germany breathed new life into it by upsetting Australia to reach the final, where they gave the Americans a stern test. Helga Niessen, one of the most astute clay-court players of the period, was close to beating Julie Heldman before going down 4-6, 7-5, 6-1, and Billie Jean King lost the middle set to Edda Buding. The Germans were rewarded with the honour of staging the 1967 event in West Berlin, though this time they got only as far as the semi-finals. Great Britain reached the final over Australia, but the US retained the trophy as Rosemary Casals defeated Virginia Wade and King overcame Ann Jones — which was rather surprising as the British might have been expected to handle their opponents on clay.

Order amidst chaos

The 1968 event in Paris took place in the middle of the student riots that brought chaos to the city that spring. With all public services suspended it was a miracle that the event took place at all, and even more surprising that of the 23 teams entered, only West Germany failed to appear. The previous year's finalists, the US and Great Britain, were both weakened by the fact that King, Casals and Jones, as contract professionals, were ineligible, and both countries went down in the semi-finals.

Australia, led by Margaret Court, who had been missing the previous year, overcame the British, while an unseeded Dutch team shocked the US in the other tie. Richey and Mary Ann Eisel looked well on the way to victory with a 6-2, 4-2 lead, then Astrid Suurbeek and Lidy Jansen-Venneboer adopted such an effective lobbing campaign that they settled the tie 2-6, 8-6, 6-0. As Eisel had lost her singles to the ambidextrous Marijke Jansen, the Netherlands went through 2-1. Miss Jansen nearly beat Kerry Melville in the opening rubber of the final, but the Australian recovered to win 4-6, 7-5, 6-3, and Court regained the trophy with an easy defeat of Suurbeek.

The US came back at Athens in 1969 to take a surprise win over Australia in the final. It all hinged on the deciding doubles, where two baseliners (and a scratch partnership), Richey and Peaches Bartkowicz, outlobbed Court and Judy Tegart. Yet in 1970, when the competition returned to a German venue at Freiburg, a second-rank Australian team emerged as winners. Court and Melville were both sidelined with injury, but Judy Dalton (the former Miss Tegart) and Karen Krantzcke surprised Great Britain in the semi-final, at the same time as the home team were winning through against the US. The Germans then suffered the disappointment of seeing Helga Hoesl lose to Krantzcke and Niessen submit to Dalton.

The 1971 competition, in Perth, was actually played at the end of December 1970. Because most of their leading players were in dispute with the US Tennis Association, the Americans were represented by Patti Hogan and Sharon Walsh, who were no match for Jones and Wade of Great Britain in the semi-finals. For the home team, Court was supported by a new star, Evonne Goolagong — who was to win her first Wimbledon title six months later. By beating Françoise Durr of France in the semi-finals and Wade in the final, Goolagong enabled Australia to retain the trophy.

Political overtones

The 1972 event was laden with political overtones. South Africa had been banned from the Davis Cup that year, but the ILTF granted a South African request to stage the Federation Cup. The host nation were anxious to prove that progress was being made to integrate non-white races into sporting competition in the Republic, and as a result, they were readmitted into the Davis Cup in 1973. There was a record Federation Cup entry of 30 that year (although no Communist nation took part) and the final result was an extraordinary victory for the home team.

The two leading nations were both under-strength: Court was having a baby, and America once again had to rely on low-ranked players. In the semi-finals, Australia lost to Great Britain, with Virginia Wade and Joyce Williams taking the doubles over Goolagong and Helen Gourlay, while South Africa eliminated the US, with Brenda Kirk and Pat Pretorius taking the decider over Walsh and Valerie Ziegenfuss. The final, before a vociferous and partisan crowd on the cement centre court of Ellis Park, Johannesburg, was a real thriller. Pretorius lost the opening rubber to Virginia Wade, and Winnie Shaw was poised to win the cup for Britain for the first time as she led Brenda Kirk by a set and 4-2. Then she lost her nerve, Kirk recovered to win, and the South Africans easily took the doubles.

Quickest final on record

The British had never lost before the semi-finals in the ten-year history of the event, but in 1973, at Bad Homburg, Germany, they went down to a young Romanian team in the last eight. West Germany overwhelmed the US at the same stage, then in the semi-finals Australia beat the Germans and South Africa narrowly overcame Romania. The final was the quickest on record, with Goolagong, Pat Coleman and Janet Young dropping only 13 games in three rubbers.

Australia won again at Naples in 1974, though in the final they were tested by a stronger US team than of late. After Goolagong had beaten Heldman, Dianne Fromholtz lost to Chris Evert's younger sister, Jeanne, and Goolagong and Young only defeated Heldman and Walsh 7-5, 8-6 in the doubles.

There was an exciting new winning team at the 1975 competition in Aix-en-Provence. Czechoslovakia, represented by 18-year-old Martina Navratilova and 21-year-old Renata Tomanova, dropped a rubber to West Germany in the quarter-finals, but in the semis they handed France a 3-0 defeat. The French, whose team included the Australian-born Gail Chanfreau and the Mexican-born Rosa Darmon, had beaten the second-seeded British the previous round. Australia beat the US in the other semi, but they were not able to take even a set from the bouncing Czechs in the final.

New-look Cup

Navratilova's defection later that year deprived Czechoslovakia of any more wins for the time being, and the 1976 Cup had a whole new look about it. After years of being

a low-key event, it gained sponsorship from Colgate and was held indoors at the vast Spectrum in Philadelphia (although it was in August, and the week before the outdoor US Open at Forest Hills). The move was in recognition of Team Tennis, which at that time occupied most of the top women in indoor combat during the summer months. But it did mean that, after nine years, the best players were once more available for the US. Chris Evert was injured, so they relied on Casals and King for both singles and doubles.

However, the competition was disrupted by the withdrawals of Czechoslovakia, the USSR and Hungary in protest at the presence of South Africa. For the Iron Curtain countries the position was particularly delicate as Moscow was due to stage the Olympics in four years' time. Coming so soon after the African boycott of the Montreal Games, and after the major controversy that flared up in the Davis Cup that year, the ITF reacted by banning all three from the following year's competition.

Above: Chris Evert did not make her debut in the Federation Cup until 1977, whereas she made her first appearance in the Wightman Cup six years earlier. Evert was a member of seven winning Federation Cup teams.

Right: Czechoslovakia won the Federation Cup three years running, from 1983 to 1985. Their winning team in the 1985 event at Nagoya, Japan, pictured with their non-playing captain, is (left to right): Hana Mandlikova, Helena Sukova, Regina Marsikova and Andrea Holikova.

US resurgence

That year the US easily regained the trophy after a gap of seven years, and this was the first of seven successive wins for them.

In 1977 the competition returned to English grass. Played at Eastbourne in place of the usual pre-Wimbledon women's tournament, it was held alongside the Wimbledon women's qualifying tournament, as many of the players were required for both. The British, with two players among the top four in the world — Wade and Sue Barker — had high hopes of winning, but they failed in the semi-finals against Australia's Kerry Reid and Dianne Fromholtz. America, with Chris Evert joining Casals and King for the first time, swept through without dropping a rubber until the final, where they lost the dead doubles to Australia ('dead' meaning the result had already been decided and did not depend on the outcome of this rubber).

There was an exciting finish to the 1978 event at Melbourne. Tracy Austin lost to Kerry Reid in the opening rubber, then Evert levelled the match over Wendy Turnbull. In the doubles, Reid and Turnbull won the opening set before Evert and King fought back to retain the trophy. In 1979, in Madrid, Austin took advantage of the switch from grass to clay and this time beat Reid decisively. But Chris Lloyd, as she now was, needed to draw on all her experience to overcome Fromholtz 2-6, 6-3, 8-6 and clinch another US victory.

America beat Australia for the fifth year running in the final in 1980 at Berlin. Once again, Lloyd and Austin took both singles to render the doubles academic. In 1981 the tournament was held in Tokyo in recognition of the fact that NEC had taken over sponsorship. This time Australia lost to Great Britain in the semi-finals, but Wade could gain only four games against Andrea Jaeger and Barker only three against Lloyd in the final.

Martina Navratilova, having become an American citizen, was available to represent her adopted homeland in the 1982 competition at Santa Clara, California. By now, new generations of leading Czechs and Germans had emerged, and these two nations reached the semi-finals. Navratilova led her team to victory over the nation she had won the trophy for in 1975, while West Germany upset the Australians to reach the final for the first time since 1970. Claudia Kohde beat Fromholtz, and Bettina Bunge (who was born in Peru, raised in Florida and later moved to Monaco) overcame the former Evonne Goolagong, now Mrs Cawley. The Americans took the final and the trophy for the seventh year running, 3-0.

Return to Europe

The Federation Cup returned to Europe in every respect in 1983. Held in Zurich, it was notable for the defeat of Australia by Switzerland in the quarter-finals and of the US by Czechoslovakia in the semis. With Lloyd, Navratilova and Austin all missing,

Jaeger was supported by a lowly player indeed, Candy Reynolds. They went down to Hana Mandlikova and Helena Sukova, while West Germany ended Switzerland's run in the other semi-final. Czechoslovakia regained the trophy — the first of three successive wins — with Sukova beating Kohde and Bunge retiring against Mandlikova with a pulled muscle.

In 1984 the tournament was staged in South America, at São Paulo. It was rather a weak year, with several countries — most notably West Germany — without their leading players. The US, with a second-line team of Kathy Jordan, Kathleen Horvath, Zina Garrison and Anne Smith, were top-seeded, but they always looked shaky and were seen off in the semi-finals by a new-look Australian team with Anne Minter and Elizabeth Sayers playing singles. Fourth-seeded Britain lost to Bulgaria in the first round, and the Bulgarians went on to beat the USSR before falling to Yugoslavia in the quarter-finals. Czechoslovakia struggled to beat the Yugoslavs, who won a set in all three rubbers, then blazed past Australia after Minter had defeated Sukova in the opening rubber.

Czechoslovakia secured a hat-trick of wins at Nagoya in 1985. Although they once again lacked their leading players, the US managed to reach the final with Kathy Jordan and Elise Burgin, but here they could only take the dead doubles. Sukova and Mandlikova were the architects of their team's

triumph, and they were rewarded by the selection of Prague as Federation Cup venue for 1986.

Two dramatic finals

This was notable not only for the fact that the competition was staged in a Communist country for the first time, but it also marked Navratilova's first return to her homeland since her defection 11 years earlier. The US were at full strength, with Lloyd and Pam Shriver making up the team. In a joyous and emotional final, they beat the Czechs, although in the quarter-finals against Italy Lloyd had suffered her first singles defeat in the competition at the hand of Sandra Cecchini.

The 1987 event, at Vancouver, was a personal triumph for Steffi Graf. The young West German, who was about to take over from Navratilova as No 1 in the world, struggled in her opening rubber against Patricia Hy of Hong Kong, but after that she did not drop a set. The Germans beat Argentina and Czechoslovakia to reach the final, while the US, with Navratilova side-lined by injury, overcame Great Britain and Bulgaria. The final was the most dramatic since South Africa's recovery against Britain in 1972. Claudia Kohde-Kilsch lost the first singles to Shriver, then Graf trounced Evert (now divorced from John Lloyd) to make it 1-1. In the deciding doubles, Evert and Shriver led 6-1, 4-0, before Graf and Kohde made an almost impossible comeback. In one

Above: The US sent their strongest possible team to Prague for the 1986 Federation Cup, which marked Martina Navratilova's first visit to her homeland since she defected in 1975. Pictured (left to right), the winning US team were: Pam Shriver, Chris Evert Lloyd, Zina Garrison, Navratilova and Marty Riessen (trainer).

of the most exciting women's doubles matches ever seen, the German pair ultimately triumphed 1-6, 7-5, 6-4, to give their country victory in the Federation Cup for the first time.

WIGHTMAN CUP

The original international team competition for women, the Wightman Cup has, in fact, always been a purely two-way annual contest between the top players of the United States and Great Britain. Hazel Hotchkiss Wightman, a notable American player before and after the First World War, donated a tall, elaborately decorated silver vase to the US Lawn Tennis Association in 1920 for all nations to challenge. Three years later, the British LTA agreed to send a team to play for it, and those have been the only teams in contention. Wightman had hoped that other nations — particularly the French, who had the great Suzanne Lenglen at the time — would also take part, but it was not until 1963, and the institution of the Federation Cup, that other countries began competing internationally in women's team events.

Right: The Wightman Cup, a huge silver vase, was donated for women's international team play by Mrs Hazel Wightman (née Hotchkiss), who was a leading American player of the 1920s.

Although known as 'The Wightman Cup', the trophy is actually inscribed: 'The Women's Lawn Tennis Team Championship between Great Britain and the United States'. The format of the match, which is played each year alternately in the two countries, has remained unchanged. Teams consist of up to seven players (though most have about five): a No 1 singles player, who plays the No 1 and No 2 of the opposing side; a No 2 singles player, who likewise plays the opposite No 1 and No 2; a No 3 singles player; a No 1 doubles pair and a No 2 doubles pair, who just play their opposite numbers. A draw takes place at the start to determine the order of top singles rubbers.

The series of seven rubbers is now played over three days. Early on it was a two-day affair, with three rubbers on the first day and four on the second. From 1965, in the US, and from 1974, in Great Britain, the matches have been extended to three days. Since 1978, the order has been standardized as follows: Day 1 — First or second string vs first or second (depending on the draw); three vs three. Day 2 — First or second vs first or second; second doubles vs second doubles. Day 3 — First or second vs first or second; first or second vs first or second; first doubles vs first doubles.

The matches were played on grass every year until 1957, when they were staged on cement. They have been held indoors in Great Britain since 1974, and since 1983 all matches have been in the autumn. The inaugural contest of 1923 opened the new Stadium Court at the West Side Club, Forest Hills, New York. In Britain, the matches were at the All England Club, Wimbledon — at first on the Centre Court, but later on Court One. The Americans began varying their venues from 1949, and the British left Wimbledon in 1974, trying one year in North Wales and another in southeast London before settling at the Royal Albert Hall, London. Since 1983, the Americans have established a permanent home for their matches at Williamsburg, Virginia, where a special Wightman Cup Museum has been set up.

American domination

The Americans have had by far the better of the encounters, leading overall by 49 wins to Britain's 10. In the early years, honours were evenly balanced, with either nation winning four times up to 1930. Then the US won 21 times without loss (there was a six-year break during the Second World War) before the British finally regained the trophy in 1958. There have been only two occasions that the British have won on American soil — in 1925 and 1975. However, the biggest shock was probably in 1961, when a side of inexperienced American teenagers faced a visiting team that boasted both Wimbledon singles finalists and the French singles champion of that year. The British gained only one rubber.

In recent years, as the British have fallen further and further behind in calibre of players, the matches have become embarrassingly one-sided. The US only lost one rubber on home soil between 1975 and 1987. In an attempt to make it more competitive, they have scaled down the standard of their players. A full-strength US team has not been turned out since 1981, in which year they did not drop even a set.

Possible changes

Under these acutely ill-matched circumstances, the Wightman Cup is looked on by many as an anachronism and an absurdity. Calls are made regularly either to abandon it or to open out the contest as a US vs Europe confrontation, as has been done successfully in golf's Ryder Cup. Neither the USTA nor the LTA is sympathetic to this view. Unless an outstanding British player comes along, no British player would qualify for a European team, and they argue that without the element of patriotism, the traditional excitement of the match would be lost.

An alternative would be for the American team to consist only of players from the original 13 states, or for the British team to include players from the rest of the Commonwealth. The latter suggestion is perhaps the most viable, as it would greatly improve the British team, and maintain old links between the mother country and her former dominions of Australia and Canada. Nevertheless, it is a fact that, however traditional and nostalgic the contest might be, the original situation of the two nations being of equal strength in women's tennis no longer applies.

Leading players

As in the Federation Cup, the most prolific participant has been Britain's Virginia Wade. She appeared in 21 consecutive matches from 1965 to 1985, playing 56 rubbers and winning 19. She was on the winning side in 1968 (when she was unbeaten), 1974, 1975 and 1978. The leading American has been Chris Evert, who took part in 13 matches between 1971 and 1985. She never lost a singles, and her overall tally is 34 wins and four losses. Evert was on the losing teams of 1975 and 1978.

The other British stalwarts were Ann Haydon Jones (13 contests between 1957 and 1975), Christine Truman Janes (11 contests between 1957 and 1971) and Sue Barker (10 contests in a row, 1974 to 1983). The leading Americans after Evert were Helen Wills Moody (10 between 1923 and 1938), Helen Jacobs (12 between 1927 and 1939), and Billie Jean King (10 between 1961 and 1978).

The oldest player to take part was Britain's Dorothea Lambert Chambers, who was 47 when she appeared in 1926 (she won both a singles and a doubles the previous year). For the US, Hazel Wightman and Margaret du Pont were both 44 when they took part in 1931 and 1962 respectively. At the other end of the age scale, three 15-year-olds — Andrea Jaeger (the youngest, in 1980), Jeanne Evert (1973) and Tracy Austin (1978) — have been in action. Sixteen-year-old first-timers were Betty Nuthall and Christine Truman of Great Britain (1927 and 1957 respectively), and Pam Shriver (1978), Chris Evert (1971), and Maureen Connolly (1951) of the United States.

As a commercial proposition, the match was usually more rewarding in Britain, where the ties held at Wimbledon were popular days out for schoolgirls. However, in the 1977 American fixture the match was promoted by Larry King (Billie Jean's husband) at Oakland, California, along the lines of a Team Tennis event, with much razzmatazz. The increasing disparity of the teams in recent years has resulted in declining support, even though the Royal Albert Hall ties in London are renowned for a full panoply of pomp and splendour along the lines of that famous venue's jingoistic Last Night of the Proms festival, when they sing *Rule Britannia* and

Above: Christine Truman was only 16 when she made her Wightman Cup debut in 1957. The following year, she played a major part in Great Britain's first victory in the two-nation contest for 28 years.

Above: Broadcaster Pete Murray 'brought the house down' while Great Britain were celebrating a win over the US in the 1978 Wightman Cup match in London. He embraced British team trainer, Roger Taylor — much to the amusement of referee Bea Seal (left) and players Anne Hobbs, Sue Mappin, Michele Tyler, Sue Barker and Virginia Wade.

other Edwardian anthems redolent of the lost days of the British Empire.

Cliff-hangers

At its best, the Wightman Cup is a wonderful sporting event, full of excitement and drama. There have been ten occasions when the outcome hinged on the seventh rubber, and seven when the ultimate winners recovered from a match deficit of 2-3 to take the final two. The most recent was in 1978, when the two countries went into the final day's play with two rubbers apiece. Evert overwhelmed Wade 6-0, 6-1, but Barker played the match of her life to beat Austin 6-3, 3-6, 6-0. In the decider, the British went almost apopleptic with excitement as Barker and Wade defeated Evert and Shriver 6-0, 5-7, 6-4. Two years later there was another nerve-jangling match when, with the US leading 3-2, Wade led Evert 5-1 in the final set and had two match points before the American recovered to win the last six games.

Against such an overwhelming catalogue of American success, it is worth recalling the other few British victories. Having lost the opening series in 1923 7-0, Britain struck back the next year to win 6-1 at the Wimbledon venue and then retained the trophy at Forest Hills in 1925, with the indestructible

Lambert Chambers playing a major part. The British also took the decisive seventh rubbers in 1928 and 1930.

Twenty-eight years later, Christine Truman became the first player to beat the reigning Wimbledon champion Althea Gibson, to set up a match-clinching victory for Ann Haydon over Mimi Arnold. In 1960, even though one British pair lost a rubber 6-0, 6-0, the final doubles was won by Truman and Shirley Brasher over Janet Hopps and Dorothy Knode to clinch the trophy for Britain. Truman, now Mrs Janes, was also involved in the deciding rubber of 1968, when she joined her sister Nell to beat Stephanie de Fina and Kathy Harter.

The 1974 series saw the British team win 6-1. They won each of the first four rubbers after losing the first set, and they lost only the last rubber, when Julie Heldman and Mona Schallau salvaged some American pride by defeating Wade and Glynis Coles. The British registered an historic 5-2 win in America the following year, the only two American points being scored by Evert.

There were also four occasions when the Americans won on the deciding rubber. In 1926 and 1936 they recovered from 2-3 down, and in 1966 the British lost after establishing a 3-1 lead. This was the closest match ever, because Wade actually led Nancy Richey 5-3 in the final set and was within three points of giving Britain a winning lead. She lost, 6-2, 2-6, 5-7. Four years later, Wade and Winnie Shaw led 2-0 in the final set of the deciding rubber against King and Peaches Bartkowicz. They lost 5-7, 8-6, 2-6, with Bartkowicz never leaving the baseline and King taking all the volleys.

The Wightman Cup has such a long and illustrious history that it should not be allowed to perish. But if only there was some way of ensuring that the teams were of comparable standard! At least its immediate future is assured financially — it is now sponsored on both sides of the Atlantic by Nabisco.

Younger versions

The contest has had two imitators. One was the Bonne Bell Cup, a match played along similar lines between the US and Australia in 1972, 1973 and 1974. The top women players from either country turned out for the first two matches, but the 1974 version was less attractive, and it was then turned into a junior event. The other, the Maureen Connolly Memorial Trophy, is an under-21 version of the Wightman Cup between the US and Great Britain, held in each country in alternate years. In this, a scrupulous effort is made by the Americans to select teams of an equal standard to the British. The only major American players to have taken part were Pam Shriver and Kathy Jordan in 1978. The format consists of 11 rubbers, two of which are doubles. The British have won twice — in 1975 and 1987 — in 15 contests. In complete contrast to the Americans, the British have always seen fit to field full-strength teams.

WORLD TEAM CUP

Formerly known as the Nations Cup, this is an annual competition played in May, the week before the French Open, at Dusseldorf, West Germany. It is restricted to the seven countries with the combined highest-ranked players on the ATP men's computer ranking list, plus one wild-card entry decided by the organizers. It is divided into two round-robin groups of four, the winners playing off for the trophy. Like the Federation Cup, matches consist of two singles and one doubles rubber, and there are up to four players in a team.

The original competition was held at Kingston, Jamaica, in 1975. It was won by the US, represented by Arthur Ashe and Roscoe Tanner, who beat Great Britain (Buster Mottram and Roger Taylor) 2-1 in the final.

There was no competition in 1976 or 1977, but in 1978 the event was revived as an official ATP team championship, sponsored by Ambre Solaire, at Dusseldorf. Winners were Spain (Manuel Orantes and Jose Higueras), who beat Australia (Phil Dent and John Newcombe) 2-1 in the final. Australia, with John Alexander replacing Newcombe, went one better in 1979, with a 2-1 final win over

Below: A young American team ruthlessly retained the Wightman Cup in 1986 without dropping a rubber. Seen with the trophy are (left to right): Kathy Rinaldi, Bonnie Gadusek, Stephanie Rehe, Elise Burgin, Anne White and Marty Riessen (trainer).

Italy (Adriano Panatta, Corrado Barazzutti and Paolo Bertolucci). Italy were also runners-up in 1980, losing 3-0 to Argentina (Guillermo Vilas and Jose Luis Clerc).

Czechoslovakia got their name on the trophy in 1981 with a 2-1 defeat of Australia. Although Ivan Lendl was beaten by Peter McNamara in the opening rubber, Tomas Smid levelled the score by defeating Paul McNamee, and the Czechs took the deciding doubles. The 1982 competition went to the US, represented by Gene Mayer, Eliot Teltscher and Sherwood Stewart, with a 2-1 verdict over Australia (McNamara, Kim Warwick and Mark Edmondson). The Australians, represented by Edmondson and Pat Cash, lost their third successive final in 1983, this time to Spain, who used Manuel Orantes, José Higueras and Angel Gimenez.

The US beat Czechoslovakia 2-1 in the finals of both 1984 and 1985. In the earlier year, John McEnroe beat Lendl in the opening rubber, Jimmy Arias lost to Smid in the second, and McEnroe and Peter Fleming took the deciding doubles. The following year, Czechoslovakia were close to taking the trophy. Lendl beat McEnroe, then Miloslav Mecir led Jimmy Connors 5-2 in the final set. However, the elegant Mecir became paralyzed with nerves and let his opponent off the hook. Ken Flach and Robert Seguso readily took the doubles against Lendl and Smid.

France were the surprise winners of the 1986 event. Although lacking Yannick Noah, their team of Henri Leconte, Thierry Tulasne and Guy Forget defeated Sweden 2-1 in the final, with Forget and Leconte taking a three-set deciding doubles over Anders Jarryd and Mats Wilander.

Czechoslovakia regained the trophy in tempestuous circumstances in 1987 when Mecir beat McEnroe 7-6, 2-6, 2-1, 40-0 rtd, with McEnroe plumbing new depths in tantrums. He was disqualified. Brad Gilbert levelled the final by beating Milan Srejber, but the Czechs took the doubles. Afterwards there were calls for McEnroe to be suspended, but he got away with a meaningless fine.

EUROPEAN CUP

This competition was known as the King's Cup until 1986. It is an international team championship for European nations held each winter, though it was originally intended as a worldwide indoor equivalent to the Davis Cup. The trophy was donated in 1936 by King Gustav V of Sweden, himself a keen tournament player. In its early years the competition was played in November and December of each year on a knock-out basis. (A challenge round was abolished after the Second World War.) In 1976, however, the format was transformed into a league competition with divisions and a promotion-relegation system. From 1984, the ties in each division have been held concurrently at one venue. Up to 1959, each match consisted of four singles and a doubles, as in the Davis Cup, but since then it has been two singles and a doubles. (A team consists of from two to four players, like the Davis Cup.)

Appropriately, Sweden have won the event most often, with nine victories. Denmark come second with seven, although all of these were between 1952 (when the event was resumed after the Second World War) and 1962. West Germany, Great Britain and Czechoslovakia have four wins apiece, France three, Italy two and Yugoslavia, Spain, Hungary and Switzerland one each. Countries to have reached the final without winning are the Netherlands and the USSR.

Below: Jimmy Connors in characteristic pose. He recovered from a losing position in the 1985 World Team Cup against Miloslav Mecir and enabled the US to win the trophy for the third time.
Opposite: Bjorn Borg was a member of the Swedish team that regained the King's Cup (now known as the European Cup) in 1973.

In recent years, most nations have not selected their top players for this competition. But in the 1960s and early 1970s some of the best names of that era took part. The best final was probably in 1971, when Italy, represented by Adriano Panatta and Nicola Pietrangeli, beat Spain (Manuel Orantes and José Gisbert). Andres Gimeno joined the Spanish team to win the trophy in 1972, while in 1973 Bjorn Borg helped the Swedes regain it.

Great Britain won the King's Cup four years running, from 1964 to 1967. During those years, the event saw the longest singles match ever played, when Roger Taylor beat Wieslaw Gasiorek of Poland 27-29, 31-29, 6-4 in a tie in Warsaw. The playing time (4 hours 35 minutes) has since been exceeded, but the number of games — 126 — has not. The reason for those two incredibly long sets was that the rubber was played on ultra-fast wood, and it was almost impossible to break service. Wood became virtually extinct as a playing surface after the mid 1970s, and nowadays the matches are played on carpet.

A women's equivalent European Cup was introduced in 1986, and the inaugural competition was won by Sweden, represented by Catarina Lindquist and Carina Karlsson. They beat West Germany 2-0 in the final at Eindhoven, Netherlands.

OTHER TEAM EVENTS

The World Cup, a men's team event between the United States and Australia, was played annually at Hartford, Connecticut, between 1970 and 1980, when it became an over-35 event. Each nation won it five times, though the US took the last four series. The format was five singles and two doubles rubbers, as in the Wightman Cup.

The BP Cup was a worldwide international competition with separate men's and women's events for players aged 20 and under. It ran for eight years from 1973 to 1980; the first six competitions were held indoors at Torquay, England, and the last two at Hamburg, West Germany. Participation was by invitation, and restricted to six men's teams and four women's. On the men's side, the US won the competition four times, Great Britain three times, and Sweden once. Britain's women won their event five times, and Czechoslovakia, the US and Sweden once each. It was notable for the international debuts of several leading players, including Martina Navratilova, Sue Barker, Vitas Gerulaitis, and Peter Fleming.

The Galea Cup is the oldest international team event for young players. Men's teams of players aged under 21 have been competing for the trophy since 1950. It is played in zones, and the final rounds are held annually at Vichy, France. In the early years, entries came

almost entirely from European nations, though more recently other countries like Argentina and Australia have taken part, and won. The United States has participated since 1985.

The Annie Soisbault Cup, for women's teams aged under 21, has been running since 1965. Like the Galea Cup, it is played in zones, with the final stages at Le Touquet, France, each July. Entries were confined to European nations until the late 1970s, when Australia, Argentina and the US began to take part.

The Sunshine Cup, for boys aged 18 and under, has been played along Federation Cup lines in one week at Miami Beach each December since 1959. It is a curtain-raiser to the Orange Bowl, the unofficial world junior championships that have been held in Miami at Christmas time since 1947.

The Continental Players' Cup, for girls' teams aged 18 and under, has been played at various venues in the southeastern United States since 1976, also in the week prior to the Orange Bowl. But whereas the Sunshine Cup has always been outdoors on clay, this event has usually been held indoors.

The Dubler Cup is the oldest international team event for veterans. Men aged 45 and over take part. It dates from 1958. Until 1979 the early rounds were played zonally; since then the matches have all been played in one week at the same venue.

Other international team competitions for specific age groups are: Italia Cup (men 35 and over), Austria Cup (men 55 and over), Britannia Cup (men 65 and over), Crawford Cup (men 75 and over), Young Cup (women 40 and over), Maria Esther Bueno Cup (women 50 and over); Valerio Cup (boys 18 and under), Jean Borotra Cup (boys 16 and under), Del Sol Cup (boys 14 and under), HM Queen Sofia Cup (girls 18 and under), Helvetie Cup (girls 16 and under), Europa Cup (girls under 14), Alice Marble Cup (women 60+).

Below: Miloslav Mecir of Czechoslovakia became the first tennis player to win an Olympic gold medal for 64 years when he triumphed in the men's singles at Seoul.

WORLD TEAM TENNIS

The concept of lawn tennis as a team form within national confines goes right back almost to the dawn of the game. In England, matches on grass and clay between the counties have been played since 1895. These competitions, sponsored by a leading assurance company since 1972, are now regarded as the last bastion of the amateur game in the country that did the most to bring about open tennis.

In America, team matches have also been the bedrock of the amateur game for many years, particularly at collegiate level, where players are still required to have amateur status and to forfeit any prize money from any event. But in 1974, a movement began in the US which had dramatic and far-reaching consequences in world tennis. A group of promoters decided to institute a professional league system along the lines of other major sports in America — and indeed around the world — like football, baseball, basketball and ice hockey.

The World Team Tennis league was designed to bring the game to the American public at large. In order to do so, it was decided that tennis as played along conventional lines was too confusing and boring. So they revised the scoring system — 15, 30 and 40 were abandoned in favour of 1, 2 and 3; deuce was abolished; and the court was marked out in different colours. No longer were audiences required to be quiet and restrained: they were encouraged to shout and cheer, and the players of each team, sitting on the bench beside the court, participated vociferously as well.

Players of both sexes were signed to play for a team in either the Eastern or Western division of the league. Each team played out of a major city, and had names like the Philadelphia Freedoms, the New York Apples, the Hawaii Leis, the San Francisco Golden Gaters, and the San Diego Friars. Matches consisted of a set each of men's singles and doubles, women's singles and doubles, and mixed doubles. Players could be replaced in mid-set if the trainer felt they were not doing well enough. There were cheerleaders, music and all types of razzmatazz, and the players were offered lucrative guarantees.

Most of the leading stars — particularly the women — took part at various stages during the league's six-year history. It was played during the summer months, from May to August, with three weeks off in the middle for Wimbledon, and it decimated the quality of players available for the major European events like the French and Italian Opens. The matches were all played indoors in huge coliseums like the Spectrum in Philadelphia and Madison Square Garden, which were free at that time of year. Some of the teams were fairly successful, and some made money, but others were not and failed spectacularly.

There were a number of changes during the period, as franchises were sold, and at one time there was the extraordinary presence of a team of Russians in the league, known as the Soviets, in this very capitalistic cultural circus. The league's commissioner was Larry King, husband of Billie Jean, and he continued to run it in a modified form when the original system collapsed after the 1979 series. The purists were horrified by this grotesque reincarnation of a genteel sport, but it did have a following of some strength at its height.

Team Tennis never became the dominant form of professional tennis that was hoped for, but it was imitated on a less extreme basis elsewhere. Professional leagues sprang up in countries like West Germany and the Netherlands, guaranteeing a substantial income for lesser-grade players. A format began in Britain in 1987 which, by the following year, was offering top players like Ivan Lendl and Pat Cash huge sums of money to appear in small stadia half a dozen times during the late winter. The idea of giving an audience a complete evening's entertainment with plenty of variety appeared to have caught on, and Team Tennis looks like being a viable alternative to tournament play for the next century.

OLYMPIC GAMES

The reappearance of tennis as a full discipline at the Seoul Olympics in 1988 was the culmination of many years of effort by the International Tennis Federation and in particular by its President, Philippe Chatrier.

For the last decade Chatrier has campaigned determinedly to restore tennis to a place in the world's greatest sporting showcase. Tennis is perhaps the most international of all sports, and it is only right that it should be included in this superlative festival. The Federation's main platform was for the furtherance of the game in Third World countries, as in many of these it is only the sports with Olympic status that receive government backing.

The biggest hurdle that had to be overcome was the fact that tennis has become one of the most lucrative of all sports, and its professionalism is light years away from the original amateur ethos envisaged by the Olympics' modern founder, Baron Pierre de Coubertin. How could the tennis millionaires rub shoulders with true-blue amateurs representing their countries in the disciplines of swimming, wrestling and modern pentathlon?

On the other hand, the most heavily publicized of all Olympic sports, athletics, has also become heavily professionalized in recent years, and the rules of entry are determined by the individual sports in the Games. So, after protracted negotiations, a compromise has been effected for tennis whereby all players are eligible regardless of status, although they will receive no direct financial recompense for their participation.

Tennis was part of the Olympics from 1896 to 1924, with varying degrees of support. The best celebrations in terms of quality of entry were at Antwerp in 1920 and at Paris in 1924, with players of the calibre of Suzanne Lenglen and Helen Wills winning gold medals. The ILTF withdrew after the latter year because they were locked in dispute with the International Olympic Committee over control of the organization and the definition of an amateur. Tennis was held to be purely a demonstration sport at Mexico City in 1968, with Manuel Santana and Helga Niessen taking the singles golds. Then in 1984, by which time the sport had been readmitted in principle, there were tennis events for players aged 21 and under; Stefan Edberg and Steffi Graf were the winners.

The majority of the world's leading players were enthusiastic about taking part at Seoul. Teams had to be nominated by the end of 1987, and the number of acceptances per country depended on performances in the 1987 Davis and Federation Cups. There were also wild cards and qualifying competitions at various venues around the world.

Mats Wilander, Boris Becker and Pat Cash (injured) and Ivan Lendl, Martina Navratilova and Andre Agassi (ineligible) were missing from Seoul. In the end, medals went to the following players: Men's Singles: Miloslav Mecir (gold), Tim Mayotte (silver), Stefan Edberg and Brad Gilbert (bronze). Women's Singles: Steffi Graf (gold), Gabriela Sabatini (silver), Zina Garrison and Manuela Maleeva (bronze). Doubles golds went to Ken Flach/Robert Seguso and Pam Shriver/Zina Garrison.

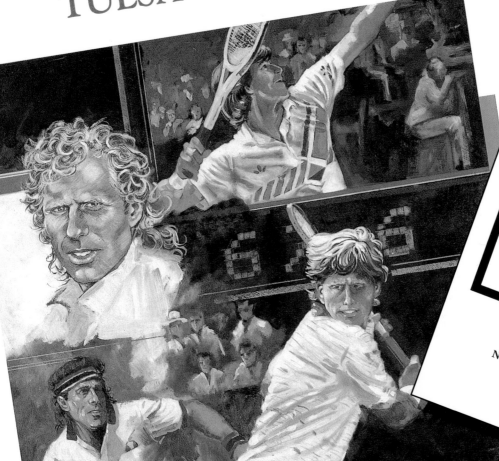

TULSA CHALLENGE '85

An International Tennis Event

Boris **BECKER**

Kevin **CURREN**

Vitas **GERULAITIS**

Guillermo **VILAS**

TULSA CONVENTION CENTER

September 17 - 18, 1985

First Tulsa
A Bank of Mid-America

KELI 1430
Tulsa's Radio Station

PEPSI

Precision
Imports

The Tulsa Tri

SIX EAST 39TH STREET
NEW YORK, NEW YORK 10016
(212) 696 - 4884

DECEMBER 2-

Understanding Modern Tennis

For many millions of people around the world, tennis is a pleasant activity that is purely and simply to be enjoyed. It is a healthy, outdoor pastime, less restricted by the seasons than other sports identified with summer — you can play it at any time of year in most parts of the world, provided it is not snowing or raining — and it is not particularly expensive. It can be played by people of all ages and social backgrounds, and you don't have to be exceptionally fit or mobile for an agreeable game of doubles.

But as a professional sport, tennis is big business. The international calendar is solid with tournaments and team competitions, ranging from the Grand Slam championships and the Masters through various grades of Grand Prix events, challenger tournaments and satellites.

The Top 20 or so of either sex are among the highest-earning sports performers in the world, banking millions of dollars through prize money and product endorsements. Lucrative exhibition matches with guaranteed appearance fees are available for a select few.

And even when a player becomes too old to keep up with the rest of the pack, avenues for future high earnings are there in off-court capacities such as coaching, business consultancy or media careers. Once you have made your name in tennis, shrewd marketing can keep you in the limelight long after your playing days are over. But no player can do it on their own, and this is where the army of lawyers, marketing personnel and managers come in.

For those who do become superstars, the sky's the limit. But the demands of modern tennis are harsh, and much needs to be sacrificed before the material rewards can be reaped. This chapter examines the contemporary tennis scene and describes the drawbacks as well as the benefits of being a professional player.

Left: Modern tennis means big money. In the US, where more top-class tournaments take place than anywhere else, corporations are enlisted in droves to act as sponsors.

As competitive tennis has expanded dramatically in the last 20 years, with thousands playing the game worldwide at a high level whereas at one time there were only a few hundred, a fair and logical method of sorting them out and determining entries for the various strata of tournaments has had to be devised. And as no individual or committee could possibly collate the myriad of results that flood in from all corners of the globe, tennis organizers have come to rely upon computers to assimilate the mass of data, and produce regularly updated ranking lists to determine acceptances and seeding.

Computer rankings

Computer rankings date from 1973. Prior to that, national associations ranked their players annually by committee, but there were no official world rankings — merely lists of the top ten of either sex compiled by journalists for reviews of the past season in newspaper and magazine articles. Silicon-chip technology was originally used by the United States Tennis Association for the practical purpose of ranking players, on their results over a year's competition, for tournament acceptance.

The Association of Tennis Professionals — the men's player union formed in 1972 to represent its members' interests in a sport beset by political squabbles between professional promoters and the traditional amateur authorities — quickly adopted the concept and requested that computer rankings be used for all professional tournaments. In due course the female equivalent, the Women's Tennis Association, formed in 1973, endorsed this policy, and set up their own ranking system in 1975. From initial print-

Right: Television plays a crucial role in the professional game. In Paris, cameras record every angle of play as Yannick Noah lunges acrobatically for a volley.

outs of only a hundred or so names, the ever-increasing numbers of tournaments now return data for nearly 2,000 men and women to be listed in this way.

Computer rankings have evolved over the years, using different systems, and using separate specifications for either sex. Both the ATP and WITA (the word 'International' was added to the WTA's title in 1986) currently use systems designed by Hewlett-Packard, but whereas male players can get on to the ATP ranking from results in one tournament, the women only qualify from their record in at least three.

ATP ranking system

The ATP list is updated each week, following the assimilation of whatever results have been recorded in that time. Overall, the rankings reflect a 12-month period, so a performance

by a player will continue to be counted until more than a year has elapsed.

No result will count unless it has been achieved in a recognized tournament that qualifies for ranking status. This is determined by the prize money available. There are three distinct levels: tournaments that are part of the Nabisco Grand Prix, which must have prize money totalling at least $100,000; challenger tournaments, where the total is a minimum of $25,000; and satellite circuits of four qualifying events plus a Masters final for the leading finishers, where minimum overall prize money is also $25,000. Through all these events there is a rigid system of a main draw, qualifying rounds, and sometimes pre-qualifying rounds.

The level of prize money, the size of the draw and the strength of the field determine the rating a tournament receives, and the value of computer points to be awarded. The number of points depends upon the round a player reaches — for example, he could win 10 points for winning a tournament, eight points as runner-up, six points as a semi-finalist, etc. He can also win bonus points for beating a player ranked among the top 150 in the world.

A player's ranking is based on his average (total number of points divided by the total number of tournaments he has played over the 12 months). If he has played more than 12 tournaments, the divisor is one number less than the total, so if, for example, he has played 20 tournaments during the previous 12 months, his points total is divided by 19 to give his ranking average. This is the fairest method of ranking, because the players who competed most would have an obvious advantage if a simple aggregate were used. If a player is injured and unable to compete, his ranking will only suffer gradually, because his existing points total is divided by the number of events he has played.

To show how this system works, here are the top ten positions in the final year-end ranking of 1986:

Position	Player	Tournaments played	Average
1	Ivan Lendl	14	187.36
2	Boris Becker	17	104.12
3	Mats Wilander	12	92.25
4	Yannick Noah	12	88.58
5	Stefan Edberg	20	86.53
6	Henri Leconte	13	76.85
7	Joakim Nystrom	19	71.41
8	Jimmy Connors	16	68.00
9	Miloslav Mecir	17	63.81
10	Andres Gomez	22	53.80

This is comparatively straightforward in the upper echelons of the list, because the volume of results produced by these players makes for clear-cut numerical differences to determine their rankings. But further down, bunches of players appear with identical averages. In order to sort these competitors' relative merits into an order of ranking, the computer takes into account every possible nuance. Even then, in positions below 400 or thereabouts, it is not always possible to separate them, so a few positions are tied.

WITA ranking system

The women, however, have an even more efficient system, which rules out ties completely. This is preferable, as a position can mean the difference between having to qualify for a tournament or being accepted straight into the main draw. The WITA rankings are revised every two weeks.

There are 10 categories of tournament counted for computer rankings, from Category 1 (with total prize money of $10,000, and where the winner receives 3 points) through Category 10 (with prize money of $750,000, where the winner is awarded 300 points). The rules and regulations that apply are complicated and involve all sorts of mathematical calculations, with percentages of points awarded through qualifying and main draw rounds. Bonus points can be won for a player beating another ranked in the top 300, scaled according to the loser's ranking at the time the tournament results are fed into the database.

Short cuts

It is easier for a player to make a sharp rise in the rankings if he or she had little previous data. So if someone has been off the circuit for whatever reason, then wins through a qualifying draw and beats a few good opponents in a tournament with valuable points allocation, he or she can go on to reach the top 100 or better in a comparatively short space of time.

There are, however, exceptions to these rules. All tournaments are allowed a number of wild cards in the draw. A wild card is a player who has entered that, for various reasons, is a desirable competitor to have in the main draw without a sufficient ranking to qualify automatically. A 32-draw tournament will normally have an allowance of four wild cards. These special places are awarded at the discretion of the tournament director, who might give them to local players, or perhaps a great name from the past who is no longer ranked high enough but whose presence and charisma might help ticket sales and media coverage.

At Wimbledon, for example, there might be only two or three British players high enough on the computer to gain direct acceptance. So the wild cards go to young unranked or low-ranked British players, and maybe a former leading player whose past record should exempt him from having to qualify. Alternatively, a leading current player who did not enter before the deadline (usually three weeks before the start of the tournament, but in some cases much earlier) might ask to have a wild card reserved for him in case he decides to take part at the last minute.

Finding a place

To illustrate how the rankings determine acceptances for tournaments, let us take an imaginary $100,000 Grand Prix tournament. There is a singles draw of 32 players, and a qualifying draw of 32. Because there are several other similar tournaments taking place elsewhere in the world that week, the entry is not particularly strong.

Of those players that have entered, the top 24 off the latest computer ranking list go straight into the main draw, and the top eight of these are seeded, so they each go into a separate section of the main draw in order to be apart until the quarter-finals. (The seeding follows the order of the computer rankings exactly. The top seed automatically goes to the top of the draw, and the second highest is placed at the bottom. Numbers three and four are drawn to see which goes to position 16, and which to position 17. Then the next four seeds are drawn for a place in each quarter.) Four wild cards are selected also to go into the draw, and four places are left for qualifiers to fill.

The qualifying draw is also seeded from

Left: Player turns interviewer: John Newcombe (left) seeks comments from doubles partner Fred Stolle after the veteran pair went all the way to a final set tiebreak in the semi-finals at Flushing Meadow in 1981.

the computer, and from the 32 players in this, four wild cards can also be allowed. Should one of the acceptances in the main draw then scratch (ie withdraw without playing), the highest-ranked loser in the third (qualifying) round will replace him as a Lucky Loser.

This is the system that applies in all professional tournaments that count towards ranking points. If a young player without points is to break into it, he must either start right at the bottom, qualifying for the lowest level of satellite tournament and working his way up or, alternatively, if he has performed well in a local or junior event, he can be awarded a wild card and take a short cut into the upper strata. Because tennis is such an unpredictable game, it is often possible for a comparatively unknown player to get far quickly, provided he has the right breaks. John McEnroe reached as far as the semi-finals as a qualifier at his first Wimbledon in 1977, and in 1984 a young Swedish girl, Carina Karlsson, went through the qualifying and got to the last eight at Wimbledon despite a very low ranking.

For several years in women's tennis there was a circuit called the Futures which ran concurrently with the first three months of the main professional tour. It was possible for anyone to enter the pre-qualifying round of a Futures event, win her way through qualifying and the main draw and, if she reached the semi-finals, be automatically into the following week's main circuit tournament among some of the best players in the world.

Reaching the Virginia Slims

This system has now been replaced by four levels of tournament below the main Virginia Slims Women's Series. (1) The $20,000 development circuits are linked series of three tournaments, each with $5,000 prize money, plus a $5,000 Masters event at the end for the 16 leading finishers from the circuit. Players receive computer points from the Masters event only. (2) The $10,000 satellite tournaments have total prize money of $10,000, with computer points available for players in the main draw. (3) The satellite circuits consist of at least three tournaments, each worth $10,000 and each with ranking points to be gained, plus a Masters event worth $10,000.

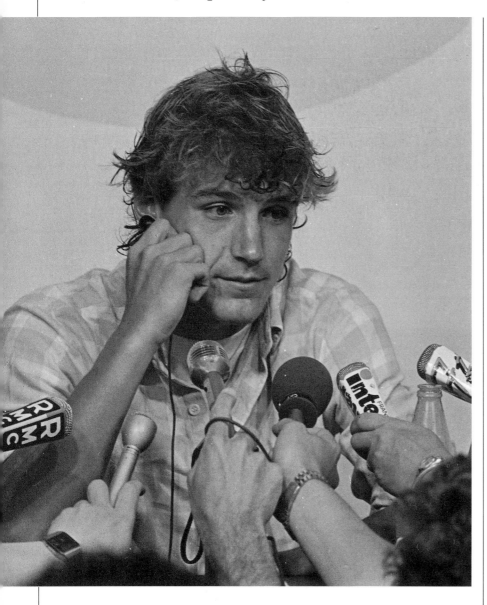

Above: A 17-year-old Mats Wilander faces a battery of microphones as he tells the world's press how it feels to be the youngest ever winner of a Grand Slam men's singles title (Paris, 1982).

association of the country where it is taking place. Or it may come out of grants from the Grand Slam Trust Fund, which is administered by the ITF on behalf of the Big Four championships, who donate a portion of their not inconsiderable profits for this purpose.

Tennis at this level is far from glamorous and lucrative. A player must realistically give himself only two or three years of trying to scratch a living around the satellites. If he has not made any significant progress in that time, he should give up. The prize money is not enough to provide more than a hand-to-mouth existence, and anyone below about 250 on the computer is unlikely to be showing much of a profit, once travelling and accommodation expenses are accounted for. Some players may have wealthy parents, and others may have private sponsorship, but unless they win lots of matches, these funds are likely to dry up. Remote and unpublicized satellite tournaments are often depressing places to be at, with no audiences, no well-known players, and no luxurious surroundings. It is a side of tennis not known to the followers of the multi-million dollar pro circuit and all its glittering accoutrements.

Playing the computer

It is, however, possible for a 'journeyman' pro, a player who is not well known and who rarely, if ever, hits the headlines, to make a respectable living from the game. There are team leagues in countries like the US, Germany, the Netherlands and Great Britain where players are guaranteed fees for a certain number of matches each year. It is also possible to 'play the computer', in other words to pick your tournaments carefully, bearing in mind the points available and the likely standard of entry, in order to achieve and maintain a position on the rankings. Players will usually enter only the sort of tournament that will suit them, so a grass and cement-court specialist will avoid the clay-court circuits of Europe and South America, and vice-versa. A former high-ranking star that has fallen way down the list because of illness, injury or other reasons will select his tournaments strategically in order to regain a high position. He will be helped on his way by wild cards and special exemptions that prevent him from competing at the lowest levels.

The rules can be bent in accommodating ways. One of the most notable comebacks was made by a Czech player, Regina Marsikova. Once ranked as high as 11th in the world, she was implicated in a fatal car accident in her native country and spent a time in prison. Because of her past record, she was actually given an 'honorary' computer ranking on her return to competition and worked her way back through wild cards and qualifying events. Similar comebacks have been made by Dianne Balestrat and Terry Holladay. Should Tracy Austin or Andrea Jaeger wish to return, they could do so.

(4) The challenger tournaments have prize money totalling $25,000 and ranking points for both the qualifying and the main draw; these are usually the springboard for the Virginia Slims tournaments, which must have minimum prize money of $50,000.

Prize money

Where does all the prize money come from? In the case of big events likely to be televised and attended by the press, it comes from sponsors. A company will agree to put up the required amount of cash for prize money and running expenses in exchange for having its name officially in the title of the tournament and its logo displayed prominently around the courts and in all publicity material. Television coverage usually guarantees sponsorship, because at the price it is cheaper than direct advertising. And the healthy, youthful image of tennis is appealing to many companies who would like their product identified in public consciousness with something like that.

But for the lower grade of tournament, where media interest is slight, prize money may often be provided by the national tennis

Above: The pressures of being a star: Adriano Panatta is besieged by autograph hunters after a notable win at Wimbledon in 1979.

Burn-out

The last two players have been the most notable victims of a notorious contemporary problem known as 'burn-out'. Both were remarkably precocious girls who were among the best four players in the world while still teenagers. Austin, who at 16 was the youngest-ever player to win a Grand Slam singles title (the 1979 US Open), played too much too soon and was sidelined by chronic sciatica by the time she was 21. She made a few comeback attempts but was forced to retire permanently in 1984. Jaeger, the youngest-ever seed at Wimbledon at the age of 15, simply lost interest and retired to go to college when she was only 19 and already a millionairess.

There have been many other cases of children attempting to play at adult level. It has been argued that, before it is fully developed, the human body cannot take the amount of punishment inflicted by the continuous competitive tennis required by the circuit, which is why injuries and 'burn-out' occur. Extensive campaigning and lobbying has taken place on this issue, and in recent years the ITF have set limits on the number of pro tournaments young players can take part in.

It has always been easier for girls to do well in women's tournaments than for boys in men's play, which is why this is mainly a female problem. However, two notable precocious young men — Jimmy Arias and Aaron Krickstein — achieved remarkable early success before falling back with loss of form and injury. At one time they represented the future of American tennis: now they are also-rans.

Prodigies in tennis, therefore, must shape their careers with caution. Too many have attempted to emulate the unparalleled progress of Chris Evert, herself a teenage sensation, who went on to enjoy the most consistently successful career in the history of professional tennis. Nobody else can match her record of at least one Grand Slam singles title every year for 13 years, and only two failures to reach the semi-finals of 50 Grand Slam events. During her magnificent 16-year pro career, Evert has seldom been injured, and by taking long breaks from competition from time to time she has never lost her enthusiasm for the game. For her,

Above: Although deadly serious on court, Chris Evert is renowned for her charm and good humour elsewhere. Here she responds at a dinner in Paris in 1983 for the International Tennis Federation's official World Champions.
Opposite: Face to face: Jimmy Connors provides a light-hearted moment on the Centre Court at Wimbledon.

financial considerations are of little consequence — she has won over $8 million in prize money, not to mention product endorsement. Her much-publicized divorce settlement with John Lloyd reportedly cost her $2 million, but she did not suffer any hardship in paying it.

Her parents, Jimmy and Colette, must be regarded as model tennis parents, having played a low-profile role in helping to shape her career. Far too many of the talented young players that have fallen off the treadmill through 'burn-out' have had greedy, dictatorial parents pushing them too hard.

Player managers

But parents are essentially amateurs in this business, and it is the professional managers and agents that have more effectively come into the reckoning in recent years. Ranging from the petty businessman to the experienced management organizations, there is one behind virtually every top player these days.

There are three major player management groups in tennis: IMG, the highly successful outfit run for many years,

beginning with golf and moving into other sports and branches of entertainment, headed by Mark McCormack; ProServ, founded by Donald Dell; and Advantage International, a more recent force whose clients include the current world No. 1, Steffi Graf. These companies sign players and advise them where to play and when to rest, arrange endorsement contracts and promotional appearances for them, and in return take a percentage of their earnings. In a sport where so much money can be won and so many avenues of marketing potential can be exploited, they have a necessary part to play.

It should not be forgotten that there are still good amateur players left in this dollar-ruled environment. Some Eastern European countries still expect their players to give their prize money to their national associations, which pay the players allowances, though in some Communist regimes, most notably Czechoslovakia, the players have complete freedom to keep the cash and come and go as they please. Attitudes there have come a long way since Martina Navratilova, frustrated and tormented by a lack of control over her own destiny, defected to the US in 1975. Ivan Lendl and Hana Mandlikova are both extremely wealthy and prefer to live outside their homeland; indeed, Lendl has applied for US citizenship, and Mandlikova has now become an Australian, like her husband.

Production line

Amateurs also remain in the US, where young people taking up scholarships at colleges and universities must retain this status and forfeit prize money in open events. The collegiate system has always been the principal production line of American tennis, with players like Jimmy Connors and John McEnroe attending at least as freshmen before pursuing full-time careers as professionals.

Another area in which budding champions are trained and prepared for the rigours of competitive play are tennis academies such as those at Port Washington and Bradenton, Florida. The latter, run by renowned coach Nick Bolettieri, has turned out useful starlets like Arias, Carling Bassett and Kathy Horvath. Coaches such as Bolettieri and Dennis van der Meer, author of several well-known instructional books, have followed in the footsteps of Harry Hopman, perhaps the greatest coach in the history of tennis, and former champions like Lew Hoad and John Newcombe, who invested some of their winnings in successful centres with highly efficient training programmes.

The growth of the junior game is of paramount importance, as it provides a vital competitive structure for the development of young talent. Most countries in the world have national junior schemes which take children displaying exceptional talent at an early age, place them under the guidance of experienced coaches, and help them through schooling and training.

State-run schemes have proved extremely successful in Czechoslovakia, where a never-ending stream of top-class players has emerged since the early 1970s. National schemes in Sweden, France and West Germany have also lifted the overall playing standard in these countries to such an extent that they are among the strongest in the world.

Considerable funds are now being channelled into this area by Australia and Great Britain although, with the exception of Pat Cash, no major players have yet emerged. Australia, which produced so many champions during the 1950s and 1960s that it could afford to become complacent, has high hopes about its new National Tennis Centre.

Britain, traditionally among the strongest tennis nations in Europe, has been slow to move with the times, and has watched most of its neighbours overtake it. Endless debate and speculation has taken place as to the reasons for this decline. Lack of finance can hardly be an excuse, as its Lawn Tennis Association receives millions each year from the profits of the Wimbledon Championships. Britain is still woefully short of indoor tennis courts, although the number has increased substantially in recent years. Strenuous efforts by the LTA to revive the country's flagging fortunes are underway, but it would be as well if some of the intense hyping of a new star by the media each time they have any sort of success were muted.

The most notable recent victim of this excessive publicity was Annabel Croft, a glamorous young woman who achieved sufficiently good results in 1984/5 for the British press to pin all their hopes on her and subject her to unnecessary pressure. Croft's form and confidence suffered so disastrously that she took a long break from the game in the autumn of 1987 and requested that she be left out of her country's annually trounced Wightman Cup team.

Junior and senior circuits

Juniors now have as highly organized an international circuit as their senior counterparts. The ITF Junior Rankings are based on a circuit of over 100 tournaments in over 60 countries, with points to be awarded and regularly updated lists to determine seeding and acceptances. There are junior events in both singles and doubles at all Grand Slam championships, plus international team competitions along the lines of the Davis and Federation Cups.

This circuit provides useful experience for the lucrative opportunities of the Nabisco Grand Prix (for men) and the Virginia Slims World Series (for women). Both of these worldwide, year-long circuits involve points totals and aggregate rankings that provide additional prize money at the end of the year. In 1986, Ivan Lendl topped the men's final standings with 4,801 points and received a bonus payment of $800,000. He then went into the Masters tournament in New York along with the other top eight finishers, playing for (and winning) total prize money of $500,000. Martina Navratilova topped the Virginia Slims standings for 1986 with 4,825 points and a bonus of $225,000. Whereas the Masters has reverted to being an eight-man round-robin (ie all-play-all) event, the VS championships is a 16-draw knockout, also worth $500,000, with a best-of-five-set final. In this, Navratilova was the winner in both singles and doubles.

Administered by the Men's International Professional Council, a body made up of representatives from the ITF, players and tournament directors, the Grand Prix has an elaborate set of rules. Each player taking part must commit himself to at least 14 tournaments each year. If he does not agree to play this number, he must qualify, whatever his computer ranking. This was one of the rules that forced Bjorn Borg's premature retirement in 1982. Borg only wanted to play a few tournaments, but the MIPC were inflexible. The rule was devised to counter the threat of unofficial tournaments and exhibitions not sanctioned by the ITF, which are counter-productive to a healthy, well-supported circuit.

Each Grand Prix event is manned by MIPC-appointed Supervisors and Chair Umpires who have the power to impose penalty points for various transgressions of conduct — such as racket abuse, audible obscenity, etc. If a player tots up sufficient penalty points to go over the limit, he is automatically suspended. John McEnroe has done so more than once, but even if he is banned from the Grand Prix, he is still able to earn vast sums competing in unofficial events and exhibitions. This is an anomaly that has been a thorn in the ITF's side for many years.

The Grand Prix takes in tournaments all over the world and is played on a variety of surfaces — most notably clay, carpet, cement and grass. A comparison with the old calendar of the pre-open years is worthwhile, as it shows how much the international circuit has changed over the last 20 years.

Pre-open tennis circuit

For most of the history of tennis up to 1968 the traditional amateur calendar began in Australia in January with state meetings and the Australian championships, which rotated between Melbourne, Sydney, Brisbane, Adelaide and Perth. It moved in February to a few indoor events in the US before returning outdoors to the popular Caribbean circuit, which took in such exotic venues as Kingston, Caracas, Barranquilla and Mexico City. At the same time, many European players were sunning themselves on the French Riviera, on the courts once trodden by the great Suzanne Lenglen, at places like Nice, Cannes, Menton and Monte Carlo. An important venue in April would be Johannesburg, for the South African Championships — once among the

top seven tournaments in the world — where leading players gathered from the Caribbean and notable tournaments in Egypt and Kenya.

As spring arrived, the place to be was Europe. The English outdoor circuit started with well-supported tournaments in London suburbs like Hampstead, Chingford and Sutton, then the once-important British Hard Court Championships at Bournemouth, which was in fact the world's first open meeting in 1968. The English circuit continued on shale (their version of clay) and then grass through and beyond Wimbledon. There used to be tournaments like the London Hard Court Championships at the Hurlingham Club and the Surrey Championships at Surbiton which attracted entries of the highest class. Across the Channel, major events like the Italian championships in Rome and the French championships in Paris were being held.

All itineraries converged on England for the run-up to Wimbledon at Beckenham and Queen's Club (London), then the Championships themselves. In those days, the majority of the best players stayed on in Britain for several more weeks of grass-court play after Wimbledon. There were the Scottish Championships at Edinburgh, the Welsh Championships at Newport, and tournaments at Hoylake (northern England), and Eastbourne. Over in Europe, clay-court competition resumed for the Swedish, Swiss, Dutch and German championships. By mid-August, many players had crossed the Atlantic for the US Eastern Grass Court circuit. Played at exclusive country clubs along the coast at venues like Newport (Rhode Island), Essex (Massachusetts), Merion (Pennsylvania) and South Orange (New Jersey), they led up to the National Doubles Championships at Boston and the singles events at Forest Hills.

In mid-September, the circuit moved west for the Pacific Coast Championships at Berkeley, and the Pacific South-West at Los Angeles. Both these were on cement. October was a quiet time, with little important activity, but in November and December there were indoor tournaments in Europe and the Sugar circuit in South Africa. By Christmas, the tour had returned to Australia for the journey around the state capitals.

Start of the Grand Prix year

Some of these fixtures remain on today's calendar. Australia is still the place to be in January, with grass-court tournaments at Adelaide and Sydney, and the newly resited Australian Open on rubberized hard courts at Melbourne. After comparatively minor events at Auckland and São Paulo, the main circuit moves to the US, with the well-established US Pro Indoor Championships at the Spectrum, Philadelphia, and the US Indoor Open at Memphis, Tennessee. It then goes outdoors for a few weeks. The Pilot Pen Classic at Indian Wells, California, a mar-

Opposite: Martina Navratilova entrances the knowledgeable tennis spectators at Eastbourne. This sedate resort on the English south coast hosts a major women's grass court tournament the week before Wimbledon.

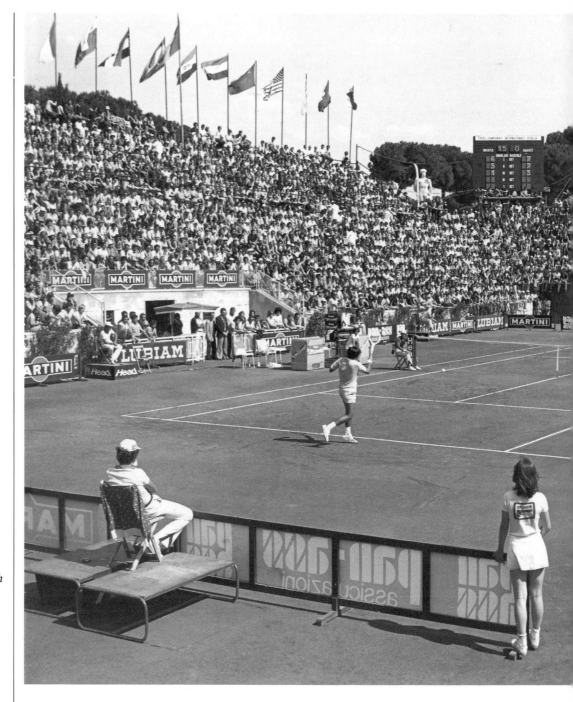

Right: Foro Italico, Rome, is venue for the Italian Open each year. Built in Mussolini's time, it is dramatically sited near the River Tiber, and with its huge marble statues and vociferous crowds evokes the atmosphere of the Coliseum of Ancient Rome.

vellous new desert facility that has inherited the event from earlier venues at Palm Springs and La Quinta, is followed by the biggest and most lucrative tournament after the four Grand Slam events.

This is the Lipton International Players Championships at Key Biscayne, Florida. It began in 1985 and is a two-week tournament for men and women with draws of 128 in each singles (other Grand Prix events do not exceed 64) plus men's, women's and mixed doubles. The prize money for both sexes is $750,000, which puts it in the second highest category for computer rankings and Grand Prix points after the Grand Slams. The standard of entries is correspondingly high, with almost all the top players taking part (although John McEnroe has been a notable absentee).

There is one more tournament in Florida before the circuit moves to Europe for a series of indoor meetings. Rotterdam, Brussels, Nancy and Milan all stage big prize-money spectaculars on Supreme, a carpet court most commonly used indoors, while simultaneously with Milan there is an indoor tournament in Chicago.

Grand Prix spring circuit

The first week of April sees the first outdoor European fixture at Bari, Italy, and the Buick WCT finals at Dallas. This used to be the culmination of a rival Grand Prix which, in its heyday, was as extensive as the ITF-approved circuit. But nowadays players qualifying for Dallas do so from just three tournaments — at Atlanta, Forest Hills and Houston. WCT has vastly diminished as a major part of professional tennis, and Dallas has nothing like the prestige it once enjoyed.

There are outdoor tournaments in the Far

(London) and Bristol, as well as a continuation of clay-court play at Bologna and Athens. But no Grand Prix event runs in opposition to the two weeks of Wimbledon, which like the French and US Opens has never varied its position on the calendar.

Grand Prix summer circuit

No more major competition takes place in England for the summer, as the tour moves in two directions, east back to Europe — for the championships of Switzerland at Gstaad, Sweden at Bastad, the Netherlands at Hilversum, and Austria at Kitzbuhel — and west for the US summer circuit.

This segment of the Grand Prix now includes a variety of surfaces. There is grass (a delightful anachronism) at the shrine of American tennis, Newport (Rhode Island), scene of the first US Nationals back in 1881. Clay is used for the US Pro Championships at the Longwood Cricket Club, Boston, another famous old venue where the surface has been changed, and for the US Clay Court Championships at Indianapolis. This is a long-established tournament dating back to 1910, and until 1986 the programme included both men's and women's events.

Cement comes into use at Livingston (New Jersey), Schenectady (New York), Washington DC, Stratton Mountain (Vermont), the Canadian Open in Montreal, the ATP Championships at Cincinnati (Ohio) and Rye Brook (New York). While these tournaments are taking place, European competition continues at Stuttgart, St Vincent (Italy) and Prague. The US Open during the first two weeks of September is followed by further European clay-court fixtures at Geneva, Madrid, Barcelona and Palermo (Sicily). Back on the West Coast, the old Pacific Coast and South West championships have been replaced by an outdoor tournament in Los Angeles and an indoor one, the Transamerica Open, at San Francisco's Cow Palace.

End of the Grand Prix year

In October there are indoor events in Europe at Basle, Toulouse, and Vienna, and in Australia at Brisbane, Sydney and Melbourne. Outdoor tournaments at this time are on cement at Scottsdale (Arizona) and Tel Aviv. Big prize-money tournaments sponsored by Seiko can be found at Tokyo (indoors) and Hong Kong (outdoors) in late October, then the European indoor circuit resumes with tournaments in Paris, Stockholm, Cologne and Wembley (London).

South America gets three weeks of Grand Prix action with tournaments at São Paulo, Buenos Aires and Itaparica (Brazil) at the same time as the evocatively named 'WCT Shootout' in Houston and the South African Open in Johannesburg.

South Africa's current situation in tennis is that its players compete wherever they can obtain visas. (This rules out many countries,

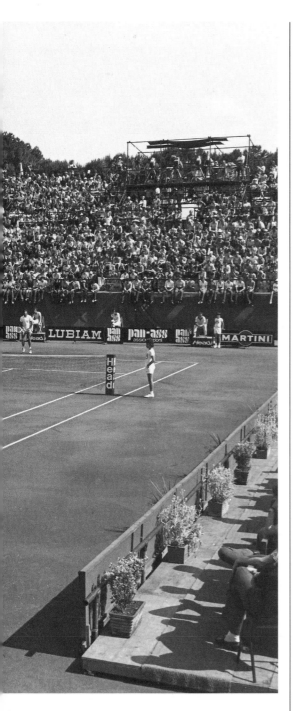

East at Seoul and Tokyo, at the same time as the surviving remnants of the old French Riviera circuit at Nice and Monte Carlo (albeit for men only). With the exception of the WCT Tournament of Champions at the old US Open venue of Forest Hills, the Grand Prix stays solidly in Europe until midsummer. A brace of meetings in West Germany — the German Open at the Club an der Alster, Hamburg, and the Bavarian Open in Munich, are followed by two in Italy — the Italian Open at Foro Italico, Rome (a magnificent setting for tennis, rivalled on the Continent only by Monte Carlo) and the Florence Open. The following week is left free for the World Team Cup in Dusseldorf, then comes the two-week French Open in Paris, where the women once more join the men.

The second and third weeks in June see grass-court tournaments at Queen's Club

but they are still welcome in the US, Britain, Australia and France.) Some of their leading players have obtained US citizenship (most notably Kevin Curren and Johan Kriek) or live abroad. South African teams have been barred from the Davis and Federation Cups for nearly 10 years, and participation by individual players occasionally causes disturbances — in 1987, for example, Bristol City Council in England withdrew financial support for a tournament there because South Africans were taking part. Overseas entries for the South African Open are much weaker than they used to be, and players that do go are named on the United Nations cultural blacklist. President Botha's reaffirmation of apartheid policies has rebounded on efforts towards racial integration by the South African Tennis Union, and no notable black player has ever emerged from the Republic.

The first two weeks of December see the culmination of the Grand Prix with the Masters singles at Madison Square Garden, followed by the Masters doubles at London's Royal Albert Hall. The latter event was previously identified as the WCT World Doubles Championship, and until 1985 doubles play took place alongside the singles in New York.

Challengers and satellites

Running simultaneously with the Grand Prix through the year are lower strata of tournaments, with prize money of $25,000 or $50,000 in the challenger series, and satellite circuits of four tournaments plus a Masters totalling $25,000, for players ranked too low on the computer to qualify for the major tour.

The challenger series include venues in Chile, Kenya, Nigeria, Brazil, France, Egypt, Morocco, Austria, Israel, Italy, Mexico, Portugal, West Germany, US, Finland, Ireland, Belgium, Turkey, Hungary, Greece, Norway, Singapore and the Netherlands.

Satellite circuits take place in 18 countries, some of them with more than one series: Australia (2), Austria, Belgium (2), Bulgaria, Canada, France (3), Great Britain (2), Hungary, Israel, Italy (2), Japan, Netherlands, Portugal, Spain (4), Switzerland (2), US (7), West Germany (3) and Yugoslavia.

Some challenger and satellite events are the modern versions of traditional tournaments, but only in very few cases do the circuits bear any resemblance to competitive activity dating back more than a few years, particularly as many of them are in indoor venues.

The Virginia Slims circuit

The women's Virginia Slims schedule has some similarity to the men's, with action in the same parts of the world at certain times, plus of course joint competition at the Grand Slam and Lipton championships. Like the men, they begin in Australia in January with grass-court tournaments at Brisbane and Sydney, and the Australian Open in Melbourne, moving on to Auckland in the last week of the month.

The Bridgestone Doubles in Tokyo is a long-standing invitation event for eight pairs. Then begin 12 weeks of tournaments exclusively in the United States. This segment starts indoors at Kansas, San Francisco and Oklahoma City, then moves south-east for the Virginia Slims of Florida at Boca Raton and the Lipton Championships at Key Biscayne. It stays outdoors on cement for the Arizona and Marco Island (Florida) events, then returns inside for Dallas, Washington DC and the US Women's Indoor Championships at Piscataway, New Jersey. The tour heads back to the sunshine for a small event at Wild Dunes (South Carolina) and two big ones, the Family Circle Cup at Hilton Head Island (South Carolina) and the WITA Championships, Amelia Island (Florida).

A little piece of history was made at the latter in 1981 when Chris Evert beat Martina

Below: Ivan Lendl launches into a serve at the Lipton International Players' Championships. This important new tournament was begun in 1985 along the lines of the Grand Slam competitions, with events for both men and women, big drawsheets, and two weeks' duration.

Navratilova 6-0, 6-0 in the final. Although Navratilova has beaten Evert marginally more times than she has lost to her, she has never duplicated that devastating scoreline, and the only historical parallel between the world's two best players happened when Suzanne Lenglen beat Kitty McKane, the holder, 6-0, 6-0 in the 1925 Wimbledon semi-finals.

The tour splits in mid-April with tournaments continuing in America at Houston and Tampa, while three Far East events take place in Tokyo, Taipei (Taiwan) and Singapore. Then action transfers to Europe, with the Italian Open in Rome, a small event in Barcelona, the German Open at West Berlin, a $75,000 week in Corsica, the European Open in Geneva, a $50,000 tournament in Strasbourg, and the French Open in Paris. These competitions, all on clay, are followed by four weeks on English grass at Edgbaston, Eastbourne, and Wimbledon.

The main tour switches back to the US for the summer segment in early July, although there are three more European tournaments, at Knokke (Belgium), Bregenz (Austria) and Bastad (Sweden). The women follow the men on to the grass courts at Newport (Rhode Island), then it's back to cement for the USTA Hard Court Championships at Seattle, the North Face Open at Berkeley, a $75,000 event at San Diego, a very big tournament at Los Angeles, the Canadian Open in Toronto and a smaller one at Mahwah (New Jersey). This series of North American action ends with the US Open at Flushing Meadow.

The Pan Pacific Open, indoors, is sited in Tokyo, while September outdoor play takes place in Hamburg, Athens and Menorca (Spain). New Orleans hosts an indoor event, and the tour remains under cover for the rest of the year with a European phase taking in Hilversum (Netherlands), Filderstadt (West Germany), Brighton (England) and Zurich. Then back west for Indianapolis, Worcester (Massachusetts), Little Rock (Arkansas) and Chicago, with the alternative of an outdoor tourney in San Juan (Puerto Rico). The climax for the points leaders is the Virginia Slims championships at Madison Square Garden in late November.

As with the Grand Prix, there are constant changes in this schedule from year to year, but the main trends remain the same.

Women's lower-level tournaments

Women's $25,000 challenger tournaments are less numerous than for the men. In 1986, they took place at Canberra (Australia), Taranto (Italy), Lee-on-Solent (Great Britain), Charleston (South Carolina), Bastad and Landskrona (Sweden), Zagreb (Yugoslavia), Sofia (Bulgaria), Bethesda (Maryland), Chiba (Japan) and Johannesburg.

Development circuits, worth $20,000, were held in Tel Aviv, Brindisi (Italy), Amersfoort (Netherlands), Tulln (Austria), Jerusalem, Buenos Aires and Rio de Janeiro.

Satellites were to be found in Florida, Texas, Sweden, Italy, Australia, England, France, Alabama, North Carolina, Michigan, West Germany, Mexico, Pennsylvania, New Jersey, Austria, New York State, Portugal, Spain, Venezuela, Yugoslavia, Colombia, Peru, Hawaii and South Africa.

ITF members

This proliferation of tournaments for all levels of computer-ranked players in all corners of the globe justifies the claim that tennis is the most international of sports. Indeed, there must be few countries in the world that do not possess at least one court. The International Tennis Federation has 147 members, 88 of them with voting rights. Countries whose national associations are affiliated (with non-voting members indicated by an asterisk) are: Afghanistan*, Algeria, American Samoa*, Argentina, Australia, Austria, Bahamas, Bahrain, Bangladesh, Barbados*, Belgium, Benin*, Bermuda*, Bhutan*, Bolivia, Botswana*,

Below: Stefan Edberg displays a healthy set of sponsors' logos on his tennis outfit. The colourful design of his shirt is a personalized commercial line, and like that of Ivan Lendl opposite, made by Adidas. Edberg is well reimbursed for endorsing the product.

Brazil, British Virgin Islands*, Brunei Darussalem*, Bulgaria, Burkina Faso*, Burma*, Cameroon, Canada, Cayman Islands*, Chile, Chinese People's Republic, Chinese Taipei, Colombia, Congo*, Cook Islands*, Costa Rica*, Côte d'Ivoire, Cuba, Cyprus, Czechoslovakia, Denmark, Djibouti, Dominica*, Dominican Republic, Ecuador, Egypt, El Salvador*, Ethiopia*, Fiji*, Finland, France, Gambia*, German Democratic Republic, German Federal Republic, Ghana, Great Britain, Greece, Guam*, Guatemala*, Guinee Conakry*, Guyana*, Haiti, Hong Kong, Hungary, India, Indonesia, Iran, Iraq, Ireland, Israel, Italy, Jamaica, Japan, Jordan, Kenya, North Korea*, South Korea, Kuwait, Lebanon, Lesotho*, Libya, Luxembourg, Malawi*, Malaysia, Mali*, Malta, Mauritius*,

Mexico, Monaco, Montserrat*, Morocco, Mozambique*, Nepal*, Netherlands, Netherlands Antilles*, New Zealand, Nigeria, North Mariana Islands*, Norway, Pakistan, Panama*, Paraguay, Peru, Philippines, Poland, Portugal, Puerto Rico*, Qatar*, Romania, St. Lucia*, San Marino*, Saudi Arabia, Senegal, Seychelles*, Sierra Leone*, Singapore, Somali*, South Africa, Spain, Sri Lanka, Sudan, Surinam*, Swaziland*, Sweden, Switzerland, Syria, Tanzania*, Thailand, Togo*, Tonga*, Trinidad & Tobago, Tunisia, Turkey, United Arab Emirates*, USSR, United States, Uruguay, Venezuela, Virgin Islands (US)*, Western Samoa*, Yemen*, Yugoslavia, Zaire*, Zambia* and Zimbabwe.

The original founder members in 1913 were Australasia, Austria, Belgium, British Isles, Denmark, France, Germany, Holland, Russia, South Africa, Sweden and Switzerland.

Although this shows that tennis is well-established just about everywhere except Greenland, Antarctica and Outer Mongolia, it must be acknowledged that it is still comparatively undeveloped in the Third World. Tennis is universally perceived as an affluent sport, and this is why up-market, luxury-orientated companies wish to be involved with it.

Nabisco, one of the world's leading food industry groups, has taken over sponsorship of the Grand Prix from Pepsi-Cola, Commercial Union, Colgate and Volvo, who backed it successively from 1970. The women's version, originally also known as the Grand Prix, began in 1973 with Commercial Union, switching to Colgate in 1977 (when it was renamed the Women's Series), Toyota in 1981 and Virginia Slims in 1983.

The women's circuit was, from 1971 to 1984, split into two separate series. Virginia Slims, the original women's pro circuit sponsors, ran an indoor tour during the first three months of the year in the US up to 1979, when Avon, who had backed the Futures circuit for three years, took over the whole segment. In 1983 Avon declined to renew their option, and Virginia Slims returned to support the entire year's schedule, which was merged into one.

There are many who regret the association of a tobacco company with the sport, but for Phillip Morris, who manufacture the Slims brand, it was an ideal marketing venture, as they based their advertising slogan 'You've come a long way, baby' on the parallel between the emancipated woman of the 1920s (for whom smoking was a symbol of independence) with the emancipated women tennis players.

Avon, whose own slogan, 'You never looked so good', emphasized women's femininity rather than their independence, backed out in 1983 when women's tennis was getting bad publicity, particularly over the unconventional lifestyles of leading players like Billie Jean King and Martina Navrati-

Opposite: John McEnroe became the first player to be paid a million dollars a year to endorse a racket made to his specifications.
Below: Pat Cash, like McEnroe, endorses the Sergio Tacchini clothing line. Also like McEnroe, he shunned convention and fathered a child out of wedlock (though McEnroe did later marry actress Tatum O'Neal).

lova. It was not something with which wholesome product companies like Avon and Colgate wished to be associated.

However, the slurs of the early 1980s have done no lasting damage to the game. Sponsors representing many luxury goods are plentiful, and they not only want to back tournaments and circuits but also wish to sign up leading players for use in consumer promotions.

Chris Evert, for example, has been paid millions by Lipton for appearances in iced-tea commercials, while Bjorn Borg still works extensively for Scandinavian Airlines, and Steffi Graf for Porsche cars. All sporting goods producers employ the stars to advertise their products: Ivan Lendl and Stefan Edberg for Adidas, Navratilova for Puma and Yonex, Connors and Evert for Converse shoes and Wilson rackets, etc. John McEnroe made history in 1980 when he was signed for $1m a year to use Dunlop rackets — nowadays these sums for top players always run into telephone-number figures.

Watches, cars, cosmetics, foodstuffs — any type of luxury goods and financial concerns cash in, except, of course, cigarettes, which still rely on tournament sponsorship, although Marlboro have developed a successful sportswear arm.

Players' agents negotiate the contracts, and it is commonplace for special lines of clothing, rackets and shoes to be marketed in association with particular players.

A player is exceptionally marketable if he or she is good-looking, or is regarded as a 'sex symbol' by the young, which is why Bjorn Borg has done so well. His many business interests nowadays include modelling his own line of leisureware fashions, and glamorous young women like Gabriela Sabatini, Carling Bassett and Andrea Temesvari have added to their income in this capacity too.

Bonanzas

Prize-money levels in tennis continue to inflate to ludicrous extents. The Grand Slam tournaments have all long since broken through the million-dollar barrier, but there are other, unofficial bonanzas as well. The European Community Championship, a men's tournament that takes place in Antwerp each autumn, offers in addition to huge prize money a diamond-encrusted racket worth $750,000 to the player that can win the tournament three times. It is hard to justify such riches for players of a game compared with the remuneration available to ordinary people.

Tennis has not yet eclipsed the sort of money to be won by world title fight boxers, but it overtook golf a long time ago and there are few other sports that can offer similar rewards. The message is clear: if you can break into the Top 100 on the computer, you can make a comfortable living; if you can make the Top 10, you are certain of becoming a millionaire.

Above: Gabriela Sabatini is the contemporary counterpart of stars like Suzanne Lenglen and Maria Bueno, who combined great tennis skill with grace and glamour. Sabatini, from Argentina, looks set to rival Steffi Graf at the top of the women's game into the 1990s.

Media attention

There have been warning signs that the bubble could burst. Television ratings in the US have slumped since a peak in the late 1970s, and whereas the networks were once prepared to show any professional tournament, they are now only interested in the Grand Slams; the rest go out on cable. In Britain, where the number of pro events is limited anyway, the only tournaments with heavy coverage are Wimbledon and Wembley. The BBC dropped the richest European indoor tournament for women at Brighton altogether. Channel 4, a minority station roughly equivalent to PBS in America, gave up on the British National Championships, which accordingly lost its sponsor.

Other media remain more loyal. British newspapers are the only ones in the world with specialist tennis writers, although Bud Collins of the *Boston Globe* is an exception to the rule in America. Tournaments like Antwerp, Dallas and a short-lived extrava-ganza in the Arabian Gulf, which like the other two was not sanctioned by the ITF, invited the British press corps to attend at their expense, so guaranteed coverage that way.

Tennis magazines have flourished in the open era. In the US, the most successful current title is *Tennis*, a glossy monthly owned by the New York Times group, which figures among America's 50 top-selling magazines. *World Tennis*, founded by Gladys Heldman in 1952 and the campaigning organ of the players, which played a crucial role in setting up the women's pro tour, has changed hands several times, and is now the official journal of the USTA. Magazines have also proved extremely successful in countries like France, Germany and Italy, though in Britain they have never secured high circulations partly because coverage in the newspapers is better there than anywhere else.

Fact and fiction

Books have also become a major growth industry for tennis. The best annual publication for reference is the ITF *World of Tennis*, which has been appearing each year since 1969. The USTA and British LTA both produce thick, informative handbooks, and coffee-table tomes are regular best-sellers.

Player biographies and autobiographies are also certain moneyspinners. In 1982, no less than four major works about John McEnroe were published simultaneously. One of them was by Richard Evans, co-author of the present book, who also wrote a major biography of Ilie Nastase in 1978. Virginia Wade published her autobiography, *Courting Triumph*, the same year, while two books about Billie Jean King appeared in 1974 and 1982. Frank DeFord has published works on Bill Tilden, Arthur Ashe and Martina Navratilova, Bud Collins wrote up the life of Evonne Goolagong, and two books on Chris Evert — by Neil Amdur (1982) and Carol Thatcher (daughter of the British Prime Minister, in 1985) — have sold well.

Tennis as a subject for fiction has produced nothing of any great literary distinction. Perhaps the most notable have been novels by feminist author Rita Mae Brown, one-time friend of Navratilova, whose tale of the women's tour featured characters whose models were not hard to discern. And Ilie Nastase has turned his hand to writing, the results of which have followed familiar plot devices that have been used many times before.

Films about tennis have likewise failed to excite the critics or ring the box-office tills. *Players*, a Paramount release in 1979 which starred the late Dean Paul Martin (a useful tennis player who had a dual career as a minor actor), Ali McGraw and, playing himself, Pancho Gonzales, went to great lengths to attain authenticity. The day after the real Wimbledon finals of 1978, a film crew took over the Centre Court and shot a scripted final between Martin and Guillermo Vilas. Similarly, the best film to use tennis as a background, Alfred Hitchcock's 1951 *Strangers on a Train*, was partly filmed at Forest Hills.

Two notable bio-pics made for television were on Maureen Connolly and Renee Richards. The former, starring Glynnis O'Connor, used the same — and highly inaccurate — set to represent a variety of different tennis stadia, while the latter, starring Vanessa Redgrave, chose as its subject the life of perhaps the most unusual person ever to figure prominently in the game.

Controversy

Renee Richards was born Richard Raskind in 1934. A successful New York eye surgeon, Dr Raskind was a good tennis player and took part in the men's singles at the US championships in 1960. He was beaten by the defending champion and reigning Wimbledon champion, Neale Fraser, in the first round.

In 1976, Raskind had an operation to change sex. Adopting the name Renee Richards, she played in the *Tennis Week* Open at Orange, New Jersey, that August and reached the semi-finals. Richards's attempts to enter more important events initially met with failure, so she took her case to a High Court judge. He ruled that she be allowed to play in women's events anywhere in the US. Accordingly, she took part on the circuit, earned a computer ranking, and was accepted for the 1977 US Open. She lost in the first round to the reigning Wimbledon champion, Virginia Wade, so earned a unique niche for herself in the annals of tennis.

At the age of 43, she was stronger than many of the women on the circuit, and at one time was ranked in the top 30, but never made a significant impact. Her best achievement was reaching the final of the 1977 US Open doubles with Betty Ann Stuart.

During her several years on the circuit, Richards encountered much prejudice and resentment in some quarters, where it was rather naively feared that her example might unleash a flood of transsexuals on to the women's circuit, and she was never accepted as a competitor outside the Americas.

In 1981 she was taken on as a travelling consultant by Navratilova and ceased playing herself. The partnership was cancelled in 1983, when Navratilova suffered her one loss that year — to Kathleen Horvath in Paris — but it was reformed in 1987 on Navratilova's break with her then coach, Mike Estep. Prior to that, Richards had resumed her ophthalmic practice in New York.

If Richards was one unusual phenomenon of 1977, another was a fad for unconventional racket adornment known as 'spaghetti' stringing. Originated by an obscure American player, Mike Fishbach, it involved a network of grommets and interlacing wires that produced an extraordinary effect on the ball,

exaggerating spin and making it impossible to predict which way the ball was going to bounce. It caused the only equipment controversy that has ever surfaced in tennis, and it was swiftly banned.

Tennis is a game of constant development, controversy and excitement. Few sports are as volatile, as unpredictable and as absorbing. By the time you read this book, some new monster may have reared its head, some new political row may be raging, the latest outburst by one of the game's 'bad boys' may be filling the headlines. But the game itself has a quality that will always surpass these ephemeral distractions. The crowds will continue to pour into the grounds of the All England Club, Stade Roland Garros, and the National Tennis Centres at Flushing Meadow and Flinders Park. Millions around the world will continue to enjoy their Saturday morning doubles. From its early origins as the Sport of Kings, tennis has become, unquestionably and everlastingly, the Sport for All.

Above: Pancho Gonzales turned in a better performance than most of the bona-fide actors in an undistinguished 1979 film about professional tennis, Players. *A climactic Wimbledon final was actually filmed on the Centre Court.*

Equipment and Clothing

Tennis equipment has come a long way since the wooden tennis racket made its first appearance towards the end of the 15th century. The introduction of space-age materials such as graphite, Boron and Kevlar has increased the number of ways a tennis ball can be projected over a net, whilst the manufacture of tennis clothing has become a highly competitive industry.
With many companies battling for a share of a lucrative market, sponsorship deals have become a large part of a top player's income.

Left: Men's tennis clothing has probably never been as stylish as in the 1920s, when this fashion plate was drawn. The lady is clearly not dressed for tennis, although some top players regularly appeared on court in fur-trimmed coats and other accoutrements. A leading British player of the time, Eileen Bennett, is reputed to have played on the French Riviera wearing a full string of pearls!

RACKETS

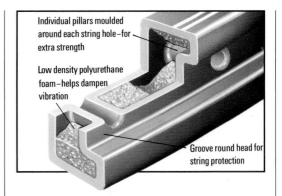

Individual pillars moulded around each string hole – for extra strength

Low density polyurethane foam – helps dampen vibration

Groove round head for string protection

'If Boris Becker had been playing with a wood-framed racket he would not have won Wimbledon at the age of 17.'

This was the outspoken opinion of Becker's predecessor as Wimbledon champion, John McEnroe, and it was not the result of sour grapes. It was the view of a player who regrets the passing of a vintage era, when power complemented, rather than dominated, the game's more delicate skills. At heart a traditionalist, he would have liked nothing better than to throw out his modern equipment and return to the Dunlop Maxply with which he first cut, drove and sliced his way into the tennis record books with feathery drop shots and perfectly placed stop volleys. But this master tactician was well aware of the extent to which modern technology has changed the game.

'I am not suggesting Becker would not have won Wimbledon eventually,' said McEnroe. 'He is a great grass-court player. But even though he was an incredibly strong 17-year-old he could not have blitzed his way

Below: Pam Shriver is smartly and functionally attired in a typical modern women's two-piece outfit made by Fila of Italy. Her racket, a Prince, is one of the most popular on the market today.
Opposite: Early lawn tennis rackets were fashioned from a single piece of wood — usually hickory or ash — by a craftsman often working alone.
Right: Cross-section of a modern-construction composite racket.

through the Wimbledon draw with that serve had he not had the extra power a graphite racket gives you.'

By 1982, McEnroe, already champion at Wimbledon and Flushing Meadow, realized he could no longer ignore the technological benefits offered by the new-style rackets. Jimmy Connors still remained loyal to his steel-framed Wilson, a notoriously difficult racket for the average player to control. But space-age materials like graphite, Boron, Kevlar and, most recently, ceramic were increasing the number of ways in which a tennis ball could be projected over a net.

To remain at the very top of the modern game, McEnroe needed power, and Dunlop produced it for him by designing the MAX 200G which he used until the 1987 US Open. Then he switched to the latest Dunlop frame, believing that it gave him an extra edge.

Tennis players have long been convinced that one racket or another was more suited to their individual style of play. For no very discernible reason Martina Navratilova suddenly discarded her large framed Yonex two weeks before the 1987 French Open, much to the despair of her agents who had just renewed her contract with the Japanese manufacturers. Martina switched to the MAX 200G, the same racket being used by her new rival Steffi Graf and, despite a loss to Graf in Paris, went on to win Wimbledon and the US Open with her new-found weapon.

It was, of course, a personal whim that brought about Martina's decision to change rackets at a particularly stressful moment in her career. Yonex quickly saved face by signing up the champion's doubles partner, Pam Shriver, who proceeded to prove the quality of their product by beating Chris Evert for the first time in her career and winning the Canadian Open singles title.

The fact is that, as soon as tennis became a multi-million dollar industry in the 1970s, the manufacturers began to spend time and money on research that they would not have bothered with before. Today's rackets, many of which are produced for a variety of companies from the same vast factory in Taiwan, are virtually all of such high quality that the choice becomes simply a matter of personal preference.

Competitors at the first Wimbledon in 1877 were still using rackets whose shape bore a marked affinity to the lop-sided head of the rackets used for real tennis. Over the years the racket gradually evolved, until the recent rush of new materials transformed it so dramatically — making the favourite pastime of comparing past and present champions even more difficult. If McEnroe rightly feels that Becker gained an immediate advantage from his graphite Puma, what might it have done for Bill Tilden or Fred Perry? The answer, of course, can never be established.

The first rackets

In the Middle Ages, long before lawn tennis was invented, players would hit a soft leather ball back and forth with their bare (later gloved) hands. Some time later a bat was introduced and, finally, towards the end of the 15th century, a racket was used, in the indoor game of real tennis.

The first rackets used for lawn tennis were modelled on those used for the indoor game and bear little resemblance to the ones used today. They were rather flat at the top until it was discovered that the tensions of the strings in a racket of this shape caused the wood to split and the frame to break. Consequently, an oval shape was developed that allowed the stringing pattern to be more easily distributed around the whole head. The racket was fashioned from a single piece of wood — usually hickory or ash — by a craftsman working either alone or in partnership with just two or three others. Such a workshop produced about ten to 15 rackets a week. The wood was cut, steamed and bent into shape, then the throat piece was assembled, glued and firmly fixed by means of a brass screw. Grips were simply scoured in a mahogany overlay on the handle.

The art of stringing

In the 1880s, tennis racket strings were made from leather, then subsequently from natural gut. (Experiments were carried out with the strings used for musical instruments, but these were abandoned; piano wire, for instance, soon damaged the tennis balls.)

Stringing was carried out by hand, the gut being threaded through holes in the frame and tightened by force of arm strength, until the invention of stringing machines in the late 1930s. This development helped to stabilize the racket head shape by ensuring even distribution of tension to a degree that hand stringers could not match.

Since those early days, the art of stringing has come a long way, and such has been the ingenuity of manufacturers in devising new refinements that the International Tennis Federation had to draw up a new ruling stating that the strings must be evenly spaced and should not tamper with the flight of the ball. The need for such a regulation became apparent during a match between Guillermo Vilas and Ilie Nastase, when the latter played with a 'spaghetti' racket (two sets of strings, fitted with plastic tubes and woven into an unusual formation). This formation caused

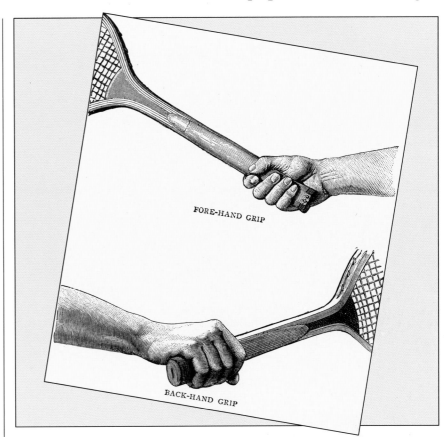

FORE-HAND GRIP

BACK-HAND GRIP

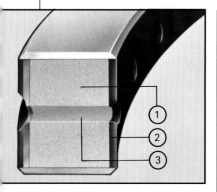

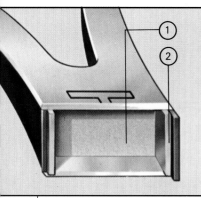

Above: Cross-section of the Arthur Ashe Competition 1 racket, made by Head. 1 – Glass fibre, the main component of the racket's construction. 2 – Outer skin of aluminium alloy for strength and rigidity. 3 – Bore hole for strings.

the ball to shoot off with unreturnable top-spin on every contact. Small wonder that Vilas stormed off the court.

Gut reactions

Following the adoption of gut as the most appropriate material for racket strings, no real alternative was developed for about 70 years. Produced from the stomach and intestinal linings of sheep and cows, gut has never been cheap, but it can be strung to tensions suitable for standard wooden rackets and is extremely responsive.

However, the advent of oversize and then mid-size rackets in the late 1970s and early 1980s provoked something of a revolution in racket stringing. It was found that natural gut broke under the higher tensions required for these rackets, and the search commenced for a synthetic equivalent to gut which would perform well. Many companies came up with products which have been progressively improved over the last decade, and some of the best synthetic 'gut' is almost indistinguishable from its natural counterpart in everything but price. Also, the synthetic product is more weather-resistant. Manufacturers of natural gut responded by producing a toughened and weatherproofed natural-gut string.

Many brands of synthetic racket string are textured in various ways or have different combinations of core materials, and new patterns of stringing are constantly being investigated and promoted. It is doubtful, however, whether any particular stringing

system is influential enough in itself to turn an ordinary player into a Wimbledon champion.

Increasing the tension

String tension has been a contentious issue practically since tennis began. Current thinking suggests that low tension — 27.3 kg (60 lb) or less — means that the ball deforms less on contact and retains more kinetic energy; therefore, it possesses more rebound. Balls hitting strings strung at high tensions — 31.7 kg (70 lb) plus — flatten more on impact and thus create extra top spin, which is used as a weapon in tennis more than ever.

Bjorn Borg, the greatest male player of the 1970s, was famous for the high tension of his racket stringing — up to 36 kg (80 lb) — and for the phenomenal control he exercised over his ground-stroke game. Borg, of course, could afford to replace his rackets and their strings after every game. (More often than not the manufacturer did so for him.) Even then, the strings were known to snap when they were not in use, so great was the tension he insisted upon.

For the present, the trend is towards slacker stringing, a weight of 25 kg (55 lb) being considered ideal for an average player. Essential for the serious player is a good professional stringer who will know the latest products available and their suitability for individual players and their rackets. Some

Right: The Dunlop Max 150G, forerunner to the now bestselling Max 200G model, was manufactured using a hollow injection moulding technique.

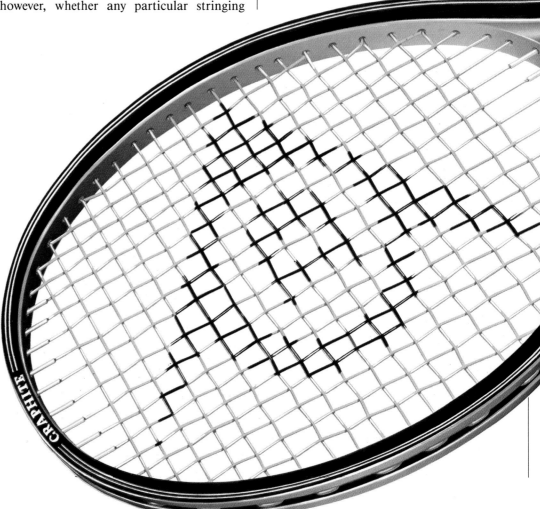

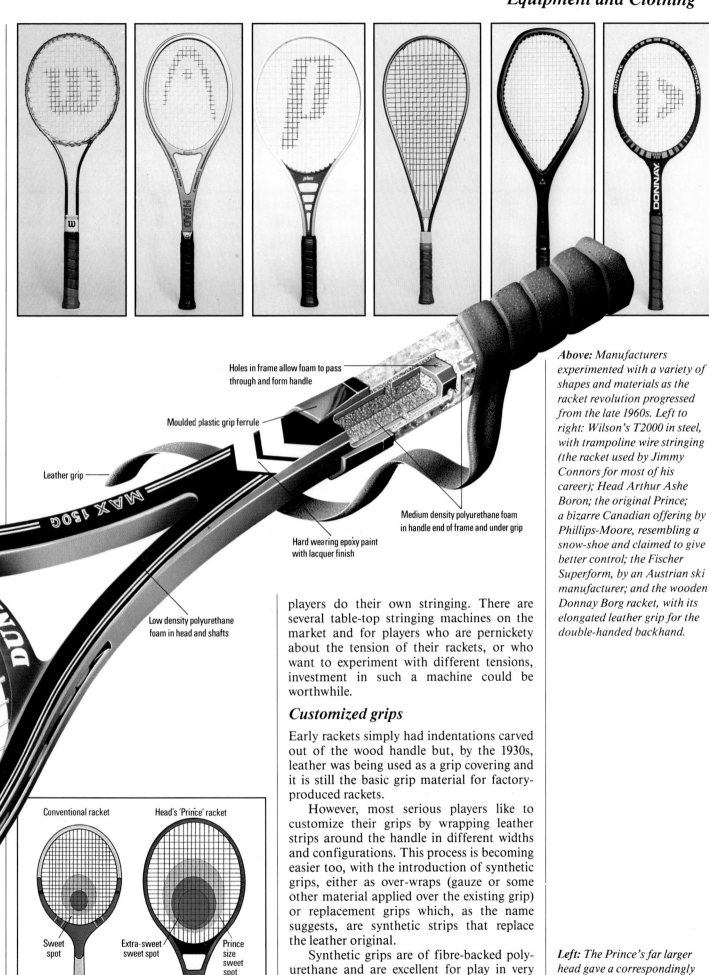

Holes in frame allow foam to pass through and form handle

Moulded plastic grip ferrule

Leather grip

Low density polyurethane foam in head and shafts

Hard wearing epoxy paint with lacquer finish

Medium density polyurethane foam in handle end of frame and under grip

Above: Manufacturers experimented with a variety of shapes and materials as the racket revolution progressed from the late 1960s. Left to right: Wilson's T2000 in steel, with trampoline wire stringing (the racket used by Jimmy Connors for most of his career); Head Arthur Ashe Boron; the original Prince; a bizarre Canadian offering by Phillips-Moore, resembling a snow-shoe and claimed to give better control; the Fischer Superform, by an Austrian ski manufacturer; and the wooden Donnay Borg racket, with its elongated leather grip for the double-handed backhand.

Conventional racket

Head's 'Prince' racket

Sweet spot

Extra-sweet sweet spot

Prince size sweet spot

players do their own stringing. There are several table-top stringing machines on the market and for players who are pernickety about the tension of their rackets, or who want to experiment with different tensions, investment in such a machine could be worthwhile.

Customized grips

Early rackets simply had indentations carved out of the wood handle but, by the 1930s, leather was being used as a grip covering and it is still the basic grip material for factory-produced rackets.

However, most serious players like to customize their grips by wrapping leather strips around the handle in different widths and configurations. This process is becoming easier too, with the introduction of synthetic grips, either as over-wraps (gauze or some other material applied over the existing grip) or replacement grips which, as the name suggests, are synthetic strips that replace the leather original.

Synthetic grips are of fibre-backed polyurethane and are excellent for play in very high temperatures because the synthetic material is a highly efficient absorber of moisture. Synthetics also come in a range of

Left: The Prince's far larger head gave a correspondingly bigger 'sweet spot' — the point where the ball should be hit — than a conventional size racket.

Above: Tennis players often like to wind their own gauze grips around the handles of their rackets, exactly how they want them. Guillermo Vilas finds the occupation therapeutic before playing a match in a head-to-head series against John McEnroe.

any rate, once a top player has signed a sponsorship agreement with a particular manufacturer, he or she usually cannot be seen using other brands.

Earlier players may not have had such constraints, but they did have to contend with other pressures — such as experimental new materials. Metal rackets were manufactured briefly in the 1920s but there were inherent problems which were at that time insuperable. The sharp-edged holes in the frame meant that gut strings quickly wore through and had to be replaced every few games, and the vibrating qualities of metal quickly caused painful arm and elbow injuries. Another reason for the failure of metal rackets when they were first introduced was the public's reluctance to accept such developments. Without wide mass appeal there was no incentive to continue research into metal frames and the idea was dropped. Lawn tennis was still a fairly conservative game, played mainly by the privileged classes, and most merely recreational players were not ready for 'flashy' innovations.

Major breakthrough

Thus rackets changed very little until the 1930s, when the single most important breakthrough in the game's history occurred: laminated wood was used instead of a single piece of ash. Thanks to the power of the new synthetic adhesives, which were far stronger than the animal glues previously available, it was at last possible to bond together strips of, say, ash, beech and hickory.

The wood lamination process proved to be very adaptable and ideal for producing rackets of various weights and stiffness. Each wood has its own special qualities; for example, bamboo is the most flexible and maple the stiffest and hardest. By using layers of wood in different combinations, increased strength could be achieved without adding to the total weight or bulk.

Laminating also made it possible to string gut at a much higher tension than had previously been possible, and the search began — and still continues — for a string that gives 'touch' and power at the tensions players prefer. For all these reasons, the laminated racket quickly prevailed and continued to do so, with ever more refinements, virtually until the 1960s.

Over the years, advances in tennis racket manufacture have kept pace with relevant new materials introduced in fields outside that of sport. Just as synthetic glues revolutionized the design of wood rackets, and the invention of rubber enabled tennis to be successfully played on grass with a bouncing ball, so in the 1970s and 1980s the aerospace industry was to contribute decisively to further changes in racket design.

It was these fundamental changes in racket manufacturing technology which led to the increased development of the 'power' game of tennis, with harder serving and more

attractive, bright colours which can again provide a distinguishing note for individual players.

One player's grip may not suit another. The grip is generally the most personal part of the racket — and is likely to become even more so as experiments are being made with brightly coloured string and even towelling grips in attempts to improve and personalize the visual appeal of tennis rackets.

Material benefits

For the tennis champion of 100 years ago, the racket was a very personal item of equipment. Players rarely owned more than one or two at any time and those were built to individual requirements of weight and balance. Because rackets were virtually custom-made, they were seldom loaned or shared between players. Today's mass production methods have made available a vast range of rackets for both professionals and club players — but, of course, top professionals still rarely use another player's rackets once they have become accustomed to a particular make. At

aggressive volleying than had previously been possible.

The age of professionalism

By the 1960s, technological innovation was unstoppable. The newer and more advanced a product was, the greater the likelihood that it would be adopted by a public no longer shackled by outmoded traditions of garden-party lawn tennis. The age of professional tennis was imminent.

In this atmosphere, René Lacoste, the French Davis Cup player of the pre-war years, gained initial acceptance for his unique, round-head, 'trampoline'-strung, silver aluminium racket. Lacoste had solved the stringing problems of metal by suspending the strings from the frame rather than stringing them directly through it. This new method prevented chafing and breaking of the gut. The racket was also light, moved fast through the air and made the traditional wooden frames seem clumsy in comparison; and it was relatively inexpensive to make.

Unfortunately, the market became flooded with poor imitations of Lacoste's

model, most of which presented horrendous vibrations and broke easily. Among professional players the original metal racket went out of fashion quite quickly, although Jimmy Connors continued to use Wilson's T2000 model until the mid-1980s, long after Wilson had officially stopped making it. (Although Wilson tried to introduce Connors to a more updated version, Connors's exceptional ball control with the T2000 suited his game best, making it extremely difficult for him to adapt to another type of racket.) But the floodgates had been opened, and racket manufacture changed more profoundly in the following decade than it had in the previous half century.

Space-age technology

Wood was still the popular choice of many players in the early 1970s, but two factors were responsible for the racket makers' sudden swing away from wood towards hitherto untried materials. First, the tennis boom in the United States suddenly produced an apparently unlimited market. Second, the aerospace industry had introduced substances which, when refined and developed, seemed to solve some of the greatest obstacles to modern racket design.

The established tennis companies came under tremendous pressure as the US boom proceeded apace. Other, smaller companies began to compete for a slice of the market. To achieve this they had to come up with a racket that was strikingly different.

Wood rackets, apart from their high cost of manufacture, had a major disadvantage — wood could not be changed significantly in terms of strength, weight, or balance. The head of the racket, for example, could not be increased in size without the racket breaking or becoming unmanageable. But new alloys and materials such as glass fibre and graphite *could* be used in such ways. Howard Head, who had made his name as a ski manufacturer, was the first to introduce a racket — the Prince — with a larger-than-normal size head, designed to include a larger 'sweet spot' (the primary hitting area) and generally excellent playing qualities. The long reign of the wooden racket with the standard head size was over.

Other companies were quick to take advantage of the boom. Ski manufacturers like Howard Head were in the forefront of the new racket technology thanks to their experience in the use of lightweight but strong materials. Unable to imitate the exact size of the original Prince racket for reasons of patent, most companies saw an answer in the mid-size racket, and it is this which presently dominates the market.

Rackets are now produced in many sizes and colours, in all sorts of space-age materials, such as Boron and Kevlar, and with different stringing systems. These artificial materials are similar to wood but much stronger — and they are predictable in their behaviour. They can also be used in many different combinations to capitalize on their individual qualities.

To give but a few examples, glass fibre has a resistance to stretching equal to that of steel; it is also extremely resistant to twisting of the racket head. Boron, which is chemically related to aluminium, is similarly light and stiff, but much harder. (It is also much more expensive.) Both glass fibre and Boron may be combined with such materials as graphite (pure crystalline carbon), wood, nylon and aluminium, to produce composite rackets — and these are taking an increasingly large share of the world market.

One such composite racket has a light-weight yet extremely strong foam core combined with glass-fibre laminate encased in aluminium alloy for extra strength and rigidity. Another has a carbon fibre-reinforced nylon core filled with low-density polyurethane foam. In the shaft and handle, medium-density foam is used to provide a good feel and balance.

Recent innovations have also included adjustable weights, either built into the frame or attached outside it, adjustable string tension apparatus and handles that can be shortened and lengthened.

Mass production methods, in particular in the Far East, have meant that even rackets which are made of expensive graphites and other fibres have now become affordable to the general public.

The modern racket

The virtues of the modern tennis racket are its strength and lightness, power and durability. There are different manufacturing methods, such as injection moulding, laminating and extruding (for metal alloys) but, apart from fluctuations in head size, the actual outline of the tennis racket has really not changed a great deal.

Today's racket must meet certain specifications: it must have the right degree of stiffness combined with flexibility, and the tension of the strings must give the player maximum control as well as giving the ball maximum thrust. Also, the 'sweet spot' must be as large as possible to allow margin for error.

Following the development of rackets with an increased face size, the ever vigilant International Tennis Federation limited the size of rackets from July 1981. The maximum overall length is 81.28 cm (32 in), the maximum overall width is 31.75 cm (12½ in) and the strung surface should be a maximum 39.37 cm (15½ in) by 29.21 cm (11½ in).

Grip sizes range from the smallest, 3½, to the largest, 5¼.

The actual demands of the game make it unlikely that a racket much bigger, heavier or more complicated would find favour with players. As with the ski and the cricket bat, the basic design has proved the best for the job.

Opposite: Jimmy Connors defied convention by continuing to use the Wilson T2000, without an endorsement fee, long after the company had ceased producing them. He claimed it was the only racket that enabled him to hit the ball how he wanted.

TENNIS BALLS

For real tennis, the balls were (and still are) made of wool wrapped in leather. They lasted virtually forever — some of the balls used in real tennis today are over 100 years old. But they lacked much bounce and were very heavy. (The French King Charles VIII actually died after being hit on the head by one.)

The balls used for lawn tennis were the modern hollow indiarubber balls. Initially, these were uncovered, but by the time of the first Wimbledon Championship, in 1877, they were being covered with white wool, which was shaped and stitched over the rubber core. No cross-stitching was permitted, and unbleached carpet thread was compulsory. In order to ensure that pressure inside the balls was uniform, they were inflated by gas released from a pellet inside the core.

Towards the end of the 1920s, stitching gave way to a special cement. Wool as a covering was largely superseded after the Second World War by mixtures of wool and manmade fibres, which makes the balls longer-lasting (though pure wool remains the most responsive surface). The few companies who make covering cloth for balls supply many brands from the same factory.

Stringent, internationally accepted regulations govern the construction, size, weight, compression, etc., of tennis balls. Those used in top-class tournaments must be stored at a constant temperature of 20°C (68°F).

Tennis balls come in two varieties: pressurized and pressureless. Pressurized balls have to be packed in sealed, air-tight tins because the internal pressure introduced during the manufacturing process must be kept constant. These balls have a lively bounce but the pressure declines with use and they end up flat and lifeless. Traditionally, most players prefer the pressurized ball for its responsive qualities but it does wear out fast, particularly when used on hard courts.

Pressureless balls, originally developed for play at high altitudes, are also popular on the continent. The ball has no internal pressure, the composition of the core providing the necessary firmness. These balls are slightly heavier in play and have a lower bounce, but they last much longer. Consequently, they are gaining in popularity around the world and all of the major ball manufacturers now produce a pressureless range.

Tennis balls are also more colourful now; they used to be white, but the advent of television and different-coloured courts has lead to the gradual adoption of the yellow ball, which has a significantly higher visibility, both for the player on court and viewers watching the match on television. Wimbledon, one of the last bastions of the white ball, started using yellow balls in 1986. Very few white balls are now made.

SHOES

The sensitivity and vulnerability of grass-court surfaces meant that from the earliest days special shoes were worn for tennis. Canvas tops and rubber soles were the popular choice until after the Second World War, when technological advances produced materials that could be used to fashion a shoe that was light, yet strong enough to efficiently support the most athletic of power players.

Modern shoes can be made of canvas but the better players and all professionals prefer a high-quality leather upper and a polyurethane sole. Leather is flexible and 'breathes' well, ensuring good air circulation inside the shoes; the polyurethane is strong, can be moulded into different patterns and is much

LAWN TENNIS BALLS.

THE CHAMPIONSHIP.

(Registered, 5 & 6 Vict., cap. 100.)

EACH BALL HAS A FAC-SIMILE OF MY SIGNATURE STAMPED THUS ON THE CLOTH—

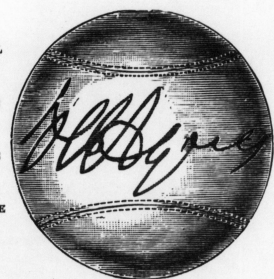

EACH BALL HAS ALSO THE YEAR OF MANUFACTURE STAMPED UPON IT.

As used in the principal Tournaments throughout England Ireland Scotland, America, and Australia.

These balls have now stood the test of twenty seasons, and their superiority has been universally admitted. The most flattering testimonials have been received by the manufacturer from some of the most eminent players, all speaking as to the excellence of their qualities, as well in accuracy as in elasticity, reliability, and finish. This opinion is further confirmed by the fact that the "Championship Lawn-Tennis Ball" has been selected for use in all the great Tournaments that have taken place, not only in the United Kingdom but in all foreign countries where the game has any votaries.

For Grass or Asphalte.

lighter than the thick rubber previously used for soles.

Tennis shoes are also available with shock-absorbent insoles — usually made from ethylene vinyl acetate (EVA) which is a synthetic foam produced in various densities — and padding around the uppers to prevent chafing. A firm cup in the back of the shoe (known as a heel counter) protects the player's heel and Achilles tendon. Lacing can be either variable lacing, in which the pairs of grommets are alternately narrow- and wide-spaced to permit a custom fit when tied, or speed lacing, which uses plastic rings instead of grommets to facilitate easier, speedier lacing up.

The insole is a contoured insert which can be fixed or removable, and the outsole (the outer base of the shoe) may have toe and pivot areas of hard, high-density structure for durability combined with a grooved area or areas to allow flexibility.

Sports footwear manufacturers now also offer designs for three different types of foot structure. These are: the normal arched foot with no tendency to 'go over' at the ankle; the low, flat arch combined with a tendency for the heels to swing outwards, and the high arch associated with heels that swing inward.

Design also takes into account the different surfaces on which players may now find themselves competing: grass, clay, indoor carpet and so on. Specific patterns on the soles take into account the characteristics of these various courts and provide optimum foothold.

Tennis shoes principally made of kangaroo skin because of its breathing qualities are used especially for playing on grass. The rubber sole has thick, semi-circular grooved patterns that give players more grip on slippery surfaces. Tennis shoes for clay have fewer grooves on the soles but are patterned in such a way that they enable players literally to slide into strokes, which is part of the clay-court playing technique. Indoor tennis shoes have a much flatter, grooveless sole.

Some players now use built-up boot-style tennis shoes, which are especially beneficial to those prone to ankle injuries.

In trying to give the foot adequate protection and support, some shoes now tend to be rather bulky and cumbersome in appearance. Future developments in design will probably be concentrated more on the production of lighter, tougher shoes with effective cushioning qualities and visually appealing 'extras' such as inset strips of coloured leather or canvas.

Right: Three court surfaces from British manufacturers En-tout-cas. Tennisquick (top) gives a consistent bounce at all times and is said to be ideal for beginners. Tenniprene (middle) is porous, so can be used immediately after rain. Sporturf (bottom) resembles and plays like grass. It is a bladed granular surface and one of many being developed as a more viable alternative to natural turf.

SURFACES

Although the game of tennis first became popular on the grass lawns of Victorian country houses, its rapid spread throughout the world meant that, of necessity, other court surfaces were soon adapted.

The need for different tactics in competing on different types of surface has led to a diversification in technique and strategy, adding to the immense appeal of the game. There has always been a call for the development of a uniform surface throughout the world, but such a change would very likely also encourage a uniform style of game and that could ultimately harm rather than help the sport from the entertainment angle. And if it ceased to attract an enthusiastic audience, as well as players, sponsorship would also become more difficult.

Grass courts

Grass courts of the standard required for tennis, which are only possible in temperate climates, are only found to any extent in Britain and Australia, and on the east coast of the United States. Grass is also expensive to maintain and only playable in the summer months. It is consequently not a practical investment for the average tennis club and is gradually disappearing even from the international tournament circuit. Wimbledon is the only major event played on grass and, in turn, the Championships support a small circuit of pre-Wimbledon grass tournaments. Within a few years the British summer circuit may well be the only one in the world where top-class tennis is played on grass.

Clay and shale surfaces

In Europe and South America, the most popular surface is the loose-top, reddish clay which encourages a steady baseline game. The bounce of the ball on this surface is low and slow and the top layer of the court is loose, which means that the ability to slide into shots becomes a vital part of a player's technique. The speed of continental clay varies slightly according to the country and local conditions. Clay courts in Italy, for example, are often slower than those in France. But the basic characteristics of play are the same. Clay courts are vulnerable to rain and frost and generally cannot be used in the winter.

Shale is a surface found mainly in Britain; loose-topped and brick-coloured, it resembles continental clay but is faster to play on. This court was first introduced and patented by the enterprising En-tout-cas Company and a great number were put down between the wars.

Tarmac courts

After the Second World War, maintenance-free surfaces became a priority for any new courts that were built, as the high cost of labour priced both grass and continental clay courts out of reach.

The most popular surface, particularly for public parks and schools, where many courts were required, was the bitumen macadam, or 'tarmac'. This court sometimes has a loose surface grit, or it can be treated with coloured paint. Bitumen courts are constructed in porous or non-porous form, the non-porous or impervious kind being cheaper to build but liable to 'puddling' after rain. Nevertheless, it is quicker-drying than other surfaces. The playing qualities of tarmac have improved over the years but it is still not considered the ideal surface for top-class players.

Porous and non-porous concrete

One company that has apparently come close to solving the problem of an ideal court surface is the En-tout-cas Company. Certainly the introduction of their porous concrete in the early 1960s solved many problems of playing outdoors in rainswept countries, although it took long periods of experimentation before a satisfactory solution was achieved.

To demonstrate the properties of their new surface when it was first launched, En-tout-cas hired a fire engine to flood the surface. Onlookers observed that the water soaked straight through the concrete, leaving the top surface almost instantly playable. The porous concrete court was copied by other manufacturers and has been widely used ever since. It does have certain drawbacks, however, especially when played on continuously. The unyielding surface causes strain to players' arms and legs, wears out shoes and tennis balls quickly and, unless constructed to high standards, tends to crack. Nevertheless, no other maintenance-free surface has approached it in terms of popularity.

The non-porous concrete, or cement, surface, originated in California, where it became very popular. Its medium-fast playing qualities and regular bounce were probably responsible for the distinctive 'Californian' style of aggressive serve-volley players, both male and female.

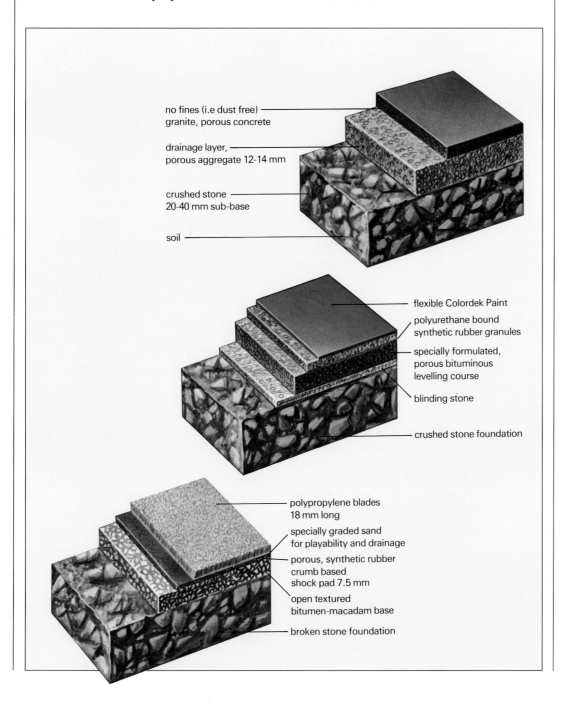

no fines (i.e dust free) granite, porous concrete

drainage layer, porous aggregate 12-14 mm

crushed stone 20-40 mm sub-base

soil

flexible Colordek Paint

polyurethane bound synthetic rubber granules

specially formulated, porous bituminous levelling course

blinding stone

crushed stone foundation

polypropylene blades 18 mm long

specially graded sand for playability and drainage

porous, synthetic rubber crumb based shock pad 7.5 mm

open textured bitumen-macadam base

broken stone foundation

Often painted in attractive colours, non-porous concrete is not just the preserve of Californians. It was adopted as the surface of the United States Open, held annually in Flushing Meadow in New York, and is now very popular all over the world.

The advantage of this type of court is that the speed at which the ball comes off the court can to some extent be manipulated by changing the consistency of the acrylic-painted surface applied as a top coat. Non-porous concrete is normally faster than the porous kind, has a medium-high bounce and favours both a baseline and net game. A disadvantage is that rain tends to collect in pools and the surface becomes slippery when wet. At the US Open even perspiration dripping from players on to the court has to be regularly mopped up to prevent the risk of skidding and injurious falls! The court also has to be renovated every year, to maintain it at a sufficiently high standard for a Grand Slam event such as the US Open.

Artificial surfaces

'Artificial' is a word normally used to describe courts which make use of synthetic materials such as plastics and the various by-products of modern chemical industries. Early plastic tennis courts tended to be sticky underfoot, particularly in hot weather, but these problems have now been overcome.

Right: If the All England Club, Wimbledon, is Britain's most famous tennis club, then Queen's Club, west London, is not far behind. Venue each year for the pre-Wimbledon Stella Artois Championships, it boasts a sea of tennis courts with several different surfaces, including grass, clay, wood, carpet and synthetic.

Outdoor artificial courts are most commonly made of perforated plastic, interlocking tiles (matting) or synthetic grass. The latter is becoming more popular as research continues to improve its quality. It consists of polypropylene tufted carpet on a sand-filled base, and the speed of the court varies according to the ratio of sand to pile. A good synthetic grass surface is similar to porous concrete in its ability to cope with rain and requires minimum maintenance. As you would expect, it is also much kinder to arms and legs than concrete and is probably *the* surface of the future.

Some courts are now covered by a layer of crumb rubber, bound by polyurethane. However, this surface is rather expensive. Initially used at Queen's Club, London, it was later abandoned principally because of cost, and replaced by a similar surface, but with a hard, rubberized top layer.

Indoor surfaces are generally either textile (woven carpet) or polymeric (rubberized carpet). The playing characteristics of these materials largely depend on the type of foundation, but on the whole they are medium-fast with a lowish bounce. Examples of such courts can be found at many indoor tennis centres. One of the advantages of this type of court is its portability, particularly when tennis events are held in arenas and sports halls where there isn't a permanent court.

Continuing competition between manufacturers should ensure that the present diversity of surfaces continues, thereby helping to retain the fascinating variety of the game. The sign of a great tennis player is the ability to adapt his or her game to whatever surface happens to be underfoot, and the records of the truly great champions bear this out.

TENNIS FASHIONS

Early tennis fashions varied little from clothes worn in everyday life. Men wore knickerbockers or long trousers and rolled up their shirt-sleeves. Some wore all-white outfits, but such attire was the exception rather than the rule.

Petticoats and stays

Women players favoured styles suited to the garden parties at which tennis was so often played in the latter years of the 19th century. Floor-length dresses, mostly of lightweight wool and in elaborately flounced styles with fitted waists, ornamental sleeves and high necks, were worn over steel-boned corsets, layers of petticoats, and long bloomers. Well-bred Victorian ladies were not supposed to perspire or appear in any way dishevelled, so tennis was a fairly leisurely, gentle game.

However, for women to be accepted as competitors they had to prove themselves on the court, and in attempting to do so it became clear that the rigid dress protocol of the time would have to be relaxed so they could play a more vigorous game.

The first concession was to adopt flat, indiarubber-soled shoes, invariably black to disguise 'unsightly' grass stains, but often decorated with pink or pale blue ribbons.

By 1877, *Queen* magazine was offering regular advice on 'Lawn Tennis Costume'. All-white outfits designed specifically for 'good' players came into vogue in the early 1880s, although in design they still resembled everyday fashions of the time. (Men's fashions had quickly become practical — white cotton shirts and long white trousers with turn-ups being *de rigeur*.)

Below: Two generations meet on the eve of the first open Wimbledon in 1968. Roger Taylor, three times a semi-finalist and Britain's top player of the period, admires the stylish outfit of 1940s star Gussy Moran. They are on the rooftop of Simpson's, a leading sports clothes store in London.

Left: *This tranquil study is a far cry from later players whose clothing was designed to be functional. The print, dated 1885, shows a lady who would certainly not have wanted to do too much running around!*

When Maud Watson won her first Wimbledon women's singles title in 1884, she wore a high-necked, long-sleeved dress, and sported a man's straw boater. Lottie Dod, who first won Wimbledon in 1887 at the age of 15 years and ten months, provided a fashion breakthrough with her loose-fitting, long-sleeved, terracotta blouse and full dark skirt worn calf-length in deference to her schoolgirl status.

Practical, dark-coloured wool blouses with tightly cinched waists and flannel skirts appeared in many early American photographs of tennis players. However, the Americans — first introduced to the game by Mary Ewing Outerbridge who had seen it played abroad — soon adopted more functional styles than their English counterparts.

In 1903, the five-times Wimbledon champion, Charlotte Sterry, recommended 'a nice hanging, white skirt, about two inches off the ground, with white blouse, white collar and pale silk neck-band.' In 1905, May Sutton, of the United States, who was the first Wimbledon champion from overseas (and thus uninhibited by British etiquette), caused a small sensation simply by rolling back her sleeves because she was 'too hot'. That was the first time a woman player put performance before appearance and, in its way, it was an important milestone.

Skirts remained floor-length and flared from the hips for the next decade at least, and although blouses were looser, they still had high necklines, starched collars and cuffs. After her first Wimbledon appearance, the American Elizabeth Ryan, referring to the special rails provided in the Ladies dressing room on which players' corsets were hung to dry, remarked, 'It was not a pretty sight, as many were blood stained from the wounds they had inflicted.' That was in 1914, just before the start of the First World War, and although corsets were still in fashion, the war did put an end to the wearing of hats on court, principally through a shortage of materials with which to make them.

The Lenglen look

In 1919 when the Wimbledon Championships reconvened after the war years, the somewhat straitlaced world of tennis fashion was shocked by the emergence of a new, flamboyant French star, Suzanne Lenglen, who not only revolutionized on-court tennis wear but had a great influence on style outside the world of sport.

At the age of 20, Suzanne appeared at Wimbledon for the first time, wearing a one-piece, flimsy cotton frock with long sleeves but *no* petticoats. She had also defiantly discarded the restricting corsets of a previous age — though she did wear long, white stockings. The effect, in contrast to other women still in their bulky, starched clothing, was staggering.

Suzanne was labelled 'indecent' and 'shocking' but her supremacy in the game inevitably led to many imitators and a consequent general relaxation of the constraints that had hampered the design of practical tennis wear for women. Suzanne's daring soon set a new trend. Shorter, mid-calf dresses with long sleeves were subsequently designed, as women players realized the practicality — and fashion appeal — of wearing 'comfortable' clothing on court. Also, the 1920s ushered in shorter skirts for everyday wear and this supported the new look. By the time fashion decreed longer lengths again, the practicality of shorter tennis styles was too well established to be changed by mere whims of style.

Both press and public were enthusiastic about the 'Lenglen Look', but it took the Wimbledon authorities somewhat longer to accept this new image. In 1920, Suzanne appeared at Wimbledon wearing the colourful bandeau which was to become her trademark and also, as a result, the rage of the early 1920s. The 'Lenglen Bandeau', created simply by wrapping round her head several metres of brightly coloured silk chiffon, achieved worldwide fame.

In 1923, Lenglen appeared at Wimbledon with yet another new look: a *toile de soie*, white dress. This was the first time a silk dress had been worn for tennis. Her matching, colourful silk cardigan and bandeau contributed a new, glamorous and luxurious image to tennis. Suzanne Lenglen thus became the first tennis 'star' in the star-struck decade of the 1920s and she continued to dress appropriately.

Many years later Elizabeth Ryan who, in

Opposite: It seems unlikely that these ladies could have played tennis in anything but an extremely dainty and decorous manner. These styles from the 1890s feature high collars, cuffs, ankle-length skirts and tightly cinched waists.

Below: A mixed doubles at St Rejchan in 1894. The ladies are no longer required to wear hats, but they are most likely to leave the major share of action to their partners.

1914, first won Wimbledon at the age of 19, declared, 'All women should go on their knees in thankfulness to Suzanne for delivering them from the tyranny of corsets.'

In her seven years' reign, Suzanne Lenglen was the prima donna of lawn tennis. Her extraordinarily graceful and balletic style demanded complete freedom of movement on court, and in tossing aside previous fashion convention she changed forever the appearance of women players. The demands of the sport would henceforth dictate the shape and style of clothes. Fashion could become the servant of the player and allow exciting, innovative styles.

Right: Women's tennis outfits underwent a dramatic transformation after the First World War. Out went stays, petticoats, collars and cuffs, and in came simple clothing like this, which enabled players to move freely and energetically.

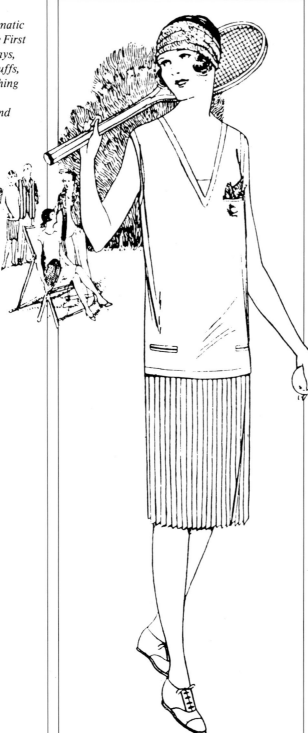

Bare legs appear

Over the next decade, however, little really changed in women's on-court tennis fashions, although in 1929 the Spanish player Lilli de Alvarez introduced the first culottes to be seen at Wimbledon, in an experimental outfit consisting of a two-tiered, pagoda-type tunic with flared trousers. In the same year, Billie Tapscott from South Africa turned heads when she played on a back court at Wimbledon without stockings — the first time a woman player had ever done so.

In the 1930s skirts became shorter still, rising from just below the knee to just above, but the fashion was mainly for culottes, principally for the sake of decency on court. Despite the Lenglen years, tradition was still strong, particularly at Wimbledon, the sport's premier championship.

It was not for another two years, in 1931, that the pioneering Joan Lycett (sister of the equally audacious Bunny Austin, the first male player to appear in tennis shorts), braved the All England Management Committee by daring to appear on Centre Court without stockings — and bare legs were finally approved.

By 1939, most men in tennis had forsaken long trousers for shorts, although as early as 1927, S.B. Wood — a 15-year-old American schoolboy — created a sensation by appearing on Wimbledon's Centre Court in knickerbockers and golfing stockings. Despite his attire he lost in the first round against René Lacoste. The first short-sleeved, knitted white shirt was introduced by the three-times Wimbledon champion Fred Perry.

The years immediately following the Second World War were a time of austerity for tennis fashions as for much else. Rationing made the purchase of materials very difficult, and styles tended to the utilitarian. Looking back, tennis wear of the late 1940s seems regimented, monotonous and unflattering.

Tinling's creations

Nevertheless, those were the years which saw the rise of Teddy Tinling, doyen of tennis designers. The time of shortages acted as a challenge to Tinling, who purposefully sought out new fabrics and stimulating designs as a cheering contrast to the bleak background of rationing and restrictions.

Sometimes he simply added pastel ribbons to the otherwise stark outfits worn by women players at that time, but his great flair for making the simplest dress look feminine and appealing began to win him many admirers. The flowing Lenglen dresses of the 1920s had not been seen for many years on Wimbledon's Centre Court, and they were very much missed. Most women in the 1940s wore all-white culottes and baggy shirt tops with split-cap sleeves.

In 1948, Tinling was asked to design a special dress for the then top British player, Betty Hilton. Unfortunately, she wore the

Above: Suzanne Lenglen was no beauty, but she revelled in the image of a glamorous star. In this carefully posed portrait she might have been an actress — and indeed she did appear in a British movie in 1935.
Left: Lenglen almost single-handedly revolutionized tennis fashions, with her loose-fitting, one-piece dresses, ending just below the knee, and her much-copied bandeau.
Overleaf, left: Tennis was being linked with up-market products such as luxury cars as long ago as the 1920s.
Overleaf, opposite: Gussy Moran models an outfit called the 'Tennis Temptress' in 1950. Incorporating bloomers, it was specially designed for her by Pierre Balmain.

dress for a disastrous loss to American Louise Brough in a Wightman Cup tie, and her defeat was later attributed to 'self-consciousness' about the colour on her dress. The Wimbledon Committee concluded therefore that tennis clothing should henceforth be 'all-white'. Not until 1972 was the rule relaxed and coloured tennis outfits officially sanctioned.

Gorgeous Gussy's panties

The most famous of Tinling's creations was undoubtedly 'Gorgeous' Gussy Moran's lace panties which she wore at Wimbledon in 1948.

With these Tinling was perhaps ahead of his time, but in his attempts to add a distinctively feminine touch to basic tennis fashions, he brought to a logical conclusion the process begun by Suzanne Lenglen, whom he had idolized from his earliest youth.

Tinling's designs showed convincingly that to be functionally attired on the tennis court did not mean that women could not also dress attractively to contribute to that elusive star quality inherent in tennis. Teddy Tinling always saw sport as a part of show business and created tennis fashions that reflected that belief.

Unfortunately, Gussy Moran's lace panties led to a 20-year difference of opinion between Tinling and the All England Club. The Committee judged Gussy's lace frills to be 'unnecessarily attracting the eye to the sexual area', and Tinling's services as an umpire were terminated. Lace, however, continued to adorn the panties of many top tennis players until well into the 1980s.

The designer era

As the 1960s dawned, the severely tailored shorts and shirts favoured by many top players in the 1950s began to give way to more diverse styles.

One of Teddy Tinling's favourite clients was the new rising star from Brazil, Maria Bueno. This glamorous player won Wimbledon in 1959, 1960 and 1964, and she was in many ways the Suzanne Lenglen of her day, graceful, balletic and flamboyant in appearance. Maria's exotic Tinling dresses were thrown into greater relief by the somewhat pedestrian Fred Perry shirts and skirts favoured by Billie Jean King and Margaret Court. For men, Fred Perry sportswear was virtually a uniform.

In 1971, the refreshingly young Australian, Evonne Goolagong, played her Wimbledon final in a dress typical of the Tinling design — and won! A short time later Billie Jean King also succumbed and became one of Tinling's clients for the closing stages of her career. For her famous 1973 match against Bobby Riggs, she wore a rhinestone-studded Tinling creation, seen on television by millions worldwide.

Teddy Tinling reached the peak of his career when women's professional tennis

Right: Ted Tinling, famed couturier of women's tennis, gave up designing dresses for the top players when they abandoned one-piece outfits for 'separates' in the late 1970s.
Below: Trey Waltke brought a touch of nostalgia to the Centre Court at Wimbledon in 1983 when he wore old-fashioned tennis clothes for a match against Ivan Lendl.

was launched in the 1970s. As the official designer to the Virginia Slims circuit he allowed his imagination full reign, and women players appeared on court in dresses embroidered with sequins, sewn with silver threads and in a wide range of colours.

In 1972, Wimbledon abandoned the 'All-white Rule', beginning to allow the tiniest hint of colour. When Chris Evert first appeared at Wimbledon she wore a brightly motifed, straight dress created by Florida designer Mondessa Swift. Her grace and popularity gave Mondessa's designs an immediate worldwide impact and their brightly coloured geometric and flowered motifs became the best selling tennis dresses of the early 1970s.

Unisex look

But the day of the individual designer seems to have passed, along with the rest of the more *outré* styles. Tennis clothing has almost returned to the post-war unisex look. Mass-produced tennis clothes have flooded the markets. Italian companies dominate sales with their interchangeable tops, shorts and shirts.

Martina Navratilova, who has won the Wimbledon women's singles title many times, last wore a dress for victory in 1979. Ever since, she has worn co-ordinating shirt and skirt outfits. Fortunately for those who like variety, dresses have not completely disappeared. In 1987, Dianne Balestrat of Australia wore a sleeveless V-neck dress that she designed herself, 'for luck', at Wimbledon. Though fashion is now an important consideration, no major tennis clothing company has dresses featured in their catalogues.

Men's fashion too is now important; top players have special lines designed for them and have become major influences in the sale of sports clothing to the general public. It could be said that Bjorn Borg pioneered such transactions when he became the first top tennis professional to sign a big-money clothing contract with Fila. His Wimbledon-winning outfits soon became Fila's best-selling lines, and it was not long before other similar clothing manufacturers followed suit. It has become very important for top tennis wear companies to be aware of popular tastes and current trends and dress their star players accordingly. A close relationship now exists between fashionable leisurewear and sports wear in general, both having become integral parts of the everyday wardrobe.

Headbands and sweatbands

Headbands for both men and women, in either brightly coloured or plain white towelling, have also become an accepted fashion both on and off the tennis court.

Originally, headbands were worn by players with long hair, as means of keeping their hair from falling into their eyes during play. Bjorn Borg and Guillermo Vilas were followers of the headband trend; and Suzanne Lenglen's famous bandeau en-

*Left: Anne White caused a
sensation at Wimbledon in
1985 when she appeared on
an outside court in a catsuit.
White, a part-time model and
US Wightman Cup player,
claimed it was too cold for
normal attire; but the
authorities asked her not
to wear the outfit again.*

couraged women to wear them, though it was
in the 1960s and 1970s that the fashion
became widespread. Chris Evert went
through a phase of wearing colourful headbands, as did Martina Navratilova, but both
have dropped this fashion. Several other
women players still wear headbands.

Similarly, sweatbands — originally used to
stop sweat rolling down the arm to the racket
hand — are now extensively used as a means

of advertising a particular tennis fashion line.

Both headbands and sweatbands present
an excellent opportunity for sponsorship, and
the sportswear makers have not been slow to
make the most of it. Sponsorship, like technology, has invaded every facet of the game of
tennis. On a positive note, both of these
modern influences have added new dimen-
sions to an already compulsively playable and
watchable sport.

The Major Records

On the following pages we give records of the premier events of tennis: the four Grand Slam championships — Wimbledon, the United States, France and Australia — together with the Grand Slam winners; the Grand Prix Masters and the Women's International Series; and the three senior team competitions, the Davis Cup, Wightman Cup and Federation Cup.

These records start from 1919, the end of the First World War, and are complete to date as far as championship status is concerned. There are no records of the French championships before 1925, because it was only in that year that they were thrown open to all-comers.

Married women players' maiden names are included as well as their married names. In the mixed doubles the woman's name is listed after the man's.

Left: Called by some a 'concrete monstrosity', Flushing Meadow in New York City is host to the final Grand Slam event of the year.

THE CHAMPIONSHIPS, WIMBLEDON
(NB: The challenge round in all events was discontinued in 1922.)

MEN'S SINGLES

YEAR	WINNER	RUNNER-UP	SCORE	YEAR	WINNER	RUNNER-UP	SCORE
1919	G.L. Patterson (AUS)	N.E. Brookes (AUS)	6-3,7-5,6-2	1966	M. Santana (SPA)	R.D. Ralston (US)	6-4,11-9,6-4
1920	W.T. Tilden (US)	G.L. Patterson (AUS)	2-6,6-3,6-2, 6-4	1967	J.D. Newcombe (AUS)	W.P. Bungert (W.GER)	6-3,6-1,6-1
1921	W.T. Tilden (US)	B.I.C. Norton (SA)	4-6,2-6,6-1, 6-0,7-5	1968	R.G. Laver (AUS)	A.D. Roche (AUS)	6-3,6-4,6-2
1922	G.L. Patterson (AUS)	R. Lycett (GB)	6-3,6-4,6-2	1969	R.G. Laver (AUS)	J.D. Newcombe (AUS)	6-4,5-7,6-4, 6-4
1923	W.M. Johnston (US)	F.T. Hunter (US)	6-0,6-3,6-1	1970	J.D. Newcombe (AUS)	K.R. Rosewall (AUS)	5-7,6-3,6-2, 3-6,6-1
1924	J. Borotra (FRA)	J.R. Lacoste (FRA)	6-1,3-6,6-1, 3-6,6-4	1971	J.D. Newcombe (AUS)	S.R. Smith (US)	6-3,5-7,2-6, 6-4,6-4
1925	J.R. Lacoste (FRA)	J. Borotra (FRA)	6-3,6-3,4-6, 8-6	1972	S.R. Smith (US)	I. Nastase (ROM)	4-6,6-3,6-3, 4-6,7-5
1926	J. Borotra (FRA)	H. Kinsey (US)	8-6,6-1,6-3	1973	J. Kodes (CZ)	A. Metreveli (USSR)	6-1,9-8,6-3
1927	H. Cochet (FRA)	J. Borotra (FRA)	4-6,4-6,6-3, 6-4,7-5	1974	J.S. Connors (US)	K.R. Rosewall (AUS)	6-1,6-1,6-4
1928	J.R. Lacoste (FRA)	H. Cochet (FRA)	6-1,4-6,6-4, 6-2	1975	A.R. Ashe (US)	J.S. Connors (US)	6-1,6-1,5-7, 6-4
1929	H. Cochet (FRA)	J. Borotra (FRA)	6-4,6-3,6-4	1976	B. Borg (SWE)	I. Nastase (ROM)	6-4,6-2,9-7
1930	W.T. Tilden (US)	W.L. Allison (US)	6-3,9-7,6-4	1977	B. Borg (SWE)	J.S. Connors (US)	3-6,6-2,6-1, 5-7,6-4
1931	S.B. Wood (US)	F.X. Shields (US)	walkover	1978	B. Borg (SWE)	J.S. Connors (US)	6-2,6-2,6-3
1932	H.E. Vines (US)	H.W. Austin (GB)	6-4,6-2,6-0	1979	B. Borg (SWE)	R. Tanner (US)	6-7,6-1,3-6, 6-3,6-4
1933	J.H. Crawford (AUS)	H.E. Vines (US)	4-6,11-9,6-2, 2-6,6-4	1980	B. Borg (SWE)	J.P. McEnroe (US)	1-6,7-5,6-3, 6-7,8-6
1934	F.J. Perry (GB)	J.H. Crawford (AUS)	6-3,6-0,7-5	1981	J.P. McEnroe (US)	B. Borg (SWE)	4-6,7-6,7-6, 6-4
1935	F.J. Perry (GB)	G. von Cramm (GER)	6-2,6-4,6-4	1982	J.S. Connors (US)	J.P. McEnroe (US)	3-6,6-3,6-7, 7-6,6-4
1936	F.J. Perry (GB)	G. von Cramm (GER)	6-1,6-1,6-0	1983	J.P. McEnroe (US)	C.J. Lewis (NZ)	6-2,6-2,6-2
1937	J.D. Budge (US)	G. von Cramm (GER)	6-3,6-4,6-2	1984	J.P. McEnroe (US)	J.S. Connors (US)	6-1,6-1,6-2
1938	J.D. Budge (US)	H.W. Austin (GB)	6-1,6-0,6-3	1985	B. Becker (W.GER)	K. Curren (US)	6-3,6-7,7-6, 6-4
1939	R.L. Riggs (US)	E.T. Cooke (US)	2-6,8-6,3-6, 6-3,6-2	1986	B. Becker (W.GER)	I. Lendl (CZ)	6-4,6-3,7-5
1940-45	No competition			1987	P. Cash (AUS)	I. Lendl (CZ)	7-6,6-2,7-5
1946	Y. Petra (FRA)	G.E. Brown (AUS)	6-2,6-4,7-9, 5-7,6-4	1988	S. Edberg (SWE)	B. Becker (W.GER)	4-6,7-6,6-4, 6-2
1947	J.A. Kramer (US)	T.P. Brown (US)	6-1,6-3,6-2				
1948	R. Falkenburg (US)	J.E. Bromwich (AUS)	7-5,0-6,6-2, 3-6,7-5				
1949	F.R. Schroeder (US)	J. Drobny (CZ)	3-6,6-0,6-3, 4-6,6-4				
1950	J.E. Patty (US)	F.A. Sedgman (AUS)	6-1,8-10,6-2, 6-3				
1951	R. Savitt (US)	K. McGregor (AUS)	6-4,6-4,6-4				
1952	F.A. Sedgman (AUS)	J. Drobny (EG)	4-6,6-2,6-3, 6-2				
1953	E.V. Seixas (US)	K. Nielsen (DEN)	9-7,6-3,6-4				
1954	J. Drobny (EG)	K.R. Rosewall (AUS)	13-11,4-6, 6-2,9-7				
1955	M.A. Trabert (US)	K. Nielsen (DEN)	6-3,7-5,5-1				
1956	L.A. Hoad (AUS)	K.R. Rosewall (AUS)	6-2,4-6,7-5, 6-4				
1957	L.A. Hoad (AUS)	A.J. Cooper (AUS)	6-2,6-1,6-2				
1958	A.J. Cooper (AUS)	N.A. Fraser (AUS)	3-6,6-3,6-4, 13-11				
1959	A. Olmedo (US)	R.G. Laver (AUS)	6-4,6-3,6-4				
1960	N.A. Fraser (AUS)	R.G. Laver (AUS)	6-4,3-6,9-7, 7-5				
1961	R.G. Laver (AUS)	C.R. McKinley (US)	6-3,6-1,6-4				
1962	R.G. Laver (AUS)	M.F. Mulligan (AUS)	6-2,6-2,6-1				
1963	C.R. McKinley (US)	F.S. Stolle (AUS)	9-7,6-1,6-4				
1964	R.S. Emerson (AUS)	F.S. Stolle (AUS)	6-4,12-10, 4-6,6-3				
1965	R.S. Emerson (AUS)	F.S. Stolle (AUS)	6-2,6-4,6-4				

WOMEN'S SINGLES

YEAR	WINNER	RUNNER-UP	SCORE
1919	S. Lenglen (FRA)	D.K. Lambert Chambers (née Douglass) (GB)	10-8,4-6,9-7
1920	S. Lenglen (FRA)	D.K. Lambert Chambers (née Douglass) (GB)	6-3,6-0
1921	S. Lenglen (FRA)	E. Ryan (US)	6-2,6-0
1922	S. Lenglen (FRA)	M. Mallory (US)	6-2,6-0
1923	S. Lenglen (FRA)	K. McKane (GB)	6-2,6-2
1924	K. McKane (GB)	H.N. Wills (US)	4-6,6-4,6-4
1925	S. Lenglen (FRA)	J. Fry (GB)	6-2,6-0
1926	K. Godfree (née McKane) (GB)	L. de Alvarez (SPA)	6-2,4-6,6-3
1927	H.N. Wills (US)	L. de Alvarez (SPA)	6-2,6-4
1928	H.N. Wills (US)	L. de Alvarez (SPA)	6-2,6-3
1929	H.N. Wills (US)	H.H. Jacobs (US)	6-1,6-2
1930	H.N. Moody (née Wills) (US)	E. Ryan (US)	6-2,6-2
1931	C. Aussem (GER)	H. Krahwinkel (GER)	6-2,7-5
1932	H.N. Moody (née Wills) (US)	H.H. Jacobs (US)	6-3,6-1
1933	H.N. Moody (née Wills) (US)	D.E. Round (GB)	6-4,6-8,6-3
1934	D.E. Round (GB)	H.H. Jacobs (US)	6-2,5-7,6-3
1935	H.N. Moody (née Wills) (US)	H.H. Jacobs (US)	6-3,3-6,7-5
1936	H.H. Jacobs (US)	H. Sperling (née Krahwinkel) (DEN)	6-2,4-6,7-5
1937	D.E. Round (GB)	J. Jedrejowska (POL)	6-2,2-6,7-5
1938	H.N. Moody (née Wills) (US)	H.H. Jacobs (US)	6-4,6-0
1939	A. Marble (US)	K.E. Stammers (GB)	6-2,6-0
1940-45	No competition		
1946	P.M. Betz (US)	M.E. Osborne (US)	6-2,6-4
1947	M.E. Osborne (US)	D.J. Hart (US)	6-2,6-4
1948	A.L. Brough (US)	D.J. Hart (US)	6-3,8-6
1949	A.L. Brough (US)	M.E. DuPont (née Osborne) (US)	10-8,1-6, 10-8
1950	A.L. Brough (US)	M.E. du Pont (née Osborne) (US)	6-1,3-6,6-1
1951	D.J. Hart (US)	S.J. Fry (US)	6-1,6-0
1952	M.C. Connolly (US)	A.L. Brough (US)	7-5,6-3
1953	M.C. Connolly (US)	D.J. Hart (US)	8-6,7-5
1954	M.C. Connolly (US)	A.L. Brough (US)	6-2,7-5
1955	A.L. Brough (US)	B. Fleitz (US)	7-5,8-6
1956	S.J. Fry (US)	A. Buxton (GB)	6-3,6-1
1957	A. Gibson (US)	D.R. Hard (US)	6-3,6-2
1958	A. Gibson (US)	A. Mortimer (GB)	8-6,6-2
1959	M.E. Bueno (BRA)	D.R. Hard (US)	6-4,6-3
1960	M.E. Bueno (BRA)	S. Reynolds (SA)	8-6,6-0
1961	A. Mortimer (GB)	C.C. Truman (GB)	4-6,6-4,7-5
1962	K.M. Susman (née Hantze) (US)	V. Sukova (née Puzejova) (CZ)	6-4,6-4
1963	M. Smith (AUS)	B.J. Moffitt (US)	6-3,6-4
1964	M.E. Bueno (BRA)	M. Smith (AUS)	6-4,7-9,6-3
1965	M. Smith (AUS)	M.E. Bueno (BRA)	6-4,7-5
1966	B.J. King (née Moffitt) (US)	M.E. Bueno (BRA)	6-3,3-6,6-1
1967	B.J. King (née Moffitt) (US)	A.S. Jones (née Haydon) (GB)	6-3,6-4

YEAR	WINNER	RUNNER-UP	SCORE
1968	B.J. King (née Moffitt) (US)	J.A.M. Tegart (AUS)	9-7,7-5
1969	A.S. Jones (née Haydon) (GB)	B.J. King (née Moffitt) (US)	3-6,6-3,6-2
1970	M. Court (née Smith) (AUS)	B.J. King (née Moffitt) (US)	14-12,11-9
1971	E.F. Goolagong (AUS)	M. Court (née Smith) (AUS)	6-4,6-1
1972	B.J. King (née Moffitt) (US)	E.F. Goolagong (AUS)	6-3,6-3
1973	B.J. King (née Moffitt) (US)	C.M. Evert (US)	6-0,7-5
1974	C.M. Evert (US)	O. Morozova (USSR)	6-0,6-4
1975	B.J. King (née Moffitt) (US)	E.F. Cawley (née Goolagong) (AUS)	6-0,6-1
1976	C.M. Evert (US)	E.F. Cawley (née Goolagong) (AUS)	6-3,4-6,8-6
1977	S.V. Wade (GB)	B.F. Stove (NETH)	4-6,6-3,6-1
1978	M. Navratilova (US)	C.M. Evert (US)	2-6,6-4,7-5
1979	M. Navratilova (US)	C. Lloyd (née Evert) (US)	6-4,6-4
1980	E.F. Cawley (née Goolagong) (AUS)	C. Lloyd (née Evert) (US)	6-1,7-6
1981	C. Lloyd (née Evert) (US)	H. Mandlikova (CZ)	6-2,6-2
1982	M. Navratilova (US)	C. Lloyd (née Evert) (US)	6-1,3-6,6-2
1983	M. Navratilova (US)	A. Jaeger (US)	6-0,6-3
1984	M. Navratilova (US)	C. Lloyd (née Evert) (US)	7-6,6-2
1985	M. Navratilova (US)	C. Lloyd (née Evert) (US)	4-6,6-3,6-2
1986	M. Navratilova (US)	H. Mandlikova (CZ)	7-6,6-3
1987	M. Navratilova (US)	S. Graf (W.GER)	7-5,6-3
1988	S. Graf (W.GER)	M. Navratilova (US)	5-7,6-2,6-1

Players' countries are shown in brackets after the players' names. Abbreviations used are as follows (the capital letters denote the abbreviation): ARGentina, AUStralia, BELgium, BRAzil, BULgaria, CHIle, CZechoslovakia, DENmark, ECUador, EGypt, FRAnce, GERmany, Great Britain, HUNgary, INDia, IRELand, ITAly, JaPaN, MEXico, NETHerlands, New Zealand, PARaguay, POLand, ROMania, South Africa, SPAin, SWEden, SWItzerland, URUguay, United States, USSR, W. GERmany, YUGoslavia.

THE CHAMPIONSHIPS, WIMBLEDON continued

MEN'S DOUBLES

YEAR	WINNERS	YEAR	WINNERS
1919	P. O'Hara Wood & R.V. Thomas (AUS)	1961	R.S. Emerson & N.A. Fraser (AUS)
1920	C.S. Garland & R.N. Williams (US)	1962	R.A.J. Hewitt & F.S. Stolle (AUS)
1921	R. Lycett & M. Woosnam (GB)	1963	R.H. Osuna & A. Palafox (MEX)
1922	J.O. Anderson (AUS) & R. Lycett (GB)	1964	R.A.J. Hewitt & F.S. Stolle (AUS)
1923	L.A. Godfree & R. Lycett (GB)	1965	J.D. Newcombe & A.D. Roche (AUS)
1924	F.T. Hunter & V. Richards (US)	1966	K.N. Fletcher & J.D. Newcombe (AUS)
1925	J. Borotra & R. Lacoste (FRA)	1967	R.A.J. Hewitt & F.D. McMillan (SA)
1926	J. Brugnon & H. Cochet (FRA)	1968	J.D. Newcombe & A.D. Roche (AUS)
1927	F.T. Hunter & W.T. Tilden (US)	1969	J.D. Newcombe & A.D. Roche (AUS)
1928	J. Brugnon & H. Cochet (FRA)	1970	J.D. Newcombe & A.D. Roche (AUS)
1929	W.L. Allison & J. Van Ryn (US)	1971	R.S. Emerson & R.G. Laver (AUS)
1930	W.L. Allison & J. Van Ryn (US)	1972	R.A.J. Hewitt & F.D. McMillan (SA)
1931	G.M. Lott & J. Van Ryn (US)	1973	J.S. Connors (US) & I. Nastase (ROM)
1932	J. Borotra & J. Brugnon (FRA)	1974	J.D. Newcombe & A.D. Roche (AUS)
1933	J. Borotra & J. Brugnon (FRA)	1975	V. Gerulaitis & A.A. Mayer (US)
1934	G.M. Lott & L.R. Stoefen (US)	1976	B.E. Gottfried (US) & R. Ramirez (MEX)
1935	J.H. Crawford & A.K. Quist (AUS)	1977	R.L. Case & G. Masters (AUS)
1936	G.P. Hughes & C.R.D. Tuckey (GB)	1978	R.A.J. Hewitt & F.D. McMillan (SA)
1937	J.D. Budge & G. Mako (US)	1979	P. Fleming & J.P. McEnroe (US)
1938	J.D. Budge & G. Mako (US)	1980	P. McNamara & P. McNamee (AUS)
1939	E.T. Cooke & R.L. Riggs (US)	1981	P. Fleming & J.P. McEnroe (US)
1940-45	No competition	1982	P. McNamara & P. McNamee (AUS)
1946	T. Brown & J.A. Kramer (US)	1983	P. Fleming & J.P. McEnroe (US)
1947	R. Falkenburg & J.A. Kramer (US)	1984	P. Fleming & J.P. McEnroe (US)
1948	J.E. Bromwich & F.A. Sedgman (AUS)	1985	H.P Guenthardt (SWI) & B. Taroczy (HUN)
1949	R.A. Gonzales & F.A. Parker (US)	1986	J. Nystrom & M. Wilander (SWE)
1950	J.E. Bromwich & A.K. Quist (AUS)	1987	K. Flach & R. Seguso (US)
1951	K. McGregor & F.A. Sedgman (AUS)	1988	K. Flach & R. Seguso (US)
1952	K. McGregor & F.A. Sedgman (AUS)		
1953	L.A. Hoad & K.R. Rosewall (AUS)		
1954	R.N. Hartwig & M.G. Rose (AUS)		
1955	R.N. Hartwig & L.A. Hoad (AUS)		
1956	L.A. Hoad & K.R. Rosewall (AUS)		
1957	G. Mulloy & J.E. Patty (US)		
1958	S. Davidson & U. Schmidt (SWE)		
1959	R.S. Emerson & N.A. Fraser (AUS)		
1960	R.H. Osuna (MEX) & R.D. Ralston (US)		

WOMEN'S DOUBLES

YEAR	WINNERS	YEAR	WINNERS
1919	S. Lenglen (FRA) & E. Ryan (US)	1937	S. Mathieu (FRA) & A.M. Yorke (GB)
1920	S. Lenglen (FRA) & E. Ryan (US)	1938	S. Fabyan (née Palfrey) & A. Marble (US)
1921	S. Lenglen (FRA) & E. Ryan (US)	1939	S. Fabyan (née Palfrey) & A. Marble (US)
1922	S. Lenglen (FRA) & E. Ryan (US)	1940-45	No competition
1923	S. Lenglen (FRA) & E. Ryan (US)	1946	A.L. Brough & M.E. Osborne (US)
1924	H.V. Wightman (née Hotchkiss) & H.N. Wills (US)	1947	D.J. Hart & P.C. Todd (US)
1925	S. Lenglen (FRA) & E. Ryan (US)	1948	A.L. Brough & M.E. du Pont (née Osborne) (US)
1926	M.K. Browne & E. Ryan (US)	1949	A.L. Brough & M.E. du Pont (née Osborne) (US)
1927	E. Ryan & H.N. Wills (US)	1950	A.L. Brough & M.E. du Pont (née Osborne) (US)
1928	P.H. Watson & P. Saunders (GB)	1951	S.J. Fry & D.J. Hart (US)
1929	P.H. Watson & P. Michel (née Saunders) (GB)	1952	S.J. Fry & D.J. Hart (US)
1930	H.N. Moody (née Wills) & E. Ryan (US)	1953	S.J. Fry & D.J. Hart (US)
1931	D.C. Shepherd Barron & P.E. Mudford (GB)	1954	A.L. Brough & M.E. du Pont (née Osborne) (US)
1932	D. Metaxa (FRA) & J. Sigart (BEL)	1955	A. Mortimer & J.A. Shilcock (GB)
1933	S. Mathieu (FRA) & E. Ryan (US)	1956	A. Buxton (GB) & A. Gibson (US)
1934	S. Mathieu (FRA) & E. Ryan (US)	1957	A. Gibson & D.R. Hard (US)
1935	F. James & K.E. Stammers (GB)	1958	M.E. Bueno (BRA) & A. Gibson (US)
1936	F. James & K.E. Stammers (GB)	1959	J. Arth & D.R. Hard (US)

MIXED DOUBLES

YEAR	WINNERS	YEAR	WINNERS
1919	R. Lycett (GB) & E. Ryan (US)	1961	F.S. Stolle & L.R. Turner (AUS)
1920	G.L. Patterson (AUS) & S. Lenglen (FRA)	1962	N.A. Fraser (AUS) & M.E. du Pont (née Osborne) (US)
1921	R. Lycett (GB) & E. Ryan (US)	1963	K.N. Fletcher & M. Smith (AUS)
1922	P. O'Hara Wood (AUS) & S. Lenglen (FRA)	1964	F.S. Stolle & L.R. Turner (AUS)
1923	R. Lycett (GB) & E. Ryan (US)	1965	K.N. Fletcher & M. Smith (AUS)
1924	J.B. Gilbert & K. McKane (GB)	1966	K.N. Fletcher & M. Smith (AUS)
1925	J. Borotra & S. Lenglen (FRA)	1967	O.K. Davidson (AUS) & B.J. King (née Moffitt) (US)
1926	L.A. Godfree & K. Godfree (née McKane) (GB)	1968	K.N. Fletcher & M. Court (née Smith) (AUS)
1927	F.T. Hunter & E. Ryan (US)	1969	F.S. Stolle (AUS) & A.S. Jones (née Haydon) (GB)
1928	P.D.B. Spence (SA) & E. Ryan (US)	1970	I. Nastase (ROM) & R. Casals (US)
1929	F.T. Hunter & H.N. Wills (US)	1971	O.K. Davidson (AUS) & B.J. King (née Moffitt) (US)
1930	J.H. Crawford (AUS) & E. Ryan (US)	1972	I. Nastase (ROM) & R. Casals (US)
1931	G.M. Lott & A. Harper (US)	1973	O.K. Davidson (AUS) & B.J. King (née Moffitt) (US)
1932	E. Maier (SPA) & E. Ryan (US)	1974	O.K. Davidson (AUS) & B.J. King (née Moffitt) (US)
1933	G. von Cramm & H. Krahwinkel (GER)	1975	M.C. Riessen (US) & M. Court (née Smith) (AUS)
1934	R. Miki (JPN) & D.E. Round (GB)	1976	A.D. Roche (AUS) & F. Durr (FRA)
1935	F.J. Perry & D.E. Round (GB)	1977	R.A.J. Hewitt & G.R. Stevens (SA)
1936	F.J. Perry & D.E. Round (GB)	1978	F.D. McMillan (SA) & B.F. Stove (NETH)
1937	J.D. Budge & A. Marble (US)	1979	R.A.J. Hewitt & G.R. Stevens (SA)
1938	J.D. Budge & A. Marble (US)	1980	J.R. Austin & T.A. Austin (US)
1939	R.L. Riggs & A. Marble (US)	1981	F.D. McMillan (SA) & B.F. Stove (NETH)
1940-45	No competition	1982	K. Curren (SA) & A.E. Smith (US)
1946	T.P. Brown & A.L. Brough (US)	1983	J.M. Lloyd (GB) & W.M. Turnbull (AUS)
1947	J.E. Bromwich (AUS) & A.L. Brough (US)	1984	J.M. Lloyd (GB) & W.M. Turnbull (AUS)
1948	J.E. Bromwich (AUS) & A.L. Brough (US)	1985	P. McNamee (AUS) & M. Navratilova (US)
1949	E.W. Sturgess & S.P. Summers (SA)	1986	K. Flach & K. Jordan (US)
1950	E.W. Sturgess (SA) & A.L. Brough (US)	1987	M.J. Bates & J.M. Durie (GB)
1951	F.A. Sedgman (AUS) & D.J. Hart (US)	1988	S. Stewart & Z.L. Garrison (US)
1952	F.A. Sedgman (AUS) & D.J. Hart (US)		
1953	E.V. Seixas & D.J. Hart (US)		
1954	E.V. Seixas & D.J. Hart (US)		
1955	E.V. Seixas & D.J. Hart (US)		
1956	E.V. Seixas & S.J. Fry (US)		
1957	M.G. Rose (AUS) & D.R. Hard (US)		
1958	R.N. Howe & L. Coghlan (AUS)		
1959	R.G. Laver (AUS) & D.R. Hard (US)		
1960	R.G. Laver (AUS) & D.R. Hard (US)		

YEAR	WINNERS	YEAR	WINNERS
1960	M.E. Bueno (BRA) & D.R. Hard (US)	1978	K. Reid (née Melville) & W.M. Turnbull (AUS)
1961	K. Hantze & B.J. Moffitt (US)	1979	B.J. King (née Moffitt) & M. Navratilova (US)
1962	B.J. Moffitt & K.M. Susman (née Hantze) (US)	1980	K. Jordan & A.E. Smith (US)
1963	M.E. Bueno (BRA) & D.R. Hard (US)	1981	M. Navratilova & P.H. Shriver (US)
1964	M. Smith & L.R. Turner (AUS)	1982	M. Navratilova & P.H. Shriver (US)
1965	M.E. Bueno (BRA) & B.J. Moffitt (US)	1983	M. Navratilova & P.H. Shriver (US)
1966	M.E. Bueno (BRA) & N. Richey (US)	1984	M. Navratilova & P.H. Shriver (US)
1967	R. Casals & B.J. King (née Moffitt) (US)	1985	K. Jordan (US) & E. Smylie (AUS)
1968	R. Casals & B.J. King (née Moffitt) (US)	1986	M. Navratilova & P.H. Shriver (US)
1969	M. Court (née Smith) & J.A.M. Tegart (AUS)	1987	C. Kohde-Kilsch (W.GER) & H. Sukova (CZ)
1970	R. Casals & B.J. King (née Moffitt) (US)	1988	S. Graf (W.GER) & G. Sabatini (ARG)
1971	R. Casals & B.J. King (née Moffitt) (US)		
1972	B.J. King (née Moffitt) (US) & B.F. Stove (NETH)		
1973	R. Casals & B.J. King (née Moffitt) (US)		
1974	E.F. Goolagong (AUS) & M. Michel (US)		
1975	A.K. Kiyomura (US) & K. Sawamatsu (JPN)		
1976	C.M. Evert (US) & M. Navratilova (CZ)		
1977	H.F. Cawley (née Gourlay) (AUS) & J.C. Russell (US)		

UNITED STATES CHAMPIONSHIPS
(NB: In 1968 and 1969 both Amateur and Open championships were held.)

MEN'S SINGLES

YEAR	WINNER	RUNNER-UP	SCORE
1919	W.M. Johnston (US)	W.T. Tilden (US)	6-4,6-4,6-3
1920	W.T. Tilden (US)	W.M. Johnston (US)	6-1,1-6,7-5, 5-7,6-3
1921	W.T. Tilden (US)	W.F. Johnson (US)	6-1,6-3,6-1
1922	W.T. Tilden (US)	W.M. Johnston (US)	4-6,3-6,6-2, 6-3,6-4
1923	W.T. Tilden (US)	W.M. Johnston (US)	6-4,6-1,6-4
1924	W.T. Tilden (US)	W.M. Johnston (US)	6-1,9-7,6-2
1925	W.T. Tilden (US)	W.M. Johnston (US)	4-6,11-9,6-3, 4-6,6-3
1926	R. Lacoste (FRA)	J. Borotra (FRA)	6-4,6-0,6-4
1927	R. Lacoste (FRA)	W.T. Tilden (US)	11-9,6-3, 11-9
1928	H. Cochet (FRA)	F.T. Hunter (US)	4-6,6-4,3-6, 7-5,6-3
1929	W.T. Tilden (US)	F.T. Hunter (US)	3-6,6-3,4-6, 6-2,6-4
1930	J.H. Doeg (US)	F.X. Shields (US)	10-8,1-6,6-4, 16-14
1931	H.E. Vines (US)	G.M. Lott (US)	7-9,6-3,9-7, 7-5
1932	H.E. Vines (US)	H. Cochet (FRA)	6-4,6-4,6-4
1933	F.J. Perry (GB)	J.H. Crawford (AUS)	6-3,11-13, 4-6,6-0,6-1
1934	F.J. Perry (GB)	W.L. Allison (US)	6-4,6-3,3-6, 1-6,8-6
1935	W.L. Allison (US)	S.B. Wood (US)	6-2,6-2,6-3
1936	F.J. Perry (GB)	J.D. Budge (US)	2-6,6-2,8-6, 1-6,10-8
1937	J.D. Budge (US)	G. von Cramm (GER)	6-1,7-9,6-1, 3-6,6-1
1938	J.D. Budge (US)	C.G. Mako (US)	6-3,6-8,6-2, 6-1
1939	R.L. Riggs (US)	S.W. Van Horn (US)	6-4,6-2,6-4
1940	W.D. McNeill (US)	R.L. Riggs (US)	8-6,6-8,6-3, 7-5
1941	R.L. Riggs (US)	F. Kovacs (US)	5-7,6-1,6-3, 6-3
1942	F.R. Schroeder (US)	F.A. Parker (US)	8-6,7-5,3-6, 4-6,6-2
1943	J.R. Hunt (US)	J.A. Kramer (US)	6-3,6-8,10-8, 6-0
1944	F.A. Parker (US)	W.F. Talbert (US)	6-4,3-6,6-3, 6-3
1945	F.A. Parker (US)	W.F. Talbert (US)	14-12,6-1, 6-2
1946	J.A. Kramer (US)	T. Brown (US)	9-7,6-3,6-0
1947	J.A. Kramer (US)	F.A. Parker (US)	4-6,2-6,6-1, 6-0,6-3
1948	R.A. Gonzales (US)	E.W. Sturgess (SA)	6-2,6-3, 14-12
1949	R.A. Gonzales (US)	F.R. Schroeder (US)	16-18,2-6, 6-1,6-2,6-4
1950	A. Larsen (US)	H. Flam (US)	6-3,4-6,5-7, 6-4,6-3
1951	F.A. Sedgman (AUS)	E.V. Seixas (US)	6-4,6-1,6-1
1952	F.A. Sedgman (AUS)	G. Mulloy (US)	6-1,6-2,6-3
1953	M.A. Trabert (US)	E.V. Seixas (US)	6-3,6-2,6-3
1954	E.V. Seixas (US)	R.N. Hartwig (AUS)	3-6,6-2,6-4, 6-4

YEAR	WINNER	RUNNER-UP	SCORE
1955	M.A. Trabert (US)	K.R. Rosewall (AUS)	9-7,6-3,6-3
1956	K.R. Rosewall (AUS)	L.A. Hoad (AUS)	4-6,6-2,6-3, 6-3
1957	M.J. Anderson (AUS)	A.J. Cooper (AUS)	10-8,7-5,6-4
1958	A.J. Cooper (AUS)	M.J. Anderson (AUS)	6-2,3-6,4-6, 10-8,8-6
1959	N.A. Fraser (AUS)	A. Olmedo (US)	6-3,5-7,6-2, 6-4
1960	N.A. Fraser (AUS)	R.G. Laver (AUS)	6-4,6-4,10-8
1961	R.S. Emerson (AUS)	R.G. Laver (AUS)	7-5,6-3,6-2
1962	R.G. Laver (AUS)	R.S. Emerson (AUS)	6-2,6-4,5-7, 6-4
1963	R.H. Osuna (MEX)	F.R. Froehling (US)	7-5,6-4,6-2
1964	R.S. Emerson (AUS)	F.S. Stolle (AUS)	6-4,6-1,6-4
1965	M. Santana (SPA)	E.C. Drysdale (SA)	6-2,7-9,7-5, 6-1
1966	F.S. Stolle (AUS)	J.D. Newcombe (AUS)	4-6,12-10, 6-3,6-4
1967	J.D. Newcombe (AUS)	C.E. Graebner (US)	6-4,6-4,8-6
1968	A.R. Ashe (US) (Amateur)	R.C. Lutz (US)	4-6,6-3,8-10, 6-0,6-4
1968	A.R. Ashe (US) (Open)	T.S. Okker (NETH)	14-12,5-7, 6-3,3-6,6-3
1969	S.R. Smith (US) (Amateur)	R.C. Lutz (US)	9-7,6-3,6-1
1969	R.G. Laver (AUS) (Open)	A.D. Roche (AUS)	7-9,6-1,6-3, 6-2
1970	K.R. Rosewall (AUS)	A.D. Roche (AUS)	2-6,6-4,7-6, 6-3
1971	S.R. Smith (US)	J. Kodes (CZ)	3-6,6-3,6-2, 7-6
1972	I. Nastase (ROM)	A.R. Ashe (US)	3-6,6-3,6-7, 6-4,6-3
1973	J.D. Newcombe (AUS)	J. Kodes (CZ)	6-4,1-6,4-6, 6-2,6-3
1974	J.S. Connors (US)	K.R. Rosewall (AUS)	6-1,6-0,6-1
1975	M. Orantes (SPA)	J.S. Connors (US)	6-4,6-3,6-3
1976	J.S. Connors (US)	B. Borg (SWE)	6-4,3-6,7-6, 6-4
1977	G. Vilas (ARG)	J.S. Connors (US)	2-6,6-3,7-6, 6-0
1978	J.S. Connors (US)	B. Borg (SWE)	6-4,6-2,6-2
1979	J.P. McEnroe (US)	V. Gerulaitis (US)	7-5,6-3,6-3
1980	J.P. McEnroe (US)	B. Borg (SWE)	7-6,6-1,6-7, 5-7,6-4
1981	J.P. McEnroe (US)	B. Borg (SWE)	4-6,6-2,6-4, 6-3
1982	J.S. Connors (US)	I. Lendl (CZ)	6-3,6-2,4-6, 6-4
1983	J.S. Connors (US)	I. Lendl (CZ)	6-3,6-7,7-5, 6-0
1984	J.P. McEnroe (US)	I. Lendl (CZ)	6-3,6-4,6-1
1985	I. Lendl (CZ)	J.P. McEnroe (US)	7-6,6-3,6-4
1986	I. Lendl (CZ)	M. Mecir (CZ)	6-4,6-2,6-0
1987	I. Lendl (CZ)	M. Wilander (SWE)	6-7,6-0,7-6, 6-4
1988	M. Wilander (SWE)	I. Lendl (CZ)	6-4,4-6,6-3, 5-7,6-4

WOMEN'S SINGLES

YEAR	WINNER	RUNNER-UP	SCORE
1919	H.V. Wightman (née Hotchkiss) (US)	M. Zinderstein (US)	6-1,6-2
1920	M. Mallory (née Bjurstedt) (US)	M. Zinderstein (US)	6-3,6-1
1921	M. Mallory (née Bjurstedt) (US)	M.K. Browne (US)	4-6,6-4,6-2
1922	M. Mallory (née Bjurstedt) (US)	H.N. Wills (US)	6-3,6-1
1923	H.N. Wills (US)	M. Mallory (née Bjurstedt) (US)	6-2,6-1
1924	H.N. Wills (US)	M. Mallory (née Bjurstedt) (US)	6-1,6-2
1925	H.N. Wills (US)	K. McKane (GB)	3-6,6-0,6-2
1926	M. Mallory (née Bjurstedt) (US)	E. Ryan (US)	4-6,6-4,9-7
1927	H.N. Wills (US)	B. Nuthall (GB)	6-1,6-4
1928	H.N. Wills (US)	H.H. Jacobs (US)	6-2,6-1
1929	H.N. Wills (US)	P.H. Watson (GB)	6-4,6-2
1930	B. Nuthall (GB)	A. Harper (US)	6-4,6-1
1931	H.N. Moody (née Wills) (US)	E. Whittingstall (née Bennett) (GB)	6-4,6-1
1932	H.H. Jacobs (US)	C.A. Babcock (US)	6-2,6-2
1933	H.H. Jacobs (US)	H.N. Moody (née Wills) (US)	8-6,3-6,3-0, retired
1934	H.H. Jacobs (US)	S. Palfrey (US)	6-1,6-4
1935	H.H. Jacobs (US)	S. Fabyan (née Palfrey) (US)	6-1,6-4
1936	A. Marble (US)	H.H. Jacobs (US)	4-6,6-3,6-2
1937	A. Lizana (CHI)	J. Jedrejowska (POL)	6-4,6-2
1938	A. Marble (US)	N. Wynne (AUS)	6-0,6-3
1939	A. Marble (US)	H.H. Jacobs (US)	6-0,8-10,6-4
1940	A. Marble (US)	H.H. Jacobs (US)	6-2,6-3
1941	S. Cooke (née Palfrey) (US)	P.M. Betz (US)	6-1,6-4
1942	P.M. Betz (US)	A.L. Brough (US)	4-6,6-1,6-4
1943	P.M. Betz (US)	A.L. Brough (US)	6-3,5-7,6-3
1944	P.M. Betz (US)	M.E. Osborne (US)	6-3,8-6
1945	S. Cooke (née Palfrey) (US)	P.M. Betz (US)	3-6,8-6,6-4
1946	P.M. Betz (US)	D.J. Hart (US)	11-9,6-3
1947	A.L. Brough (US)	M.E. Osborne (US)	8-6,4-6,6-1
1948	M.E. du Pont (née Osborne) (US)	A.L. Brough (US)	4-6,6-4, 15-13
1949	M.E. du Pont (née Osborne) (US)	D.J. Hart (US)	6-4,6-1
1950	M.E. du Pont (née Osborne) (US)	D.J. Hart (US)	6-3,6-3
1951	M.C. Connolly (US)	S.J. Fry (US)	6-3,1-6,6-4
1952	M.C. Connolly (US)	D.J. Hart (US)	6-3,7-5
1953	M.C. Connolly (US)	D.J. Hart (US)	6-2,6-4
1954	D.J. Hart (US)	A.L. Brough (US)	6-8,6-1,8-6
1955	D.J. Hart (US)	P.E. Ward (GB)	6-4,6-2
1956	S.J. Fry (US)	A. Gibson (US)	6-3,6-4
1957	A. Gibson (US)	A.L. Brough (US)	6-3,6-2
1958	A. Gibson (US)	D.R. Hard (US)	3-6,6-1,6-2
1959	M.E. Bueno (BRA)	C.C. Truman (GB)	6-1,6-4
1960	D.R. Hard (US)	M.E. Bueno (BRA)	6-4,10-12, 6-4
1961	D.R. Hard (US)	A.S. Haydon (GB)	6-3,6-4
1962	M. Smith (AUS)	D.R. Hard (US)	9-7,6-4
1963	M.E. Bueno (BRA)	M. Smith (AUS)	7-5,6-4
1964	M.E. Bueno (BRA)	C.E. Graebner (US)	6-1,6-0
1965	M. Smith (US)	B.J. Moffitt (US)	8-6,7-5
1966	M.E. Bueno (BRA)	N. Richey (US)	6-3,6-1
1967	B.J. King (née Moffitt) (US)	A.S. Jones (née Haydon) (GB)	11-9,6-4
1968	M. Court (née Smith) (AUS) (Amateur)	M.E. Bueno (BRA)	6-2,6-2
1968	S.V. Wade (GB) (Open)	B.J. King (née Moffitt) (US)	6-4,6-2
1969	M. Court (née Smith) (AUS) (Amateur)	S.V. Wade (GB)	4-6,6-3,6-0
1969	M. Court (née Smith) (AUS) (Open)	N. Richey (US)	6-2,6-2
1970	M. Court (née Smith) (AUS)	R. Casals (US)	6-2,2-6,6-1
1971	B.J. King (née Moffitt) (US)	R. Casals (US)	6-4,7-6
1972	B.J. King (née Moffitt) (US)	K.A. Melville (AUS)	6-3,7-5
1973	M. Court (née Smith) (AUS)	E.F. Goolagong (AUS)	7-6,5-7,6-2
1974	B.J. King (née Moffitt) (US)	E.F. Goolagong (AUS)	3-6,6-3,7-5
1975	C.M. Evert (US)	E.F. Cawley (née Goolagong) (AUS)	5-7,6-4,6-2
1976	C.M. Evert (US)	E.F. Cawley (née Goolagong) (AUS)	6-3,6-0
1977	C.M. Evert (US)	W.M. Turnbull (AUS)	7-6,6-2
1978	C.M. Evert (US)	P.H. Shriver (US)	7-5,6-4
1979	T.A. Austin (US)	C. Lloyd (née Evert) (US)	6-4,6-3
1980	C. Lloyd (née Evert) (US)	H. Mandlikova (CZ)	5-7,6-1,6-1
1981	T.A. Austin (US)	M. Navratilova (US)	1-6,7-6,7-6
1982	C. Lloyd (née Evert) (US)	H. Mandlikova (CZ)	6-3,6-1
1983	M. Navratilova (US)	C. Lloyd (née Evert) (US)	6-1,6-3
1984	M. Navratilova (US)	C. Lloyd (née Evert) (US)	4-6,6-4,6-4
1985	H. Mandlikova (CZ)	M. Navratilova (US)	7-6,1-6,7-6
1986	M. Navratilova (US)	H. Sukova (CZ)	6-3,6-2
1987	M. Navratilova (US)	S. Graf (W.GER)	7-6,6-1
1988	S. Graf (W.GER)	G. Sabatini (ARG)	6-3,3-6,6-1

UNITED STATES CHAMPIONSHIPS continued

MEN'S DOUBLES

YEAR	WINNERS		YEAR	WINNERS
1919	N.E. Brookes & G.L. Patterson (AUS)		1955	K. Kamo & A. Miyagi (JPN)
1920	W.M. Johnston & C.J. Griffin (US)		1956	L.A. Hoad & K.R. Rosewall (AUS)
1921	W.T. Tilden & V. Richards (US)		1957	A.J. Cooper & N.A. Fraser (AUS)
1922	W.T. Tilden & V. Richards (US)		1958	H. Richardson & A. Olmedo (US)
1923	W.T. Tilden (US) & B.I.C. Norton (SA)		1959	R.S. Emerson & N.A. Fraser (AUS)
1924	R.G. Kinsey & H.O. Kinsey (US)		1960	R.S. Emerson & N.A. Fraser (AUS)
1925	R.N. Williams & V. Richards (US)		1961	C.R. McKinley & R.D. Ralston (US)
1926	R.N. Williams & V. Richards (US)		1962	R.H. Osuna & A. Palafox (MEX)
1927	W.T. Tilden & F.T. Hunter (US)		1963	C.R. McKinley & R.D. Ralston (US)
1928	G.M. Lott & J.F. Hennessey (US)		1964	C.R. McKinley & R.D. Ralston (US)
1929	G.M. Lott & J.H. Doeg (US)		1965	R.S. Emerson & F.S. Stolle (AUS)
1930	G.M. Lott & J.H. Doeg (US)		1966	R.S. Emerson & F.S. Stolle (AUS)
1931	W.L. Allison & J. Van Ryn (US)		1967	J.D. Newcombe & A.D. Roche (AUS)
1932	H.E. Vines & K. Gledhill (US)		1968	R.C. Lutz & S.R. Smith (US) (Amateur)
1933	G.M. Lott & L.R. Stoefen (US)		1968	R.C. Lutz & S.R. Smith (US) (Open)
1934	G.M. Lott & L.R. Stoefen (US)		1969	R.D. Crealy & A.J. Stone (AUS) (Amateur)
1935	W.L. Allison & J. Van Ryn (US)		1969	K.R. Rosewall & F.S. Stolle (AUS) (Open)
1936	J.D. Budge & C.G. Mako (US)		1970	P. Barthes (FRA) & N. Pilic (YUG)
1937	G. von Cramm & H. Henkel (GER)		1971	J.D. Newcombe (AUS) & R. Taylor (GB)
1938	J.D. Budge & C.G. Mako (US)		1972	E.C. Drysdale (SA) & R. Taylor (GB)
1939	A.K. Quist & J.E. Bromwich (AUS)		1973	O.K. Davidson & J.D. Newcombe (AUS)
1940	J.A. Kramer & F.R. Schroeder (US)		1974	R.C. Lutz & S.R. Smith (US)
1941	J.A. Kramer & F.R. Schroeder (US)		1975	J.S. Connors (US) & I. Nastase (ROM)
1942	G. Mulloy & W.F. Talbert (US)		1976	T.S. Okker (NETH) & M.C. Riessen (US)
1943	J.A. Kramer & F.A. Parker (US)		1977	R.A.J. Hewitt & F.D. McMillan (SA)
1944	W.D. McNeill & R. Falkenburg (US)		1978	R.C. Lutz & S.R. Smith (US)
1945	G. Mulloy & W.F. Talbert (US)		1979	P. Fleming & J.P. McEnroe (US)
1946	G. Mulloy & W.F. Talbert (US)		1980	R.C. Lutz & S.R. Smith (US)
1947	J.A. Kramer & F.R. Schroeder (US)		1981	P. Fleming & J.P. McEnroe (US)
1948	G. Mulloy & W.F. Talbert (US)		1982	K. Curren (SA) & S. Denton (US)
1949	O.W. Sidwell & J.E. Bromwich (AUS)		1983	P. Fleming & J.P. McEnroe (US)
1950	J.E. Bromwich & F.A. Sedgman (AUS)		1984	J. Fitzgerald (AUS) & T. Smid (CZ)
1951	K. McGregor & F.A. Sedgman (AUS)		1985	K. Flach & R. Seguso (US)
1952	M.G. Rose (AUS) & E.V. Seixas (US)		1986	A. Gomez (ECU) & S. Zivojinovic (YUG)
1953	M.G. Rose & R.N. Hartwig (AUS)		1987	S. Edberg & A. Jarryd (SWE)
1954	E.V. Seixas & M.A. Trabert (US)		1988	S. Casal & E. Sanchez (SPA)

MIXED DOUBLES

YEAR	WINNERS		YEAR	WINNERS
1919	V. Richards & M. Zinderstein (US)		1938	J.D. Budge & A. Marble (US)
1920	W.F. Johnson & H.V. Wightman (née Hotchkiss) (US)		1939	H.C. Hopman (AUS) & A. Marble (US)
1921	W.M. Johnston & M.K. Browne (US)		1940	R.L. Riggs & A. Marble (US)
1922	W.T. Tilden & M. Mallory (née Bjurstedt) (US)		1941	J.A. Kramer & S. Cooke (née Palfrey) (US)
1923	W.T. Tilden & M. Mallory (née Bjurstedt) (US)		1942	F.R. Schroeder & A.L. Brough (US)
1924	V. Richards & H.N. Wills (US)		1943	W.F. Talbert & M.E. Osborne (US)
1925	J.B. Hawkes (AUS) & K. McKane (GB)		1944	W.F. Talbert & M.E. Osborne (US)
1926	J. Borotra (FRA) & E. Ryan (US)		1945	W.F. Talbert & M.E. Osborne (US)
1927	H. Cochet (FRA) & E. Bennett (GB)		1946	W.F. Talbert & M.E. Osborne (US)
1928	J.B. Hawkes (AUS) & H.N. Wills (US)		1947	J.E. Bromwich (AUS) & A.L. Brough (US)
1929	G.M. Lott (US) & B. Nuthall (GB)		1948	T.P. Brown & A.L. Brough (US)
1930	W.L. Allison & E. Cross (US)		1949	E.W. Sturgess (SA) & A.L. Brough (US)
1931	G.M. Lott (US) & B.Nuthall (GB)		1950	K. McGregor (AUS) & M.E. du Pont (née Osborne) (US)
1932	F.J. Perry (GB) & S. Palfrey (US)		1951	F.A. Sedgman (AUS) & D.J. Hart (US)
1933	H.E. Vines & E. Ryan (US)		1952	F.A. Sedgman (AUS) & D.J. Hart (US)
1934	G.M. Lott & H.H. Jacobs (US)		1953	E.V. Seixas & D.J. Hart (US)
1935	E. Maier (SPA) & S. Fabyan (née Palfrey) (US)		1954	E.V. Seixas & D.J. Hart (US)
1936	G.C. Mako & A. Marble (US)		1955	E.V. Seixas & D.J. Hart (US)
1937	J.D. Budge & S. Fabyan (née Palfrey) (US)		1956	K.R. Rosewall (AUS) & M.E. du Pont (née Osborne) (US)

WOMEN'S DOUBLES

YEAR	WINNERS	YEAR	WINNERS
1919	E.E. Goss & M. Zinderstein (US)	1955	A.L. Brough & M.E. du Pont (née Osborne) (US)
1920	E.E. Goss & M. Zinderstein (US)	1956	A.L. Brough & M.E. du Pont (née Osborne) (US)
1921	M.K. Browne & L. Williams (US)	1957	A.L. Brough & M.E. du Pont (née Osborne) (US)
1922	M. Jessup (née Zinderstein) & H.N. Wills (US)	1958	J. Arth & D.R. Hard (US)
1923	P. Covell (née Howkins) & K. McKane (GB)	1959	J. Arth & D.R. Hard (US)
1924	H.V. Wightman (née Hotchkiss) & H.N. Wills (US)	1960	M.E. Bueno (BRA) & D.R. Hard (US)
1925	M.K. Browne & H.N. Wills (US)	1961	D.R. Hard (US) & L.R. Turner (AUS)
1926	E.E. Goss & E. Ryan (US)	1962	M.E. Bueno (BRA) & D.R. Hard (US)
1927	K. Godfree (née McKane) & E.H. Harvey (GB)	1963	R.A. Ebbern & M. Smith (AUS)
1928	H.V. Wightman (née Hotchkiss) & H.N. Wills (US)	1964	B.J. Moffitt & K.M. Susman (née Hantze) (US)
1929	P. Michel (née Saunders) & P.H. Watson (GB)	1965	C.E. Graebner & N. Richey (US)
1930	B. Nuthall (GB) & S. Palfrey (US)	1966	M.E. Bueno (BRA) & N. Richey (US)
1931	B. Nuthall & E. Whittingstall (née Bennett) (GB)	1967	R. Casals & B.J. King (née Moffitt) (US)
1932	H.H. Jacobs & S. Palfrey (US)	1968	M.E. Bueno (BRA) & M. Court (née Smith) (AUS) (Amateur)
1933	F. James & B. Nuthall (GB)	1968	M.E. Bueno (BRA) & M. Court (née Smith) (AUS) (Open)
1934	H.H. Jacobs & S. Palfrey (US)	1969	M. Court (née Smith) (AUS) & S.V. Wade (GB) (Amateur)
1935	H.H. Jacobs & S. Fabyan (née Palfrey) (US)	1969	F. Durr (FRA) & D.R. Hard (US) (Open)
1936	C.A. Babcock & M. Van Ryn (née Gladman) (US)	1970	M. Court (née Smith) & J.A.M. Dalton (née Tegart) (AUS)
1937	S. Fabyan (née Palfrey) & A. Marble (US)	1971	R. Casals (US) & J.A.M. Dalton (née Tegart) (AUS)
1938	S. Fabyan (née Palfrey) & A. Marble (US)	1972	F. Durr (FRA) & B.F. Stove (NETH)
1939	S. Fabyan (née Palfrey) & A. Marble (US)	1973	M. Court (née Smith) (AUS) & S.V. Wade (GB)
1940	S. Fabyan (née Palfrey) & A. Marble (US)	1974	R. Casals & B.J. King (née Moffitt) (US)
1941	S. Cooke (née Palfrey) & M.E. Osborne (US)	1975	M. Court (née Smith) (AUS) & S.V. Wade (GB)
1942	A.L. Brough & M.E. Osborne (US)	1976	D.A. Boshoff & I.S. Kloss (SA)
1943	A.L. Brough & M.E. Osborne (US)	1977	M. Navratilova (CZ) & B.F. Stove (NETH)
1944	A.L. Brough & M.E. Osborne (US)	1978	B.J. King (née Moffitt) (US) & M. Navratilova (CZ)
1945	A.L. Brough & M.E. Osborne (US)	1979	B.F. Stove (NETH) & W.M. Turnbull (AUS)
1946	A.L. Brough & M.E. Osborne (US)	1980	B.J. King (née Moffitt) (US) & M. Navratilova (CZ)
1947	A.L. Brough & M.E. Osborne (US)	1981	K. Jordan & A.E. Smith (US)
1948	A.L. Brough & M.E. du Pont (née Osborne) (US)	1982	R. Casals (US) & W.M. Turnbull (AUS)
1949	A.L. Brough & M.E. du Pont (née Osborne) (US)	1983	M. Navratilova & P.H. Shriver (US)
1950	A.L. Brough & M.E. du Pont (née Osborne) (US)	1984	M. Navratilova & P.H. Shriver (US)
1951	D.J. Hart & S.J. Fry (US)	1985	C. Kohde-Kilsch (W.GER) & H. Sukova (CZ)
1952	D.J. Hart & S.J. Fry (US)	1986	M. Navratilova & P.H. Shriver (US)
1953	D.J. Hart & S.J. Fry (US)	1987	M. Navratilova & P.H. Shriver (US)
1954	D.J. Hart & S.J. Fry (US)	1988	G. Fernandez (P.RICO) & R. White (US)

YEAR	WINNERS	YEAR	WINNERS
1957	K. Nielsen (DEN) & A. Gibson (US)	1974	G. Masters (AUS) & P. Teeguarden (US)
1958	N.A. Fraser (AUS) & M.E. du Pont (née Osborne) (US)	1975	R.L. Stockton & R. Casals (US)
1959	N.A. Fraser (AUS) & M.E. du Pont (née Osborne) (US)	1976	P.C. Dent (AUS) & B.J. King (née Moffitt) (US)
1960	N.A. Fraser (AUS) & M.E. du Pont (née Osborne) (US)	1977	F.D. McMillan (SA) & B.F. Stove (NETH)
1961	R. Mark & M. Smith (AUS)	1978	F.D. McMillan (SA) & B.F. Stove (NETH)
1962	F.S. Stolle & M. Smith (AUS)	1979	R.A.J. Hewitt & G.R. Stevens (SA)
1963	K.N. Fletcher & M. Smith (AUS)	1980	M.C. Riessen (US) & W.M. Turnbull (AUS)
1964	J.D. Newcombe & M. Smith (AUS)	1981	K. Curren (SA) & A.E. Smith (US)
1965	F.S. Stolle & M. Smith (AUS)	1982	K. Curren (SA) & A.E. Smith (US)
1966	O.K. Davidson (AUS) & D. Fales (née Floyd) (US)	1983	J. Fitzgerald & E. Sayers (AUS)
1967	O.K. Davidson (AUS) & B.J. King (née Moffitt) (US)	1984	T. Gullikson (US) & M. Maleeva (BUL)
1968	P.W. Curtis (GB) & M.A. Eisel (US) (Amateur)	1985	H. Guenthardt (SWI) & M. Navratilova (US)
1968	(Open) No event held	1986	S. Casal (SPA) & R. Reggi (ITA)
1969	P. Sullivan & P.S.A. Hogan (US) (Amateur)	1987	E. Sanchez (SPA) & M. Navratilova (US)
1969	M.C. Riessen (US) & M. Court (née Smith) (AUS) (Open)	1988	J. Pugh (US) & J. Novotna (CZ)
1970	M.C. Riessen (US) & M. Court (née Smith) (AUS)		
1971	O.K. Davidson (AUS) & B.J. King (née Moffitt) (US)		
1972	M.C. Riessen (US) & M. Court (née Smith) (AUS)		
1973	O.K. Davidson (AUS) & B.J. King (née Moffitt) (US)		

FRENCH CHAMPIONSHIPS
(NB: Prior to 1925, the entry was restricted to members of French clubs.)

MEN'S SINGLES

YEAR	WINNER	RUNNER-UP	SCORE
1925	R. Lacoste (FRA)	J. Borotra (FRA)	7-5,6-1,6-4
1926	H. Cochet (FRA)	R. Lacoste (FRA)	6-2,6-4,6-3
1927	R. Lacoste (FRA)	W.T. Tilden (US)	6-4,4-6,5-7, 6-3,11-9
1928	H. Cochet (FRA)	R. Lacoste (FRA)	5-7,6-3,6-1, 6-3
1929	R. Lacoste (FRA)	J. Borotra (FRA)	6-3,2-6,6-0, 2-6,8-6
1930	H. Cochet (FRA)	W.T. Tilden (US)	3-6,8-6,6-3, 6-1
1931	J. Borotra (FRA)	C. Boussus (FRA)	2-6,6-4,7-5, 6-4
1932	H. Cochet (FRA)	G. de Stefani (ITA)	6-0,6-4,4-6, 6-3
1933	J.H. Crawford (AUS)	H. Cochet (FRA)	8-6,6-1,6-3
1934	G. von Cramm (GER)	J.H. Crawford (AUS)	6-4,7-9,3-6, 7-5,6-3
1935	F.J. Perry (GB)	G. von Cramm (GER)	6-3,3-6,6-1, 6-3
1936	G. von Cramm (GER)	F.J. Perry (GB)	6-0,2-6,6-2, 2-6,6-0
1937	H. Henkel (GER)	H.W. Austin (GB)	6-1,6-4,6-3
1938	J.D. Budge (US)	R. Menzel (CZ)	6-3,6-2,6-4
1939	W.D. McNeill (US)	R.L. Riggs (US)	7-5,6-0,6-3
1940-45	No competition		
1946	M. Bernard (FRA)	J. Drobny (CZ)	3-6,2-6,6-1, 6-4,6-3
1947	J. Asboth (HUN)	E.W. Sturgess (SA)	8-6,7-5,6-4
1948	F.A. Parker (US)	J. Drobny (CZ)	6-4,7-5,5-7, 8-6
1949	F.A. Parker (US)	J.E. Patty (US)	6-3,1-6,6-1, 6-4
1950	J.E. Patty (US)	J. Drobny (EG)	6-1,6-2,3-6, 5-7,7-5
1951	J. Drobny (EG)	E.W. Sturgess (SA)	6-3,6-3,6-3
1952	J. Drobny (EG)	F.A. Sedgman (AUS)	6-2,6-0,3-6, 6-4
1953	K.R. Rosewall (AUS)	E.V. Seixas (US)	6-3,6-4,1-6, 6-2
1954	M.A. Trabert (US)	A. Larsen (US)	6-4,7-5,6-1
1955	M.A. Trabert (US)	S. Davidson (SWE)	2-6,6-1,6-4, 6-2
1956	L.A. Hoad (AUS)	S. Davidson (SWE)	6-4,8-6,6-3
1957	S. Davidson (SWE)	H. Flam (US)	6-3,6-4,6-4
1958	M.G. Rose (AUS)	L. Ayala (CHI)	6-3,6-4,6-4
1959	N. Pietrangeli (ITA)	E.C. Vermaak (SA)	3-6,6-3,6-4, 6-1
1960	N. Pietrangeli (ITA)	L. Ayala (CHI)	3-6,6-3,6-4, 4-6,6-3
1961	M. Santana (SPA)	N. Pietrangeli (ITA)	4-6,6-1,3-6, 6-0,6-2
1962	R.G. Laver (AUS)	R.S. Emerson (AUS)	3-6,2-6,6-3, 9-7,6-2
1963	R.S. Emerson (AUS)	P. Darmon (FRA)	3-6,6-1,6-4, 6-4
1964	M. Santana (SPA)	N. Pietrangeli (ITA)	6-3,6-1,4-6, 7-5
1965	F.S. Stolle (AUS)	A.D. Roche (AUS)	3-6,6-0,6-2, 6-3
1966	A.D. Roche (AUS)	I. Gulyas (HUN)	6-1,6-4,7-5

YEAR	WINNER	RUNNER-UP	SCORE
1967	R.S. Emerson (AUS)	A.D. Roche (AUS)	6-1,6-4,2-6, 6-2
1968	K.R. Rosewall (AUS)	R.G. Laver (AUS)	6-3,6-1,2-6, 6-2
1969	R.G. Laver (AUS)	K.R. Rosewall (AUS)	6-4,6-3,6-4
1970	J. Kodes (CZ)	Z. Franulovic (YUG)	6-2,6-4,6-0
1971	J. Kodes (CZ)	I. Nastase (ROM)	8-6,6-2,2-6, 7-5
1972	A. Gimeno (SPA)	P. Proisy (FRA)	4-6,6-3,6-1, 6-1
1973	I. Nastase (ROM)	N. Pilic (YUG)	6-3,6-3,6-0
1974	B. Borg (SWE)	M. Orantes (SPA)	2-6,6-7,6-0, 6-1,6-1
1975	B. Borg (SWE)	G. Vilas (ARG)	6-2,6-3,6-4
1976	A. Panatta (ITA)	H. Solomon (US)	6-1,6-4,4-6, 7-6
1977	G. Vilas (ARG)	B. Gottfried (US)	6-0,6-3,6-0
1978	B. Borg (SWE)	G. Vilas (ARG)	6-1,6-1,6-3
1979	B. Borg (SWE)	V. Pecci (PAR)	6-3,6-1,6-7, 6-4
1980	B. Borg (SWE)	V. Gerulaitis (US)	6-4,6-1,6-2
1981	B. Borg (SWE)	I. Lendl (CZ)	6-1,4-6,6-2, 3-6,6-1
1982	M. Wilander (SWE)	G. Vilas (ARG)	1-6,7-6,6-0, 6-4
1983	Y. Noah (FRA)	M. Wilander (SWE)	6-2,7-5,7-6
1984	I. Lendl (CZ)	J.P. McEnroe (US)	3-6,2-6,6-4, 7-5,7-5
1985	M. Wilander (SWE)	I. Lendl (CZ)	3-6,6-4,6-2, 6-2
1986	I. Lendl (CZ)	M. Pernfors (SWE)	6-3,6-2,6-4
1987	I. Lendl (CZ)	M. Wilander (SWE)	7-5,6-2,3-6, 7-6
1988	M. Wilander (SWE)	H. Leconte (FRA)	7-5,6-2,6-1

WOMEN'S SINGLES

YEAR	WINNER	RUNNER-UP	SCORE	YEAR	WINNER	RUNNER-UP	SCORE
1925	S. Lenglen (FRA)	K. McKane (GB)	6-1,6-2	1973	M. Court (née Smith) (AUS)	C.M. Evert (US)	6-7,7-6,6-4
1926	S. Lenglen (FRA)	M.K. Browne (US)	6-1,6-0	1974	C.M. Evert (US)	O. Morozova (USSR)	6-1,6-2
1927	K. Bouman (NETH)	G. Peacock (IND)	6-2,6-4	1975	C.M. Evert (US)	M. Navratilova (CZ)	2-6,6-2,6-1
1928	H.N. Wills (US)	E. Bennett (GB)	6-1,6-2	1976	S. Barker (GB)	R. Tomanova (CZ)	6-2,0-6,6-2
1929	H.N. Wills (US)	S. Mathieu (FRA)	6-3,6-4	1977	M. Jausovec (YUG)	F. Mihai (ROM)	6-2,6-7,6-1
1930	H.N. Moody (née Wills) (US)	H.H. Jacobs (US)	6-2,6-1	1978	V. Ruzici (ROM)	M. Jausovec (YUG)	6-2,6-2
1931	C. Aussem (GER)	B. Nuthall (GB)	8-6,6-1	1979	C. Lloyd (née Evert) (US)	W.M. Turnbull (AUS)	6-2,6-0
1932	H.N. Moody (née Wills) (US)	S. Mathieu (FRA)	7-5,6-1	1980	C. Lloyd (née Evert) (US)	V. Ruzici (ROM)	6-0,6-3
1933	M.C. Scriven (GB)	S. Mathieu (FRA)	6-2,4-6,6-4	1981	H. Mandlikova (CZ)	S. Hanika (W.GER)	6-2,6-4
1934	M.C. Scriven (GB)	H.H. Jacobs (US)	7-5,4-6,6-1	1982	M. Navratilova (US)	A. Jaeger (US)	7-6,6-1
1935	H. Sperling (née Krahwinkel) (DEN)	S. Mathieu (FRA)	6-2,6-1	1983	C. Lloyd (née Evert) (US)	M. Jausovec (YUG)	6-1,6-2
1936	H. Sperling (née Krahwinkel) (DEN)	S. Mathieu (FRA)	6-3,6-4	1984	M. Navratilova (US)	C. Lloyd (née Evert) (US)	6-3,6-1
1937	H. Sperling (née Krahwinkel) (DEN)	S. Mathieu (FRA)	6-2,6-4	1985	C. Lloyd (née Evert) (US)	M. Navratilova (US)	6-3,6-7,7-5
1938	S. Mathieu (FRA)	N. Landry (née Adamson) (FRA)	6-0,6-3	1986	C. Lloyd (née Evert) (US)	M. Navratilova (US)	2-6,6-3,6-3
1939	S. Mathieu (FRA)	J. Jedrejowska (POL)	6-3,8-6	1987	S. Graf (W.GER)	M. Navratilova (US)	6-4,4-6,8-6
1940-45	No competition			1988	S. Graf (W.GER)	N. Zvereva (USSR)	6-0,6-0
1946	M.E. Osborne (US)	P.M. Betz (US)	1-6,8-6,7-5				
1947	P.C. Todd (US)	D.J. Hart (US)	6-3,3-6,6-4				
1948	N. Landry (née Adamson) (FRA)	S.J. Fry (US)	6-2,0-6,6-0				
1949	M.E. du Pont (née Osborne) (US)	N. Adamson (FRA)	7-5,6-2				
1950	D.J. Hart (US)	P.C. Todd (US)	6-4,4-6,6-2				
1951	S.J. Fry (US)	D.J. Hart (US)	6-3,3-6,6-3				
1952	D.J. Hart (US)	S.J. Fry (US)	6-4,6-4				
1953	M.C. Connolly (US)	D.J. Hart (US)	6-2,6-4				
1954	M.C. Connolly (US)	G. Bucaille (FRA)	6-4,6-1				
1955	A. Mortimer (GB)	D.P. Knode (née Head) (US)	2-6,7-5,10-8				
1956	A. Gibson (US)	A. Mortimer (GB)	6-0,12-10				
1957	S.J. Bloomer (GB)	D.P. Knode (née Head) (US)	6-1,6-3				
1958	S.Kormoczy (HUN)	S.J. Bloomer (GB)	6-4,1-6,6-2				
1959	C.C. Truman (GB)	S. Kormoczy (HUN)	6-4,7-5				
1960	D.R. Hard (US)	Y. Ramirez (MEX)	6-3,6-4				
1961	A.S. Haydon (GB)	Y. Ramirez (MEX)	6-2,6-1				
1962	M. Smith (AUS)	L.R. Turner (AUS)	6-3,3-6,7-5				
1963	L.R. Turner (AUS)	A.S. Jones (née Haydon) (GB)	2-6,6-3,7-5				
1964	M. Smith (AUS)	M.E. Bueno (BRA)	5-7,6-1,6-2				
1965	L.R. Turner (AUS)	M. Smith (AUS)	6-3,6-4				
1966	A.S. Jones (née Haydon) (GB)	N. Richey (US)	6-3,6-1				
1967	F. Durr (FRA)	L.R. Turner (AUS)	4-6,6-3,6-4				
1968	N. Richey (US)	A.S. Jones (née Haydon) (GB)	5-7,6-4,6-1				
1969	M. Court (née Smith) (AUS)	A.S. Jones (née Haydon) (GB)	6-1,4-6,6-3				
1970	M. Court (née Smith) (AUS)	H. Niessen (W.GER)	6-2,6-4				
1971	E.F. Goolagong (AUS)	H.F. Gourlay (AUS)	6-3,7-5				
1972	B.J. King (née Moffitt) (US)	E.F. Goolagong (AUS)	6-3,6-3				

FRENCH CHAMPIONSHIPS *continued*

MEN'S DOUBLES

YEAR	WINNERS	YEAR	WINNERS
1925	J. Borotra & R. Lacoste (FRA)	1967	J.D. Newcombe & A.D. Roche (AUS)
1926	H. Kinsey & V. Richards (US)	1968	K.R. Rosewall & F.S. Stolle (AUS)
1927	J. Brugnon & H. Cochet (FRA)	1969	J.D. Newcombe & A.D. Roche (AUS)
1928	J. Borotra & J. Brugnon (FRA)	1970	I. Nastase & I. Tiriac (ROM)
1929	J. Borotra & R. Lacoste (FRA)	1971	A.R. Ashe & M.C. Riessen (US)
1930	J. Brugnon & H. Cochet (FRA)	1972	R.A.J. Hewitt & F.D. McMillan (SA)
1931	G.M. Lott & J. Van Ryn (US)	1973	J.D. Newcombe (AUS) & T.S. Okker (NETH)
1932	J. Brugnon & H. Cochet (FRA)	1974	R.D. Crealy (AUS) & O. Parun (NZ)
1933	G.P. Hughes & F.J. Perry (GB)	1975	B.E. Gottfried (US) & R. Ramirez (MEX)
1934	J. Borotra & J. Brugnon (FRA)	1976	F. McNair & S.E. Stewart (US)
1935	J.H. Crawford & A.K. Quist (AUS)	1977	B.E. Gottfried (US) & R. Ramirez (MEX)
1936	M. Bernard & J. Borotra (FRA)	1978	G. Mayer & H. Pfister (US)
1937	H. Henkel & G. von Cramm (GER)	1979	A.A. Mayer & G. Mayer (US)
1938	B. Destremau & Y. Petra (FRA)	1980	V. Amaya & H.Pfister (US)
1939	C. Harris & W.D. McNeill (US)	1981	H. Guenthardt (SWI) & B. Taroczy (HUN)
1940-45	No competition	1982	S.E. Stewart & F. Taygan (US)
1946	M. Bernard & Y. Petra (FRA)	1983	A. Jarryd & H. Simonsson (SWE)
1947	E. Fannin & E.W. Sturgess (SA)	1984	H. Leconte & Y. Noah (FRA)
1948	L. Bergelin (SWE) & J. Drobny (CZ)	1985	M.R. Edmondson & K.G. Warwick (AUS)
1949	R.A. Gonzales & F.A. Parker (US)	1986	J. Fitzgerald (AUS) & T. Smid (CZ)
1950	W.F. Talbert & M.A. Trabert (US)	1987	A. Jarryd (SWE) & R. Seguso (US)
1951	K. McGregor & F.A. Sedgman (AUS)	1988	A. Gomez (ECU) & E. Sanchez (SPA)
1952	K. McGregor & F.A. Sedgman (AUS)		
1953	L.A. Hoad & K.R. Rosewall (AUS)		
1954	E.V. Seixas & M.A. Trabert (US)		
1955	E.V. Seixas & M.A. Trabert (US)		
1956	D.W. Candy (AUS) & R.M. Perry (US)		
1957	M.J. Anderson & A.J. Cooper (AUS)		
1958	A.J. Cooper & N.A. Fraser (AUS)		
1959	N. Pietrangeli & O. Sirola (ITA)		
1960	R.S. Emerson & N.A. Fraser (AUS)		
1961	R.S. Emerson & R.G. Laver (AUS)		
1962	R.S. Emerson & N.A. Fraser (AUS)		
1963	R.S. Emerson (AUS) & M. Santana (SPA)		
1964	R.S. Emerson & K.N. Fletcher (AUS)		
1965	R.S. Emerson & F.S. Stolle (AUS)		
1966	C.E. Graebner & R.D. Ralston (US)		

MIXED DOUBLES

YEAR	WINNERS	YEAR	WINNERS
1925	J. Brugnon & S. Lenglen (FRA)	1948	J. Drobny (CZ) & P.C. Todd (US)
1926	J. Brugnon & S. Lenglen (FRA)	1949	E.W. Sturgess & S.P. Summers (née Piercy) (SA)
1927	J. Borotra & M. Bordes (FRA)	1950	E. Morea (ARG) & B. Scofield (US)
1928	H. Cochet (FRA) & E. Bennett (GB)	1951	F.A. Sedgman (AUS) & D.J. Hart (US)
1929	H. Cochet (FRA) & E. Bennett (GB)	1952	F.A. Sedgman (AUS) & D.J. Hart (US)
1930	W.T. Tilden (US) & C. Aussem (GER)	1953	E.V. Seixas & D.J. Hart (US)
1931	P.D.B. Spence (SA) & B. Nuthall (GB)	1954	L.A. Hoad (AUS) & M.C. Connolly (US)
1932	F.J. Perry & B. Nuthall (GB)	1955	G.L. Forbes (SA) & D.R. Hard (US)
1933	J.H. Crawford (AUS) & M.C. Scriven (GB)	1956	L. Ayala (CHI) & T. Long (née Coyne) (AUS)
1934	J. Borotra & C. Rosambert (FRA)	1957	J. Javorsky & V. Puzejova (CZ)
1935	M. Bernard (FRA) & L. Payot (SWI)	1958	N. Pietrangeli (ITA) & S.J. Bloomer (GB)
1936	M. Bernard (FRA) & A.M. Yorke (GB)	1959	W.A. Knight (GB) & Y. Ramirez (MEX)
1937	Y. Petra & S. Mathieu (FRA)	1960	R.N. Howe (AUS) & M.E. Bueno (BRA)
1938	D. Mitic (YUG) & S. Mathieu (FRA)	1961	R.G. Laver (AUS) & D.R. Hard (US)
1939	E.T. Cooke & S. Fabyan (née Palfrey) (US)	1962	R.N. Howe (AUS) & R. Schuurman (SA)
1940-45	No competition	1963	K.N. Fletcher & M. Smith (AUS)
1946	J.E. Patty & P.M. Betz (US)	1964	K.N. Fletcher & M. Smith (AUS)
1947	E.W. Sturgess & S.P. Summers (née Piercy) (SA)	1965	K.N. Fletcher & M. Smith (AUS)

WOMEN'S DOUBLES

YEAR	WINNERS
1925	S. Lenglen & D. Vlasto (FRA)
1926	S. Lenglen & D. Vlasto (FRA)
1927	E.L. Heine (SA) & G. Peacock (IND)
1928	E. Bennett & P.H. Watson (GB)
1929	K. Bouman (NETH) & E. de Alvarez (SPA)
1930	H.N. Moody (née Wills) & E. Ryan (US)
1931	B. Nuthall & E. Whittingstall (née Bennett) (GB)
1932	H.N. Moody (née Wills) & E. Ryan (US)
1933	S. Mathieu (FRA) & E. Ryan (US)
1934	S. Mathieu (FRA) & E. Ryan (US)
1935	M.C. Scriven & K.E. Stammers (GB)
1936	S. Mathieu (FRA) & A.M. Yorke (GB)
1937	S. Mathieu (FRA) & A.M. Yorke (GB)
1938	S. Mathieu (FRA) & A.M. Yorke (GB)
1939	S. Mathieu (FRA) & J. Jedrejowska (POL)
1940-45	No competition
1946	A.L. Brough & M.E. Osborne (US)
1947	A.L. Brough & M.E. Osborne (US)
1948	D.J. Hart & P.C. Todd (US)
1949	A.L. Brough & M.E. du Pont (née Osborne) (US)
1950	S.J. Fry & D.J. Hart (US)
1951	S.J. Fry & D.J. Hart (US)
1952	S.J. Fry & D.J. Hart (US)
1953	S.J. Fry & D.J. Hart (US)
1954	M.C. Connolly (US) & N. Hopman (née Hall) (AUS)
1955	B. Fleitz & D.R. Hard (US)
1956	A. Buxton (GB) & A. Gibson (US)
1957	S.J. Bloomer (GB) & D.R. Hard (US)
1958	Y. Ramirez & R.M. Reyes (MEX)
1959	S. Reynolds & R. Schuurman (SA)
1960	M.E. Bueno (BRA) & D.R. Hard (US)
1961	S. Reynolds & R. Schuurman (SA)
1962	S. Price (née Reynolds) & R. Schuurman (SA)
1963	A.S. Jones (née Haydon) (GB) & R. Schuurman (SA)
1964	M. Smith & L.R. Turner (AUS)
1965	M. Smith & L.R. Turner (AUS)
1966	M. Smith & J.A.M. Tegart (AUS)

YEAR	WINNERS
1967	F. Durr (FRA) & G.V. Sherriff (AUS)
1968	F. Durr (FRA) & A.S. Jones (née Haydon) (GB)
1969	F. Durr (FRA) & A.S. Jones (née Haydon) (GB)
1970	F. Durr & G.V. Chanfreau (née Sherriff) (FRA)
1971	F. Durr & G.V. Chanfreau (née Sherriff) (FRA)
1972	B.J. King (née Moffitt) (US) & B.F. Stove (NETH)
1973	M. Court (née Smith) (AUS) & S.V. Wade (GB)
1974	C.M. Evert (US) & O. Morozova (USSR)
1975	C.M. Evert (US) & M. Navratilova (CZ)
1976	F. Bonicelli (URU) & G.V. Lovera (née Sherriff) (FRA)
1977	R. Marsikova (CZ) & P. Teeguarden (US)
1978	M. Jausovec (YUG) & V. Ruzici (ROM)
1979	B.F. Stove (NETH) & W.M. Turnbull (AUS)
1980	K. Jordan & A.E. Smith (US)
1981	R. Fairbank & T.J. Harford (SA)
1982	M. Navratilova & A.E. Smith (US)
1983	R. Fairbank (SA) & C.S. Reynolds (US)
1984	M. Navratilova & P.H. Shriver (US)
1985	M. Navratilova & P.H. Shriver (US)
1986	M. Navratilova (US) & A. Temesvari (HUN)
1987	M. Navratilova & P.H. Shriver (US)
1988	M. Navratilova & P.H. Shriver (US)

YEAR	WINNERS
1966	F.D. McMillan & A.M. van Zyl (SA)
1967	O.K. Davidson (AUS) & B.J. King (née Moffitt) (US)
1968	J.C. Barclay & F. Durr (FRA)
1969	M.C. Riessen (US) & M. Court (née Smith) (AUS)
1970	R.A.J. Hewitt (SA) & B.J. King (née Moffitt) (US)
1971	J. Barclay & F. Durr (FRA)
1972	K.G. Warwick & E.F. Goolagong (AUS)
1973	J.C. Barclay & F. Durr (FRA)
1974	I. Molina (COL) & M. Navratilova (CZ)
1975	T. Koch (BRA) & F. Bonicelli (URU)
1976	K.G. Warwick (AUS) & I.S. Kloss (SA)
1977	J.P. McEnroe & M. Carillo (US)
1978	P. Slozil & R. Tomanova (CZ)
1979	R.A.J. Hewitt (SA) & W.M. Turnbull (AUS)
1980	W. Martin & A.E. Smith (US)
1981	J. Arias & A. Jaeger (US)
1982	J.M. Lloyd (GB) & W.M. Turnbull (AUS)
1983	E. Teltscher & B.S. Jordan (US)

YEAR	WINNERS
1984	R.L. Stockton & A.E. Smith (US)
1985	H.P. Guenthardt (SWI) & M. Navratilova (US)
1986	K. Flach & K. Jordan (US)
1987	E. Sanchez (SPA) & P.H. Shriver (US)
1988	J. Lozano (MEX) & L. McNeil (US)

AUSTRALIAN CHAMPIONSHIPS

MEN'S SINGLES

YEAR	WINNER	RUNNER-UP	SCORE	YEAR	WINNER	RUNNER-UP	SCORE
1919	A.R.F. Kingscote (GB)	E.O Pockley (AUS)	6-4,6-0,6-3	1959	A. Olmedo (US)	N.A. Fraser (AUS)	6-1,6-2,3-6, 6-3
1920	P. O'Hara Wood (AUS)	R.V. Thomas (AUS)	6-3,4-6,6-8, 6-1,6-3	1960	R.G. Laver (AUS)	N.A. Fraser (AUS)	5-7,3-6,6-3, 8-6,8-6
1921	R.H. Gemmell (AUS)	A. Hedeman (AUS)	7-5,6-1,6-4	1961	R.S. Emerson (AUS)	R.G. Laver (AUS)	1-6,6-3,7-5, 6-4
1922	J.O. Anderson (AUS)	G.L. Patterson (AUS)	6-0,3-6,3-6, 6-3,6-2	1962	R.G. Laver (AUS)	R.S. Emerson (AUS)	8-6,0-6,6-4, 6-4
1923	P. O'Hara Wood (AUS)	C.B. St John (AUS)	6-1,6-1,6-3	1963	R.S. Emerson (AUS)	K.N. Fletcher (AUS)	6-3,6-3,6-1
1924	J.O. Anderson (AUS)	R.E. Schlesinger (AUS)	6-3,6-4,3-6, 5-7,6-3	1964	R.S. Emerson (AUS)	F.S. Stolle (AUS)	6-3,6-4,6-2
1925	J.O. Anderson (AUS)	G.L. Patterson (AUS)	11-9,2-6,6-2, 6-3	1965	R.S. Emerson (AUS)	F.S. Stolle (AUS)	7-9,2-6,6-4, 7-5,6-1
1926	J.B. Hawkes (AUS)	J. Willard (AUS)	6-1,6-3,6-1	1966	R.S. Emerson (AUS)	A.R. Ashe (US)	6-4,6-8,6-2, 6-3
1927	G.L. Patterson (AUS)	J.B. Hawkes (AUS)	3-6,6-4,3-6, 18-16,6-3	1967	R.S. Emerson (AUS)	A.R. Ashe (US)	6-4,6-1,6-4
1928	J. Borotra (FRA)	R.O. Cummings (AUS)	6-4,6-1,4-6, 5-7,6-3	1968	W.W. Bowrey (AUS)	J.M. Gisbert (SPA)	7-5,2-6,9-7, 6-4
1929	J.C. Gregory (GB)	R.E. Schlesinger (AUS)	6-2,6-2,5-7, 7-5	1969	R.G. Laver (AUS)	A. Gimeno (SPA)	6-3,6-4,7-5
1930	E.F. Moon (AUS)	H.C. Hopman (AUS)	6-3,6-1,6-3	1970	A.R. Ashe (US)	R.D. Crealy (AUS)	6-4,9-7,6-2
1931	J.H. Crawford (AUS)	H.C. Hopman (AUS)	6-4,6-2,2-6, 6-1	1971	K.R. Rosewall (AUS)	A.R. Ashe (US)	6-1,7-5,6-3
1932	J.H. Crawford (AUS)	H.C. Hopman (AUS)	4-6,6-3,3-6, 6-3,6-1	1972	K.R. Rosewall (AUS)	M.J. Anderson (AUS)	7-6,6-3,7-5
1933	J.H. Crawford (AUS)	K. Gledhill (US)	2-6,7-5,6-3, 6-2	1973	J.D. Newcombe (AUS)	O. Parun (NZ)	6-3,6-7,7-5, 6-1
1934	F.J. Perry (GB)	J.H. Crawford (AUS)	6-3,7-5,6-1	1974	J.S. Connors (US)	P.C. Dent (AUS)	7-6,6-4,4-6, 6-3
1935	J.H. Crawford (AUS)	F.J. Perry (GB)	2-6,6-4,6-4, 6-4	1975	J.D. Newcombe (AUS)	J.S. Connors (US)	7-5,3-6,6-4, 7-5
1936	A.K. Quist (AUS)	J.H. Crawford (AUS)	6-2,6-3,4-6, 3-6,9-7	1976	M.R. Edmondson (AUS)	J.D. Newcombe (AUS)	6-7,6-3,7-6, 6-1
1937	V.B. McGrath (AUS)	J.E. Bromwich (AUS)	6-3,1-6,6-0, 2-6,6-1	1977	R. Tanner (US) (January)	G. Vilas (ARG)	6-3,6-3,6-3
1938	J.D. Budge (US)	J.E. Bromwich (AUS)	6-4,6-2,6-1	1977	V. Gerulaitis (US) (December)	J.M. Lloyd (GB)	6-3,7-6,5-7, 3-6,6-2
1939	J.E. Bromwich (AUS)	A.K. Quist (AUS)	6-4,6-1,6-3	1978	G. Vilas (ARG)	J. Marks (AUS)	6-4,6-4,3-6, 6-3
1940	A.K. Quist (AUS)	J.H. Crawford (AUS)	6-3,6-1,6-2	1979	G. Vilas (ARG)	J. Sadri (US)	7-6,6-3,6-2
1941-45	No competition			1980	B. Teacher (US)	K.G. Warwick (AUS)	7-5,7-6,6-3
1946	J.E. Bromwich (AUS)	D. Pails (AUS)	5-7,6-3,7-5, 3-6,6-2	1981	J.C. Kriek (SA)	S. Denton (US)	6-2,7-6,6-7, 6-4
1947	D. Pails (AUS)	J.E. Bromwich (AUS)	4-6,6-4,3-6, 7-5,8-6	1982	J.C. Kriek (SA)	S. Denton (US)	6-3,6-3,6-2
1948	A.K. Quist (AUS)	J.E. Bromwich (AUS)	6-4,3-6,6-3, 2-6,6-3	1983	M. Wilander (SWE)	I. Lendl (CZ)	6-1,6-4,6-4
1949	F.A. Sedgman (AUS)	J.E. Bromwich (AUS)	6-3,6-3,6-2	1984	M. Wilander (SWE)	K. Curren (US)	6-7,6-4,7-6, 6-2
1950	F.A. Sedgman (AUS)	K. McGregor (AUS)	6-3,6-4,4-6, 6-1	1985	S. Edberg (SWE)	M. Wilander (SWE)	6-4,6-3,6-3
1951	R. Savitt (US)	K. McGregor (AUS)	6-3,2-6,6-3, 6-1	1986	Not held within the calendar year		
1952	K. McGregor (AUS)	F.A. Sedgman (AUS)	7-5,12-10, 2-6,6-2	1987	S. Edberg (SWE)	P. Cash (AUS)	6-3,6-4,3-6, 5-7,6-3
1953	K.R. Rosewall (AUS)	M.G. Rose (AUS)	6-0,6-3,6-4	1988	M. Wilander (SWE)	P. Cash (AUS)	6-3,6-7,3-6, 6-1,8-6
1954	M.G. Rose (AUS)	R.N. Hartwig (AUS)	6-2,0-6,6-4, 6-2				
1955	K.R. Rosewall (AUS)	L.A. Hoad (AUS)	9-7,6-4,6-4				
1956	L.A. Hoad (AUS)	K.R. Rosewall (AUS)	6-4,3-6,6-4, 7-5				
1957	A.J. Cooper (AUS)	N.A. Fraser (AUS)	6-3,9-11,6-4, 6-2				
1958	A.J. Cooper (AUS)	M.J. Anderson (AUS)	7-5,6-3,6-4				

WOMEN'S SINGLES

YEAR	WINNER	RUNNER-UP	SCORE	YEAR	WINNER	RUNNER-UP	SCORE
1922	M. Molesworth (AUS)	E.F. Boyd (AUS)	6-3,10-8	1969	M. Court (née Smith) (AUS)	B.J. King (née Moffitt) (US)	6-4,6-1
1923	M. Molesworth (AUS)	E.F. Boyd (AUS)	6-1,7-5	1970	M. Court (née Smith) (AUS)	K.A. Melville (AUS)	6-1,6-3
1924	S. Lance (AUS)	E.F. Boyd (AUS)	6-3,3-6,6-4	1971	M. Court (née Smith) (AUS)	E.F. Goolagong (AUS)	2-6,7-6,7-5
1925	D. Akhurst (AUS)	E.F. Boyd (AUS)	1-6,8-6,6-4	1972	S.V. Wade (GB)	E.F. Goolagong (AUS)	6-4,6-4
1926	D. Akhurst (AUS)	E.F. Boyd (AUS)	6-1,6-3	1973	M. Court (née Smith) (AUS)	E.F. Goolagong (AUS)	6-4,7-5
1927	E.F. Boyd (AUS)	S. Harper (née Lance) (AUS)	5-7,6-1,6-2	1974	E.F. Goolagong (AUS)	C.M. Evert (US)	7-6,4-6,6-0
1928	D. Akhurst (AUS)	E.F. Boyd (AUS)	7-5,6-2	1975	E.F. Goolagong (AUS)	M. Navratilova (CZ)	6-3,6-2
1929	D. Akhurst (AUS)	L.M. Bickerton (AUS)	6-1,5-7,6-2	1976	E.F. Cawley (née Goolagong) (AUS)	R. Tomanova (CZ)	6-2,6-2
1930	D. Akhurst (AUS)	S. Harper (née Lance) (AUS)	10-8,2-6,7-5	1977	K. Reid (née Melville) (AUS) (January)	D.L. Fromholtz (AUS)	7-5,6-2
1931	C. Buttsworth (AUS)	M. Crawford (née Cox) (AUS)	1-6,6-3,6-4	1977	E.F. Cawley (née Goolagong) (AUS) (December)	H.F. Cawley (née Gourlay) (AUS)	6-3,6-0
1932	C. Buttsworth (AUS)	K. Le Messurier (AUS)	9-7,6-4	1978	C. O'Neil (AUS)	B. Nagelsen (US)	6-3,7-6
1933	J. Hartigan (AUS)	C. Buttsworth (AUS)	6-4,6-3	1979	B.K. Jordan (US)	S.A. Walsh (US)	6-3,6-3
1934	J. Hartigan (AUS)	M. Molesworth (AUS)	6-1,6-4	1980	H. Mandlikova (CZ)	W.M. Turnbull (AUS)	6-0,7-5
1935	D.E. Round (GB)	N.M. Lyle (GB)	1-6,6-1,6-3	1981	M. Navratilova (US)	C. Lloyd (née Evert) (US)	6-7,6-4,7-5
1936	J. Hartigan (AUS)	N. Wynne (AUS)	6-4,6-4	1982	C. Lloyd (née Evert) (US)	M. Navratilova (US)	6-3,2-6,6-3
1937	N. Wynne (AUS)	E. Westacott (AUS)	6-3,5-7,6-4	1983	M. Navratilova (US)	K. Jordan (US)	6-2,7-6
1938	D.M. Bundy (US)	D. Stevenson (AUS)	6-3,6-2	1984	C. Lloyd (née Evert) (US)	H. Sukova (CZ)	6-7,6-1,6-3
1939	E. Westacott (AUS)	N. Hopman (née Hall) (AUS)	6-1,6-2	1985	M. Navratilova (US)	C. Lloyd (née Evert) (US)	6-2,4-6,6-2
1940	N. Bolton (née Wynne) (AUS)	T. Coyne (AUS)	5-7,6-4,6-0	1986	Not held during the calendar year		
1941-45	No competition			1987	H. Mandlikova (CZ)	M. Navratilova (US)	7-5,7-6
1946	N. Bolton (née Wynne) (AUS)	J. Fitch (AUS)	6-4,6-4	1988	S. Graf (W.GER)	C. Evert (US)	6-1,7-6
1947	N. Bolton (née Wynne) (AUS)	N. Hopman (née Hall) (AUS)	6-3,6-2				
1948	N. Bolton (née Wynne) (AUS)	M. Toomey (AUS)	6-3,6-1				
1949	D.J. Hart (US)	N. Bolton (née Wynne) (AUS)	6-3,6-4				
1950	A.L. Brough (US)	D.J. Hart (US)	6-4,3-6,6-4				
1951	N. Bolton (née Wynne) (AUS)	T. Long (née Coyne) (AUS)	6-1,7-5				
1952	T. Long (née Coyne) (AUS)	H. Angwin (AUS)	6-2,6-3				
1953	M.C. Connolly (US)	J. Sampson (US)	6-3,6-2				
1954	T. Long (née Coyne) (AUS)	J. Staley (AUS)	6-3,6-4				
1955	B. Penrose (AUS)	T. Long (née Coyne) (AUS)	6-4,6-3				
1956	M. Carter (AUS)	T. Long (née Coyne) (AUS)	3-6,6-2,9-7				
1957	S.J. Fry (US)	A. Gibson (US)	6-3,6-4				
1958	A. Mortimer (GB)	L. Coghlan (AUS)	6-3,6-4				
1959	M. Reitano (née Carter) (AUS)	R. Schuurman (SA)	6-2,6-3				
1960	M. Smith (AUS)	J. Lehane (AUS)	7-5,6-2				
1961	M. Smith (AUS)	J. Lehane (AUS)	6-1,6-4				
1962	M. Smith (AUS)	J. Lehane (AUS)	6-0,6-2				
1963	M. Smith (AUS)	J. Lehane (AUS)	6-2,6-2				
1964	M. Smith (AUS)	L.R. Turner (AUS)	6-3,6-2				
1965	M. Smith (AUS)	M.E. Bueno (BRA)	5-7,6-4,5-2, retired				
1966	M. Smith (AUS)	N. Richey (US)	default				
1967	N. Richey (US)	L.R. Turner (AUS)	6-1,6-4				
1968	B.J. King (née Moffitt) (US)	M. Court (née Smith) (AUS)	6-1,6-2				

AUSTRALIAN CHAMPIONSHIPS *continued*

MEN'S DOUBLES

YEAR	WINNERS		YEAR	WINNERS
1919	P. O'Hara Wood & R.V. Thomas (AUS)		1964	R.A.J. Hewitt & F.S. Stolle (AUS)
1920	P. O'Hara Wood & R.V. Thomas (AUS)		1965	J.D. Newcombe & A.D. Roche (AUS)
1921	S.H. Eaton & R.H. Gemmell (AUS)		1966	R.S. Emerson & F.S. Stolle (AUS)
1922	J.B. Hawkes & G.L. Patterson (AUS)		1967	J.D. Newcombe & A.D. Roche (AUS)
1923	P. O'Hara Wood & C.B. St John (AUS)		1968	R.D. Crealy & A.J. Stone (AUS)
1924	J.O. Anderson & N.E. Brookes (AUS)		1969	R.S. Emerson & R.G. Laver (AUS)
1925	P. O'Hara Wood & G.L. Patterson (AUS)		1970	R.C. Lutz & S.R Smith (US)
1926	J.B. Hawkes & G.L. Patterson (AUS)		1971	J.D. Newcombe & A.D. Roche (AUS)
1927	J.B. Hawkes & G.L. Patterson (AUS)		1972	O.K. Davidson & K.R. Rosewall (AUS)
1928	J. Borotra & J. Brugnon (FRA)		1973	M.J. Anderson & J.D. Newcombe (AUS)
1929	J.H. Crawford & H.C. Hopman (AUS)		1974	R.L. Case & G. Masters (AUS)
1930	J.H. Crawford & H.C. Hopman (AUS)		1975	J.G. Alexander & P.C. Dent (AUS)
1931	C. Donohue & R. Dunlop (AUS)		1976	J.D. Newcombe & A. D. Roche (AUS)
1932	J.H. Crawford & E.F. Moon (AUS)		1977	A.R. Ashe (US) & A.D. Roche (AUS) (January)
1933	K. Gledhill & H.E. Vines (US)		1977	R.O. Ruffels & A.J. Stone (AUS) (December)
1934	G.P. Hughes & F.J. Perry (GB)		1978	W. Fibak (POL) & K.G. Warwick (AUS)
1935	J.H. Crawford & V.B. McGrath (AUS)		1979	P. McNamara & P. McNamee (AUS)
1936	A.K. Quist & D.P. Turnbull (AUS)		1980	M.R. Edmondson & K.G. Warwick (AUS)
1937	A.K. Quist & D.P. Turnbull (AUS)		1981	M.R. Edmondson & K.G. Warwick (AUS)
1938	J.E. Bromwich & A.K. Quist (AUS)		1982	J.G. Alexander & J. Fitzgerald (AUS)
1939	J.E. Bromwich & A.K. Quist (AUS)		1983	M.R. Edmondson & P. McNamee (AUS)
1940	J.E. Bromwich & A.K. Quist (AUS)		1984	M.R. Edmondson & S.E. Stewart (US)
1941-45	No competition		1985	P. Annacone (US) & C.J. Van Rensburg (SA)
1946	J.E. Bromwich & A.K. Quist (AUS)		1986	Not held during the calendar year
1947	J.E. Bromwich & A.K. Quist (AUS)		1987	S. Edberg & A. Jarryd (SWE)
1948	J.E. Bromwich & A.K. Quist (AUS)		1988	R. Leach & J. Pugh (US)
1949	J.E. Bromwich & A.K. Quist (AUS)			
1950	J.E. Bromwich & A.K. Quist (AUS)			
1951	K. McGregor & F.A. Sedgman (AUS)			
1952	K. McGregor & F.A. Sedgman (AUS)			
1953	L.A. Hoad & K.R. Rosewall (AUS)			
1954	R.N. Hartwig & M.G. Rose (AUS)			
1955	E.V. Seixas & M.A. Trabert (US)			
1956	L.A. Hoad & K.R. Rosewall (AUS)			
1957	L.A. Hoad & N.A. Fraser (AUS)			
1958	A.J. Cooper & N.A. Fraser (AUS)			
1959	R.G. Laver & R. Mark (AUS)			
1960	R.G. Laver & R. Mark (AUS)			
1961	R.G. Laver & R. Mark (AUS)			
1962	R.S. Emerson & N.A. Fraser (AUS)			
1963	R.A.J. Hewitt & F.S. Stolle (AUS)			

MIXED DOUBLES

YEAR	WINNERS		YEAR	WINNERS
1922	J.B. Hawkes & E.F. Boyd (AUS)		1936	H.C. Hopman & N. Hopman (née Hall) (AUS)
1923	H.M. Rice & S. Lance (AUS)		1937	H.C. Hopman & N. Hopman (née Hall) (AUS)
1924	J. Willard & D. Akhurst (AUS)		1938	J.E. Bromwich & M. Wilson (AUS)
1925	J. Willard & D. Akhurst (AUS)		1939	H.C. Hopman & N. Hopman (née Hall) (AUS)
1926	J.B. Hawkes & E.F. Boyd (AUS)		1940	C. Long & N. Bolton (née Wynne) (AUS)
1927	J.B. Hawkes & E.F. Boyd (AUS)		1941-45	No competition
1928	J. Borotra (FRA) & D. Akhurst (AUS)		1946	C. Long & N. Bolton (née Wynne) (AUS)
1929	E.F. Moon & D. Akhurst (AUS)		1947	C. Long & N. Bolton (née Wynne) (AUS)
1930	H.C. Hopman & N. Hall (AUS)		1948	C. Long & N. Bolton (née Wynne) (AUS)
1931	J.H. Crawford & M. Crawford (née Cox) (AUS)		1949	F.A. Sedgman (AUS) & D.J. Hart (US)
1932	J.H. Crawford & M. Crawford (née Cox) (AUS)		1950	F.A. Sedgman (AUS) & D.J. Hart (US)
1933	J.H. Crawford & M. Crawford (née Cox) (AUS)		1951	G.A. Worthington & T. Long (née Coyne) (AUS)
1934	E.F. Moon & J. Hartigan (AUS)		1952	G.A. Worthington & T. Long (née Coyne) (AUS)
1935	C. Boussus (FRA) & L.M. Bickerton (AUS)		1953	R.N. Hartwig (AUS) & J. Sampson (US)

WOMEN'S DOUBLES

YEAR	WINNERS	YEAR	WINNERS
1922	E.F. Boyd & M. Mountain (AUS)	1967	J.A.M. Tegart & L.R. Turner (AUS)
1923	E.F. Boyd & S. Lance (AUS)	1968	K.M. Krantzcke & K.A. Melville (AUS)
1924	D. Akhurst & S. Lance (AUS)	1969	M. Court (née Smith) & J.A.M. Tegart (AUS)
1925	D. Akhurst & S. Harper (née Lance) (AUS)	1970	M. Court (née Smith) & D.E. Dalton (née Tegart) (AUS)
1926	E.F. Boyd & P. O'Hara Wood (AUS)	1971	M. Court (née Smith) & E.F. Goolagong (AUS)
1927	L.M. Bickerton & P. O'Hara Wood (AUS)	1972	H.F. Gourlay & K. Harris (AUS)
1928	D. Akhurst & E.F. Boyd (AUS)	1973	M. Court (née Smith) (AUS) & S.V. Wade (GB)
1929	D. Akhurst & L.M. Bickerton (AUS)	1974	E.F. Goolagong (AUS) & M. Michel (US)
1930	E. Hood & M. Molesworth (AUS)	1975	E.F. Goolagong (AUS) & M. Michel (US)
1931	L.M. Bickerton & D. Cozens (née Akhurst) (AUS)	1976	E.F. Cawley (née Goolagong) & H.F. Gourlay (AUS)
1932	C. Buttsworth & M. Crawford (née Cox) (AUS)	1977	D.L. Fromholtz & H.F. Gourlay (AUS) (January)
1933	M. Molesworth & E. Westacott (AUS)	1977	E.F. Cawley (née Goolagong) & H.F. Cawley (née Gourlay) (AUS) (December)
1934	M. Molesworth & E. Westacott (AUS)		
1935	E.M. Dearman & N.M. Lyle (GB)	1978	B. Nagelsen (US) & R. Tomanova (CZ)
1936	T. Coyne & N. Wynne (AUS)	1979	J. Chaloner (NZ) & D.R. Evers (AUS)
1937	T. Coyne & N. Wynne (AUS)	1980	B. Nagelsen & M. Navratilova (US)
1938	T. Coyne & N. Wynne (AUS)	1981	K. Jordan & A.E. Smith (US)
1939	T. Coyne & N. Wynne (AUS)	1982	M. Navratilova & P.H. Shriver (US)
1940	T. Coyne & N. Bolton (née Wynne) (AUS)	1983	M. Navratilova & P.H. Shriver (US)
1941-45	No competition	1984	M. Navratilova & P.H. Shriver (US)
1946	M. Bevis & J. Fitch (AUS)	1985	M. Navratilova & P.H. Shriver (US)
1947	N. Bolton (née Wynne) & T. Long (née Coyne) (AUS)	1986	Not held during the calendar year
1948	N. Bolton (née Wynne) & T. Long (née Coyne) (AUS)	1987	M. Navratilova & P.H. Shriver (US)
1949	N. Bolton (née Wynne) & T. Long (née Coyne) (AUS)	1988	M. Navratilova & P.H. Shriver (US)
1950	A.L. Brough & D.J. Hart (US)		
1951	N. Bolton (née Wynne) & T. Long (née Coyne) (AUS)		
1952	N. Bolton (née Wynne) & T. Long (née Coyne) (AUS)		
1953	M.C. Connolly & J. Sampson (US)		
1954	M.K. Hawton & B. Penrose (AUS)		
1955	M.K. Hawton & B. Penrose (AUS)		
1956	M.K. Hawton & T. Long (née Coyne) (AUS)		
1957	S.J. Fry & A. Gibson (US)		
1958	M.K. Hawton & T. Long (née Coyne) (AUS)		
1959	S. Reynolds & R. Schuurman (SA)		
1960	M.E. Bueno (BRA) & C.C. Truman (GB)		
1961	M. Reitano (née Carter) & M. Smith (AUS)		
1962	R.A. Ebbern & M. Smith (AUS)		
1963	R.A. Ebbern & M. Smith (AUS)		
1964	J.A.M. Tegart & L.R. Turner (AUS)		
1965	M. Smith & L.R. Turner (AUS)		
1966	C.E. Graebner & N. Richey (US)		

YEAR	WINNERS	YEAR	WINNERS
1954	R.N. Hartwig & T. Long (née Coyne) (AUS)	1967	O.K. Davidson & L.R. Turner (AUS)
1955	G.A. Worthington & T. Long (née Coyne) (AUS)	1968	R.D. Crealy & B.J. King (née Moffitt) (US)
1956	N.A. Fraser & B. Penrose (AUS)	1969	M.C. Riessen (US) & M. Court (née Smith) (AUS) divided with F.S. Stolle (AUS) & A.S. Jones (née Haydon) (GB)
1957	M.J. Anderson & F. Muller (AUS)		
1958	R.N. Howe & M.K. Hawton (AUS)	1970-86	No event held
1959	R. Mark & S. Reynolds (SA)	1987	S.E. Stewart & Z.L. Garrison (US)
1960	T. Fancutt (SA) & J. Lehane (AUS)	1988	J. Pugh (US) & J. Novotna (CZ)
1961	R.A.J. Hewitt & J. Lehane (AUS)		
1962	F.S. Stolle & L.R. Turner (AUS)		
1963	K.N. Fletcher & M. Smith (AUS)		
1964	K.N. Fletcher & M. Smith (AUS)		
1965	J.D. Newcombe & M. Smith (AUS) divided with O.K. Davidson & R. Ebbern (AUS)		
1966	A.D. Roche & J.A.M. Tegart (AUS)		

WIGHTMAN CUP
(International match between women players from United States and Great Britain)

YEAR	WINNER	SCORE	VENUE
1923	United States	7-0	New York
1924	Great Britain	6-1	Wimbledon
1925	Great Britain	4-3	New York
1926	United States	4-3	Wimbledon
1927	United States	5-2	New York
1928	Great Britain	4-3	Wimbledon
1929	United States	4-3	New York
1930	Great Britain	4-3	Wimbledon
1931	United States	5-2	New York
1932	United States	4-3	Wimbledon
1933	United States	4-3	New York
1934	United States	5-2	Wimbledon
1935	United States	4-3	New York
1936	United States	4-3	Wimbledon
1937	United States	6-1	New York
1938	United States	5-2	Wimbledon
1939	United States	5-2	New York
1940-45	No competition		
1946	United States	7-0	Wimbledon
1947	United States	7-0	New York
1948	United States	6-1	Wimbledon
1949	United States	7-0	Philadelphia
1950	United States	7-0	Wimbledon
1951	United States	6-1	Boston
1952	United States	7-0	Wimbledon
1953	United States	7-0	Rye
1954	United States	6-0	Wimbledon
1955	United States	6-1	Rye
1956	United States	5-2	Wimbledon
1957	United States	6-1	Sewickley
1958	Great Britain	4-3	Wimbledon
1959	United States	4-3	Sewickley
1960	Great Britain	4-3	Wimbledon
1961	United States	6-1	Chicago
1962	United States	4-3	Wimbledon
1963	United States	6-1	Cleveland
1964	United States	5-2	Wimbledon
1965	United States	5-2	Cleveland
1966	United States	4-3	Wimbledon
1967	United States	6-1	Cleveland
1968	Great Britain	4-3	Wimbledon
1969	United States	5-2	Cleveland
1970	United States	4-3	Wimbledon
1971	United States	4-3	Cleveland
1972	United States	5-2	Wimbledon
1973	United States	5-2	Boston
1974	Great Britain	6-1	Deeside
1975	Great Britain	5-2	Cleveland
1976	United States	5-2	London
1977	United States	7-0	Oakland
1978	Great Britain	4-3	London
1979	United States	7-0	West Palm Beach
1980	United States	5-2	London
1981	United States	7-0	Chicago
1982	United States	6-1	London
1983	United States	6-1	Williamsburg
1984	United States	5-2	London
1985	United States	7-0	Williamsburg
1986	United States	7-0	London
1987	United States	5-2	Williamsburg

THE FEDERATION CUP
(Women's world international team championship)

YEAR	WINNER	RUNNER-UP	SCORE	VENUE
1963	United States	Australia	2-1	Queen's Club, London
1964	Australia	United States	2-1	Philadelphia
1965	Australia	United States	2-1	Melbourne
1966	United States	West Germany	3-0	Turin
1967	United States	Great Britain	2-0	West Berlin
1968	Australia	Netherlands	3-0	Paris
1969	United States	Australia	2-1	Athens
1970	Australia	West Germany	3-0	Freiburg
1971	Australia	Great Britain	3-0	Perth
1972	South Africa	Great Britain	2-1	Johannesburg
1973	Australia	South Africa	3-0	Bad Homburg
1974	Australia	United States	2-1	Naples
1975	Czechoslovakia	Australia	3-0	Aix-en-Provence
1976	United States	Australia	2-1	Philadelphia
1977	United States	Australia	2-1	Eastbourne
1978	United States	Australia	2-1	Melbourne
1979	United States	Australia	3-0	Madrid
1980	United States	Australia	3-0	West Berlin
1981	United States	Great Britain	3-0	Tokyo
1982	United States	West Germany	3-0	Santa Clara
1983	Czechoslovakia	West Germany	2-1	Zurich
1984	Czechoslovakia	Australia	2-1	Sao Paulo
1985	Czechoslovakia	United States	2-1	Nagoya
1986	United States	Czechoslovakia	3-0	Prague
1987	West Germany	United States	2-1	Vancouver

GRAND SLAM
The following players have held the championships of Australia, France, Wimbledon and the United States in the same calendar year.

YEAR	WINNER

MEN'S SINGLES

YEAR	WINNER
1938	J.D. Budge (US)
1962	R.G. Laver (AUS)
1969	R.G. Laver (AUS)

WOMEN'S SINGLES

1953	M.C. Connolly (US)
1970	M. Court (née Smith) (AUS)
1988	S. Graf (W.GER)

MEN'S DOUBLES

1951	F.A. Sedgman & K. McGregor (AUS)

MIXED DOUBLES

1963	K.N. Fletcher & M. Smith (AUS)

WOMEN'S DOUBLES

1949-50	A.L. Brough (US)[1]
1960	M.E. Bueno (BRA)[2]
1984	M. Navratilova & P.H. Shriver (US)

[1] Brough won the French, Wimbledon and US titles with M. du Pont (née Osborne) in 1949, and the 1950 Australian women's doubles with D. Hart.
[2] Bueno won the Australian with C. Truman and the other three with D. Hard.

THE DAVIS CUP
(Men's international team championship)

CHALLENGE ROUNDS 1919–1971

YEAR	WINNER	RUNNER-UP	SCORE	VENUE
1919	Australasia	British Isles	4-1	Sydney
1920	United States	Australasia	5-0	Auckland
1921	United States	Japan	5-0	New York
1922	United States	Australasia	4-1	New York
1923	United States	Australia	4-1	New York
1924	United States	Australia	5-0	Philadelphia
1925	United States	France	5-0	Philadelphia
1926	United States	France	4-1	Philadelphia
1927	France	United States	3-2	Philadelphia
1928	France	United States	4-1	Paris
1929	France	United States	3-2	Paris
1930	France	United States	4-1	Paris
1931	France	Great Britain	3-2	Paris
1932	France	United States	3-2	Paris
1933	Great Britain	France	3-2	Paris
1934	Great Britain	United States	4-1	Wimbledon
1935	Great Britain	United States	5-0	Wimbledon
1936	Great Britain	Australia	3-2	Wimbledon
1937	United States	Great Britain	4-1	Wimbledon
1938	United States	Australia	3-2	Philadelphia
1939	Australia	United States	3-2	Philadelphia
1940-45	No competition			
1946	United States	Australia	5-0	Melbourne
1947	United States	Australia	4-1	New York
1948	United States	Australia	5-0	New York
1949	United States	Australia	4-1	New York
1950	Australia	United States	4-1	New York
1951	Australia	United States	3-2	Sydney
1952	Australia	United States	4-1	Adelaide
1953	Australia	United States	3-2	Melbourne
1954	United States	Australia	3-2	Sydney
1955	Australia	United States	5-0	New York
1956	Australia	United States	5-0	Adelaide
1957	Australia	United States	3-2	Melbourne
1958	United States	Australia	3-2	Brisbane
1959	Australia	United States	3-2	New York
1960	Australia	Italy	4-1	Sydney

YEAR	WINNER	RUNNER-UP	SCORE	VENUE
1961	Australia	Italy	5-0	Melbourne
1962	Australia	Mexico	5-0	Brisbane
1963	United States	Australia	3-2	Adelaide
1964	Australia	United States	3-2	Cleveland
1965	Australia	Spain	4-1	Sydney
1966	Australia	India	4-1	Melbourne
1967	Australia	Spain	4-1	Brisbane
1968	United States	Australia	4-1	Adelaide
1969	United States	Romania	5-0	Cleveland
1970	United States	West Germany	5-0	Cleveland
1971	United States	Romania	3-2	Charlotte

FINALS

YEAR	WINNER	RUNNER-UP	SCORE	VENUE
1972	United States	Romania	3-2	Bucharest
1973	Australia	United States	5-0	Cleveland
1974	South Africa	India	walkover	
1975	Sweden	Czechoslovakia	3-2	Stockholm
1976	Italy	Chile	4-1	Santiago
1977	Australia	Italy	3-1	Sydney
1978	United States	Great Britain	4-1	Palm Springs
1979	United States	Italy	5-0	San Francisco
1980	Czechoslovakia	Italy	4-1	Prague
1981	United States	Argentina	3-1	Cincinnati
1982	United States	France	4-1	Grenoble
1983	Australia	Sweden	3-2	Melbourne
1984	Sweden	United States	4-1	Gothenburg
1985	Sweden	West Germany	3-2	Munich
1986	Australia	Sweden	3-2	Melbourne
1987	Sweden	India	5-0	Gothenburg

WOMEN'S SERIES
(NB: Final played over best of five sets since 1983.)

YEAR	WINNER	RUNNER-UP	SCORE
1977	C.M. Evert (US)	B.J. King (née Moffitt) (US)	6-2,6-2
1978	C.M. Evert (US)	M. Navratilova (CZ)	6-3,6-3
1979	M. Navratilova (US)	T.A. Austin (US)	6-2,6-1
1980	T.A. Austin (US)	A. Jaeger (US)	6-2,6-2
1981	T.A. Austin (US)	M. Navratilova (US)	2-6,6-4,6-2
1982	M. Navratilova (US)	C. Lloyd (née Evert) (US)	4-6,6-1,6-2
1983	M. Navratilova (US)	C. Lloyd (née Evert) (US)	6-3,7-5,6-1
1984	M. Navratilova (US)	H. Sukova (CZ)	6-3,7-5,6-4
1985	M. Navratilova (US)	H. Mandlikova (CZ)	6-2,6-0,3-6, 6-1
1986	M. Navratilova (US)	S. Graf (W.GER)	7-6,6-3,6-2
1987	S. Graf (W.GER)	G. Sabatini (ARG)	4-6,6-4,6-0, 6-4

THE GRAND PRIX MASTERS

MEN'S SINGLES

YEAR	WINNER	RUNNER-UP	SCORE
1970	S.R. Smith (US)	R.G. Laver (AUS)	(Round Robin)
1971	I. Nastase (ROM)	S.R. Smith (US)	(Round Robin)
1972	I. Nastase (ROM)	S.R. Smith (US)	6-3,6-2,3-6, 2-6,6-3
1973	I. Nastase (ROM)	T.S. Okker (NETH)	6-3,7-5,4-6, 6-3
1974	G. Vilas (ARG)	I. Nastase (ROM)	7-6,6-2,3-6, 3-6,6-4
1975	I. Nastase (ROM)	B. Borg (SWE)	6-2,6-2,6-1
1976	M. Orantes (SPA)	W. Fibak (POL)	5-7,6-2,0-6, 7-6,6-1
1977	J.S. Connors (US)	B. Borg (SWE)	6-4,1-6,6-4
1978	J.P. McEnroe (US)	A.R. Ashe (US)	6-7,6-3,7-5
1979	B. Borg (SWE)	V. Gerulaitis (US)	6-2,6-2
1980	B. Borg (SWE)	I. Lendl (CZ)	6-4,6-2,6-2
1981	I. Lendl (CZ)	V. Gerulaitis (US)	6-7,2-6,7-6, 6-2,6-4
1982	I. Lendl (CZ)	J.P. McEnroe (US)	6-4,6-4,6-2
1983	J.P. McEnroe (US)	I. Lendl (CZ)	6-3,6-4,6-4
1984	J.P. McEnroe (US)	I. Lendl (CZ)	7-5,6-0,6-4
1985	I. Lendl (CZ)	B. Becker (W.GER)	6-2,7-6,6-3
1986	I. Lendl (CZ)	B. Becker (W.GER)	6-4,6-4,6-4
1987	I. Lendl (CZ)	M. Wilander (SWE)	6-2,6-2,6-3

PICTURE CREDITS

Russ Adams: 171. Allsport: 124(bl,br) 124/5(t,b), 144/5, 145, 146/7, 153(c,b), 158, 159, 176, 177, 178, 181, 232/3. BBC Hulton Picture Library: 10, 16, 20/1, 22/3, 24, 86, 120/1, 121, 213. Gus Bower: 104. Michael Cole Camerawork: 15, 22, 28, 34, 35, 36, 38, 48, 50, 53, 55, 56, 57, 60, 61, 71, 74/5, 80, 81, 84, 85, 89, 92, 95, 97, 101, 110, 112, 114, 116/17, 124(l), 129, 132, 134, 135, 136/7, 138/9, 142/3, 144, 148/9, 152(t,b), 134, 135, 136/7, 138/9, 142/3, 144, 148/9, 152(t,b), 156, 162, 164, 169, 170(t), 172, 173, 175, 179, 196, 200, 201, 212, 220/1. Colorsport: 184. Melchior DiGiacoma: 204, 216. Dunlop Slazenger: 210. Mary Evans Picture Library: 6/7, 8/9, 14, 17, 19, 118, 119, 206/7, 209(t,b), 217, 223, 224, 225, 226, 228. Richard Evans: 40, 47, 165, 204, 212. Bill Hickley: 208. Mansell Collection: 12/13, 66, 227(t). Nabisco Masters: 185(r). Linda Pentz: 46, 190. The Photo Source: 11, 26/7, 31, 32, 43, 54, 58, 59, 63, 67, 69(t), 72, 73, 76, 79, 83, 91, 93, 94, 103, 106, 109, 111, 115, 122, 126, 128/9, 130, 131, 166/7, 168, 183, 188, 202, 203, 222, 229. R & A Photofeatures: 44, 49, 62, 64/5, 68, 69(b), 77, 98, 99, 113, 123, 127, 128, 133, 140/1, 148, 150, 151, 153(t), 170(b), 174, 180, 182, 192, 193, 194, 195, 198/9, 205, 214, 230(t,b), 231. Tennis Australia: 154/5. Tennis Week: 185(c). Challenge: 185(r).